CHAMPAGNE

ALSACE AND LORRAINE

JURA AND SAVOIE

BURGUNDY

THE RHÔNE VALLEY

FRENCH WINES

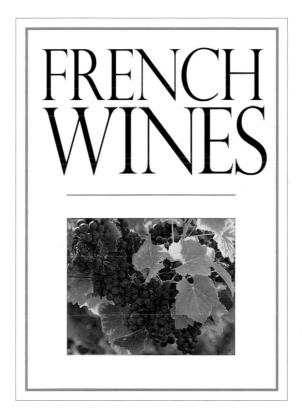

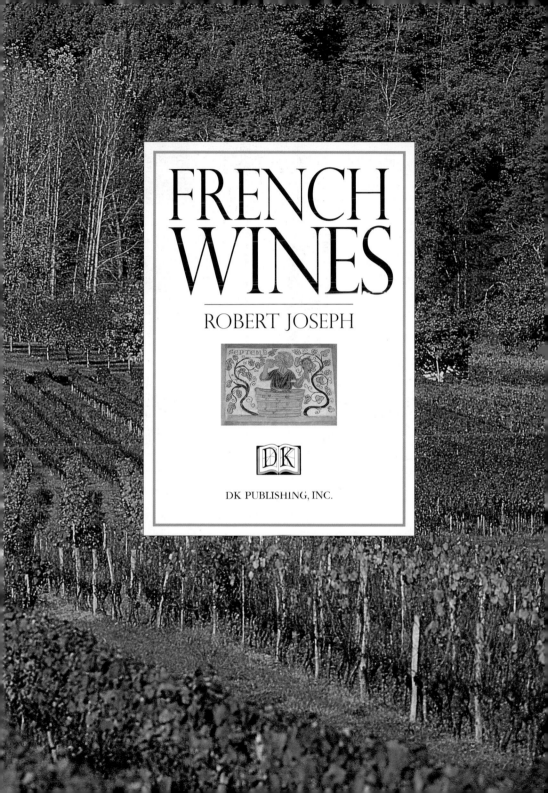

FRENCH WINES

ROBERT JOSEPH

DK PUBLISHING, INC.

A DK Publishing Book
www.dk.com

Project Editor Marcus Hardy
Art Editor Tessa Bindloss
Editors Nancy Jones, Jane Bolton,
Edward Bunting
Designers Catherine MacKenzie, Tim Mann
Managing Editor Francis Ritter
Managing Art Editor Derek Coombes
DTP Designer Sonia Charbonnier

Picture Research Brigitte Aurora
Maps James Anderson
Illustrations Claire Littlejohn
Wine Photography Steve Gorton
Production Manager Julian Deeming

Robert Joseph's Team Kitty Johnson,
Jane Boyce, Richard Royds

First American Edition, 1999
2 4 6 8 10 9 7 5 3 1

Published in the United States by
DK Publishing, Inc.
95 Madison Avenue
New York, New York 10016

Library of Congress Cataloging-in-Publication Data
Joseph, Robert.
 French wines: an information-packed handbook
for anyone enjoying French wine at home or
planning a gastronomic visit / Robert Joseph.
 – 1st American ed.
  p.   cm.
Includes index.
ISBN 0-7894-4625-1 (alk. paper)
1. Wine and winemaking – France. I. Title.
TP553.J66 1999
641.2'2'0944–dc21   99-23325
                                CIP

Reproduced by Colourscan
Printed and bound in Italy by LEGO

Contents

Vineyard sign in Riquewihr, Alsace

Introducing French Wines

Grape pickers enjoy a well-earned lunch among the vines

Oak barrel at Champagne Mercier

THE FRENCH WINE REGIONS

Carefully tended vineyards in the foothills of the French Alps

HOW TO USE THIS GUIDE

FOR LOVE OR MONEY
Whether you are buying wine for investment or for pure enjoyment, this book provides a wealth of knowledge on the varying wines of France.

WHETHER YOU ARE A WINE BUFF or simply enjoy a glass of wine with a meal, this book will provide a comprehensive guide to the world of French wines.

Highlights of the introductory section include an informative outline of the history of wine, detailed information on how wine is made, step-by-step instructions in the art of wine tasting, a useful guide to starting a cellar, and handy hints for cooking with wine.

The bulk of the book is divided alphabetically into the 10 wine-making regions of France, with full-color photographs through-out. Each regional chapter opens with an introduction to the region

as a whole, followed by a driving tour that encompasses some of the region's highlights. The pages that follow provide an insight into Robert Joseph's choices among the region's *appellations*, and include recommended producers, examples of good vintages, ideal wine and food partnerships, and tasting tips.

Because wine and food are inextricably linked, each chapter closes with a mouth-watering introduction to the local dishes, together with a separate box on the cheeses of the region.

As you delve into the world of French wines, this book will be use-ful both at home and on your travels through the vineyards of France.

THE WINE-PRODUCING REGIONS

Locator Map
On each introductory spread to the 10 wine regions, the region in question is shown on a map of France.

Regional Map
This map locates the region's main wine-producing areas and gives you an idea of the size of each area.

Color Photographs
As well as providing a wealth of information, the introductory spreads provide a visual taste of the region.

Key to Regional Map
The key to the regional map is color-coded by wine-growing area for easy reference.

Key Facts Box
Here you will find information on how much wine a region produces, its climate, soil types, and the main grape varieties.

Description of Region
The introductory spreads provide background information on each wine-producing region as a whole.

SYMBOLS FOR TOURS

- 🍷 Tasting possible
- 🏛 Places to eat
- ★ Site of interest
- ℹ Tourist information
- ☀ Viewpoint

Locator Map
This locator map pinpoints
the part of the region covered
by the driving tour.

Touring Tips Box
Here you will find addresses and
telephone numbers for tourist
offices, hotels and restaurants,
and dates of local wine events.

THE REGIONAL TOURS

Driving Tour Map
A suggested route for a driving tour
of the region is plotted on this map.

Description of Tour
Here you will find details of the sites and
places covered by the driving tour.

THE INDIVIDUAL APPELLATIONS

Name of Appellation
In bands color-coded by region, the main appellations appear in alphabetical order.

Description of Appellation
This text describes the appellation and the styles and qualities of its wines.

Locator Map
The locator map pinpoints the appellation on a map of the region.

Key Facts Box
This fact box systematically provides further information about the appellation.

Illustrated Wine
An important wine from the appellation is shown.

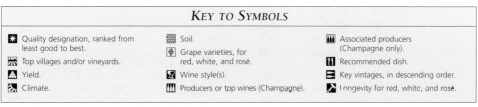

KEY TO SYMBOLS

- ✴ Quality designation, ranked from least good to best.
- ☷ Top villages and/or vineyards.
- ▲ Yield.
- ⚡ Climate.
- ▦ Soil.
- ✤ Grape varieties, for red, white, and rosé.
- ✶ Wine style(s).
- ⦀ Producers or top wines (Champagne).
- ⦀ Associated producers (Champagne only).
- ☰ Recommended dish.
- ☰ Key vintages, in descending order.
- ↗ Longevity for red, white, and rosé.

FOREWORD

I FIRST FELL IN LOVE WITH the wines of France as an adolescent while exploring the cellar of my parents' country hotel. Wine, I imagined then, came in four colors: red, white, pink, and brown, and in various levels of sweetness. Pulling a few corks, however, I discovered an extraordinary range of flavors concealed behind the green and clear glass of the bottles. There was young, red Burgundy, its raspberry tang contrasting with the gamey flavor of older vintages. There was flinty Chablis and nutty Meursault, red Bordeaux full of blackcurrants from the Médoc and full of plums from St. Émilion. I discovered gooseberries in Sancerre and spring flowers in wine from Condrieu in the Rhône.

NATURAL ALCHEMY

I continued my education on youthful trips to France with the help of a book or two and many generous wine makers. Both well-known and lesser-known wines, including Jurançon, Château Chalon, and Banyuls, gave me a combined course in geography and history. I discovered the tastes of different grape varieties and the effects of changing soils, climates, and vintages. Even more important, both then and later when I was living in Burgundy, I learned about the vital role of the wine maker in the alchemy that transforms a simple fruit into a drink that can somehow touch the emotions and linger for decades in the memory of the drinker.

The story of a wine cannot be fully understood without proper reference to the place where it is made, the people who make it, and the local food with which it is drunk. Celebrating all of these things in this book, I have chosen some of France's best-known wines – and some of the least known – from the merchant's shelf and restaurant wine list, and endeavored to set them in a context that makes the most sense of their flavor and style.

PITFALLS TO AVOID

As well as exploring the flavors and styles of French wines, I have also drawn attention to some of the pitfalls that you may encounter when you come to buying your own wine. Critics now agree that the famous French system of *appellations contrôlées* is in urgent need of a thorough overhaul. The name of a region on a wine label provides no guarantee of its quality. One bottle of Champagne or Bordeaux may be a delight, the next may be a disaster. A supposedly basic Burgundy made by a skilled and diligent wine maker often tastes much better than an expensive wine made to less exacting standards using grapes from a neighboring *grand cru appellation*. Besides its inadequacy as an indicator of quality, the *appellation* system can also be extremely confusing. Cheverny and Cour-Cheverny, for example, are both white wines, made in the same place but from different grape varieties, resulting in wines with completely different flavors. Further, the wines made in Rully taste nothing like the wines made in Reuilly, and likewise, the wines made in Pouilly-Fumé, Pouilly-sur-Loire, and Pouilly-Fuissé have very little in common beyond the first part of their name.

COMPLEX BUT REWARDING

With problems like these, it is easy to understand why a growing number of people choose wine that is labeled simply by grape variety, such as Chardonnay, Cabernet Sauvignon, or Merlot. By doing so, however, they are missing out on the enormous range of subtle flavors that set wine apart from almost anything else you can drink. The myriad variables of the French climate, microclimates, soils, grapes, wine makers and wine-making traditions come together to create an ever-changing maze of different wines, each with its own unique flavors. Despite, and perhaps because of, its complexity, France's long wine-making tradition still offers surprises and delights to match, and often surpass, those of any other wine-producing country in the world.

A PATH THROUGH THE MAZE

My aim in this book is to provide you with a few paths through the exciting maze of French wine, and a few detours around its potential pitfalls. More important, perhaps, I want to provide you with the confidence and the knowledge that will enable you to anticipate the qualities of almost any French wine that you may encounter. I hope you enjoy reading this book half as much as I have enjoyed researching and writing it.

INTRODUCING
FRENCH WINES

THE HISTORY OF WINE

THE OLD TESTAMENT ACKNOWLEDGES THE PLEASURE AND THE

POWER OF THE DRINK DERIVED FROM FERMENTED GRAPES, BUT

IT WAS THE FRENCH WHO PERFECTED THE ART OF WINE MAKING.

NOAH'S ART
According to the Old Testament, Noah was the first person ever to make wine. This 14th-century relief by Andrea Pisano records the aftermath.

FOR THOSE OF US WHO NOW HEED medical warnings about the minimum and maximum weekly consumption of wine, it is worth pausing to recall that, for most of man's history, wine tended to be the safest, healthiest drink available. It was finding water pure enough to drink that was the luxury.

To listen to some of France's more chauvinist wine growers, it would be easy to believe that it was their ancestors who first had the notion of turning grapes into wine. In fact, while it was the French who most successfully developed the art of wine making and created what are now regarded as the world's most famous wines, credit for the actual invention must go elsewhere. The Biblical legend says that it was Noah who first drank wine. According to the Bible, soon after Noah's boat had come aground in the country that we now know as Turkey, he noticed the giddy antics of a goat that had been eating over-ripe grapes that had started to ferment. Encouraged by the sight, he planted a vineyard and, to the shame of his sons, Noah "drank of the wine and was drunk, and became uncovered in his tent." If this story is to be believed, not only was Noah the first wine maker, he was also the first person ever to get drunk. Wine is constantly

WINE AS AN APHRODISIAC
Rubens' painting of Lot and his daughters shows the two women getting their father drunk in order to maintain the family lineage.

featured in the Bible. In one case, Lot's two daughters are described as making their father, with whom they were hiding in a cave, drink wine on two successive nights so that they could "lay with him" and "preserve [his] lineage."

The Persians, however, tell a very different story. For them, the person who invented wine was not Noah, but a sad princess who was intent on doing away with herself. Assuming that a jar full of frothing grape juice was poisonous, she drank what she believed to be a deadly dose. The pleasurable effects that immediately followed, and indeed her survival, must have come as quite a surprise to the young princess. Sadly, her reaction to what was presumably the first hangover has gone unrecorded.

SURVIVAL OF THE COOLEST

Whatever story you prefer, it cannot have taken long for people to discover that grape juice, given half a chance, ferments into something alcoholic. With a bit of luck, the beverage may even be pleasant to drink. At the same time, experience would have taught him that fermented grape juice, though generally more robust and longer-lived than in its natural state, is vulnerable to bacteria that have the ability to convert it into vinegar. We now know that these bacteria are most active at warmer temperatures so, in the absence of the refrigeration and sulphur dioxide that are used today to protect wine against these bacteria, there is no question that the wines with the greatest chance of remaining drinkable from one vintage to the

next would have been the ones produced and stored in regions that were relatively cool.

From the earliest vintages that were made in what is now called the Middle East, the story of wine can be traced alongside the history of most of the civilized world. Archaeological discoveries suggest that wine has been made in Egypt for at least 3,000 years, and according to records, Marco Polo enjoyed wine that was imported into China from Persia in the 1400s. The Romans were very serious about their wine drinking and laid down the best vintages for as long as 100 years. They are known to have planted vines even in Britain. However, archaeological finds suggest that then, as now, imported wine was more popular.

European emigrants traveling to the New World took both wines and vines with them, so that by the late 19th century it was clear that nothing could stand in the way of the production and gradual spread of wine around the world.

PORT OF BORDEAUX
Monet's 1871 painting of the busy port of Bordeaux, depicting the forest of masts belonging to cargo vessels, shows the potential for trade at this time.

PERSIANS
Wine has always been a symbol of civilized, courtly life, as in this painting of a Persian prince drinking wine in his harem.

THE HISTORY OF FRENCH WINE

Monks, emperors, and revolutionaries all had a hand in shaping France's wine industry. However, more recently, the industry has been ravaged by disease and transformed by supermarkets.

EARLY CONNOISSEURS
Roman citizens, like this first-century couple and their slave, depicted in a painting at Herculaneum, were as interested in imported wines as they were in homegrown ones.

We HAVE NO WAY of knowing exactly when anyone enjoyed the first mouthful of wine produced from French grapes that were grown on French soil, but we can be pretty sure that there was plenty of wine being drunk in France more than 500 years before the birth of Christ. Some of the first drinkers would have been the Phoenicians and the Greeks in their trading posts on the Mediterranean coast. The climate of this region, the presence of indigenous vines, and the difficulties of transporting wine in amphorae from their homelands meant that it was inevitable that the newcomers would soon turn their hands to the making of wine. By the time the Romans occupied the northern part of the country in the first century, vines were growing and wine was being produced in many of the regions that have since become synonymous with wine. The men who made these wines were often members of tribes who took to the ways of the Romans and continued to make and trade wine following the collapse of the Roman Empire. From the outset, the vine growers sought pieces of land where the vines stood the greatest likelihood of ripening successfully. According to local legend, in the 9th century the French emperor Charlemagne is said to have chosen a particular slope on the hill of Corton, in Burgundy (*see pp.98–141*), on which to plant a vineyard. He had noticed that, due to regular exposure to sunlight, the snows on that slope were always the first to thaw.

THE OBSERVANT CHARLEMAGNE
Emperor Charlemagne is said to have spent much time selecting new sites for vineyards.

MEDIEVAL HARVEST
This scene is somewhat idealized, as the 15th-century French nobility did not really stage mass invasions of the harvest in their best clothes.

PAVING THE WAY

The churches and monasteries established between the 10th and 13th centuries throughout France played a crucial role in the further development of wine in France and beyond. However, France is a fairly large country, and transporting wine over poor roads limited the markets that the wine could reach. Places with river access, such as Alsace (*see pp.58–69*), and sea ports, like Bordeaux (*see pp.70–97*), clearly had the greatest advantage.

The arrival of the cork around 1650 further increased the popularity of wine. In the 1780s, the French Revolution removed the church from the industry. Vineyards that had once been owned by the monks were sold to the middle class, and even to peasants. In 1804 the Code Napoléon was introduced, stating that all heirs, regardless of their age or sex, would share any inheritance equally between them.

A BREAK FROM TRADITION

The fragmentation of the vineyards, coupled with the arrival of a new breed of landowners, opened the way for merchants whose role lay in blending and selling the wines of numerous small producers. The merchants also benefited from access to new markets as a result of better roads, canals, and railways.

A century after the revolution, France's wine industry was thrown into turmoil by the vine diseases mildew, oidium, and – worst of all – the phylloxera louse, which affected almost every vine.

The vineyards that were replanted or, to be more precise, grafted with phylloxera-resistant vines, were often very different from the ones that had gone before. Once-famous vineyards shrank, once-familiar grape varieties disappeared, and between the two world wars, fraudulent labeling was rife. This latter practice was countered in the 1930s when the *appellation contrôlée* legislation was introduced.

During the second half of the 20th century, unprecedented competition from the New World resulted in extensive research into the "how" and "why" of vine growing and wine making. As the evolution of French wine accelerated, previously neglected vineyards in the south were given a new lease on life.

If the way in which wine is made has changed as a result of increased competition, so too has the way that it is bought and drunk. The rapid growth in the number of supermarkets in France has led wine drinkers to try wines from other regions. Most French wine drinkers now drink less, but better, wine. However, many young French do not drink wine at all, which helps to explain why many French wine makers may now be more focused on selling their wines overseas.

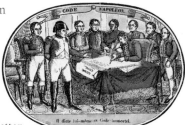

NAPOLEONIC INHERITANCE
Here Napoleon is pictured signing the Code Napoléon, the law that splits every inheritance, including any vineyards, equally between all the heirs.

SUPERMARKET REVOLUTION
Today, we buy wine with an ease that was undreamed of by the Romans or Charlemagne, and at far lower prices for the quality on offer.

How Wine is Made

WINE MAKING IS BOTH ONE OF THE SIMPLEST AND MOST COMPLEX

ACTIVITIES KNOWN TO MAN, BRINGING TOGETHER THE SKILLS OF

THE FARMER, THE HORTICULTURIST, THE COOK, AND THE CHEMIST.

THE FRENCH LANGUAGE HAS NO commonly used translation for "wine maker" or "winery," terms that are used frequently throughout the English-speaking world. For the French, the person who turns grapes into wine is the *vigneron* or *viticulteur*, terms that refer to the vineyard rather than the actual process of converting the harvested grapes into wine. As far as the term winery is concerned, a state-of-the-art, computerized establishment is still usually known in France as a *cave*, or a cellar, even when it could be mistaken by passersby for a semiconductor factory.

In France, traditionally at least, outside of Bordeaux, Champagne, and Alsace the most visible words on a wine label refer to the place where the grapes were grown. The name of the producer appears only in small print. In the New World, by contrast, it is the wine maker or winery that takes center stage.

DIFFERENCE OF OPINION

These differences reveal the French producers' sense of tradition and their belief that wine is, as they say, "made in the vineyard." Few New World producers would disagree with this view, but in the US and Australia the emphasis has often been on what happens to grapes at the winery. In the 1990s, the two attitudes collided when, unhappy with the wine they were getting from some French regions, British retailers sent "flying wine makers,"

THE OLD WAY
Wine presses, like this one at Kientzheim in Alsace, were built to last for centuries. Until recently, wine-making techniques had altered very little over the years.

WINE PRESS
Basket presses are still used in Champagne. Old ones, like this, are operated by hand.

who were often Australian or had been trained in Australia, to the *coopératives* in France to make the wine for them.

BOTTLING IT UP

Historically, grape growers could not afford wooden presses, barrels, and fermenting vats, so they had little to do with the making of wine. Grapes went to the monastery or château that served as a central processing plant. Even when, as in Burgundy, individual estates did make their own wine, they sold it on to merchants and *négociants* who blended and bottled it. Today, Burgundies bottled at a *domaine* are increasingly popular and represent a growing proportion of the region's wine. Even in Bordeaux, where châteaux have held on to the good reputations they have gained for centuries, the idea of the wine

maker bottling the wine, rather than a merchant, only dates back to the end of World War II The 1970s and 1980s brought the arrival of New World competition and of a new generation of *vignerons* who had learned their skills at college. Unlike their parents, they know how things are done in other regions of France and have often worked in Australia or California. They prefer to deal with customers worldwide than to be restricted to a local merchant or *coopérative,* and they want to see their own labels on their bottles. Even 20 years ago, it was a rare Champagne that was not produced by a big merchant or *coopérative.* Today, however, it is as though every second cottage in the region houses a small grower with wine to sell.

Competition among *vignerons* is fierce. They know the value of a good rating from an influential critic and are aware that skillful grape growing is only the first step on the journey to success. They appreciate that how they treat those grapes will have a crucial influence on the quality and flavor of the wine. A wine may be made in the vineyard, but it can be improved in the *cave*.

CHÂTEAU CARBONNIEUX
Bottling at the château is a relatively new idea. Before World War II, it was common for wine to be shipped in bulk for bottling by merchants.

THE NEW WAY
Modern wineries, like this one at Château Haut-Brion in Bordeaux, make use of stainless-steel vats.

Grape Varieties

The character of any wine is influenced by the soil, the climate, and the art of the wine maker; but nothing will dictate its flavor more than the variety, or varieties, of grape from which it is made.

Gamay
Grown in several regions, the Gamay performs at its best in the granite soil of Beaujolais.

Merlot and Cabernet Sauvignon
These Bordeaux grape varieties need very different soils. The Merlot (left) likes clay, while the Cabernet Sauvignon (right) prefers gravel.

STRINGENT RULES APPLIED OVER THE centuries have decreed precisely which varieties of grape might be planted where; but despite them, wine growers in France obstinately continued to experiment with new grape varieties. All that was stopped, however, by the establishment of a countrywide *appellation contrôlée* system set up in 1935 to control the origin and quality of French wines. Pomerol *(see p.87)*, for example, which produced white wine before 1935, is now a red-only zone; the only area of choice left open to its wine growers is the precise proportion of the Merlot, Cabernet Franc, and Cabernet Sauvignon grapes that they grow. In regions such as Burgundy *(see pp.98–141)*, where only one grape variety is used in each style of wine, all the wine growers can choose is the specific clone, or group of clones, with which to replant their vineyards. The

appellation rules have undoubtedly, and laudably, helped to protect the individuality of France's best-known wines and encouraged the adoption of traditional French grape varieties in the New World. Less positively, however, they have also effectively halted experimentation in the vineyards, stopping vinous evolution in its tracks.

There are, fortunately, some welcome exceptions to this state of affairs. In southern France, for example, recent moves have been made to acknowledge the improvement that judicious change can bring to wines. Quality has improved following a reduction in the use of traditional, rather dull grape varieties, such as the Carignan, and the introduction of proven alternatives, such as the Syrah and the Mourvèdre. Other more famous regions, such as Muscadet, could benefit from similarly innovative thinking.

THE BEST-KNOWN GRAPE VARIETIES OF FRANCE

A **Aligoté** Acidic white grape grown in Burgundy, where it is used to produce good white wine, especially in the village of Bouzeron.

C **Cabernet Franc** A component of red Bordeaux, this grassy cousin of the Cabernet Sauvignon is most interesting in red wines from the Loire, such as Chinon and Bourgueil.

Cabernet Sauvignon The major component of Bordeaux from the Médoc. This blackcurranty, bell-peppery grape is also widely used for southern *appellation* blends and for *vins de pays*.

Carignan The mainstay of Languedoc-Roussillon reds such as Fitou, Corbières, and Minervois, this variety tends to produce dull, earthy flavors unless it is carefully handled.

Chardonnay The world's most popular white grape, now grown not only in Burgundy and Champagne, but also in the Loire and southern France, where it is used for *vins de pays*.

CHARDONNAY
The grape of white Burgundy and Champagne.

Chasselas A once-popular, non-aromatic white variety still used in Alsace and in Pouilly-sur-Loire.

Chenin Blanc The grape of classic white wines from the Loire, such as Vouvray, sparkling Saumur, and Bonnezeaux.

Cinsault A full-bodied and increasingly widely used component of red wines from the southern Rhône and many parts of southern France.

Colombard Basic appley grape variety grown in Gascogne in southwest France.

G **Gamay** The red grape used in the Loire, Beaujolais, Gaillac, and the Mâconnais.

Gewürztraminer Exotic white Alsatian grape with flavors of lychees, violets, and rose water.

Grenache Peppery variety used to make Côtes du Rhône in the southern Rhône and as a component in other reds from southern France.

Gros/Petit Manseng The deliciously honeyed white grape varieties of Jurançon.

Gros Plant An undeniably undistinguished grape variety used to produce the dryly acidic white wine of the same name in the Loire valley.

M **Malbec** Traditionally used as a major component in red Bordeaux blends, this spicy grape variety is now grown only in Cahors and in the Loire, where it is known as Cot.

Marsanne Flowery, limey, white variety used in the Rhône valley, often with the finer Roussanne, to make Hermitage and Châteauneuf-du-Pape.

Melon de Bourgogne A non-aromatic variety, only used to produce Muscadet.

Merlot The toffeeish, plummy variety of Bordeaux, grown especially in St. Émilion and Pomerol. Increasingly used in southern French *vins de pays*.

Mourvèdre A blackberryish component of reds in the Rhône. Also grown in the south, particularly in Bandol.

P **Pinot Blanc** Alsatian variety, producing dry, creamy, brazil-nutty wines.

Pinot Gris/Tokay Spicy white variety producing wonderful dry and late-harvest wines in Alsace.

PINOT NOIR
Used to make both red Burgundy and Champagne.

Pinot Meunier Black-skinned cousin of the Pinot Noir that is found in far more Champagne than is generally admitted.

Pinot Noir The raspberryish variety used in great red Burgundy, red and pink Sancerre, red Alsace and in southern French *vins de pays*. Also used to make Champagne and red Bouzy.

R **Riesling** A great appley, limey white grape used in both sweet and dry Alsace.

Roussanne The delicately perfumed white grape used, with the Marsanne grape, in the Rhône.

S **Sauvignon Blanc** A gooseberryish, asparagussy white grape variety used in wines from the Loire and Bordeaux.

Sémillon The peachy variety used with the Sauvignon Blanc in white Bordeaux.

Sylvaner Non-aromatic white grape used in Alsace.

Syrah Smoky, blackberryish, spicy grape used in northern Rhône reds and, increasingly, in the reds of southern French areas such as Minervois.

T **Tannat** The tough red wine grape of Madiran.

V **Viognier** Once restricted to the northern Rhône, this gloriously perfumed grape is now used in *vins de pays*.

RIESLING
One of the great Alsatian grapes, now sadly unfashionable outside France.

CLIMATE, SOIL, AND VINEYARDS

The individual flavor of every wine is created by a combination of factors. A subtle variation of soil or microclimate can make wines produced in neighboring vineyards taste quite different.

HEALTHY CHILL
While frost can cause problems in spring, cold weather in winter helps to keep vines dormant and ensures that their sap is kept down in the roots.

BLOOD OUT OF STONES
Châteauneuf-du-Pape's pebbles store and reflect heat, a process that contributes to the rich flavor of its wines.

IF THE FRENCH LANGUAGE HAS NO translation for the English term "wine maker," it has in *terroir* a far more valuable and untranslatable word of its own that is now being used throughout the wine making world. The classic definition of this term was offered by Bruno Prats, former owner of Château Cos d'Estournel in Bordeaux. For Prats, *terroir* is "the combination of the climate, the soil, and the landscape" that forms the character of a vineyard and its wines. At its simplest, *terroir* could refer to a chalky hillside in a cool region, but the term is far more precise than that. As Prats continues, "the night and day temperatures, the distribution of rainfall, hours of sunlight, the slope and drainage... All these factors react together in each part of the vineyard...."

So, although the literal meaning of *terroir* is "soil," it actually refers to far more than that. The climate, or to be more precise the macro- and microclimate, is a vital component of *terroir*. The macroclimate is the weather of a whole region, for example the sea-influenced and moderate conditions of Bordeaux, or the more extreme, continental conditions of Burgundy. The microclimate refers instead to prevailing conditions and the geographical location of a specific vineyard: the altitude of the vineyard and the proximity of hills, forests, rivers, lakes or the sea. The aspect of the vineyard, its orientation and gradient, also acts in determining its microclimate.

ASPECTS OF THE TERROIR

Vines grown on south-facing slopes get more sunshine and, as a result, ripen much better than those that are grown on flat land. While hills and woods can offer a protective "rain shadow" against storms, they can also provide shelter from winds that would otherwise blow away the pockets of cold air in which frost develops. A nearby lake or river can increase humidity, which in turn raises the likelihood of both desirable noble rot (see p.93) and undesirable gray rot developing.

The soil in which vines are grown has three sets of properties. The first, texture, is determined by the size of the particles that make up the soil. Vines can be grown in soil that is either as fine as sand or as lumpy as pebbles. However, if the particles are not to be blown or washed away by the wind or rain, they must be glued together by clay. Some soils contain more clay than others, with the clay itself varying in nature. The second property, the soil's structure, determines the way in which clay bonds particles of soil together and how water is retained in the soil or drained away. This depends also on the amount and nature of organic matter, the level of sodium and calcium, and the nature of the clay. Soil's third property, its degree of acidity, determines how acidic the wine will be.

VIEW FROM THE TERRACES
The earliest wine makers discovered that, although vines planted on steep hillside slopes ripened better, they were hard to tend and pick. To solve the problem, they soon began to lay out their vineyards on terraces.

THE PRINCIPAL SOILS OF FRANCE

CHALK BUT NO CHEESE
Champagne and other dry white wines benefit from chalky soil like this.

PRICELESS GRAVEL
Bordeaux's gravelly soil is perfect for growing the Cabernet Sauvignon.

Alluvial Potentially fertile, sandy, silty, gravelly soil laid down by rivers. At its best in the Médoc.

Argillaceous Catch-all term for sedimentary clay, siltstones, marl or shale. *Argilo-calcaire* means a combination of clay and limestone.

Clay Acid, malleable, argillaceous compound that holds water well and drains poorly. Important as subsoil in Pomerol, where it is well suited to the Merlot grape.

Granite Both quartz-rich, hard rock and the alkaline, easy-draining, low-fertility soil of the best vineyards of Beaujolais and the northern Rhône.

Gravel Easy-draining, low-fertility, pebbly topsoil that is at its best in Bordeaux and Châteauneuf-du-Pape, where it retains the heat of the sun.

Limestone Alkaline, easy-draining rock, mainly consisting of calcium carbonates. Best suited to white wines.

Loam A crumbly mixture of clay, silt, and sand. Generally too fertile for fine wine.

Marl Acidic mixture of limestone and clay that is at its best in the Côte d'Or, the Rhône, and Jura.

Sand Sandy soil has the advantage of deterring the phylloxera beetle and the disadvantage of draining too easily and storing no nutrients.

Sandstone Variable sedimentary rock that can be composed either of quartz or calcium carbonate.

Schist Crystalline rock that can be split into layers. Found beneath soil of Alsace and in the Côte Rôtie. Rich in magnesium and potassium.

Shale Crumbly, quite fertile, sedimentary rock.

Silt Quite fertile, poor-draining river deposit.

Slate Crystalline rock formed from clay, mudstone, and shale, to be found beneath the topsoil of Pouilly Fumé and parts of southern Beaujolais – known in French as *schiste*.

Tufa/Tuffeau Easy-draining limestone soil of the Loire.

Grape Growing and Harvesting

Wherever the vineyard and whatever the style of wine, the grapes develop according to an inexorable timetable, dictating what the wine grower will be doing at any given time of the year.

J ANUARY Despite low temperatures, wine growers are out pruning their vines. Traditionally, pruning was begun on the 22nd, the feast day of St. Vincent, patron saint of wine growers.

F EBRUARY A quiet month in the vineyards once the pruning is finished. There is, however, plenty of work to be done on the new wine maturing in the cellars.

M ARCH Most wine growers have finished pruning and will now be tilling the soil in order to aerate it and remove weeds. In some areas, depending on soil type and local climate, late March sees bud-break, the first sign of new growth on the woody vine.

A PRIL Rapid growth of leaves, shoots, and embryo bunches follows bud-break. The embryo bunches, which will eventually flower and become grapes, are the first indication of the size and date of the coming harvest. Cool temperatures or rain at this time may cause *millerandage*, the formation of seedless grapes that never grow to maturity. A spell of especially warm sunshine, on the other hand, encourages the vine's sap to feed the leaves rather than the embryo grapes, often leading to *coulure*, in which the embryos fail to develop, and fall off the plant.

M AY Oil stoves and windmills are often used to protect the vulnerable leafy vine from frost. The soil is tilled to remove weeds and many growers spray the vines against mildew and oidium fungus and add fertilizer to the soil.

J UNE This is the month in which the vines pollinate, fertilize, and flower. Dry, warm weather now allows the vines to flower rapidly, and the grapes on each bunch to grow simultaneously. Changeable weather produces bunches with berries of uneven ripeness, so-called "hens and chickens." After flowering, some shoots are trained to the wires and others removed. Spraying against oidium continues.

PRUNING
Trimming back the vines for spring growth is a laborious and often chilly process, but it is a job that must be done before the new season begins.

BUD-BREAK
As winter gives way to spring, fresh green leaves transform the vines from dead-looking wood into fruitful plants.

FLOWERS
The flowering of the vine is one of the most exciting moments of the growing season, providing a first glimpse of the future crop.

JULY As the vines respond to the warm weather, each fertilized berry in the embryo bunches becomes a recognizable tiny grape. This is called "fruit set." Some grape varieties, such as Merlot, set less successfully than others. The wine grower removes some bunches now to concentrate the vines' energy into the remaining fruit. Spraying against oidium continues in the vineyard and growers may clear the ground of weeds.

AUGUST This is the time for *véraison*, a series of important chemical changes marked by the changing of the color of the grape skins. The sugar content of the grapes increases dramatically at this stage. This is a critical moment for the vines: a bad storm followed by warm weather provides perfect conditions for rot, one of the reasons why growers increasingly remove some foliage to allow air and sunlight to reach the grapes. Drought conditions occurring now will slow the ripening process.

SEPTEMBER Quality-conscious growers will be trimming the vines tightly and possibly performing a *vendange verte*, or green harvest, removing a proportion of the potential crop in order to concentrate the vines' energies. Drought conditions still pose a danger to the ripening grapes. Likewise, rain or even hail at this time of year may well expose the grapes to the risk of rot. Depending on the region, the weather conditions and the grape variety, the grape harvest is usually begun in late September.

VÉRAISON
A crucial stage in the vineyard, when chemical changes cause grapes to become sweeter and black grapes to develop their color.

OCTOBER In most regions, grapes are still being picked In some years and in areas where late-harvest wines are made, the harvest may just be beginning. Once the crop is in and the grapes have been pressed, the skin, stalks and pips, known as the *marc*, are spread among the vines, often together with a combination of manure and chemical fertilizer.

NOVEMBER As cold weather returns, the sap retreats into the vines' root systems. The vineyard is tidied and the feet of the vines are cleared of soil in preparation for the rigors of winter.

DECEMBER Most wine growers are busy dispatching wines to customers in time for Christmas. A few will begin some early pruning in the vineyards.

HARVEST
While machines are widely used to pick the grapes, most quality-conscious producers still prefer to harvest their crop by hand.

How Red Wine is Made

Human skill will always be the key to transforming grapes into a well-made wine, whether the equipment and techniques used are age-old or modern, very simple or highly sophisticated.

MACHINE PICKING
Mechanical harvesters are highly efficient, picking grapes quickly, 24 hours a day.

Once the wine grower has determined the moment when the grapes are as ripe as possible, while retaining sufficient acidity, the grapes can be harvested, either manually or by machine. Many people believe that harvesting by hand makes for higher quality, but machine harvesting, in which the grapes are shaken from the vines, may be conducted both in daylight and at night.

Fermentation

Quality-conscious producers remove rotten grapes, either in the vineyard or at the *cuverie*. Stalks are also removed to avoid the harsh tannic character they might give the finished wine. The fruit is then lightly crushed and transferred into a stainless steel tank, the *cuve*, or a wooden vat, the *foudre*. The grapes are now left to macerate, or soften, for two or three days. Fermentation is kicked off using either cultured yeasts or yeasts occurring naturally in the grapes. The fruit may be heated or fermenting juice, called must, may be added. To prevent the floating skins and pips from drying out, the must is pumped over them, or they are pushed down with wooden paddles in a process known as *pigeage*. Some wine makers use rotary fermenters similar to sealed cement mixers, but some critics say this causes excessive astringency. For successful fermentation the fruit must be kept at 77–86°F (25–30°C). Soft, fruity wine such as Beaujolais (*see pp.106–7*) is made by a process known as *macération carbonique*, which involves fermenting the grapes uncrushed.

HARVESTING
BLACK GRAPES
The key to making good wine lies in the quality of the grapes. Quality-conscious producers sort the grapes in the vineyard or at the cuverie, *discarding any which are either underripe or rotten.*

Adjusting the Mixture

The alcoholic strength of the wine may be increased by adding sugar, chaptalizing, during fermentation. Likewise, acidity may be increased by adding tartaric acid, a substance that occurs naturally in the grape. Strict legislation restricts both chaptalization and acidification, but is often ignored. If the mixture is too watery, some of the part-fermented pink juice is drawn off, concentrating the remainder. The wine made from the drawn-off juice may be sold as rosé.

After Fermentation

Fermentation is complete when all the sugar has been converted into alcohol. The wine may now be left to macerate on the skins for a period of between one and four weeks, during which time the color will deepen and the tannins soften. The free-running juice, the *vin de goutte*, is then drawn off and the solids transferred to a press, which extracts from them the tougher, darker wine known as press wine or *vin de presse*. The two are kept separate until the wine maker is ready to blend them before bottling.

Following fermentation, red wine will almost always be allowed to undergo a natural process called malolactic fermentation, in which appley malic acid is transformed into creamier lactic acid.

Some wine, such as Beaujolais and basic *vin de pays*, is intended to be drunk young, but most high-quality wine will now be matured for up to 18 months in wooden casks. Increasingly, some or all of the casks will be made of new oak. When used carefully, oak gives the wine an appealing vanilla character. It can, however, easily overpower other subtler flavors.

New Wine Barrels
Good-quality red wines are increasingly matured in casks made of new French oak, which give the wine an attractive hint of vanilla.

Racking and Fining

Sulphur is used to protect the developing wine against bacteria throughout the wine-making process. If not managed carefully, though, it can combine with hydrogen to produce the stink bomb smell and flavor of hydrogen sulphide, or foul-smelling mercaptans, which are hydrogen sulphide and alcohol compounds. One way to prevent this problem is to rack the wine, transferring it from one cask to another to aerate it and prevent it from becoming stale.

Before bottling, the wine is likely to be fined or clarified with powdered clay or beaten egg whites to remove cloudiness. It may also be filtered to remove sediment, though many producers now prefer to bottle their wine unfiltered, and possibly even unfined, to preserve as much of its flavor as possible.

Egg White
When added to the wine, beaten egg whites drag suspended solids with them as they fall to the bottom of the cask.

HOW WHITE WINE IS MADE

Many factors can influence the more delicate flavors associated with white wines, and many wine makers believe that producing a really good white presents the ultimate challenge.

HARVESTING THE GRAPES
These grapes being harvested in Riquewihr, Alsace, will be used to make rich, aromatic, and slightly sweet white wines.

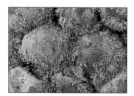

NOBLE ROT
The unattractive but highly-prized Botrytis cinerea *fungus, otherwise known as noble rot, will give the sweet wine made from these grapes a delicious apricot flavor.*

WHILE THE SKINS OF BLACK grapes provide the tannins that give red wine its longevity and are responsible for the color of the finished red wine, the skins of white grapes have little or no role to play in finished white wine. For various reasons, it is far trickier to make white wine that tastes good than it is to make a drinkable red wine. First, the thinner skins of most white grape varieties increase the risk of harmful rot in the vineyard. It is also easy for white grapes to become oxidized or "cooked" if they are left out in the sun after picking, as happens at many southern *cuveries*. Some producers reduce the risk by using machines to pick the grapes at night, but quality-conscious growers still prefer to harvest by hand.

Picking white grapes too early gives the wine a green character, while harvesting too late makes for dull wine. In some regions, however, grapes are deliberately allowed to overripen, developing as much natural sugar as possible in the hope that they will become covered by the sought-after fungus *Botrytis cinerea (see p93)* or noble rot. This fungus concentrates the flavors of the grape and adds a dried-apricot character of its own. Noble rot, however, only occurs in humid conditions in which undesirable gray rot is also a risk. For this reason, makers of sweet botrytized wines have to take special care to select only grapes with the right kind of rot.

SULPHURING AND PRESSING

One of the best ways to avoid oxidation and unwanted rot is to use sulphur dioxide, which works both as an antiseptic and as an antioxidant. Sulphur is as

SORTING THE GRAPES
Thin-skinned white grapes require careful sorting to eliminate rotten and oxidized fruit.

necessary in a *cuverie* as soap is in a kitchen; but in excess it is as unwelcome in a wine as detergent in a sauce. Nowadays, in any case, most producers also use cooling equipment that helps to keep bacteria at bay.

Having arrived at the *cuverie*, white grapes pass into the press often uncrushed and still attached to their stalks. Alternatively, in the case of less aromatic grape varieties, the wine maker may crush the grapes and leave them for several days in a vat or a cement mixer-like tank called a *vinimatic*, which extracts the aromatics stored in the skins before the grapes are pressed. Once the grapes have been pressed, the juice will be separated from the pips and skins. The juice may be chilled, fined, or filtered at this point, but many producers of quality white wines believe that these procedures remove flavor and richness from the wine.

FERMENTATION
Fermentation, using natural or cultured yeasts, now follows, either in stainless steel tanks or in wooden barrels. Fermentation takes place at anything from 41–86°F (5–30°C) and can take weeks or even months. Low temperatures produce light, crisp wines with a pear-drop character. Warmer temperatures produce richer, fatter-textured wines with less specific flavors. After fermentation, dry white wines such as Bourgogne and Bordeaux will be allowed to undergo a naturally-occurring biochemical process known as malolactic fermentation, in which appley

malic acid is transformed into richer lactic acid. For sweeter wines that benefit from the freshness of the malic acid, malolactic fermentation is prevented by adding sulphur.

Light-bodied, fruity wines will now be fined, filtered, and bottled, often within a few months of the harvest. Finer wines will be matured for up to 18 months, probably in oak barrels. Filtering may now take place. Sulphur, in as small a quantity as possible, will be added before bottling to protect the wine from oxidation as it matures.

ROSÉ WINES
Champagne rosé is made by mixing red and white wine. All other French rosé wines are made from black grape juice that is drawn off before the skins have had time to give it much color. In every other respect, rosé wine is produced in the same way as white.

VATS AND BARRELS
Modern producers such as the Château de Meursault in Burgundy use a combination of stainless steel vats and new oak barrels for fermenting and maturing their wines.

ROSÉ
Made from the juice of black grapes, like red wine, but produced in the same way as white, rosé owes its delicate color to restricted contact with the black grape skins.

CHAMPAGNE AND FORTIFIED WINES

Many areas of France produce excellent sparkling wines, including, of course, the world-famous wines of Champagne. Also of interest are the various fortified wines known as *vins doux naturels*.

CHAMPAGNE YEAST
Yeast is the secret ingredient that puts the bubbles into sparkling wine, causing it to ferment in the bottle.

MECHANICAL REMUAGE
Even in the most illustrious Champagne houses, machines have taken over over the laborious task of remuage.

BOTH COLA DRINKS AND THE FINEST Champagne contain bubbles of dissolved carbon dioxide. To make cola, the carbon dioxide is injected directly into the drink. The same method can also be used in wine making, but it will not produce a wine of any quality or longevity. Four different methods are used to produce fine sparkling wine, all of which create carbon dioxide naturally during fermentation.

The most traditional method is the now rare *méthode rurale*, which involves bottling the wine during its initial fermentation, like cider or beer. The carbon dioxide released as fermentation continues has nowhere to go and so remains dissolved in the wine. One wine produced by this method is the sweet Clairette de Die Méthode Dioise Ancestrale, from the northern Rhône. Fine dry wines are made by this method in Gaillac in southwest France, where it is known as the *méthode gaillaçoise*.

MÉTHODE CHAMPENOISE

More widely used in the production of high-quality wines than the *méthode rurale* is the *méthode champenoise*. In wines made by this method a second fermentation is induced in the bottle. To achieve this, the wine maker adds a *liqueur de tirage*, a blend of wine, sugar, and yeast, after fermentation and before bottling. As in the *méthode rurale*, the released carbon dioxide remains dissolved in the wine. Wine made by the *méthode champenoise*, however, will take flavor from the yeast solids used to kick off the second fermentation.

To avoid a gritty deposit at the bottom of your glass, the dead yeast must be removed once the second fermentation is complete. This is achieved by a process called *remuage*: by manually or mechanically turning and shaking the gradually upturned bottle, the yeast solids are made to slide down into the neck of the bottle where they are collected in a thimble-like container beneath the stopper. The upturned bottles are now aged for between one and four years, depending on the region and the style. Once the second fermentation is complete, the dead yeast cells are broken down in a process called autolysis, which gives the finished wine the biscuity character that is the hallmark of this method. The longer the aging period, the stronger the biscuity flavor. Eventually the

MANUAL REMUAGE
Only on a few estates is the skilled and lengthy task of remuage still performed by hand.

yeast is removed in a process called *dégorgement*: the wine is frozen and the stopper, usually a beer-bottle cap, is removed. The pressure that has built up in the wine propels the icy yeast out of the bottle, leaving the remaining wine clear. The bottle is now topped up and a blend of wine and sugar syrup, known as the *liqueur d'expédition*, is added. Finally, the bottle is resealed with a traditional Champagne cork.

The remaining two methods are simplifications of the *méthode champenoise* and neither is used to make *appellation contrôlée* wine. In the transfer method, instead of undergoing *remuage*, the wine and yeast are transferred into a tank before being filtered and rebottled. The *cuve close* method is similar to the transfer method, except that the second fermentation takes place in a sealed tank instead of a bottle.

FORTIFIED WINES

Less famous than port, sherry, Marsala, and Madeira, France's fortified wines, or *vins doux naturels*, deserve a larger share of the spotlight. The principle behind the production of all fortified wines is the same: the fermentation of the juice of very ripe white or black grapes is interrupted by the addition of neutral, unflavored grape spirit. This raises the alcohol content of the vat above 15 percent, killing off the yeasts and halting fermentation. Wines made in this way, such as the famous Muscat de Beaumes-de-Venise (*see p.215*), are by definition sweet and fruity. They are often fairly simple in character and rarely improve with age.

One exception is Banyuls (*see p.164*), most southerly of the French *appellations*. Red Banyuls is France's answer to vintage port, developing great complexity with age and left in the bottle for up to 40 years. Other fortified wines that age well are well-made *rancio* wines, such as Rasteau (*see p.216*) in the southern Rhône. To be labeled *rancio*, fortified wine must be stored in oak casks and exposed to heat (often sunshine) and oxygen for at least two years, during which time the wine develops its distinctive nutty, tangy, *rancio* flavor.

VIN DOUX NATUREL
France's fortified wines are appreciated by the French but often sadly overlooked by wine drinkers elsewhere.

CHAMPAGNE CORKS
Made from separate layers of cork of varying flexibility, the corks used for sparkling wines develop their mushroom shape in the bottle.

READING THE LABEL

UNDERSTANDING THE LABEL IS ESSENTIAL TO SUCCESS IN
CHOOSING WINES, AND FRENCH LABELS CAN BE SOME OF THE MOST
INFORMATIVE, AND SOME OF THE MOST CONFUSING, IN THE WORLD.

PROOF OF IDENTITY
*Producers on even the
smallest family-run
estates must comply with
labeling requirements,
which vary depending on
the country to which the
wines are exported.*

FRAUDULENT LABELING by wine merchants was not uncommon in the early 20th century, and since that time the French authorities have done their utmost to lay down labeling legislation designed to protect the consumer. The most vaunted and visible part of this legislation is the system of *appellation contrôlée*, or controlled appellation (*see pp.34–5*). Before putting the *appellation contrôlée* system under the magnifying glass, however, it is useful to understand the other pieces of information that appear on French wine labels.

The label on the front of every bottle, whether classified as a basic *vin de pays* (*see pp.230–233*), a *vin délimité de qualité supérieure* or *VDQS* (*see p.32*), or an *appellation d'origine contrôlée*, is legally required to include certain pieces

of information. First, the bottle volume, usually 37.5 cl, 75 cl, or 150 cl. Second, the name and address of the bottler, who may also be the producer. Unhelpfully, this information sometimes appears in code, as *JFV à 5600* for example, or may be one of a number of pseudonyms adopted to help sell the same wine to a variety of customers. A final piece of information required by law is the place where the wine was made. Any wine that fails to reveal its geographic origins can only be sold as a *vin de table* and, as such, is denied the right to declare a vintage or a grape variety.

Other information that often appears on the label includes: a particular brand name, such as Mouton Cadet, Malesan, or Piat d'Or; the name of a particular vine-

---

ALSACE
*This is the only major
region in France to
specify the grape variety
on almost all of its labels.
Wines, like this one,
labeled "sélection de
grains nobles," are made
from nobly rotted, or
botrytized, grapes.*

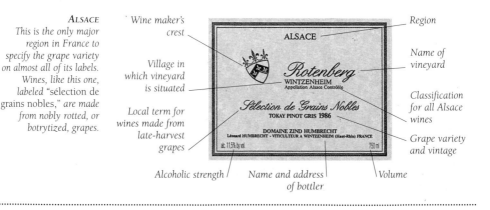

Wine maker's crest

Village in which vineyard is situated

Local term for wines made from late-harvest grapes

Alcoholic strength

Name and address of bottler

Region

Name of vineyard

Classification for all Alsace wines

Grape variety and vintage

Volume

ALSACE

Rotenberg
WINTZENHEIM
Appellation Alsace Contrôlée

Sélection de Grains Nobles
TOKAY PINOT GRIS 1986

DOMAINE ZIND HUMBRECHT
Léonard HUMBRECHT - VITICULTEUR A WINTZENHEIM (Haut-Rhin) FRANCE

alc. 11.5% by vol.   750 ml

Appellation contrôlée

Name and address of bottler

Indication that Robert Ampeau is a grower and producer, not a merchant

Wine maker's crest

Village in which wine was produced

Combettes is a premier cru vineyard, a fact that may, or may not, be mentioned on label

yard, such as Clos du Mesnil, or of an individual *cuvée*, such as Cuvée Laurence; the alcoholic strength, which is usually between 10.5 and 15 percent; the classification (*vin de table*, *vin de pays*, *VDQS*, or *appellation d'origine contrôlée*); whether or not the wine was bottled on the estate; and finally, the vintage when the wine was made.

LOCAL CLASSIFICATIONS
In addition to the terms discussed above, different regions also use particular local systems of classification. To illustrate this point, I have chosen labels from three different regions, Alsace (*see pp.58–69*), Burgundy (*see pp.98–141*), and Bordeaux (*see pp.70–97*). In Alsace, the grape variety nearly always appears on the label, and, in addition, 50 or so of the best vineyards are classified as *grand cru*. In Bordeaux and Burgundy, on the other hand, classifications of the best estates and vineyards are confusingly varied, including *cru bourgeois*, *cru classé*, *premier cru*, *grand cru*, *grand cru classé*, and *premier grand cru classé*. In the case of these wines, the grape

variety never features on the label. It is also important to be aware of a number of grand-sounding words that often appear on labels, but which should be taken with a large pinch of salt. *Grand Vin de France*, *Cuvée Prestige*, and *Réserve Speciale*, for example, are all legally meaningless terms. Likewise, while the phrase *vieilles vignes* or old vines suggests especially rich wines, no one has defined how old a vine must be to qualify as *vieille*. Finally, while a wine labeled *élevé en fûts de chêne* will have spent time in an oak barrel, there is no way of knowing the age of the barrel, important since old and young oak affects the wine in different ways.

Name of estate

Indication that Château Lynch Bages was included in 1855 classification of the Médoc

Producer's crest

Commune in which wine was made

Vintage

Name and address of bottler

Appellation contrôlée

WINES FOR EVERYDAY DRINKING

The majority of French vineyards produce wines that fall outside the prestigious *appellation contrôlée* classification system, but which can still offer enormous enjoyment and interest.

GROWING IN STATURE
At the time when this excellent wine was produced, the Corbières region was classified as vin délimité de qualité supérieure *or VDQS, but Corbières now enjoys* appellation contrôlée *status.*

ALL FRENCH WINES are classified as part of a pyramid system designed as a guide to quality. Divided into four categories, the bottom layer consists of *vin de table*, next, *vin de pays*, then *vin délimité de qualité supérieure* (VDQS) and, finally, *appellation contrôlée*.

VIN DE TABLE
Covering 28 percent of French wines, this is the most basic of the country's quality designations. There are no rules as to how *vin de table* may be produced, except that no grape variety or place of origin can be stated on the front label. *Vin de table* is rarely of great quality, but occasionally the classification includes good wines that fall foul of restrictive *appellation* rules. Examples include the innovative, sweet Pouilly-Fumé (*see p.184*) made by Didier Dagueneau, one of the best wine makers in the Loire valley, and Rebelle, the award-winning, blended red wine produced by the Bordeaux firm of Dulong.

VIN DE PAYS
The next layer in the pyramid is made up of 150 or so *vins de pays* or "country wine" *appellations*. Introduced in 1973 to promote regional wines, the *vin de pays* classification specifies grape varieties, production methods, and an area of origin for each style of wine. Unlike most *appellation contrôlée* wines, *vins de pays* are allowed to name the grape variety on their label. The wines in this fast-evolving category were not designed to be more than decent daily-drinking fare, and the fact that the best *vins de pays* now sell for more than some *appellation contrôlée* wines is something that

VIN DE TABLE
This unusual award-winning red is made with a blend of grapes from different regions. Under French law this means that the label may not identify the regions, the grapes, or the vintage, and that the wine can be sold only as vin de table.

Producer's name and logo

Brand name

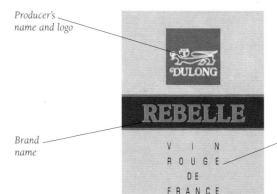

Forbidden by law to state a grape variety or an exact place of origin, this description says simply, "French red wine"

Name of estate

Cépage, or grape variety

Quality designation

Name and address of bottler

Wine style, in this case blanc (white), and moelleux (medium-sweet)

Logo indicating membership of the association of independent vine growers

Wine is estate-bottled

VIN DE PAYS
Domaine Cazes is entitled to sell many of its wines as part of the appellation contrôlée system. This unfortified Muscat, however, falls outside the appellation rules and is therefore sold as a vin de pays. Like most vins de pays, but unlike most appellation contrôlée wines, its grape variety is specified on the label.

many supporters of the *appellation contrôlée* system still find hard to swallow. To achieve this state of affairs, ambitious producers, such as Aimé Guibert of Mas de Daumas Gassac in the Hérault (*see p.232*), and Robert Skalli of Skalli Fortant de France in Languedoc-Roussillon, have applied skill and care in the production of their *vins de pays* to match that of the better producers of *appellation contrôlée* wines. Accounting for a quarter of French wine production, the success of *vins de pays* has led to the strange situation where grapes from *appellation contrôlée* vineyards in Minervois (*see p.169*) and Corbières

(*see p.165*), for example, are being used, for the time being at least, to make wines sold as *vins de pays*.

VIN DÉLIMITÉ DE QUALITÉ SUPÉRIEURE

Finally, squeezed between the *vins de pays* and the *appellations contrôlées,* is the small category of *vin délimité de qualité supérieure* or VDQS, officially due to have been phased out for some years. Most VDQS wines have now been promoted to *appellation contrôlée* status, but a few, including the well-known Sauvignon de St. Bris (*see p.136*), are still inexplicably caught in this odd administrative limbo.

Name of estate

Quality designation

Alcohol content

Name and address of bottler

Volume

Official name of district

VDQS symbol

VIN DÉLIMITÉ DE QUALITÉ SUPÉRIEUR
One of France's shrinking band of VDQS wines, Sauvignon de St. Bris is made entirely with Sauvignon Blanc grapes, as its name suggests. Other VDQS wines often make no mention of the grape variety.

Appellation d'Origine Contrôlée

Around 40 percent of all French wines are included in the *appellation d'origine contrôlée* system, which guarantees their style and geographical origin, though not their quality.

APPELLATION D'ORIGINE CONTRÔLÉE

Making the Rules
Based in Paris, the INAO, or Institut National des Appellations d'Origine, promotes and regulates the production of many French wines and a variety of other regional food products, including more than 30 cheeses.

SINCE ITS CREATION IN 1936, THE system of *appellation d'origine contrôlée,* or controlled appellation, has included all of France's best-known wines and has been widely copied around the world. The system was devised to protect honest producers and their customers by ensuring that the wine in every bottle corresponds to what is claimed on its label.

Today, as in 1936, the words *appellation contrôlée* aim to provide a guarantee of origin, style, and quality. In reality, most wine makers agree that, despite valiant efforts, the system often fails in a task fraught with pitfalls. On the plus side, the presence of an *appellation d'origine contrôlée* label will, despite a certain amount of illegal transfer of wine from one region to another,

generally guarantee that a wine comes from the region, *commune,* or vineyard on the label. In addition, it will almost certainly guarantee the variety of grape or grapes that have been used, as each *appellation* has its own list of permitted varieties. Even here, however, there are quirks in the system. Over 99 percent of the white wines of Burgundy (*see pp.98–141*), for example, are made from the Chardonnay grape, so wines made from the equally legal Pinot Blanc come as a surprise. In the same way, most wines from the *appellation* of Minervois (*see p.169*) are, like many southern French reds, made from a blend of grape varieties. Some producers, however, seeking to copy wines made in Australia and the Rhône valley (*see pp.200– 221*),

Young Vines in Muscadet
Only Melon de Bourgogne grapes can be used to make wines sold as appellation contrôlée *Muscadet. Legal restrictions on grape varieties help consumers to know what to expect from the wines of a particular* appellation.

have found a legal loophole that allows them to make their wines purely from the Syrah grape, which gives them a completely different flavor. Grape variety aside, while the *appellation d'origine contrôlée* rules do help to identify the style of a wine, they often do so in a rather irregular fashion. Didier Dagueneau's luscious, sweet, late-harvest Pouilly-Fumé (*see p.132*), for instance, is illegal, while there are plenty of producers in Vouvray (*see p.190*) and Alsace (*see pp.58–69*) who legally make sweet wines, often delicious, but which one expects from the label to be dry.

FLAWS IN THE SYSTEM

Further confusion is sown by the arcane legislation governing the way in which *premiers crus* vineyards are identified. Take, for example, the Charmes vineyard in Meursault (*see p.125*), which enjoys *premier cru* status. Producers there can label their wines either as *appellation contrôlée* Meursault Charmes Premier Cru, or as *appellation contrôlée* Meursault Charmes. Down the road from Charmes is the non-*premier cru* Clos de la Barre vineyard, whose wines may be labeled as *appellation contrôlée* Meursault or as *appellation contrôlée* Meursault Clos de la Barre. So, if you were confronted with two bottles, one Meursault Charmes and the other Meursault Clos de la Barre, how would you know which was from the *premier cru* vineyard? It's simple: according to *appellation* rules, unless the wine is from a *premier cru* vineyard, then the vineyard name must be printed in characters no more than half the height of the ones

used for the village name. Easy!! These difficulties, however, are minor in comparison with the worst failing of the system, which lies in the way it oversees quality. To carry the term *appellation contrôlée* on its label, every wine must undergo a blind tasting. The first flaw here is that the tasting is carried out by local experts who have been known to be rather generous in assessing the wines of their friends. Much more crucially, the tasting always takes place before the wine is bottled, often even before it is sold in bulk to a merchant, who will blend it with other wines. In other words, there is no reason to believe that the wine you are drinking is the one that was given its *appellation* by the tasting panel. In 1995, in an attempt to tackle the problems of the system, the head of the Institut National des Appellations d'Origine publicly acknowledged that some 15 percent of *appellation contrôlée* wines fail to come up to scratch. Shortly after making this admission, he found himself in a new job – looking after fish. Like France's farmers, her wine makers are clearly a powerful lobby.

HIDDEN QUALITY
Despite not having appellation contrôlée status, the vins de pays produced at Mas de Daumas Gassac, long-lived, top-class red and white wines, are among the most famous in France.

WINE PIONEERS
In 1923 Baron Leroy (left) sowed the seeds of what became the national appellation contrôlée system, put into practice by men such as Joseph Capus (far left), "godfather" of the appellation laws.

WINE TASTING

OF ALL THE SPECIALIZED SKILLS THAT HUMANITY HAS ACQUIRED

OVER THE CENTURIES, FEW HAVE BEEN MORE REGULARLY

LAMPOONED BY CARTOONISTS THAN THAT OF THE WINE TASTER.

LOOKING AT WINE
The appearance of a glass of wine can reveal its age and state of health, and it can even provide a hint of where it was made.

YOU CAN SEE THE CARTOONISTS' point. What, after all, is the connection between drinking and enjoying wine, and all that very serious-looking swirling, sniffing, and spitting? We in the West draw lines between the different ways in which we perceive and experience things. On one level, we see, hear, eat and drink, while on another we watch, listen, and taste. The difference is plain: sometimes we apply more of our brain to the task. A person may buy an expensive ticket and listen intently to Miles Davis, Mahler, or Mick Jagger in concert, but will, on another occasion, use the same music as the background to a social event.

Every day, all around the world, billions of mouthfuls of food and drink are eaten and drunk. How many are actually tasted, and how many are simply consumed?

Memory lies at the heart of the appreciation of almost anything. We may like or enjoy something on a first encounter, but we are bound to be setting it in the context of previous experiences. Wine tasting consists of briefly concentrating on a glass of wine sufficiently to be able to compare its characteristics with those of other wines you have tasted. The procedure, which will not look impolite in a restaurant, involves the stages shown on the right.

BEAUJOLAIS
This youthful Beaujolais, with an almost violet color that runs right to the rim, is typical of young red wine of every kind.

BURGUNDY
Burgundy can be recognized by its brick-red color. This example is three years old and already going slightly pale at the rim.

SEE

When analyzing a wine, first look at it. Whatever the style or age, it should be transparent and bright. Any cloudiness – as long as it is not simply caused by disturbing the deposit in a red wine – reveals a fault. A wine's color, and the depth of that color, indicates the wine's age, while the way in which the liquid flows down the inside of the glass will reveal its richness.

SNIFF

Swirl the wine around the glass, take a good sniff, then concentrate on what you have smelled. Does the wine seem light or intense? Fresh and clean, or musty, dirty, or vinegary? Does it smell of fruits, spices, flowers, or vegetables? Fix that smell or mixture of smells in your memory, and you will be surprised how quickly you begin to acquire the skill of guessing at the identity of a wine without having to read the label.

SIP

Wine tasters sip slowly, allowing the liquid to reveal as many layers of flavor as it has to reveal. In the past they focused on the tongue and its receptors for salt, sugar, sourness, and bitterness; now they pay more attention to aroma. To increase the effect of the oxygen, they aerate the wine by sucking air between their teeth and through the liquid. Along with the warming effect of the mouth, this will bring out flavors you might otherwise never notice.

SPIT OR SWALLOW

Spitting is a good idea if you have many wines to taste and do not want to ingest too much alcohol. Take a moment to concentrate on the flavor – if any – that the wine has left behind. One of the greatest differences between really fine wine and the ordinary stuff lies in the quality and longevity of the "finish" or aftertaste.

COLOR AND CLARITY
Is the wine bright and transparent? Youthful, or beginning to turn brown?

THE SMELL
Does it smell clean? And of what precisely? Is the aroma simple or complex?

BODY AND TEXTURE
Is the wine light and delicate, or richly full-bodied? Fat or thin?

THE FLAVOR
Does it taste of fruit? Is it spicy, gamey, or vegetal? Is there a single flavor or complex layers of flavors? Does the taste fade quickly or linger?

SAUTERNES
A three-year-old Sauternes like this, made in a good vintage, will have a lovely gold color that goes deeper with age.

RIESLING
A two-year-old dry Riesling from Alsace will have the color of pale straw. In a decade, however, this wine will turn gold.

JUDGING QUALITY

Having learned the mechanics of tasting wine, the next stage is to focus your new skills on the task of judging the quality of a wine and, just as importantly, its potential for improvement in future.

STILL GOING STRONG
Few wines have the quality needed to survive for three-quarters of a century. This one, from Château Margaux in Bordeaux, is one of the greats.

ASSUMING THAT A WINE POSSESSES attractive flavors and that they are well balanced, the feature that sets a fine wine apart from the rest is its complexity. While plenty of wines are like a melody played on a single instrument, the greatest wines have the many-layered quality of a full-blown symphony.

As it ages, the appearance of any wine will change. Try holding your glass tipped away from you against a white background, and look at the far edge of the liquid. The older the wine, the paler and more watery the edge will be. The color of the wine will give you more clues to its age, with reds beginning life violet, changing to ruby, then to brick and finally to brown. Whites

change from green-gold to gold and then to bronze. Smell and flavor also evolve. The wine loses the simple, primary characteristics derived from its grape variety and the way in which it was fermented and matured before bottling. It gains the more complex secondary smells and flavors that develop only during its time in the bottle.

Most wines today are drunk while primary characteristics are still evident. Some wines, such as Beaujolais (*see pp.106–7*), Muscadet (*see p.183*), and Vins de Pays d'Oc (*see p.233*), are actually at their best at this stage. Drinking great reds and whites in their youth, however, can be compared to going to watch a play in rehearsal rather than on its opening night.

FORECASTING THE FUTURE

To judge a wine's future potential, you look for various characteristics. Does it smell and taste fresh? Like sprightly elderly people, good wines can retain an element of freshness throughout life. Unfortunately, a

FUTURE STARS
Here, young wine of the previous year's vintage is tasted. Even expert tasters can make misjudgments at this stage.

wine that seems dull or stale today is likely to be even more so tomorrow. Does it have enough flavor to survive a few more years in the bottle? A light, delicate wine may taste good now, but after storage it may be thin and watery. There is also the matter of balance. A red wine will need a certain amount of tannin (its harshness balances the fruitiness of black grapes), and a white needs acidity to keep any tendency to sweetness in check. Neither tannin nor acid is good in excess, but it can be tricky to forecast changes in the balance between them as the wine ages.

When tasting young claret, it is difficult to assess the amount and the quality of the fruit behind the tannin. Critics who ranked the intensely tannic 1970 red Bordeaux as great when they first tasted it dismissed 1982 Bordeaux as being too short of tannin to be worth keeping. Both these assessments were wrong. The 1970 retained its toughness throughout its life and was rarely an enjoyable drink. The 1982 vintage, like an athlete with hidden reserves of strength, turned out to have more tannin than had seemed to be the case.

PATTERNS OF CHANGE

Another challenge confronting the wine taster is the unpredictable way in which wines evolve. Some grape varieties and some regions produce wines that evolve faster, or slower, than some others. Wines made from the Viognier grape in

the Rhône valley *appellation* of Condrieu *(see p.208)*, for example, age faster than than those made from the Riesling in Alsace *(see pp.58–69)*. White Rhône wines made from the Marsanne and Roussanne grapes go into decline for a few years after bottling, developing more interesting flavors when they are seven years old.

The wines of Bordeaux, too, tend to decline for a year or so at various stages of their development. This trait varies, however, from one vintage to another. The wines of 1985 went through no such sulk, for example, while good examples of the 1966 vintage have returned from apparent death on more than one occasion. Red Burgundy, which contains less tannin than many other wines, can fade from fruity drinkability to watery fragility in the space of six months. Weightier red Bordeaux generally takes rather longer to lose its appeal, but can quite often end its days with a mouth-drying, tannic edge.

BLIND TASTING
When tasting wines blind, the tasters do not know the identity of the wines, and must judge purely by their impressions on the day. Here, the labels are hidden by napkins.

THE LANGUAGE OF WINE

EVERY GENERATION AND EVERY COUNTRY DEVELOPS ITS OWN

VOCABULARY FOR THE CHALLENGING TASK OF DESCRIBING WINE.

MYRIAD STYLES
There are many, many styles of wine, and describing the unique taste and character of each one is a fine art.

TRANSLATING THE FLAVOR OF A wine into words is as difficult as trying to describe a symphony or a painting. Language is clearly not the ideal medium in which to convey physical sensations. That said, in describing a wine one is trying to define three aspects of its character. First, there is the smell and the flavor, often best evoked by reference to familiar fruits, spices, and herbs. Next, there is the style and texture. Is it tannic like stewed tea, or flabby like a dull Golden Delicious apple? Is it thin or concentrated? Last, although inextricably bound up in the description of flavor and style, there is the question of whether it is actually good to drink. Is it immature, at its peak, or past its best? Is it clean or dirty? Simple or complex? Does the flavor vanish quickly or linger in the mouth? Descriptions of wines have ranged from Michelangelo's Italian wine that "kisses, licks, bites, thrusts, and stings," through a wine described by one nameless drinker as "like the little Lord Jesus slipping down your throat in velvet pantaloons," to wines with "silky," "satiny," or even "lacy" textures. In North America, reference is frequently made to such technical terms as "malolactic fermentation" and "skin contact." The following list is a personal attempt to bring together some of the most commonly used French, US, and British terminology.

A **Acetic** Wine with a vinegary taste caused by bacteria that produce acetic acid.
Amylique The pear-drop character of wine that has been fermented at a low temperature.
Animal The character of many mature reds and of younger wines made from the Syrah grape.
Âpre Describes a bitter, harshly tannic wine.
Aromatique The spicy or perfumed character of wines made from aromatic grape varieties such as the Gewürztraminer.
Arôme Term used to describe the fresh, grapey smells of a young unbottled wine.
Austere An acidic white wine or a tannic red one.

B **Balanced** A wine whose component flavors are in harmony.
Barrique An oak barrel, usually new.
Biscuity The rich flavor of mature white Bourgogne and Champagne.
Boisé A woody-flavored wine.

Bouchon (goût de) Corked.
Bouquet The smell of a wine maturing in the bottle, as opposed to the *arôme* of a young, unbottled wine. Can also refer to the smell of a wine generally.
Buttery Describes the character of wines such as a good white Burgundy.

C *Capiteux* Describes an over-alcoholic wine.
Chaleureux Suggests a richly flavored red wine with a high alcohol content.
Chaptalisé Wine whose alcoholic strength has been increased by the addition of sugar during fermentation.
Charnu A less pronounced version of *chaleureux*.
Charpenté A full-flavored but slightly over-tannic red wine that will improve with keeping.
Chêne Oak – probably new.
Cigar box The cedar-wood character of maturing red Bordeaux.

Closed Wine whose smell and flavor are hard to discern. Such wines may well open out with time and exposure to the air.

Complet Complex and balanced.

Complex Wine with more than one flavor.

Corked Describes a musty-tasting wine, caused by a mold-infected cork. This fault affects three to six percent of bottles of wine to a lesser or greater extent.

Corsé Similar to *charnu* and *chaleureux*.

D *Dépouillé* A faded, flavorless wine.
Dilute/Dilué Wine lacking concentration because of overcropping or a rainy harvest.

E **Elegant** A subtle, well-balanced wine.
Étoffé Muscular, full-bodied wine with aging potential.

Éventé A wine that is past its best.

F **Fat** Flavorsome wine made from ripe fruit.
Féminin Delicate, light wine.

Finish The flavor that lingers in the mouth after the wine has been swallowed.

Flabby Wine lacking acidity, which will deteriorate further with time.

Fondu A mature wine that is in its prime.

Friand Wine, of any age, with a good fruity balance of ripeness and acidity.

Fumé Smoky. The term is used differently in the New World, where it refers to oaky wines.

G **Gobs of fruit** Describes a fruit-packed wine, usually a new-style red Bordeaux, or a wine from the Rhône or southern France.

Green A wine made from unripe grapes. Often the result of a cool summer.

H **Hot** Similar to *capiteux* and *chaptalisé*. A wine with too much alcohol for its flavor.

Hydrogen sulphide If wine is insufficiently aired in the cellar, the sulphur, added as an anti-oxidant when the wine is bottled, can turn into hydrogen sulphide, giving the wine a very unpleasant rotten-egg odor.

L **Long** A wine with a lingering flavor.
Louche A wine that is cloudy, usually as a result of bacterial spoilage.

M **Meaty** A wine with a texture so dense that you almost imagine you could chew it.

Mercaptan A foul-smelling chemical compound, produced once the wine is bottled when hydrogen sulphide reacts with alcohol.

Moisi A musty smell, usually caused by dirty casks or tanks.

N **Noble rot/***Pourriture noble* This benevolent fungus grows on white grapes, adding a unique and highly-prized flavor to

sweet white wines.

Nose A wine's "nose" is its smell, including both its *arôme* and its *bouquet*.

P *Pâteux* Describes a flabby, sweet white wine lacking in acidity.

Pétillant Similar in meaning to *crémant*, this describes a slightly sparkling wine. An even lighter sparkle is described as *perlant*.

Pierre-à-fusil Meaning "gun flint," this term is used to describe the steely character of some wines made from Sauvignon Blanc grapes.

Pourri Describes wines made from grapes that have been spoiled by harmful rot.

Puissant A wine with plenty of flavor and a high alcohol content.

R *Rancio* Refers to a fortified wine or *vin doux naturel* that has been stored in oak casks for at least two years, often exposed to direct sunlight. This oxidizes the wine and gives it a much-prized sherrylike character that is especially popular in the Roussillon area.

Rich English equivalent of *puissant*.

Robe The appearance, literally the dress, of a wine.

Rôti Describes the roasted character of wines made from nobly rotten grapes.

S **Short** Describes a wine whose flavor fades fast.

Soyeux Refers to a wine that is silky in texture and easy to drink.

Stalky This refers to a wine spoiled by the woody flavor of grape stalks.

Structure A wine's structure is made up of various components, including tannin, acidity, sugar, and fruitiness, in relation to its alcohol content.

Sulphur Used throughout the wine-making process as an antiseptic and an antioxidant, sulphur is cough-inducing when used excessively, especially in sweet white wines.

T **Tannic** Used to describe a tough red wine with the mouth-puckering character of strong, cold tea.

V **Vegetal** Vegetal smell and flavor of a wine made from unripe grapes.

Vif Lively, light.

Volatile acids Acids that evaporate at low temperatures. One of the most important volatile acids is acetic acid, which in excess gives wine an unpleasant vinegary character.

Voluptuous Refers to wine which is rich and flavorsome with a high alcohol content.

Y **Yeasty** The characteristic flavor of good Champagne, and of traditional Muscadet bottled *sur lie*, that is, without racking or filtering.

SERVING WINE

OVER THE CENTURIES, WINE HAS BEEN DRUNK OUT OF ALL KINDS

OF GLASSES, FROM THE MOST DELICATE CRYSTAL TO HEAVY PEWTER

BEAKERS MADE TO ENDURE THE ROUGH AND TUMBLE OF THE BAR.

CHILLING OUT
Most white wines are best served chilled, but older, finer wines should not be served too cold.

A MONG THE BEST WINE-DRINKING experiences I have ever had were drinking Champagne directly from the bottle in a cornfield with a woman with whom I was madly in love, and sipping a 50-year-old red Burgundy from a hotel room mug. On neither of these occasions was the wine served in the ideal glass, at the correct temperature, or with the appropriate dish, but that was more than compensated for by the setting, the company, and the flavor. Had I been drinking either of these wines at home, however, I would have taken the trouble to serve them at their best.

The Austrian glass manufacturer Georg Riedel has, with inventive genius, proven that by altering the form of the glass he can subtly but perceptibly bring out the flavors of different kinds of wines. So, his red Bordeaux, red Burgundy, and red Rhône glasses all have their own distinctive shape, as do those designed for an ever-growing range of other regions. If you are a fan of a particular wine, there is a lot to be said for indulging in a full set of Riedel glasses. Possessing a range of ideal glasses, however, is not unlike having an array of kitchen knives, in that you can, in fact, accomplish almost everything you want with three or four really good ones. My own quartet consists of a large red wine glass, a long-stemmed, smaller glass for white wines, a flute for Champagne, and a small, but not too small, glass for port and sweet white wines.

Whatever glass you use, it should conform to the following criteria if it is to bring out the wine's best qualities. It should be made of clear crystal and be large enough to contain a reasonable amount of wine when only a third- to half-full. The circumference of the rim should be quite a bit smaller than that of the bowl, while the bowl itself should be taller than it is wide. In other words, no wine glass is more poorly designed for the task than the traditional "saucer" Champagne glass that is said to have been modeled on Marie Antoinette's breasts. This glass's wide brim allows both the aroma and the bubbles to escape from the glass.

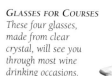

GLASSES FOR COURSES
These four glasses, made from clear crystal, will see you through most wine drinking occasions.

DECANTING WINE

The business of decanting wines and allowing them to "breathe" is a controversial one. In my opinion, opening a bottle a few hours before serving it is almost pointless, as the surface area that is open to the air is far too small. Decanting wines, however, achieves two purposes. In the case of older red wines, it offers a means of separating the wine from the deposit that has settled at the bottom of the bottle. Second, decanting is an effective way to "open out" and soften young reds, whites, and even sparkling wines, provided the wine is allowed to spread across the surface of the glass as it flows into the decanter. Young wines can be decanted two or three hours before serving, but older wines are best decanted as late as possible, since forcible exposure to air in a decanter after decades in a bottle can be tiring for a mature wine.

According to tradition, at dinner, light wines should come before full-bodied examples, whites before reds, youth before age, and dry before sweet. The wines should also improve with every course. But what if the white Burgundy is

finer than the red that it precedes, and if, as is highly likely, the old Bordeaux you have saved for the cheese is more delicate than the Hermitage you served with the venison? As in every other form of etiquette, the best rule to follow is common sense. It will do a fair wine no favors to serve it after a great one, unless that fair wine happens to be the perfect partner for the dish with which it is to be drunk. Treat a series of wines as you do a set of paintings, giving each the space and setting it needs to be enjoyed at its best.

WINE BY CANDLELIGHT
The secret of decanting lies in standing the bottle upright for at least 24 hours beforehand. With a candle or flashlight, simply pour until you see the first specks of deposit.

SCREWPULL CORKSCREW

AMERICAN STYLE AH-SO CORKSCREW

WAITER'S FRIEND

SERVING TEMPERATURES

A dry white wine served too cold will have hardly any taste, while a red served too warm will be like soup. To chill wine, put it in a bucket full of water and ice for 10 minutes before serving. Wines that are too cold can be warmed in tepid water.

Light reds such as Loires and Beaujolais	52–55° F	(11–13° C)
Younger red Burgundy and Rhônes and older Bordeaux	57–61° F	(14–16° C)
Older Burgundy, tannic young Bordeaux and Rhônes	61–64° F	(16–18° C)
Light, dry, and semi-sweet white wines such as Vouvray	43–48° F	(6–9° C)
Rosé, Champagne, aromatic white wines such as Riesling, and fuller bodied ones such as Sancerre and basic Chablis	46–52° F	(8–11° C)
Richer white Burgundies and Bordeaux	52–55° F	(11–13° C)

CHOOSING A CORKSCREW
While no corkscrew does the job better than the "Screwpull," the American "Ah-So" is useful for old corks, and the "Waiter's Friend" is also reliable. Whatever corkscrew you use, make sure it is in the form of a wire spiral.

FOOD AND WINE

IT IS NO ACCIDENT THAT A REGION'S WINES GO SO WELL WITH ITS FOOD; WINE MAKERS SUPPLY THEIR OWN TABLES FIRST. TO GET THE PERFECT MATCH, THINK OF THE WINE AS A SAUCE FOR THE DISH.

WINE AND CHEESE
Not all wines go with all types of cheese. Sauvignon Blanc is the perfect accompaniment to goats' cheese like this Chavignol.

THE EFFECTS OF WINE
Slow cooking with wine helps to tenderize a tough old bird (below left), and gives mussels (below right) added flavor and aroma.

WHEN IT COMES TO MATCHING wine to food, and vice versa, there are two very different schools of thought. On the one hand, there is what could be called the doctrinal approach of traditional *sommeliers,* who prescribe specific partnerships of wine and food as if they were holy writs. On the other, there is the laissez-faire approach that suggests there are no rules and that the choice is down to personal taste. In my experience, neither approach is as useful as a readiness to learn from both common sense and the experiences of others. It is only natural that, over the years, wine growers have more often than not produced styles of wine to suit the types of food that are laid on their tables. Burgundy (*see pp.98–141*) is the source of some of France's best beef and chicken, while the Médoc

(*see p.83*) is more famous for its lamb; Sancerre (*see p.186*) is as well known for its goat's cheese as it is for its wines.

The wine that accompanies a meal fills much the same role as a sauce. A powerful Hermitage (*see p.213*) will do no more favors for a dish of sweetbreads than *sauce poivrade* (cracked pepper sauce), and a Muscadet will be as overshadowed by venison as a creamy sauce would be. So, when choosing a wine to go with a dish, consider the intensity of its flavor. Next, bear in mind the flavor itself. Gamey dishes such as venison are complemented by spicy sauces such as *sauce poivrade* and by spicy wines like Hermitage. Fruity dishes, such as *sole Véronique,* which contains grapes, call for fruity wines like Riesling and Muscat. The textures of both dish and wine are

also important. One of the worst culinary marriages I have ever come across is the one between smoked salmon, which is an oily fish, and Gewürztraminer, a wine that has an oily texture. A crisp Sauvignon Blanc would be a far better match.

Tough, tannic red wines are a poor match for beef, which makes them taste harsher; so you'd be better off drinking Burgundy with the beef and saving your Bordeaux (see p.77) for the lamb. If this incompatibility between beef and Bordeaux comes as a surprise, just try a good, young Médoc with an unpasteurized Brie and you'll find a partnership from hell. The creamy cheese makes the tannic wine taste positively metallic, and would be far better served with a soft red Burgundy or a dry white wine.

Rich dessert wines are often laced with the scents of the fruits that share the grapes' growing space, and make ideal matches for them. Whether dessert wines should accompany a meal's sweet ending or themselves be the dessert is a debatable point. An alternative to the usual dessert is to make one from wine – a jelly of Claret and redcurrants or a Champagne sorbet.

A Classic Match
With the delicate flavors of shellfish, only the most delicate of wines will do Muscadet goes perfectly with most seafood.

Cooking with Wine

Wine is used for a wide range of purposes in the kitchen. Since the Romans, people have been making marinades from wine, olive oil, and herbs, using them to soften and flavour potentially tough meat. The best wines for this are simple, youthful, full-flavored reds from the Rhône (see pp.200–21), Bordeaux (see pp.70–97), and the south of France. Similarly, peaches improve with white Bordeaux (see p.77), strawberries with old red Bordeaux, and fruit salad with Muscat de Beaumes-de-Venise (see p.215). Fish can be poached in white wine and stock, while dishes like *coq au vin* and *boeuf Bourguignon* show what slow cooking in red wine can do for sinewy meat. When it comes to choosing the wine you are going to use in the kitchen, be rigorous – if you wouldn't choose to drink it, you should avoid cooking with it. If you want a dish to taste of vinegar or sherry, use stuff from bottles bearing those exact words on their labels. By the same token, though, ignore classic recipes that instruct you to cook with the same expensive wine you plan to enjoy with the meal. Few people today can afford even to drink the rare Grand Cru Chambertin very often, so using it in a chicken dish seems terribly extravagant.

I would instead argue that a full-bodied Vin de Pays (see pp.230–33) Pinot Noir, Mâcon Rouge, or any other soft, juicy red would be a perfectly acceptable alternative. Where a recipe specifies that red Bordeaux should be used, good Vin de Pays Cabernet Sauvignon will do more for the dish than a watery Bordeaux Rouge. Any dry sparkling wine can be used as a substitute for Champagne (see pp.142–55), as could a yeasty Muscadet (see p.183). If you do cook with wine, remember to add it to the pan early so that the alcohol has time to evaporate.

Adding Wine
Unless you are making a dish like sherry trifle, in which the alcohol is supposed to be apparent, don't add the wine right at the end of the cooking.

FOOD AND WINE GLOSSARY

The following partnerships are not necessarily ones with which every *sommelier* will agree, but they all represent the fruits of my personal experiments and experience over the years.

*WINE AND CHEESE
Although many people
believe that only red
wine should be drunk
with cheese, most creamy
cheeses are better matched
with white wines.*

STARTERS

Caviar This delicacy and Champagne were made for each other.

Eggs Burgundians poach eggs in their red wine, and Beaujolais and young basic Burgundy can go well with omelettes. Alternatively, I'd suggest *blanc de blancs* Champagne and white wine from Burgundy, the Loire valley, or Bordeaux.

Foie Gras The rich, apparently "sweet" character of *foie gras* is delicious with Sauternes or any other top-quality, late-harvest wine.

Terrine A good country terrine is best served with a rustic wine like a Madiran, a Fitou, a Provence rosé, a Côtes du Rhône, or a Beaujolais.

Melon This fruit does unexpected damage to the flavor of most wines. Quarts-de-Chaume or *vendange tardive* Riesling will fare better than most.

Salad A vinaigrette sauce will do no wine any good at all. If you must drink wine with your salad, then try a basic white.

FISH AND SHELLFISH

River fish These flavorsome fish call for flavorsome wines. White Burgundy, Riesling d'Alsace, Sancerre, and dry white Bordeaux all work well, as does dry rosé and even young red Burgundy (the Burgundians go so far as to cook trout in it).

Sea fish The key here is subtle wines to complement the light flavors of the fish. Chablis, white Hermitage, dry Jurançon, Pinot Blanc, or dry white Bordeaux all work well with most sea fish.

Smoked fish The oily character of most smoked fish needs crisp wine, so forget the recommendation to drink Alsace Gewürztraminer with smoked salmon. This is also the one type of dish that calls for oaky white wine, such as modern Pessac-Léognan, Burgundy, and *vins de pays*.

Shellfish "Sweeter" tasting shellfish such as crayfish, crab, lobster, and scallops go well with white Burgundy, Sancerre, dry Vouvray, Pinot Gris, or Riesling d'Alsace. Peppery Rhône rosés and rosé Champagne can also be delicious. Mussels are best partnered with Muscadet, Chablis, or Sauvignon de Touraine.

Oysters Chablis or Muscadet would be my choice here. Alternatively, you could opt for Champagne.

MEATS

Beef Everything depends on the way the dish is prepared. However, I believe that red Bordeaux is far less appropriate than red Burgundy or wines from the northern or southern Rhône.

Lamb Red Bordeaux is the best choice here, although red Loire like Chinon or Bourgueil can be good, as can Cahors.

Offal Liver and kidney dishes suit red Bordeaux (especially St. Émilion and Pomerol) and Châteauneuf-du-Pape.

Game Red Burgundy is good here, too, but Rhône reds are better, as are the finer wines from southwestern regions such as Cahors and Madiran.

Chicken Avoid flavors that are either too strong or too subtle. Creamy chicken dishes need the bite of dry, fruity Sauvignon, dry Vouvray, or Alsace Riesling. On the other hand, a Chardonnay or an Alsace Riesling will work better if the chicken is plainly roasted.

Duck The ideal wine here is red Burgundy, but a flavorsome Alsace Riesling or a fruity southern Rhône, such as a Gigondas or a Châteauneuf-du-Pape, will also work well.

SPICY DISHES
In India, wine has no traditional place. It can, therefore, be a challenge to select a wine to accompany a curry. Everything depends on the spiciness of the dish, but Gewürztraminer and fruity white Sancerre should work. Ginger is no friend to most wines, but seems best suited to Gewürztraminer or Clairette de Die Tradition.

VEGETABLES
Most vegetables don't dictate which type of wine would best accompany a particular dish. Some, however, have strong flavors that should be taken into account when choosing a wine. **Artichokes**, for example, are not always an easy match for wine. This flavorsome vegetable will make most reds taste metallic, especially when a Hollandaise sauce is involved. White or rosé Sancerre works well here, as does dry Tokay Pinot Gris, Cabernet d'Anjou, or rosé from the Jura or Burgundy regions. Dry white Loire Sauvignon is delicious with **asparagus**, as the wine can have an asparagus flavor of its own. Another option is unoaked Chablis or good Pouilly Fuissé. Whether they are stuffed or used in *ratatouille*, **aubergines** are well matched to reds from southern France and peppery Côtes du Rhône. The fatty character of **avocado** calls for crisp wines like Loire Sauvignon or Chablis. Pinot Gris is a good alternative. The licorice flavor of **fennel** can overpower many wines, so in this case I would suggest serving a full-bodied Pouilly-Fumé.

CHEESES
The more appealing and varied the cheese board, the greater the risk of choosing an inappropriate wine. As a rule, tannic reds such as young Bordeaux are only worth drinking with a hard, savory cheese such as **Parmesan**. Smoky and slightly sweet cheeses such as **Comté**, **Gruyère**, and **Emmenthal** go well with fruity Alsace wines such as Pinot Gris, Muscat, or Gewürztraminer, while blue cheeses such as **Roquefort** can be delicious with late-harvest wines such as Sauternes, medium-sweet Jurançon, or Bonnezeaux. Creamy cheeses such as **Brillat Savarin**, **Brie**, and **Camembert** are horrible with many red wines, but are perfect with whites such as Sancerre and Pouilly Fumé, both of which are ideal with **goat's cheese**. Because of its lack of tannin, red Burgundy is better with creamy cheese than red Bordeaux or Rhône, but strong Burgundian cheeses like **Ami du Chambertin** will overwhelm a subtle, mature Burgundy. Champagne is a good match to all sorts of cheese, as is *vin jaune* from Arbois.

DESSERTS
Chocolate-based desserts
The strong flavor of milk or plain chocolate is one of the most formidable enemies for most wines. The strongest contenders are Muscat *vins doux naturels* such as Beaumes de-Venise and Banyuls. Clairette de Die Tradition can just about handle chocolate mousse, but any kind of Champagne is a bad idea.

Cream-based desserts The best sweet wines for these dishes are not the fruitiest. Try semi-sweet Jurançon, sweet white Bordeaux, or *riche* or *doux* Champagne.

Fruit-based desserts Fruit calls for fruit, so go for *vendange tardive* Riesling or Muscat *vin doux naturel*.

A SWEET PARTNERSHIP
According to some rule books, all desserts deserve Sauternes, but there are numerous alternatives.

STARTING A CELLAR

FOR ANYONE WITH MORE THAN A PASSING INTEREST IN WINE,

STOCKING EVEN A MODEST WINE CELLAR IS AS REWARDING AS

BUILDING UP A COLLECTION OF GOOD BOOKS OR MUSIC.

WINE RACK IN A PRIVATE CELLAR
Identification tags like these can prove very useful, provided both they and the ink used to write on them are humidity-proof.

CHÂTEAU CELLAR
Major producers like this one (Château Cos d'Estournel in Bordeaux) keep reference bottles of all their old vintages.

I N AN AGE WHEN FEW OF US ARE lucky enough to live in a home with a functional basement, the term "cellar" has to be a broad one. For some, it is a rack beneath the stairs or in an unused fireplace; some will opt for a Eurocave – a commercially made, temperature- and humidity-controlled cabinet; others use a converted fridge.

A cellar should enjoy a constant, cool temperature. Around 52° F (11° C) is ideal, but constancy is more important than coolness.

A cellar should be reasonably humid, to prevent corks from drying out: aim for 75–85 percent humidity. Drier cellars should be humidified, while ones that are too humid can be improved with a bit of gravel. This also greatly reduces the risk of bottles breaking when they are dropped. Fresh air should circulate reasonably freely through the cellar. And then, a cellar must be secure. There is little point in locking up your jewelery while leaving priceless bottles at the mercy of thieves. Don't neglect to insure the cellar too, and to keep the insured value up to date. Lastly, you need racks or bins – examples are illustrated on this page.

ORGANIZING THE BOTTLES

However ideal your cellar, it is in effect only the vinous equivalent of the shelves on which you store your books. It is just as frustrating to have to search for a bottle of Musigny as for your copy of *Les Misérables*. Once, in the days when most people drank only a dozen or so different wines, keeping track of them was quite simple. Today, with an ever-growing selection of new wines to discover, it is a lot trickier.

The system I use removes the need to group together wines of similar style and allows me to fill every hole in the rack while being able to lay my hands on the bottle I want almost instantly. I use a business spreadsheet and identify the individual holes or bins with a system of numbers and letters. Numbers run horizontally, while letters run vertically. So, bottles of the same Nuits-St. Georges bought

HIDDEN TREASURE
This elegantly designed wine cellar is built into a spiral staircase and accessed by a trap door, conveniently close to the dining table.

on different occasions might, for example, be found in B45, F82, and U12. The key to the system lies in a well-kept record of what went where. For this, a computer database is easy to use.

Anyone starting a cellar should aim to have four different sets of wines: current daily drinking, current "special occasion" bottles, and a set of examples of each for the future. Muscadet, most Pinot Blanc, and most basic red Côtes du Rhône are not worth laying down, for example, while most good red Bordeaux will improve after a few years in the cellar. Some wines are supposedly ready to drink when sold but are well worth maturing for a year or two: an example of this, in my experience, is good nonvintage Champagne.

I offer the 210-bottle selection on the right as a possible starting point; an alternative might be to halve all the quantities, resulting in a total of 105 bottles.

LIST OF SUGGESTED WINES

6 Bottles of assorted, mature (or maturing) high-quality red Bordeaux.

6 Bottles of young, high-quality red Bordeaux.

12 *Cru bourgeois* or *petit-château* Bordeaux.

6 Northern Rhône reds: Hermitage, Côte Rôtie, or Cornas.

6 Southern Rhône reds: Châteauneuf-du-Pape or Gigondas.

12 Good red Côtes du Rhône-Villages.

6 Good young red Burgundies such as Beaune, Volnay, or Vosne-Romanée.

6 Older examples of the above wines.

12 Bottles of red Burgundy.

4 Bottles of Chinon or Bourgueil.

4 Bottles of Fleurie.

12 Assorted Cahors, Minervois, and Côteaux d'Aix en Provence reds.

12 Good Vin de Pays reds.

6 Bottles of top white Burgundy: Chablis Grand Cru, Meursault, or Chassagne-Montrachet.

12 Bottles of white Burgundy or good Chablis.

4 Bottles of Alsace Riesling, Pinot Gris, or Gewurztraminer.

4 Bottles of good Alsace Pinot Blanc.

4 Bottles of Alsace Vendange Tardive.

6 Bottles of Condrieu.

6 Bottles of Sancerre or Pouilly Fumé.

4 Bottles of Vouvray Sec.

4 Bottles of Vouvray Mousseux.

6 Bottles of Pessac-Léognan Blanc.

12 Bottles of good white Bordeaux (choose with particular care).

4 Bottles of young Condrieu.

4 Bottles of Sauternes or Barsac.

4 Bottles of Jurançon Sec.

12 Bottles of good white Vin de Pays Sauvignon or Chardonnay.

4 Bottles of Muscadet (useful for oysters).

6 Bottles of good nonvintage Champagne.

4 Bottles of vintage Champagne.

INGENUITY AT WORK
Wicker baskets like these work perfectly well for bottles – as do chimney pots.

INVESTING IN WINE

EVERY BOTTLE OF WINE, LIKE EVERYTHING ELSE WE BUY, COMES

AT A PRICE. IN SOME CASES, THAT PRICE, THE VALUE, RISES WITH

TIME. IN OTHERS, UNFORTUNATELY BUT INEVITABLY, IT FALLS.

SALE BY CANDLELIGHT
At the Hospices de Beaune wine auctions, auctioneers do not use a hammer. Each time a new bid is placed on a wine, a candle is lit to indicate how much time is left for a new bid to be made.

MOST OF THE WINE WE BUY IS intended for drinking. Just try auctioning off, for example, a case of basic Côtes du Rhône. If, however, in 1993 you offered an auctioneer some 1982 Château Latour in the barrel, your profit might have been as high as 1000 percent. Provided you buy the right wine and look after it, wine can be one of the best investments around.

For many producers, though, there is something unacceptable about the idea of speculating on wine. However, how many of them, when deciding the price of each year's wine, ignore the popularity of previous vintages at auction?

Unlike paintings, which can last forever, bottles of wine have a life-span that depends on the vintage and the quality of the vineyard and the wine making. It is as difficult to predict the longevity of a particular vintage as it is to foretell the racing success of a newly born foal. The 1983 Château Latour, for example, would have initially cost you around the same price as the 1982; but like other wines of that vintage, it is aging far more quickly and is worth less.

Until the early 1990s, the people who fueled the market by buying mature and maturing bottles at auction rarely strayed far beyond wines like Château Latour and a few other "blue chip" Bordeaux. This changed, however, both with the growth in popularity of American pundits who "discover" and recommend "new" wines, and with the arrival on the scene of a wave of "new" wine buyers.

VALUE JUDGEMENT
The 200-year-old company Christie's may now belong to a French-man and sell wine throughout the globe, but it remains at the heart of the London wine trade.

CHATEAU LE PIN
The value of the wines produced by this tiny, recently created estate have risen dramatically, but some observers expect them to fall again.

THE BLUE CHIP NAMES

Bordeaux: Château l'Angélus, Cheval Blanc, Cos d'Estournel, Ducru-Beaucaillou, Figeac, Grand-Puy-Lacoste, Gruaud-Larose, Haut-Brion, Lafite, Lafleur, Léoville Barton, Léoville-las-Cases, Lynch Bages, Margaux, la Mission-Haut-Brion, Montrose, Mouton Rothschild, Palmer, Pape Clément, Pétrus, Pichon-Lalande, Pichon-Longueville, Rauzan Segla, Château Église Clinet, la Mondotte, le Pin, Valandraud.
Burgundy: Drouhin Marquis de Laguiche, Gros Frères, Hospices de Beaune (Drouhin and Jadot), Lafon, Leroy, Méo Camuzet, Romanée Conti (La Tâche, Romanée Conti, Romanée St. Vivant) de Vogüe.
Rhône: Chapoutier, Chave, Guigal, Jaboulet Aîné.

THE RISING STARS

Once buyers have filled their racks with "blue chip" wines, they want to purchase novelties that their friends don't have. So, wines from the recently created Château le Pin, which produces only 25,000 bottles each year, are now worth more than the longer-established Château Margaux, which produces 10 times as many. Wines in limited production from little-known châteaux in St. Émilion and Pomerol, and *domaines* in Burgundy and the Rhône, also attract investors.

The long-term investment potential of these wines will, however, depend on whether they stand the test of time as well as the "blue chips." The one certainty is that, unless the world turns teetotal or top restaurants turn to offering cola with their meals, the value of classic, fine wines will continue to rise. The only rules for wine lovers who would like to benefit from this trend are to keep track of what influential commentators are saying about the vintages in your cellar, to look after your wine, and to buy the ones that you enjoy drinking. At least then, if the performance of the bottles is disappointing, you can always enjoy your liquid assets, which is more than can be said for underperforming stocks.

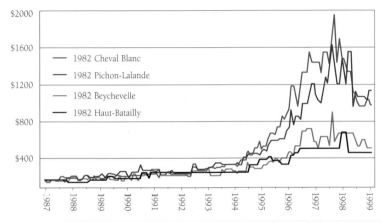

— 1982 Cheval Blanc
— 1982 Pichon-Lalande
— 1982 Beychevelle
— 1982 Haut-Batailly

TEST OF TIME
The value of the wines produced by individual châteaux can fluctuate. Recording the value of the 1982 vintage at auction, this chart, produced by wine merchants Bordeaux Index, shows that "blue chip" châteaux like Cheval Blanc and Pichon-Lalande are far more reliable than some humbler estates.

VINTAGES

ASSESSING THE POTENTIAL OF A WINE FROM A GIVEN YEAR'S GRAPES IS NEVER EASY. FAVORED VINTAGES MAY ULTIMATELY DISAPPOINT, WHILE APPARENTLY AVERAGE YEARS CAN YIELD RARE CLASSICS.

BEAUTY OR BEAST?
From the earliest stages of the growing season to the time when the wine is fermenting in the vat or barrel, it is very hard to predict the quality and longevity of a wine.

VINTAGES ARE ONE OF THE ASPECTS of wine that can confuse even experienced wine enthusiasts and professionals. Every year, in every region and every vineyard, nature provides a fresh set of challenges for the wine maker. Grapes on the vine, and wines in the bottle, develop in unpredictable ways. Add to this the fact that wine enthusiasts differ in their definition of a perfectly mature wine and it is clear that predicting the longevity of any wine is going to be tricky.

When using a vintage chart, bear in mind that it is the work of a broad brush. A chart cannot take account of the lucky or skillful producer, nor can it encompass underperforming wine makers who fail to make the most of a vintage. The vintage chart *(see opposite)* refers to better-than-average producers and indicates how good a particular vintage was and when it is best drunk. For example, 1998 was a very good vintage for Margaux and bottles made by good châteaux from this year would be best drunk between 2004 and 2020.

The first key to understanding vintages lies in appreciating that they often vary from region to region, and even within the same part of the country. So, while 1982 was a great year for Bordeaux's red wines, it was a mediocre vintage for Burgundy, on the other side of France. Years that suit the Merlot grape in Bordeaux, for example, are not always as kind to Cabernet Sauvignon, so, in 1998, it was easier to make good claret in the Merlot-filled vineyards of Pomerol and St. Émilion than in their Cabernet Sauvignon-dominated neighbors of the Médoc. Similarly, vintages that are ideal for the development of the "noble rot" that is needed for sweet white wine are often years when it is hard to make good, dry red wine.

There are different kinds of good and poor vintages. There are some years when the best wines are drinkable almost from the outset, while others from the same regions repay patience in their early life. So-called "bad" vintages may be unpalatably acidic, or simply lightweight and dilute. Some supposedly "lesser" vintages give a great deal of pleasure during their brief heyday, while so-called top-class vintages may never fulfill their initial promise.

THE TEST OF TIME
Bottles of top-class wines from great vintages can survive the test of time if laid down properly.

KEY	
**	Average
***	Good
****	Very Good
*****	Excellent
'01-'07	Best drunk between 2001 and 2007
(1987 is not included as its wines are past their prime.)	

	1998	1997	1996	1995	1994	1993	1992	1991	1990	1989	1988	1986	1985	OTHER GOOD VINTAGES
ALSACE														
Sélection de Grains Nobles/Vendange Tardive	*** '02-'10	***** '02-'20	**** '99-'10	**** '97-'08	*** '97-'02	**** '96-'08	** '95-'99	** '93-'98	***** '94-'16	**** '93-'05	**** '92-'01	*** '88-'00	***** '90-'15	'83, '76, '71,
BORDEAUX														
Margaux	**** '04-'20	*** '01-'10	**** '00-'15	**** '00-'17	*** '96-'00	*** '96-'00	** '96-'01	*** '95-'00	***** '95-'20	**** '95-'20	**** '01-'12	**** '96-'10	**** '90-'07	'83, '82, '81, '70, '61, '59
Pauillac	**** '05-'25	*** '01-'10	**** '00-'20	**** '00-'18	*** '97-'01	*** '96-'02	*** '97-'02	*** '95-'03	***** '95-'20	**** '95-'20	**** '02-'15	**** '98-'12	**** '90-'10	'83, '82, '75, '70, '61, '59
St. Estèphe	**** '05-'20	*** '02-'05	**** '02-'20	**** '01-'21	*** '98-'06	*** '97-'02	*** '98-'01	*** '95-'00	***** '97-'20	**** '97-'20	**** '03-'16	**** '99-'12	**** '90-'08	'83, '82, '70, '66, '61, '59
St. Julien	**** '05-'23	*** '01-'08	**** '02-'18	**** '01-'18	*** '97-'07	*** '96-'02	*** '97-'02	*** '95-'00	***** '96-'20	**** '97-'20	*** '02-'15	**** '98-'12	*** '90-'09	'83, '82, '70, '66, '61, '59
Pomerol	+++++ '03-'28	**** '01-'08	**** '01-'15	***** '02-'20	**** '00-'15	*** '96-'02	** '96-'02	** '94-'00	***** '95-'20	**** '95-'20	**** '00-'15	**** '93-'10	**** '90-'10	'82, '71, '70, '64, '61, '59
St. Émilion	**** '03-'28	*** '01-'05	**** '02-'15	**** '01-'12	*** '00-'10	*** '95-'01	** '95-'01	** '94-'00	**** '94-'20	***** '95-'20	**** '00-'12	**** '92-'10	**** '90-'10	'82, '71, '70, '64, '61, '59
Pessac-Léognan red	**** '04-'20	*** '01-'08	**** '02-'15	**** '01-'18	*** '98-'06	*** '96-'02	** '95-'00	** '93-'99	**** '94-'15	**** '93-'15	**** '98-'10	**** '95-'10	**** '90-'10	'83, '82, '79, '70, '64, '61
Pessac-Léognan white	**** '01-'12	*** '00-'10	*** '99-'05	*** '94-'02	*** '96-'02	*** '96-'00	*** '94-'99	*** '93-'98	*** '93-'00	** '92-'01	*** '90-'99	*** '89-'97	** '88-'95	'83, '82, '81
Sauternes/Barsac	**** '02-'25	**** '03-'22	*** '00-'12	*** '97-'05	** '96-'03	** '96-'03	** '95-'02	** '94-'00	***** '95-'17	**** '93-'12	**** '93-'14	**** '90-'10	**** '90-'09	'83, '80, '76, '75, '71, '70
BURGUNDY														
Beaujolais: Cru Villages	**** '00-'05	**** '99-'04	**** '98-'01	***** '97-'02	**** '96-'00	**** '95-'00	** '94-'97	**** '93-'00	**** '92-'00	**** '91-'98	*** '90-'97	** '88-'95	***** '87-'95	'83, '78, '71,
Chablis: Grands Crus	*** '01-'07	**** '00-'07	***** '00-'12	***** '99-'10	*** '97-'03	*** '95-'00	**** '96-'04	** '93-'99	**** '93-'03	**** '93-'02	**** '91-'02	***** '89-'00	**** '88-'00	'82, '79, '78, '73
Mâcon	*** '00-'08	**** '00-'06	**** '99-'10	**** '98-'07	*** '97-'00	**** '95-'00	*** '95-'02	** '94-'97	*** '93-'00	**** '92-'00	**** '92-'01	**** '89-'00	**** '87-'98	'82, '79,
Côte de Beaune white	*** '01-'08	**** '00-'10	***** '99-'15	**** '99-'10	*** '97-'00	*** '95-'00	***** '95-'12	** '93-'98	**** '92-'00	**** '91-'08	**** '90-'04	**** '88-'02	**** '88-'02	'83, '82, '79, '78, '73
Côte de Beaune red	*** '02-'10	**** '00-'12	**** '00-'10	**** '98-'12	** '98-'02	*** '97-'05	*** '95-'02	*** '93-'05	***** '94-'11	**** '93-'11	**** '92-'11	*** '90-'99	**** '88-'10	'78, '76, '71, '64, '61, '59
Côte de Nuits red	**** '03-'12	**** '01-'15	**** '01-'12	**** '00-'15	** '98-'03	*** '97-'06	*** '95-'02	*** '93-'05	***** '95-'12	**** '95-'12	***** '93-'11	**** '90-'01	**** '90-'11	'78, '71, '64, '61, '59, '55
CHAMPAGNE														
Vintage		***** '05-'25	***** '03-'25	**** '02-'15		**** '00-'15	**** '99-'15		***** '98-'20	**** '98-'15	***** '98-'17	*** '94-'05	***** '95-'15	'83, '82, '79, '76, '75, '70
THE LOIRE VALLEY														
Anjou Touraine red	**** '00-'10	***** '00-'15	***** '99-'14	***** '98-'04	*** '96-'00	*** '95-'00	** '94-'98	** '93-'98	***** '93-'06	***** '92-'05	**** '88-'00	**** '88-'00	***** '89-'02	'78, '71, '64, '61, '59, '55
Coteaux de Layon	**** '05-'15	***** '02-'22	***** '01-'21	**** '00-'22	*** '97-'09	**** '96-'08	** '94-'02	*** '93-'00	***** '95-'20	**** '94-'15	*** '90-'00	*** '90-'00	**** '90-'06	'78, '71, '64, '61, '59, '55
THE RHÔNE VALLEY														
Northern Rhône red	**** '02-'20	*** '00-'15	***** '02-'23	***** '00-'24	*** '98-'15	** '96-'05	**** '96-'09	***** '95-'11	***** '95-'11	**** '94-'09	***** '92-'10	**** '89-'08	***** '89-'10	'83, '79, '78, '70, '61, '59
Northern Rhône white	**** '00-'06	**** '99-'02	**** '98-'08	*** '98-'04	*** '96-'02	** '95-'01	*** '94-'03	***** '93-'06	***** '93-'06	**** '92-'04	***** '90-'04	**** '88-'02	***** '87-'04	'83, '82, '79
Southern Rhône red	**** '01-'12	*** '00-'08	*** '99-'03	**** '98-'12	*** '96-'06	*** '96-'01	** '94-'00	** '93-'99	***** '94-'06	***** '94-'08	**** '91-'00	*** '89-'99	**** '88-'00	'81, '78, '70, '67, '61

TOURING

WINE MAKERS ARE SURPRISINGLY APPROACHABLE AND MANY,

INCLUDING SOME OF THE MOST FAMOUS, WELCOME VISITORS TO

THEIR CELLARS AND ARE HAPPY TO OFFER SAMPLES OF THEIR WINE.

TAX DISC
Tax is levied on all wine sold in France. A tax disc on the top of the foil capsule is evidence that this has been paid.

THE PEBBLED VINEYARDS OF Châteauneuf-du-Pape, the chalky hills of Champagne, or the sheer slopes of the Rhône all look very different once you have tasted the wines they are instrumental in producing. The experience can be likened to watching a play performed that you have only ever seen before on paper.

The timing of your visit to any wine region depends very much on what you are planning to do there. For a sightseeing holiday, the summer is a good choice: wine makers will be delighted to welcome you into their cellars, though you may have to share a limited amount of space and attention with other tourists.

Harvest time is likely to appeal to a keen photographer. No one who has watched pickers of all ages in the vineyards, and witnessed the picnics among the vines and the banquets in the cellars, will ever forget the experience. As a general rule, most French grapes are picked at some point between September 20th and October 15th. However, timing your trip to coincide with the week or fortnight of the harvest can be very tricky. Like sailors trimming their sails to the wind, wine makers are often forced to reschedule the harvest according to the weather. If you are thinking of combining your tour with some wine buying, bear in mind that people busy picking,

PATRON SAINT OF WINE GROWERS
In many wine-growing regions, producers show off their wines on the weekend following January 22nd, feast day of St. Vincent, the patron saint of wine growers.

MOREY St DENIS

pressing, and fermenting grapes are unlikely to have time for a leisurely chat over a barrel or bottle, which means that harvest time is not a good time to fill your cellar.

In my experience, to be sure of getting the warmest possible welcome from wine growers, the best time to visit the cellars is mid-week in January or February. Most growers will be happy for an excuse to spend time in the cellar showing you wines, rather than among the freezing vines. And in addition, you run little risk of being elbowed out of the way by a succession of other visitors.

Visiting the Cellars
In New World countries like the United States and Australia, wineries often offer tasting rooms and gift shops packed with branded glasses, corkscrews, T-shirts, hats, and posters. In the vast majority of French cellars, however, the person who welcomes you will be either the wine maker or a member of his or her family. Of course, there are plenty of tourist-friendly cellars that advertise their presence at the side of the road; but, like the restaurants with the brightest neon signs, they are not always the best places in which to discover the wines that a region can offer.

It is important to remember that, when you visit the cellars of a small estate, you are entering a place that is not so much a shop or a showroom as a cross between the wine maker's home and place of work. Most producers prefer to offer tastings by appointment, restricting them to hours that do not interfere with work time or

with family time. Lunchtime, especially, is a bad part of the day to arrive at a French cellar.

One hazard to be wary of when visiting out of season is the "tired" bottle, one that has been opened some days earlier for the last people to visit the cellar. Always be politely honest about your impressions of the wines you are tasting so as to give the wine grower an idea of your tastes. If you know anything at all about the region and its wines, then tactfully ensuring that your host is aware of that knowledge may persuade him or her to open another bottle or two for you to taste. Never purchase a wine from a producer who is not willing to let you taste at least a few of his bottles. Most producers will be happy to sell you anything from a single bottle to several cases or more. If you find nothing that you like, there is no need to feel pressured into buying. At the same time, avoid wasting the producer's time by outstaying your welcome in his cellar.

LIVING HISTORY
Artifacts and wine-making equipment from Greek, Roman, and medieval times appear in many museums in wine-producing areas. Together with old maps and written records, these help to put a region's wine into context.

BAR À VIN
In the absence of a tasting room or the address of a recommended producer, your best first stop is a restaurant or bar à vin in which you can sample wines by the glass.

THE FRENCH
WINE REGIONS

ALSACE AND LORRAINE

ALSACE IS, AS ITS NEIGHBOUR LORRAINE ONCE
ALSO USED TO BE, THE SOURCE OF SOME OF THE
WORLD'S MOST EXTRAORDINARY WHITE WINES.

☐ Alsace and Lorraine regions

AᴌSACE STANDS APART from other French wine regions. Around 20 years ago, I remember judging a set of anonymous wines at a French competition, alongside wine makers from Burgundy and Bordeaux. For one member of our team in particular, this was a daunting task. Having taken a perplexed few sniffs, and an even more confused sip, he spat out the first sample, spluttering the words, *"C'est pas du vin, c'est du parfum!"* ("This isn't wine, it's perfume!"). For a man who was used to drinking Chardonnay, a wine made from the extraordinary Gewürztraminer grape, with its combined flavours of spice and perfume, simply made no sense. Fortunately, this was not my first exposure to Alsace's most characterful grape, but I could easily sympathize with the plight of that Burgundian. Today, thankfully, most French wine makers are far less insular when it comes to wine tasting. The relatively recent experience of being a territorial tug-of-love child between the Germans to the east and the French to the west has left the Alsatians with a language, cuisine and wines that are part Germanic, part

ALSATIAN WINE MERCHANT
Many of Alsace's wine merchants first opened their doors over 400 years ago.

ALMOST ALL WHITE
About 90 per cent of the grapes grown in this region are white varieties, most, like Gewürztraminer, with origins elsewhere.

Gallic and 100 per cent Alsatian. This is the only significant wine-making region in France to devote itself almost exclusively to growing white grapes. It is also the only major *appellation contrôlée* to have embraced the notion of printing the names of the grapes from which its wines are made on the labels.

So, while people buying white Burgundy may choose between wines produced from the same Chardonnay grape variety in the well-known *appellations* of Chassagne-Montrachet (*see p115*) or Puligny-Montrachet (*see p133*), for example, the Alsace wine drinker is confronted with labels like Riesling d'Alsace, Gewürztraminer d'Alsace or Tokay Pinot Gris d'Alsace. These three wines are made from very different grapes that are grown almost anywhere within an area of 13,000 ha (32,000 acres) of land, covering very diverse soils and benefiting from very diverse climates. If you are lucky, the label

⛰ 13,500 ha (33,300 acres): 157 million bottles.	▦ Very varied with granite and sandstone on the slopes of the Vosges, limestone on the hills and fertile soil on the plains.	
🌡 Northern continental, with warm summers. The Vosges mountains create a rain shadow and most vines are planted on slopes so they ripen well and allow generous yields.	🍷 White: Pinot Blanc, Tokay-Pinot Gris, Muscat, Gewürztraminer, Sylvaner, Auxerrois, Pinot Noir.	

GERARDM

BELFO

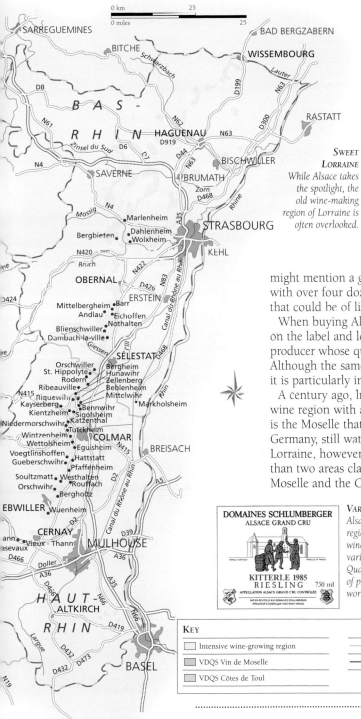

Sweet Lorraine
While Alsace takes the spotlight, the old wine-making region of Lorraine is often overlooked.

might mention a *grand cru* vineyard, but, with over four dozen of these to remember, that could be of little help.

When buying Alsace, read the small print on the label and look for the name of a producer whose quality and style you trust. Although the same can be said for all wines, it is particularly important with Alsace.

A century ago, like Alsace, Lorraine was a wine region with a difference. Its main river is the Moselle that, across the border in Germany, still waters a great wine region. Lorraine, however, now boasts little more than two areas classified as *VDQS*: Vin de Moselle and the Côtes de Toul.

DOMAINES SCHLUMBERGER
ALSACE GRAND CRU

KITTERLE 1985
RIESLING   750 ml
APPELLATION ALSACE GRAND CRU CONTRÔLÉE

VARIETALS ARE THE SPICE OF LIFE
Alsace is unique among France's wine regions for the way in which it sells its wines under the names of the grape varieties from which they are made. Quality varies, however, so the names of producers like Schlumberger are worth remembering.

KEY

☐ Intensive wine-growing region	—— *Département* boundary
☐ VDQS Vin de Moselle	—— Delimited AOC region of Alsace
☐ VDQS Côtes de Toul	

THE HISTORY OF ALSACE AND LORRAINE

Wine making in the neighboring regions of Alsace and Lorraine dates back to Roman times, since when it has had its ups and downs. The trade in both regions became depressed in the 1870s. In Alsace, a renaissance began in the mid-20th century, whereas Lorraine has yet to see a return to the levels of trade it enjoyed in the 19th century.

VINE GROWING IN THE 15TH CENTURY
Vine growing and wine making, as well as other tasks, meant that peasants in Alsace were employed throughout the year. This beautiful 15th-century tapestry shows them at work.

THE REGION OF ALSACE has been passed between France and Germany for perhaps as long as 2,000 years. The first time this is known to have happened was in the 1st century AD, when a Germanic tribe called the Suebi wrested the region from a Celtic people known as the Sequani.

The Romans under Julius Caesar reversed the situation. They ruled the region for the next 200 years, but in the 4th century another Germanic tribe, the Alemanni, overran Alsace. Later, in 496, the Alemanni in their turn were expelled from Alsace by the Franks – the ancestors of the modern French.

Fortunately for wine enthusiasts, when the Alsatians were not involved in these wars, they evidently had time to plant and grow vines. By 780 the ecclesiastical chronicler Adam the Monk was referring to wine making as the most profitable of the region's activities.

In 843 the Treaty of Verdun gave Charlemagne the right to share his pan-European empire between his three grandsons. The Alsace region was presented to Louis the German, who also received Germany, so

that, among other things, "he might have wine in his new kingdom." By the end of the 9th century, vines were tended and wine made in no fewer than 119 Alsatian villages.

Over the next 500 years vine growing had extended to over 400 villages and some 300 abbeys. According to one of the region's best-known wine merchants, Johnny Hugel, in his book *Reasons for the Renaissance of Alsace Wines*, exports had risen to the modern equivalent of nearly 80 million bottles by 1481: twice today's total.

The first wine-grape variety to be grown in Alsace was probably the Pinot Noir. This may have been introduced by the Romans, possibly to be used to make red wine.

A shift from red to white wine was already taking place during the 12th century. The "Rissling," Traminer (Gewürztraminer), and Muscat seem to have been introduced before the 15th century. These were followed by the Pinot Blanc, which was almost certainly imported from Burgundy. The Tokay Pinot Gris probably also originated there, although the Alsatians prefer to believe that an heroic Alsatian general brought it back from campaigning in Hungary. Whatever the origins of the Pinot Gris, Alsatian growers of the 16th century certainly had a sophisticated understanding of the varied potential

PICTURESQUE STREETS
In Alsace, buying from the producer is made all the more memorable by the picturesque houses of the wine makers.

WARRING NEIGHBORS
Although the war between France and Prussia was over 125 years ago, the impact it had on Alsace is still felt today.

offered by different grape varieties. They also knew plenty about the ways in which these grapes should be grown and harvested. At that time, the wine making trade was governed by a body known as the Wine Growers' Association of Riquewihr, which established rules to ensure that grapes were picked as late and as ripe as possible.

PROSPERITY, THEN DECLINE

Under Riquewihr rules, officially registered tasters – *Weinsticheren* – were given the task of rating wines as either *hüntsch* (which had to be drunk within Alsace) or *vin noble* (in German, *Edelwein*), the export variety. Sale outside Alsace was in the hands of such wine houses as Dopff, which opened in 1574 and whose name survives in the firms Dopff au Moulin and Dopff & Irion. Among other exporters, Trimbach and Hugel began trading in 1626 and 1637 respectively.

These firms thrived, but the early heyday of Alsace's wine industry was brought to a halt during the Thirty Years' War of 1618–48. By the end of the 17th century, the number of *Weinsticheren* had halved and vineyards were being taken over by settlers from other parts of France, from Switzerland, the Tyrol, and Germany, who were given land for nothing by Louis XIV of France. The newcomers were often less quality-conscious than their predecessors, preferring to plant productive vines on the fertile flat land rather than on the more demanding and labor-intensive slopes. Despite royal edicts that were issued in 1731 and 1766 to protect them, the Riesling, Muscat, and Traminer, as well as the Pinots, were steadily supplanted by the dull Elbling, Chasselas, and Sylvaner grapes.

RETURN TO FRENCH NATIONALITY

Following the French Revolution in 1790 and the break-up of ecclesiastical estates, there was another enthusiastic bout of planting, which this time involved yet another substandard variety, the Knipperlé. This soon comprised all but a fifth of the region's vines.

The banalization of Alsace's wines was exacerbated by the annexation of the region to Germany in 1871 and by the devastation caused by a set of virulent vine diseases and the spread of phylloxera. After the First World War and the return to French rule, Alsace was, as Johnny Hugel recalls, in a sorry and very confused state.

"To change nationality is not only to change flags. It is also to enter into a different economic space. They move the customs offices, you lose all of your customers and you are subjected to another set of viticultural rules . . . in 1918, we didn't have a single customer in Paris." Even if there had been Parisian customers, it is questionable how happy they would have been with the wines that the region was then making.

The survival to this day of Alsace's wine industry, with its traditional standards, is largely the work of a set of unusually dynamic and quality-conscious *coopératives*.

1911 HARVEST FESTIVAL
Costumes may have changed, but today's pickers celebrate with equal enthusiasm.

A DRIVING TOUR OF ALSACE

This tour covers part of the Alsace Route du Vin, an official scenic route meandering over 108 miles (180 km) from Marlenheim to Thann. The tour takes in some of the region's prettiest villages and towns, many of which are reminiscent of tales from the Brothers Grimm.

Alsace ☐ Tour

0 km   5
0 miles   5

COLMAR TO EGUISHEIM

Wandering around the cobbled streets of Colmar ①, past the clocks, ornate signs, and half-timbered, often pastel-colored buildings, is like listening to the overture before the opera that is the rest of Alsace. Like so many towns and villages in this region, Colmar is so idyllic that it looks as though it was put together by Walt Disney's designers. As elsewhere in Alsace, the best way to explore is on foot as the town is not made for cars. While in Colmar, make sure you visit the Petite Venise canal and the Maison Pfinster on the Rue des Marchands.

Rouffach ②, the southernmost point on your journey, is an old walled town with an impressive church that has been added to over the centuries and a 15th-century corn exchange. Husseren les Châteaux is nestled in the hills here, nearly 1300 ft (400 m) above sea level, and is distinguishable by the Tours d'Eguisheim, three ruined towers that poke through the woodland like dinosaur teeth. Kuentz-Bas makes good wine here and in the Grand Cru Eichberg, located in the nearby commune of Eguisheim ③, your next stop on this tour.

An exquisite 15th-century town, Eguisheim's château once belonged to Pope Leo IX, who was born here. Bruno Sorg and Leon Beyer are the producers to visit, but the huge coopérative also makes good wines. Nearby Wintzenheim has a pair of ruined châteaux and the great Hengst Grand Cru vineyard that makes brilliant Gewurztraminer.

TURCKHEIM TO RIQUEWIHR

Turckheim ④ offers the chance to sample and compare wines from Zind Humbrecht, one of the best producers in Alsace, and those of the excellent Turckheim coopérative. Don't forget to look up at the roofs where, with luck, you will see the white storks that nest here. Albert Schweitzer, one of Alsace's most famous sons, was born in Kaysersberg ⑤, a village that sits astride the river Weiss. The long and prosperous history of wine making here is evident in the beauty of its buildings and in the fact that there is a chapel whose statue of Christ is holding a bunch of grapes. The place of pilgrimage for wine lovers, though, is Domaine Weinbach's cellar, where Laurence Faller makes exquisite Riesling.

The twin communes of Bennwihr ⑥ and

A PEACEFUL RETREAT
Sentiers viticoles, *lovely paths that run through the vineyards, complement the charm of Alsace's towns and villages.*

KEY	
🍷	Tasting possible
🍴	Places to eat
ℹ️	Tourist information
★	Site of interest
▬	Tour route
🔆	Viewpoint

ST. HIPPOLY
🍷★

RIBEAUVILLÉ
🍷★🔆ℹ️
⑨

BERGH
🍷★

RIQUEWIHR ⑧
🍷★🍴🔆

MITTELWIHR
⑦ 🍷

KAYSERSBERG
⑤ ★

BENNWIHR
⑥ 🍷★

TURCKHEIM
🍷★🍴🔆 ④

COLMAR
🍷★🍴ℹ️ ①

EGUISHEIM
🍷★🍴 ③

② ROUFFACH
🍷★

↓ To Thann

MITTELBERGHEIM
ANDLAU ⑫ ⑬

DAMBACH-
LA-VILLE ⑪

To Marlenheim

CHÂTENOIS
TZHEIM

• SÉLESTAT

HOME TO ROOST
Stork-breeding centers in Turckheim and Molsheim have encouraged these beautiful birds to return to Alsace.

RIBEAUVILLÉ TO MITTELBERGHEIM

Ribeauvillé ⑨ still feels like the wine capital of Alsace. Here you will find lovely old churches, ruined castles, plenty of fine restaurants, wine producers, and some top-class *grands crus* vineyards. Your next stop, Bergheim ⑩, is known for its town hall and the Porte Haute gateway, through which outlaws seeking sanctuary once fled. St. Hippolyte's claim to fame lies in its stately town square and the quality of its Pinot Noir. The old watchtower is worth photographing, but save some film for the castle of Haut-Koenigsbourg that towers over the vineyards between Kintzheim and Châtenois. Dambach-la-Ville ⑪ used to be known as Dambach-la-Vigne and the importance of wine here is reflected in the 14th-century chapel to St. Sebastian that sits almost within the Frankstein *grand cru* vineyard. In Dambach itself, the half-timbered houses and flowering plants are so perfect that they look as though they are touched up daily. Andlau ⑫ is said to owe its situation to a bear which was sent by an angel to indicate the valley where a 9th-century abbey should be built, while Mittelbergheim ⑬, the historic "City of Wine," is arguably the most ornate and least changed of all the region's communes.

PRETTY AS A PICTURE
Riquewihr's narrow streets, with their gilded signs, are some of Alsace's prettiest.

Mittelwihr ⑦ are a triumph of restoration and reconstruction, following their near-destruction by war. Here, the often unloved Sylvaner grape variety gets almost as much tender loving care and attention as the buildings. Make sure your visit to Riquewihr ⑧ isn't in the summer, if you don't like rubbing shoulders with crowds of tourists. It was here that the merchants Hugel first opened their doors – and where they are still to be found. On your way through Hunawihr, note the fortified church, the clock of which has hands that look like bunches of grapes.

TOURING TIPS

INFORMATION: The best place to find information about the wines of Alsace is at the offices of the regional wine committee at 12 Avenue de la Foire au Vin, **Colmar** 🅲 03 89 20 16 20.

EVENTS: There are wine festivals almost every weekend in the region's wine villages, but the best opportunity to taste a wide range of wines is at the Foire Régionale in Colmar, which is held from August 5–16.

RESTAURANTS:
L'Auberge de l'Ill, 2 Rue de Collonges au Mont d'Or, **Illhausern** 🅲 03 89 71 89 00. One of the most famous restaurants in France, this Michelin 3-starred gastronomic Mecca offers traditional and modern versions of Alsace cuisine, and includes a brilliant wine list. *La Maison des Têtes*, 19 Rue des Têtes, **Colmar** 🅲 03 89 24 43 43. Taking its name from the heads on the facade, this national monument offers good, hearty, traditional Alsatian fare.

HOTELS:
Le Maréchal, 4–6 Place des Six Montagnes Noires, **Colmar** 🅲 03 89 41 43 07. Right on the edge of the water, this 16th-century timbered hotel in the center of the town offers almost a surfeit of romantic Alsatian atmosphere. *Château de Barembach*, 5 Rue du Maréchal de Lattre de Tassigny, **Colmar** 🅲 03 88 97 97 50. A lovely Renaissance château with grounds and tennis courts. The perfect place to relax after a long day of tasting.

TIME GOES BY
The sleepy town of Mittelbergheim is the perfect place to end this wine tour.

EDELZWICKER

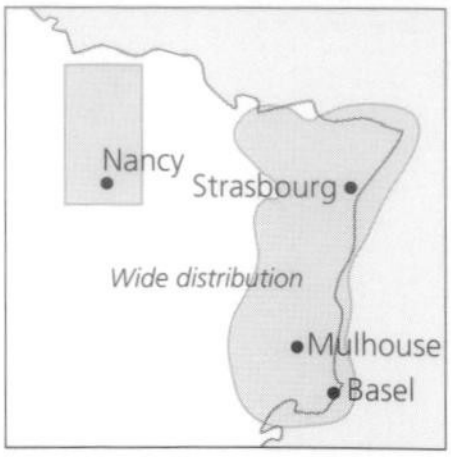
Nancy
Strasbourg
Wide distribution
Mulhouse
Basel

1995
VIN D'ALSACE
Rolly Gassmann
Edelzwicker

ALTHOUGH ALSACE WINE is commonly thought to be made from a single type of grape, the region has a strong tradition of blending. Blends of basic grape varieties were called *Zwicker* (a German word), while those made up of quality varieties were given the French name *gentil*. In 1871, when the Germans ruled Alsace, they tried to impose the term *Edelwein* in place of *gentil*. The Alsatians agreed only to the two terms *Edelzwicker* and *Zwicker*. In 1972 the French authorities banned the use of *Zwicker*, so that today all blended Alsace wine, irrespective of variety, is called *Edelzwicker*. Most of it is such ordinary wine that the more quality-conscious producers label their blends "Gentil," "Réserve," or "Côtes du," followed by the name of the relevant *commune*. Unfortunately, some downright poor wines are also sold under these labels.

ROLLY GASSMANN
Rolly Gassmann's Edelzwicker is a cut above most: it is not particularly expensive, but is nevertheless stylish.

VISITORS WELCOME
Many cellars welcome visitors, and in Alsace even the top growers often keep a shop where you can buy wine at the end of your visit.

- This wine is produced throughout the Alsace region.
- Traditional, simple, fruity, dry white wine.
- Jean-Baptiste Adam, Marcel Deiss, Jean-Pierre Dirler, Hugel, Kreydenweiss, Kuehn, Rolly Gassman, Cave de Ribeauvillé, Schlumberger, Louis Sipp, Pierre Sparr.
- Roast haunch of pork with pistachios.
- 1998, 1997, 1996.
- 2–3 years.

GEWÜRZTRAMINER

Nancy
Strasbourg
Wide distribution
Mulhouse
Basel

ALSACE GRAND CRU
Hengst
GEWURZTRAMINER
DOMAINE ZIND HUMBRECHT

THE TERM "GEWÜRZTRAMINER" refers to a grape variety that used to be known as "Traminer." The Alsatians themselves may believe that the Riesling makes the finer, longer-lived wines, but even the best of these never begin to compete with this instantly recognizable, pink-skinned grape when it comes to seductiveness and excitement. But the character of the Alsace Gewürztraminer varies enormously, depending on the site on which it is grown, the ripeness at which it is picked, and the skills and techniques of the wine makers. In the hands of careful producers such as Faller, Ostertag, Trimbach, and Zind Humbrecht, using low-cropped grapes that have grown in the soil of the best *grands crus* vineyards, Gewürztraminer can produce dry and luscious, late-harvested wines that have all the irresistible eastern aroma and appeal of the finest perfumes.

ZIND HUMBRECHT
Gewürztraminer can lack acidity in hot years, but top examples like this one can be relied on to be perfectly balanced.

HILLS OF VINES
In typical wine-growing areas of Alsace, the vines cover the slopes while the growers live close at hand in the villages below.

- Ammerschwihr, Barr, Bergheim, Guebwiller, Hunawihr, Kayserberg, Kientzheim, Mittelbergheim, Mittelwihr, Obernai, Orschwihr, Ribeauvillé, Riquewihr, Rorschwihr, Rouffach, Turckheim, Wintzenheim.
- Aromatic dry and sweet wines.
- Blanck, Deiss, J-P Dirler, Faller, Mittnacht Klack, Ostertag, Zind Humbrecht.
- Münster cheese.
- 1997, 1996, 1995, 1990.
- 5–10 years.

MUSCAT

Nancy •   Strasbourg •

Wide distribution

• Mulhouse
• Basel

ONE OF THE SURPRISES of Alsace, whose wines are often sweet, is the dryness of its Muscat – a name associated elsewhere with lusciousness. It is, however, inaccurate to refer to the Muscat as if it were a single grape variety. Alsatians grow three types of Muscat: the Muscat à Petits Grains (both white and rosé) and the Muscat Ottonel. There is little agreement over which of these makes the best wine. Despite the potentially delicious quality of Alsace Muscat, the vines are being uprooted at an alarming rate, and now cover little more land than the Chasselas. It takes dedication to keep yields down and pick at the right time to ensure that the finished wine has enough acidity not to taste flabby. Fortunately, there are producers who know this, and who allow the Muscat to reveal its grapey, appley, orange-and-mandarin perfume and flavor.

WAYSIDE SHRINE
Religious traditions live on in these deep valleys. This cross, overlooking some vines, is situated near the town of Riquewihr.

MEYER-FONNÉ
Delicate, aromatic, dry Muscat, like this one from Meyer-Fonné, is best drunk young while it retains all its freshness.

🏞 Barr, Bennwihr, Katzenthal, Mittelwihr, Riquewihr, Rorschwihr, Voegtlinshoffen, Wettolsheim, Wintzenheim.	René Muré-Clos St. Landelin, Bruno Sorg.
🍷 Light, grapey, dry white wine.	🍴 Cheesecake.
🍇 Ernest Burn, Hugel, Kitzler, Meyer-Fonné,	📅 1998, 1997, 1996, 1995.
	⌛ AC Alsace Muscat: 1–3 years. AC Alsace Grand Cru Muscat: 2–5 years.

PINOT BLANC

Nancy •   Strasbourg •

Wide distribution

• Mulhouse
• Basel

THIS COUSIN OF THE PINOT GRIS is non-aromatic – an exception to the Alsace rule. At its best, and when not overcropped, it can produce attractively creamy wines. Many of the Alsace growers use a clone of this variety that is known as the Gros Pinot Blanc. This was at one time chiefly used as a blend with the Chasselas in wines labeled as Edelzwicker. The Pinot Blanc can have so little character of its own that the *appellation contrôlée* rules permit wines to be sold as Pinot Blanc, or as the related Klevner or Clevner (*see p.67*), which are made, in whole or in part, from the Pinot Gris, Pinot Auxerrois, Chardonnay, and even Pinot Noir. This laxity has given rise to a confusing range of similarly-labeled wines, but it also allows some producers to make more interesting wines than pure Pinot Blanc might allow. The Pinot Auxerrois, in particular, brings a welcome note of Alsatian spice.

GRAND CRU
The Hengst vineyard, shown here, is one of the best in Alsace, and hence can be called grand cru.

PAUL BLANCK
The Pinot Blanc grape is generally used for everyday wines in Alsace, and at their best they are delicious: creamy, with just a touch of spice.

🏞 Mittelbergheim, Pfaffenheim, Saint Hippolyte, Westhalten, Wintzenheim.	Brecht, Kuentz-Bas, Meyer-Fonné, Cave de Turckheim, Zind Humbrecht.
🍷 Refreshing, crisp, dry white; base for crémant sparkling wines. Component in Edelzwicker blends.	🍴 Onion tart.
🍇 Paul Blanck, Henri	📅 1997, 1996, 1995, 1994.
	⌛ White: 2–8 years

PINOT GRIS

THE STORY OF HOW AN ALSATIAN wine came to share a name with a Hungarian wine-making area is full of mystery. According to a local legend, Baron Lazare de Schwendi, an Alsatian general, received 4,000 vats of wine and some cuttings of Pinot Gris vines from the town of Tokay in Hungary in 1565 as a reward for expelling a Turkish force. Today the Pinot Gris is not found in Hungary, but occupies 4 percent of Alsace's vineyards, yielding some of the region's most stylish wines. These take a middle path between the potentially acidic Riesling and the possibly oversweet Gewürztraminer or Muscat. Alsatians call the grape "the Sultan" and typically drink *vendanges tardives* and *sélection de grains nobles* examples of the wine with *foie gras*. The wines may be labeled Tokay-Pinot Gris or Pinot Gris. The illegal name "Tokay d'Alsace" is occasionally found.

TRIMBACH PINOT GRIS RÉSERVE
Of all the merchants in Alsace, none is finer than Trimbach, a firm whose Pinot Gris is always reliably well made.

Wide distribution

RIQUEWIHR
One of the most enchanting towns in Alsace, indeed in France, Riquewihr is also home to some of the region's best merchants and growers. Some great Pinot Gris can also be found here.

🏛 Barr, Dambach-la-Ville, Guebwiller (Kitterlé), Kayserberg, Kientzheim (Schlossberg), Mittelwihr (Mandelberg), Obernai, Riquewihr (Sporen), Thann (Rangen), Turckheim.	🏠 Ernest Brun, Bott-Geyl, Dopff & Irion, Kreydenweiss, Ostertag, Schleret, Sorg, Weinbach (Faller), Zind-Humbrecht.
	🍴 Sweet: *pâté de foie gras*.
	🍷 1997, 1996, 1995, 1994.
🥂 Rich, dry and sweet wines.	⏱ Dry: 3–8 years.

PINOT NOIR

Wide distribution

IF ANY BLACK GRAPE WILL PRODUCE fine wine in Alsace, this variety is admittedly the one most likely to succeed; but there are plenty of examples to prove how much of a challenge it offers wine makers. The first problem lies in producing red wine rather than pink. This has been addressed recently by introducing new clones and by the use of rotating fermenters, which extract color at the possible expense of delicacy. The Alsatian ambition to imitate red Burgundy has also led to the enthusiastic use of new oak, which is often as appropriate as a heavy gold frame around a watercolor miniature. In my opinion, it would be better if producers gave up copying Vosne-Romanée *(see p.138)* and turned more attention to their often delicious cherry and raspberryish Rosé d'Alsace, a wine that is also far more fitting to the Alsace *flûte* bottle than dark, oaky red.

ALBERT MANN
One of the most ambitious producers of this variety, Albert Mann gives his Pinot Noir a moderate length of time in new oak casks.

THE WINE IS KING
Signs like these are common in Alsace, where small producers and merchants take pride in their vinous heritage.

🏛 Dambach-la-Ville, Eguisheim, Orschwiller, Ottrot, Pfaffenheim, Ribeauvillé, Rodern, St. Hippolyte, Traenheim, Turckheim.	Eguisheim, Robert Faller, Albert Hertz, Hugel, Roger Jung, Kuentz-Bas, Pfaffenheim, de Turckheim, Charles Wantz.
🥂 Elegant, light, refreshing reds.	🍴 Meat and vegetable casserole.
🏠 J.B. Adam, Jean Becker, Joseph Cattin, Marcel Deiss, Caves de	🍷 1997, 1996, 1995.
	⏱ Red: 10–15 years.

RIESLING

T HIS, THE FAVORITE GRAPE of wine merchants and critics, is also the variety of which the Alsatians are most proud. Established here since at least the 15th century, when it was called the Rissling or *gentil* (or *noble*) *aromatique*, the Riesling has gradually supplanted the Sylvaner (*see below*) to fill some 20 percent of the vineyards, compared to 13 percent in 1969. While the Alsatian Riesling has suffered from the bad image of wines from the other side of the Rhine, it has also benefited from having its own, contrasting style. Unlike the dry German Riesling, examples from Alsace's warm climate can be richly ripe. The character of each wine varies with the soil. The richest come from clay, while the ones produced on granite or limestone take longer to develop, a quality the Alsatians readily acknowledge by selling their wine 18 months after the harvest.

Wide distribution

RIBEAUVILLÉ
Once the official "capital" of Alsace, Ribeauvillé produces some of the region's finest Rieslings from its Geisberg, Kirchberg, and Osterberg grand cru vineyards.

DOMAINE WEINBACH, CUVÉE THÉO
Laurence Faller makes extraordinarily fine wines, including individual cuvées such as this one, which was named after her father.

🌾	Barr, Deblenheim, Guebwiller, Kaysersberg, Ribeauvillé, Riquewihr, Rouffach, Turckheim, Wintzenheim.	Schlumberger, Roland Schmitt, Bruno Sorg, Trimbach, Weinbach, Zind-Humbrecht.
🍷	Dry and sweet wines.	🍴 Dry: Alsatian fish stew.
🍶	Paul Blanck, Marcel Deiss, Dirler, Albert Hertz, Kientzler, Ostertag, Rolly Gassmann,	⧗ 1997, 1996, 1995, 1994.
		🕑 Grains nobles: 5–15 years.

OTHERS

Nancy
Strasbourg

Wide distribution

Mulhouse
Basel

C HASSELAS IS MADE FROM A TABLE grape of the same name, which is now nearly extinct in Alsace (2 percent of vineyards, down from over 16 percent in 1969); a few producers, such as Schoffit and Kientzler, make light, fruity, early-drinking wine from it, but most goes into Edelzwicker (*see p.64*). Crémant d'Alsace is a series of quietly successful sparkling wines made from mixed varieties, the most successful combination being the Pinot Gris, Pinot Noir, and Chardonnay; the rosés are particularly recommendable. Klevener de Heiligenstein, both the wine and the grape variety, is unrelated to the Clevner (or Klevner) grape, but is the local form of the Savagnin Rosé, a Jura grape. Pinot Auxerrois is like a cross between the Pinots Blanc and Gris, a gently spicy variety that is officially (but wrongly) classed as Pinot Blanc; some producers ignore the legislation and print the Auxerrois name on their labels. Sylvaner is an undistinguished variety that covers 17 percent of Alsace's vineyards (down from 27 percent in 1969) but mostly ends up in Edelzwicker. In Lorraine, the Côtes de Toul *VDQS* produces tiny amounts of good light red (from Pinot Noir and Meunier) and rosé from these varieties, plus the Gamay. The red and white Vin de Moselle *VDQS* from the banks of that river are only worth buying if you are in the area, and then only the vintages from warmer years.

SIERCK-LES-BAINS
Throughout the Alsace region, the buildings have a decidedly Germanic appearance.

GENTIL HUGEL
This wine represents a welcome return to the days when grape varieties were commonly blended in Alsace.

THE FOOD OF ALSACE AND LORRAINE

Nothing more vividly illustrates the geography and history of these two regions, sandwiched between France and Germany, than the food that is eaten here. Lovers of the way in which pork and pickles are served to the east of the Rhine river will relish several Alsatian dishes, while those favouring the freshwater fish recipes of the Loire will also find much to enjoy.

PASTRY HAS ALWAYS played a large part in the cuisine of both Alsace and Lorraine, ranging from the world-famous but, sadly, often bastardized *quiche Lorraine* to *flamme-küche,* an onion, bacon and cream tart that is made, like pizza, using bread dough.

Traditional references to *le seigneur cochon,* the "lord pig", reveal how important pork is, especially in Alsace. Several of the ways in which this meat is prepared may be sampled by ordering a dish of *choucroute* (sauerkraut), which includes smoked and unsmoked pork, sausages, ham and bacon. It is, of course, the cabbage that has given this dish its fame and its place of honour in the region's households. Every autumn, after the wine harvest,

PORC AUX DEUX POMMES
Alsatian chefs have long appreciated and exploited the affinity that apples and the appley flavour of the Riesling grape both have for pork.

SALADE DE POMMES DE TERRE
Potatoes, cooked in a number of ways, are one of the major staples of Alsatian cuisine. In this recipe, they are used in a salad with pork sausages.

CHOUCROUTE GARNIE
Pickled cabbage, like sauer-kraut in Germany, is made in wooden barrels filled with salt, juniper berries and bay leaves. It is left for a month before being cooked slowly with pork, ham, sausages and Alsace wine.

TARTE ALSACIENNE
This traditional dessert can be made using apples, apricots or cherries, steeped in kirsch and sugar. Custard, flavoured with cinnamon, is poured into the crust.

a specialist *choucroute* cutter would go from door to door shredding the freshly picked cabbage, before putting it in a barrel with salt, water, cumin, juniper berries and vine or cabbage leaves. The barrel was then covered with a cloth and a lid that was weighted down with a stone. When cut and stored in this fashion, the cabbage lasted right through the cold winter.

Pork is also used with other meats, such as veal in *tourte de la vallée de Munster*, and lamb and beef in *bäckeoffe* casserole. In contrast, the Jewish population of Alsace has promoted several alternatives to pork, the most successful being goose. The goose meat is smoked, while the liver is relished in the form of *foie gras*. Popular meats with stronger flavours include wild hare and boar, both hunted in the region's forests.

Fish is also abundant in this white-wine region. Older recipes feature salmon and lampreys from the Rhine and Ill rivers. Today, however, you are more likely to find perch, pike, tench, trout and eel, which are cooked with fish stock and Riesling to make *matelote* stew.

Whatever the dish, there is a strong likelihood that spices, most notably cinnamon, cumin, caraway, coriander and nutmeg,

PASTRIES
Kugelhopf, *the most beloved of Alsatian pastries, is a rich yeast cake with raisins and almonds. Made in fluted earthenware ring moulds, this slightly sweet delicacy is intended to look like a medieval merchant's hat.*

will have been used in its preparation. These spices are also used in the desserts and cakes that swell the Alsatian waistline. However, the famous *kugelhopf* cake, an exceptionally light tube cake, owes its flavour instead to raisins and almonds.

REGIONAL CHEESES

Given the flavoursome character of Alsace's wines, it is hardly surprising that the cheeses produced here tend to be pretty pungent too. Originally, cheese was made by Alsatian monks for their own consumption. Today, inevitably, while there are still plenty of small cheese farms, a great deal of cheese is also made industrially. Factory-made, pasteurized Munster and Gérome, its cousin from Lorraine, have some of the character of the artisanal product, but they are far duller. It is worth seeking out a cheese from one of the few producers who display the fact that they are holders of the diploma of le Syndicat Interprofessionel de Munster.

MUNSTER
Produced in both Alsace and Lorraine, this smooth cheese is immediately recognizable by its pungent smell. In Alsace it is eaten with potatoes.

TRAMI D'ALSACE
This soft, slightly creamy cheese is made from unpasteurized cow's milk and washed in Gewürztraminer. It has a pungent smell and is quite spicy.

BORDEAUX

THE RED AND WHITE WINES OF BORDEAUX,

SOME OF THE WORLD'S MOST FAMOUS WINES,

OFTEN OUTLIVE THE MEN WHO MADE THEM.

ONE KEY TO UNDERSTANDING the wines of Bordeaux, and the reasons for their confusing variation in quality, lies in the vast size of the region. At 100,000 ha (247,000 acres) it is three times the size of Burgundy (*see pp98–141*). One consequence of this is that Bordeaux wines, of one style or another, are made by some 20,000 producers, of which only around 100 have achieved international fame. At least a third of Bordeaux producers bottle and label their wine under the name of their own château, which may be little bigger than a garden shed. As you might expect, the region includes a variety of soils and climates. Some areas, principally the best, most gravelly-soiled *appellations* of the Haut-Médoc (*see p81*) and Graves (*see p80*), favour red wines in which the blackcurranty Cabernet Sauvignon grape is supported by the Merlot and the Cabernet Franc, with an occasional dash of the spicy Petit Verdot. In other *appellations*, particularly St Émilion (*see p89*) and Pomerol (*see p87*), with their more clay-heavy soils, it is the plummier Merlot grape that holds sway. With the exception of the great sweet wines, produced particularly in Sauternes (*see p94*) and Barsac (*see p76*), the white wines of Bordeaux have been traditionally off-dry and mediocre. Recent technological advances, however, have helped to produce a new generation of good dry

🔺 113,000 ha (280,000 acres): 860 million bottles.	▨ There is both gravel, which suits the Cabernet Sauvignon, and clay, which is more ideal for the Merlot.
🔋 While the entire region is influenced by the proximity of the Atlantic, the climate varies greatly from one part to the next, with St Émilion and Pomerol enjoying more continental conditions.	🍇 Red: Cabernet Sauvignon, Cabernet Franc, Merlot, Malbec, Petit Verdot. White: Sauvignon Blanc, Sémillon, Muscadelle.

WATER, WATER EVERYWHERE
Fringed by forest, it is the Atlantic Ocean as well as the Gironde and Garonne rivers that give Bordeaux its mild, stable climate, ideal for vine growing.

white wines made from both the Sauvignon Blanc and Sémillon grape varieties.

Climatically, Bordeaux benefits from its position bordering the Atlantic Ocean to the west, which insulates it from extremes of temperature. Even so, the relatively northern latitude of the region means that the production of really ripe-tasting wine is possible in only around one of every three years. Confusingly, but unsurprisingly, many vintages favour only particular *appellations* or grape varieties, so that a great year for sweet white wines can be a disastrous one for reds. The much-needed map through all this confusion is a set of classifications, drawn up in 1855 and amended in the 20th century, that sets out a league table of the best châteaux in the *appellations* of Médoc,

SWEET AS HONEY
Growing on the north bank of the Garonne, these vines in Loupiac (see p81) produce luscious, sweet white wines.

Graves and Sauternes. In recent years, however, it has increasingly been acknowledged that, whatever their official ranking, individual châteaux very often over- or under-perform, depending on a number of factors, including the skill of the wine maker and the equipment at his or her disposal. True Bordeaux lovers follow the progress of a large number of châteaux every vintage, creating their own "running" classification.

RED AND WHITE
The only area in Bordeaux to produce both good red and dry white wine is the region of Graves to the south of the city of Bordeaux. Some châteaux, like La Tour Martillac, are better known for their white than their red.

KEY TO REGIONS

▢ Barsac	▢ Médoc (including Haut-Médoc, Listrac-Médoc, Margaux, Moulis, Pauillac, St Estèphe, St Julien)
▢ Côtes de Blaye	
▢ Côtes de Bourg	▢ Pessac-Léognan
▢ Cérons	▢ Pomerol
▢ Entre-Deux-Mers (including Cadillac, Loupiac, Premières Côtes de Bordeaux, Ste-Croix-du-Mont)	▢ Sauternes
	▢ St Émilion (including St Émilion satellites)
▢ Graves	— *Département* boundary
▢ Libournais (including Fronsac and Canon Fronsac, Côtes de Castillon, Côtes de Francs, Lalande de Pomerol)	— Delimited AOC Region of Bordeaux

Map labels: MONTENDRE, Larit, Dronne, COUTRAS, Isle, LALONDE-DE-POMEROL, CÔTES DE FRANCS, Fronsac, LIBOURNE, N89, CÔTES DE CASTILLON, D6708, Engranne, Sauveterre-de-Guyenne, Cadillac, Loupiac, Dropt, Ste-Croix-du-Mont, LA RÉOLE, St-Macaire, Garonne, LANGON, Ciron

0 km 20
0 miles 20

The History of Bordeaux

It was only with the 12th-century marriage between the duchess Eleanor of Aquitaine and the Norman Henry Plantagenet, heir to the throne of England, that the wine-producing history of Bordeaux really began in earnest. This alliance not only provided an instant market for the wines of Aquitaine, it also secured a crucial role for the city of Bordeaux as a port.

WHILE THE WINE INDUSTRY in most parts of France was developed by what the wine historian Hanneke Wirtjes describes as "patient monks," in Bordeaux wine production was driven by merchants looking for products with which to fill the holds of their trading ships. Bordeaux was a medieval version of today's Hong Kong, and just as the sharp businessmen of that island prefer to export clothes rather than cotton, the canny Bordelais soon learned to make money by exporting their wines rather than their grapes.

The Royal Seal
Norman duke Henry Plantagenet became King of England in 1154.

By the early 14th century, nearly half of all the wine passing through the port of Bordeaux was being exported to the British Isles. Much of it was made in the area known as the Haut Pays, to the east of the modern *appellation* of Bordeaux, in regions such as Bergerac *(see p.224)* and Gaillac *(see p.226)*. Realizing the commercial threat posed by these neighbors, the merchants and producers of Bordeaux were quick to ban the importation of their wines into the city until after November 11th, St. Martin's Day, by which time the new vintage of their own wines was safely shipped. It was this same Bordelais trading mentality that helped to create the first branded wines, that is, wines sold under the name of a single

château, rather than under the name of the village in which the grapes were grown. When the English diarist Samuel Pepys broke his vow to give up wine on April 10, 1663, it was with "a sort of French wine, called Ho Bryan." Château Haut-Brion, in what is now the *appellation* of Pessac-Léognan *(see p.86)*, enjoys the unusual distinction of naturally well-drained soil. Until the 16th century, however, most of the Médoc *(see p.83)* was swampy woodland, unsuitable for vines. Estates on slightly higher land, such as Château Margaux and Château Lafite, began to make wine in the late 17th century. The further development of the vineyards of the Médoc was made possible around this time by skilled Dutch engineers, who installed the drainage ditches that can still be seen today, and paved the way for the planting of vines in rows that could be worked with an ox-drawn plow.

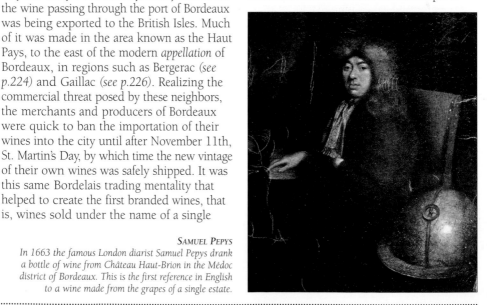

Samuel Pepys
In 1663 the famous London diarist Samuel Pepys drank a bottle of wine from Château Haut-Brion in the Médoc district of Bordeaux. This is the first reference in English to a wine made from the grapes of a single estate.

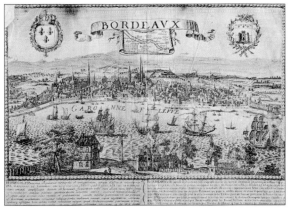

TOWARD THE MODERN APPELLATION

By the 18th century, much of the wine from the vineyards around the port of Bordeaux was passing through the hands of an increasing number of English, Irish, Dutch, German, and Danish merchants. Between them they developed a lucrative and well-organized wine trade that survived the Revolution of 1789, and of which important elements still exist today. Perhaps the most enduring legacy of these merchants is their classification of the region's wines by price, known today simply as "The Classification." Commissioned by the Bordeaux Chamber of Commerce to help with the presentation of the wines of Bordeaux at the 1855 *Exposition Universelle* in Paris, the list includes the best estates of the Médoc and Sauternes *(see p.94),* and Château Haut-Brion in Pessac Léognan. With only a few changes, the 1855 Classification is still in use today.

Since 1945, with the end of World War II, three figures in particular have shaped the *appellation* of Bordeaux as we know it today. The first is the late Philippe de Rothschild, owner of Château Mouton-Rothschild in Pauillac *(see p.84).* Rothschild was one of the first wine makers to champion the idea of bottling his own wines, rather than selling them young and leaving the task of maturing to the wine merchants. An inspired marketer, Rothschild used the name of his château to sell a mundane wine, produced from grapes grown elsewhere, which he called Mouton Cadet. The tactic proved such a success that, despite its mediocrity, Mouton Cadet is now as well known as any Bordeaux wine. Another instrumental figure is Professor Émile Peynaud, known as the father of modern oenology. Of Peynaud's many contributions, the most outstanding lies in spelling out the pitfalls of mishandling grapes and wine, and in the revival and popularization of the practice of separating the very best wine of the vintage from the rest, and selling the contents of the lesser vats as "second wine." Last but not least, there is the American contribution. In 1978 the lawyer turned wine critic Robert Parker published his first newsletter *Wine Advocate,* using an original 50–100 point scale to grade individual wines. By 1993 *Wine Advocate* had 28,000 subscribers, mainly in the United States. Without Parker's enormously popular point system, many previously little-known Bordeaux estates would not enjoy the international prestige or command the high prices that they do today.

ÉMILE PEYNAUD
As a consummate scientist, wine taster, and teacher, the influence of Professor Émile Peynaud of Bordeaux University has been immense, stretching far beyond his native Bordeaux.

A Driving Tour of Bordeaux

Unlike Burgundy, where the wine villages are often separated only by a narrow track, the villages of Bordeaux, in general, and the Médoc, in particular, are more widely dispersed. This tour takes in all of the main *appellations* of the Médoc, as well as some that are less well known.

Bordeaux ☐ Tour

To Ver

Bordeaux

You could spend several days visiting the city of Bordeaux ①, with its art galleries, museums, and wine shops. Whatever else you do, though, make sure you go to the Maison du Vin de Bordeaux to arm yourself with informative leaflets produced by the region's various vinous associations.

Bordeaux to Margaux

The first stretch of the road north to the Médoc is of little vinous interest until you get to Ludon-Médoc ②, where you pass Château la Lagune, one of the few Médoc classed estates that lie outside the *appellations* of Margaux, St. Julien, Pauillac, and St. Estèphe. The un-classed Château Cantemerle is also here, as well as the good-value Château Maucamps. In Macau ③, turn right for a brief detour down to the banks of the Gironde, where you will find a couple of cafés and an atmosphere reminiscent of the riverside excursions portrayed by the French Impressionists.

The *appellation* of Margaux begins some distance to the south of the village from which it takes its name. As you pass through Labarde ④, you are already north of Château Giscours, one of the best-known Margaux estates. I'd recommend stopping at Château Prieuré Lichine, a little further up the road in Cantenac ⑤. This is one of the châteaux most geared to welcoming visitors and offers a display of old iron fire-backs and a collection of books by the

GRAPES AND GRANDEUR
A premier cru vineyard and a grand, palatial building make Château Margaux one of the finest estates in the Médoc.

man who created the estate, the Russian-American wine merchant and author Alexis Lichine. At Issan ⑥, soon after passing the towers of Château Palmer, you can make another detour to the moated, 16th-century Château Issan. Down the road is Château Rauzan Ségla, a rising star whose vineyards and wines are benefiting from heavy investment. At Margaux ⑦, at the end of an avenue of plane trees, Château Margaux stands behind impressive gates. You can stand on the spot where Thomas Jefferson must have stood around 200 years ago to admire its classical facade.

UPPER CLASS
Owned by the Champagne house of Ayala, La Lagune is one of the few classed châteaux in the Haut-Médoc.

Lamarque and St. Julien-Beychevelle

If Château Margaux reminds you of 18th-century gentlemen, the château at Lamarque ⑧ is the kind of fortress that evokes images of knights in armor. Fort Médoc, past Lamarque and not far from battlements that were built in the 17th century to ward off the English, is worth a pause. St. Julien-Beychevelle ⑨ offers a wealth of grand châteaux, with Beychevelle being the first you will encounter. Also worth a look are Château Ducru Beaucaillou and the three Léoville châteaux – Barton, Poyferré, and Lascases – the last of which boasts a commanding stone gateway that you pass as you leave the village.

Pauillac to St. Estèphe

On entering the *appellation* of Pauillac, you will see the rival châteaux of Pichon-Longueville Baron and Pichon-Longueville-Comtesse-de-Lalande, the former proudly showing off its modern extension. To your right is Château Latour's tower and, a little further on to your left, before you head into the quiet town of Pauillac ⑩, lies Château Lynch-Bages. The road

KEY	
🍷	Tasting possible
🏠	Places to eat
ℹ	Tourist information
★	Site of interest
▬	Tour route
⸙	Viewpoint

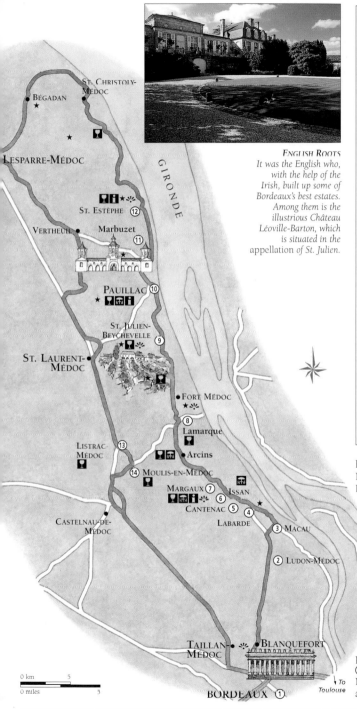

ENGLISH ROOTS
It was the English who, with the help of the Irish, built up some of Bordeaux's best estates. Among them is the illustrious Château Léoville-Barton, which is situated in the appellation of St. Julien.

TOURING TIPS

INFORMATION: Maison du Vin, 1 Cours du 30 Juillet, **Bordeaux** 05 56 00 22 66. The ideal source of information, maps, and leaflets on the region as a whole. There are also smaller *Maisons du Vin* in most of the *appellation* towns.

EVENTS: The bi-annual Vinexpo trade fair takes place in June in odd-numbered years and offers the world's biggest showcase of wines from all over the world.

RESTAURANTS:
La Tupina, 6 Rue de la Monnaie, **Bordeaux** 05 56 91 56 37. Offers some of the best-value fine cooking in Bordeaux, as well as some well-priced wines.
Le Lion d'Or, **Arcins** 05 56 58 96 79. Monsieur Barbier's roadside inn is a favorite with local producers and visiting merchants. Great rustic fare and delicious cep dishes in season.

HOTELS:
Des Quatre Soeurs, 6 Cours du 30 Juillet, **Bordeaux** 05 57 81 19 20. This quirky, inexpensive hotel is in the center of the city.
Château Cordeillan Bages, Route des Châteaux, **Pauillac** 05 56 59 24 24. Under the same ownership as nearby Château Lynch-Bages, this hotel makes an ideal base for exploring the northern Médoc.

heads north, passing Châteaux Mouton-Rothschild and Lafite-Rothschild before leading you to the oriental façade of Château Cos d'Estournel. The road beside the château goes past Marbuzet ⑪ and on to St. Estèphe ⑫.

LISTRAC-MÉDOC AND MOULIS-EN-MÉDOC

On your way back south, pause in Listrac-Médoc ⑬, where producers like Châteaux Clarke and Fonréaud are trying to make softer reds than in the past, and in Moulis-en-Médoc ⑭, where Châteaux Poujeaux, Maucaillou, and Chasse-Spleen all offer good-value wines.

BARSAC

SITUATED ON THE LEFT bank of the Garonne and separated from the larger *appellation* of Sauternes (*see p.94*) to the north by the little Ciron river, the *commune* of Barsac is entitled to sell its wines either as *appellation contrôlée* Barsac or as *appellation contrôlée* Sauternes (*see below*). The Ciron is crucial to the microclimate of the area. It is the autumnal morning mists lingering over its cool water, followed by warm, sunny after-noons, that combine to create ideal conditions for the development of *Botrytis cinerea*, or noble rot, which produces the unique sweet wines of Barsac. Richer in sandstone and limestone than neighboring Sauternes, the flat land here produces wines with a natural lightness that sets them apart from all others. As a rule, wines sold as *appellation contrôlée* Barsac are more reliable than those sold as *appellation contrôlée* Sauternes.

MAGICAL MIST
The famous mist, seen here around the vineyards of Château Myrat, is crucial to the development of the noble rot that makes these wines so special.

CHÂTEAU CLIMENS
Les Cypres is the "second wine" of Château Climens – almost as stylish as its big brother, the "grand vin" of this top estate.

✴ AC Sauternes, AC Barsac.		Doisy-Védriens, Gravas, Liot, Myrat, Nairac, Piada, de Rolland, Suau.
❁ White: Sémillon, Sauvignon Blanc, Muscadelle.		🍽 Warm duck's liver with grapes.
🍷 Elegant, lusciously sweet, white dessert wines.		📆 1997, 1996, 1995, 1990, 1989, 1988, 1986, 1983, 1976.
🍶 Ch Broustet, Caillou, Cantegril,Climens, Coutet, Doisy-Daëne, Doisy-Dubroca,		⏱ 5–20 years.

BARSAC AND THE COMMUNES OF SAUTERNES

A strangely incestuous relationship exists between the neighboring *appellations* of Sauternes and Barsac, producers of the two most famous sweet wines in Bordeaux. Since the introduction of the *appellation contrôlée* system in the 1930s, producers in Barsac have been entitled to use either the name of their own *appellation* on their bottles, or that of Sauternes, an indulgence denied to the Sauternais. Alternatively, the *vignerons* of Barsac can signify their double allegiance by using the increasingly popular name of Sauternes-Barsac. The heterogenous Sauternes *appellation* itself currently covers the four *communes* of Bommes, Fargues, Preignac, and Sauternes, producing sweet wines whose quality ranges from the dire to the sublime. I suspect, however, that as more people throughout the world begin to appreciate truly great sweet wines, as well as the pains-taking skill involved in their production, the wine makers of Barsac, together with those of Bommes, Fargues, and Preignac, will be keen to emphasize their own names. If sections of Minervois (*see p.169*), which received its own classification in 1985, are now allowed their own individual *appellations*, it seems a pity that the same kind of recognition should be denied to the *communes* listed above.

NATURAL STAR
The village of Barsac may be as quiet and remote as ever, but its wines have made it famous all over the world.

BORDEAUX

Covering 247,100 acres (100,000 ha) of vineyards, the generic Bordeaux classifications listed below are used to label a quarter of all the *appellation contrôlée* wines of France. Applied to a range of wines that come from different soils and microclimates and are made with varying skills, this is one of the most successful, but unreliable, wine names in the world.

CAUGHT BY THE RULES
Producer of some of the best sweet white wines in the world, Château d'Yquem (see p.94) is forced by appellation rules to sell its fine dry white wines as plain appellation contrôlée Bordeaux.

I F THE MARKETING GURUS responsible for promoting the wines of the region have got it right, the word Bordeaux will have you thinking of bow-ties. That, after all, is the image they have spent a king's ransom on splashing across the pages of glossy magazines. I suspect, however, that for many of us the Bordeaux region is inexorably linked to its wealth of great châteaux. The success of Mouton-Cadet, after all, owes much to the erroneous belief that it somehow offers an affordable taste of

LAND OF VINEYARDS
With vines covering both plains and hillsides and extending over the entire département of the Gironde, Bordeaux is the largest appellation in France, with more than 50 individual appellations, and eight generic ones.

Château Mouton-Rothschild. Comparison of any vintage of these two wines, however, demonstrates the problem facing anyone trying to make and sell wines under the generic Bordeaux *appellations*. In Pauillac (*see pp.84–5*), where Mouton-Rothschild is made, grapes ripen well, thanks to the position of the vineyards. This climatic advantage is the main reason why Pauillac and its châteaux have become famous. In the less favored Bordeaux vineyards, however, the fruit often fails to ripen properly, a problem exacerbated by rules encouraging over-production, and, as the grapes on thirsty vines simply stop ripening, by more rules banning any form of irrigation.

There are, of course, in humbler parts of the region, some ambitious châteaux that consistently produce good, plain *appellation contrôlée* Bordeaux, as well as Château d'Yquem in Sauternes (*see p.94*) and Château Margaux in the Médoc (*see p.83*), which are forced by quirky *appellation* rules to sell their wonderful dry white wines as plain *appellation contrôlée* Bordeaux. These, however, are exceptions to the Bordeaux rule, and the quality of most branded, merchant-bottled wines remains disappointing. The way forward for the whole of the Bordeaux region, I believe, lies in the relaxation of *appellation* rules that are stricter here than anywhere else in the world, in better wine making, and finally, in the skillful blending of the best wines from the region.

CHÂTEAU THIEULEY
Selling wines as appellation Bordeaux, rather than under the Entre-deux-Mers label to which it is entitled, this memorable château is owned by Francis Courselle.

❋ AC Bordeaux, AC Bordeaux Clairet, AC Bordeaux Sec, AC Bordeaux Rosé, AC Bordeaux Supérieur, AC Bordeaux Supérieur Clairet, AC Bordeaux Supérieur Rosé, AC Crémant de Bordeaux.	ᛁᛁᛁ Barton et Guestier, Ch Bonnet, Dourthe Frères, Maître d'Estournel, Haut Bertinerie, Landereau, Michel Lynch, Tour de Mirambeau, la Raemn, Rauzan-Despagne, Reignac, Reynon, Sirius, Thieuley.
▦ Red/ rosé: Cabernet Sauvignon, Cabernet Franc, Merlot, Malbec. White: Sémillon, Sauvignon.	ᛁᛁ White: Warm potato salad with mussels, celery, onions, and black truffles.
◪ Medium- to full-bodied reds. Dry whites. Dry rosés. Sparkling whites.	▤ Red: 1998, 1996, 1995.
	⚡ 2–5 years.

Cadillac

Stretched along the east bank of the Garonne, and centering around its namesake town, the relation of its neighbors, Loupiac to the south and Sainte Croix-du-Mont to the east. Despite the *appellation* rules which demand that wines here be made from botrytized (nobly rotted) grapes, Cadillac's wines show little evidence that this has happened. Good examples, however, can be attractively light, creamy, and raisiny, and reds; sold as Premières Côtes de Bordeaux, can also be worth buying.

✳ AC Cadillac.	**Jean du Roy**
▦ White: Sémillon, Sauvignon Blanc, Muscadelle.	*Like all good Cadillac, this*
▨ Sweet whites, which may be made from partially botrytized grapes.	*wine combines the apricot flavor of noble*
▥ Carsin, Cayla, Reynon, Jean du Roy, du Juge, Manos, Thieuley.	*rot with a lightness of touch rarely*
▮ Light fruit tart.	*found in other Sauternes.*
☰ 1998, 1997, 1996, 1995.	
➶ White: 3–8 years.	

Côtes de Blaye

First planted by the Romans, there were vineyards in Blaye and neighboring Bourg long before grapes were grown in the Médoc, on the opposite bank of the Gironde estuary. Despite a traditionally rustic character, Blaye's red wines are improving and offer good value in ripe vintages. They are sold either as AC Blaye (sometimes called AC Blayais) or as the higher-alcohol, but not always superior, Premières Côtes de Blaye. Around 10 percent of the wines made here are white, many sold under the white-only AC Côtes de Blaye label.

✳ AC Blaye, AC Côtes de Blaye, AC Premières Côtes de Blaye.	**Château Haut Sociando**
▦ Red: Merlot, Cabernet Sauvignon. White: Sauvignon Blanc.	*One of the best examples of "new wave"*
▨ Medium-bodied dry reds. Dry whites.	*wines from Blaye, this*
▥ Haut Sociando, Tourtes.	*has the elegance of many*
▮ Grilled lamb.	*Médoc wines.*
☰ Red: 1996, 1995.	
➶ Red: 2–6 years.	

Côtes de Bourg

Sometimes called the Switzerland of the Gironde because of its hilly vineyards, this small but heavily cultivated area produces more wine than the much larger Côtes de Blaye to the north. Despite similar soils to the Côtes de Blaye, it is Bourg that has traditionally made the better red wines, and improving wine-making techniques are leading to a higher public profile and the production of wines that offer excellent value. Grape varieties such as the Malbec and the Petit Verdot make an interesting addition to classic Bordeaux varieties.

✳ AC Côtes de Bourg.	**Château Falfas**
▦ Red: Merlot, Cabernet Sauvignon.	*One of the best wines in the*
▨ Medium-bodied reds.	*appellation, it offers rich,*
▥ Brûlésécaille, Falfas, Fougas, Guerry, Les Jonquières, Maldoror, Repimplet, Roc de Cambes, Rousset, Tayac.	*supple flavors that easily compete with many*
▮ Chicken with mushrooms.	*wines from St. Émilion.*
☰ 1996, 1995, 1994.	
➶ Red: 4–8 years.	

Côtes de Castillon

This is the most easterly *appellation* of the Libournais district on the north bank of the Dordogne. Both Merlot and Cabernet Franc grapes are grown here on a mixture of gravel, sand, and clay, producing supple, fruity wines that very often outclass those of the Côtes de Castillon's pricier neighbor, St. Émilion *(see p.89)*. Two thirds of wine production has long been controlled by members of the powerful *Coopérative de Castillon*, but recent investment in the area has produced a number of very promising new châteaux to look out for.

✳ AC Côtes de Castillon.	**Château Pitray**
▦ Red: Merlot, Cabernet Franc, Cabernet Sauvignon.	*One of the stronger producers of this*
▨ Sturdy, dry reds.	*appellation, this château's*
▥ Belcier, Cap de Faugères, Grand Tuillac, Grande Maye, Lapeyronie, Pitray, Poupille, Robin, Vieux Château Champ de Mars.	*wines are well worth laying down.*
▮ Duck breast.	
☰ 1996, 1995, 1994.	
➶ Red: 2–6 years.	

CÔTES DE FRANCS

ALSO KNOWN AS Bordeaux Côtes de Francs, this recently revived *appellation* lies on the eastern edge of the Libournais district, next to the Côtes de Castillon (*see p.18*) and not far from St. Émilion (*see p.89*). The soil here is similar to that of Castillon, but with more limestone and a higher altitude, which, together with the lowest rainfall and the most sunshine in the *département,* helps to produce wines of great finesse. Promising conditions here have recently attracted top producers, including the Thienpont family of Château Puygueraud

		CHÂTEAU
✳	AC Côtes de Francs, AC Côtes de Francs Liquoreux.	*LA PRADE*
🍇	Merlot, Cabernet Franc, Cabernet Sauvignon.	*Côtes de Francs is often thought of as*
🍷	Supple, plump, full-flavored reds.	*"honest" wine This château*
🏛	Charmes-Godard, de Francs, Laclaverie, la Prade, Puygueraud.	*makes a fine, blackcurranty example of the*
🍴	Kidneys with cognac	*appellation.*
▬	1996, 1995, 1994, 1990.	
📈	Red: 3–7 years.	

ENTRE-DEUX-MERS

THE LARGEST *APPELLATION* IN the Entre-Deux-Mers district, this area produces more dry white wines than any other other *appellation* in Bordeaux, apart from the generic AC Bordeaux Blanc. Some red wines are made here too, sold as AC Bordeaux or AC Bordeaux Supérieur, but the emphasis is firmly on white. Although average wine quality is now improving, thanks to better equipment and better wine-making techniques in the *coopératives*, this is a far from ideal place to grow vines and really good wines are the exception rather than the rule.

		CHÂTEAU
✳	AC Entre-Deux-Mers, AC Entre-Deux-Mers-Haut-Benauge, AC Bordeaux-Haut-Benauge.	*BONNET Fresh, flavor-some proof*
🍇	Sauvignon Blanc, Sémillon, Muscadelle, Ugni Blanc.	*of the quality that can be*
🍷	Dry white.	*produced here,*
🏛	Bonnet, la Lezardière, Sainte-Marie, Thieuley.	*given the right skill and*
🍴	Grilled trout.	*commitment*
▬	1998, 1997, 1996, 1995.	
📈	1–3 years.	

FRONSAC AND CANON-FRONSAC

THROUGHOUT THE 18th and 19th centuries, the vineyards of Fronsac and Canon-Fronsac, to the west of the town of Libourne, were better known than those of nearby Pomerol (*see p.87*). Recently rescued from obscurity, they are now once again producing wines to rival many of the best that the district has to offer. The land of Canon-Fronsac, the traditional vine-growing heart of the area, is a large bluff formed by the Dordogne, which protects the vines against frost. Much of the soil in both Fronsac and Canon-Fronsac is clay-limestone over a limestone subsoil, similar to that found on the St. Christophe plateau in St. Émilion (*see p.89*). The Merlot grape is the most widely planted here, and these wines, far better made than in the recent past, combine the Merlot's full-bodied richness with good, firm structure.

FRONSAC
The size of the church in Fronsac reveals the prosperity and importance once enjoyed by this commune, long before the Médoc as a whole began to gain international prestige.

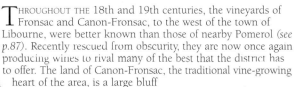

CHÂTEAU LA DAUPHINE
Good Fronsac like this offers plummy, mineral flavors that are very similar to classy and quite pricey – St. Émilion.

✳	AC Fronsac, AC Canon-Fronsac.	Rivière, la Rouselle, la Vielle Cure Villars. *Canon-Fronsac:* Barrabaque, Canon de Brem, Canon-Moueix, Moulin-Pey-Labrie, Cassagne Haut-Canon.
🍇	Red: Merlot, Cabernet Franc, Cabernet Sauvignon.	
🍷	Deep-colored reds with a powerful bouquet.	
🏛	*Fronsac:* Dalem, la Dauphine, la Fleur Cailleau, Fontenil, Moulin Haut Laroque, la	🍴 Goose breast.
		▬ 1998, 1995, 1990, 1988.
		📈 Red: 5–8 years.

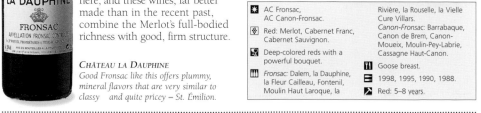

GRAVES

ONE OF THE GREAT WINE NAMES, and traditionally the only region in Bordeaux to make both top-quality reds and whites, Graves suffered the indignity in 1987 of losing all its best châteaux and land to the new *appellation* of Pessac-Léognan (*see p.86*). The Graves that remains is a part of Bordeaux whose wines have a style and quality of their own.

CHÂTEAU DE CHANTEGRIVE
Situated on ideal gravel soil, this estate produces supple reds and fine whites – especially the barrel-fermented Cuvée Caroline.

THE GRAVES REGION has been shrinking for a very long time. Before the arrival of phylloxera, its vines covered some 25,000 acres (10,000 ha), compared with less than 7,500 acres (3,000 ha) today. Some of the land simply was not replanted; other land, close to the city, was lost to suburban housing and Bordeaux's Mérignac airport.

Despite this, until 1987 the Graves *appellation* extended for nearly 38 miles (60 km) southward from Bordeaux and included châteaux such as Haut-Brion. The Pessac-Léognan *appellation* took

VILLA BEL AIR
Owner since 1990 of Villa Bel Air, Jean-Michel Cazes applies the same level of care to its reds and whites as he does to the wines of his Château Lynch-Bages in Pauillac (see p.84).

this and all the other classed growths, leaving a rump with a name but few distinguished wines.

Historically, reds have been less common than whites. Even in 1961 the volume of white wine produced was four times that of red, but as tastes grew more sophisticated there was a switch from sweet to dry white, and from white to red. Today, for every bottle of white, there are two of red. Graves *rouge* can be an attractive, sometimes long-lived, blackcurranty wine, though often lacking the richness of flavor sought by Anglo-Saxons.

The whites are a trickier business. If the sweet "ladies' wines" made here in the 19th and early 20th centuries were poor, so, too, were the dull and over-sulphured dry efforts of the 1960s and 1970s. Quality is now better, thanks to such producers as Peter Vinding-Diers and Denis Dubourdieu, who use specific yeasts that bring out the best flavors from the Sémillon and Sauvignon Blanc. The best white Graves, such as Vinding-Diers' Château Landiras, can outclass a Pessac-Léognan.

Sweet white wine – of which 2.25 million often very ordinary bottles are produced annually – is sold, somewhat confusingly, as Graves Supérieur.

DOMAINE LA GRAVE
Although relatively little-known, this is a modern estate whose wines are remarkably reliable.

CHÂTEAU DU SEUIL
This British-owned estate produces one of the region's best dry white wines.

✳ AC Graves, AC Graves Supérieur.	de Chantegrive, Clos Floridène, la Grave, Landiras, Magneau, de Malle, Millet, Rahoul, Respide Médeville, Roquetaillade la Grange, St. Robert, Tourteau-Chollet, Villa Bel Air.	
✽ Red: Merlot, Cabernet Sauvignon. White: Sémillon, Sauvignon Blanc, Muscadelle.		
▥ Medium- to full-bodied, supple, earthy, tobacco-scented reds. Medium- to full-bodied whites. Also sweet white Graves Supérieur.	❚❚ Medallions of veal.	
	▤ 1998, 1996, 1995, 1990, 1989, 1988, 1986, 1985, 1983, 1982.	
▥ Ch d'Archambeau, d'Ardennes, de Cardaillan,	▧ Red: 7–20 years. White: 3–12 years.	

HAUT-MÉDOC

COMPRISING THE SOUTHERN PART of the Médoc, this *appellation* includes Margaux (*see p.82*), Pauillac, (*see p.84*) and St. Julien (*see p.92*), whose wines are more usually sold under their own *appellations*. There are also Haut-Médoc *crus classés* and *crus bourgeois*, such as Château la Lagune, Beaumont, Cantemerle, Citran, Lanessan, Maucamps, and Sociando-Mallet, that do not have their own *appellation*. The vineyards closest to the Gironde produce wines with finesse, while those from the plateau behind tend to be more full-bodied.

✴	AC Haut-Médoc.
✦	Cabernet Sauvignon, Merlot, Cabernet Franc.
▨	Medium-bodied red.
▥	Ch Beaumont, Camensac, Cantemerle, Citran, la Lagune, Sociando-Mallet, Tour Carnet, Tour du Haut-Moulin.
▮	Rabbit casserole.
▤	1996, 1995, 1990, 1989.
▶	5–10 years.

CHÂTEAU SOCIANDO-MALLET
This modern, fast-rising, oaky star often out-classes its far pricier neighbors.

LALANDE-DE-POMEROL

LYING NORTH of Pomerol (*see p.87*), this area consists of two *communes*: Néac and Lalande-de-Pomerol itself. It covers 2,250 acres (900 ha) – far more than Pomerol itself. In Lalande the vineyards are low-lying, and situated on recent gravel and sand terraces. Some of those in Néac are on a high, south-facing plateau composed of very good gravel, like that of Pomerol across the river Barbanne. The best wines from this part of the *appellation* are readily approachable Merlot-dominant wines that can compete with far pricier Pomerol.

✴	AC Lalande-de-Pomerol.
✦	Merlot.
▨	Medium-bodied red.
▥	Ch de Bel Air, Belles-Graves, Croix-St.-André, Grand Ormeau, Haut-Chatain, Siaurac, Tournefeuille, Trocard.
▮	Roast wild boar.
▤	1998, 1996, 1995, 1990, 1989, 1988.
▶	5–10 years.

CHÂTEAU DE BEL AIR
Not to be confused with Belair in St Émilion, this estate's wines offer Pomerol quality at a price that is affordable.

LISTRAC-MÉDOC

TRADITIONALLY – BUT ERRONEOUSLY – treated as the partner of Moulis (*see p.83*) to the south, Listrac covers some 1,750 acres (700 ha) of sloping, mainly clay-limestone vineyards, rising to about 1,200 ft (400 m), among the highest in the Médoc. The lack of gravel, and the large proportion of Cabernet Sauvignon, which ripens poorly on the clay here, make for generally tough, even rustic wines, more like those of poorer-quality St. Estèphe (*see p.91*) than the wines of Moulis or other *communes* of the Haut-Médoc.

✴	AC Listrac-Médoc.
✦	Cabernet Sauvignon, Merlot, Cabernet Franc, Petit Verdot.
▨	Tannic, medium-bodied reds.
▥	Ch Clarke, Fonréaud, Fourcas-Dupré, Fourcas-Hosten.
▮	Roast guinea fowl.
▤	1996, 1995, 1990, 1989
▶	6–10 years.

CHÂTEAU FOURCAS HOSTEN
This is the perfect wine for wine drinkers who like fairly tough, long-lived, trad-itional claret.

LOUPIAC

LOUPIAC LIES ON the right bank of the river Garonne, opposite Barsac (*see p.76*). It is considered the best of a trio of dessert wine-making *communes*, the other two being its neighbors Ste. Croix-du-Mont (*see p.93*) and Cadillac (*see p.78*). Its wines have a relatively luscious character resulting from the use of botrytized grapes. While Loupiac may tend to be lighter than good examples of Sauternes (*see p.94*) and Barsac, ambitious Loupiac producers are making wine that is better than many efforts sold under these labels.

✴	AC Loupiac.
✦	Sémillon, Sauvignon Blanc, Muscadelle.
▨	Sweet whites – may be made partly from botrytized grapes.
▥	Clos-Jean, Ch du Cros, Loupiac-Gaudiet, Mazarin, du Noble, de Ricaud.
▮	Tarte Tatin (an apple tart).
▤	1998, 1997, 1996, 1995.
▶	Red: 5–15 years.

DOMAINE DU NOBLE
Sauternes-lovers should take note of this producer, whose wines, compete with all but the best of that appellation.

MARGAUX

THE ONLY *APPELLATION* IN Bordeaux to take its name from its finest estate, Margaux covers some of the most fascinatingly, and frustratingly inconsistent, wine-producing land in France. Growing in free-draining gravel soils, Cabernet Sauvignon grapes are used here to make wines with great finesse at their best, but which, at their worst, are merely light and dull.

DIGNIFIED SPLENDOR
Polished and fragrant, the red wines produced at the grand and dignified Château Margaux have enjoyed a renaissance since the late 1970s, and are now some of the very best in Bordeaux.

WHILE THERE IS INDEED a village called Margaux, whose surrounding vineyards include those of Château Margaux (the only estate in the *appellation* with the highest *premier grand cru classé* status), the *appellation* of Margaux also includes red wines made in four other villages: Soussans, Cantenac, Arsac, and Labarde. Although Bordeaux buffs like to discuss the various styles of wine produced in different parts of the *appellation*, the point of the exercise is undermined by the fact that many estates, including Margaux, make their wines from grapes grown in the vineyards of more than one *commune*.

Émile Peynaud *(see p.73)*, credited with revolutionizing the quality of Bordeaux wines in general and of those of Château Margaux in particular, has raised a more pertinent question. How much, he wonders, of the much-vaunted lightness and delicacy for which the whole *appellation* is known

is derived from the light, gravelly soil, and how much comes from the efforts of producers to make wines in a particular style? Brilliant wines made recently at Château Margaux, Château Palmer, and Château Rauzan-Ségla suggest that the answer lies with the wine maker and not with the soil, since, despite a more powerful aroma, these new wines are certainly no lighter in structure than wines from nearby Pauillac *(see p.84)* or St. Julien *(see p.92)*.

With the exceptions mentioned above, many of the wines made here leave one with the feeling of having watched a great actor on a bad day, a fact often blamed on excessive grape yields and on poor wine making. While there is a lot of truth in this, I also suspect that, even on the best-equipped, most conscientious estates, it may be harder to consistently produce top class wines here than in other *appellations* of the Médoc. When Jean-Michel Cazes bought Château Cantenac-Brown here, it took him far longer to achieve a marked improvement in its wines than it did at the châteaux he has acquired in other Bordeaux *appellations*.

CHÂTEAU LABÉGORCE-ZÉDÉ
The wines of this estate, bought by Luc Thienpont in 1979, are impressively well made.

CHÂTEAU PALMER
Bold and innovative, the wines made at Château Palmer are often as good as those of Château Margaux.

✳ AC Margaux.	Kirwan, Labégorce, Labégorce-Zédé, Lascombes, Margaux, Marquis d'Alesme Becker, Marquis de Terme, Monbrison, Palmer, Paveil de Luze, Prieuré Lichine, Rauzan-Ségla, Siran, la Tour de Mons.
❦ Red: Cabernet Sauvignon, Merlot, Petit Verdot, Cabernet Franc.	
▨ Medium- to full-bodied reds with a fragrant bouquet and relatively supple tannins.	
▥ Ch d'Angludet, d'Arsac, Bel-Air-Marquis d'Aligre, Brane-Cantenac, Ch Cantenac-Brown, Dauzac, Desmirail, Durfort-Viviens, Ferrière, Giscours, la Gurgue, d'Issan,	▮▮ Calves' sweetbreads with truffles.
	▤ 1996, 1995, 1990, 1989, 1988, 1986, 1983, 1982, 1978, 1970, 1966, 1961.
	◪ 5–25 years.

MÉDOC

COVERING THE MOST important red wine-producing area in Bordeaux, the huge, district-wide *appellation* of Médoc stretches from Bordeaux city in the south to Soulac-sur-Mer in the north, bordered to the west by the Atlantic Ocean and to the east by the Gironde river. A separate Haut-Médoc *appellation* (see p.81) for the southern half of the area, as well as six individual *commune* classifications, means that wines sold as *appellation* Médoc come mainly from the northern half of the region. A mixture of gravel, limestone, and sandy soils here makes for very varied wines, many of which have the underripe, overcropped character of wines sold as generic Bordeaux. Others, however, such as those produced at Château Potensac or Château la Tour de By, are as good as wines from much more prestigious Médoc *appellations* to the south.

CHÂTEAU ROLLAN DE BY
Part of the important wine-producing commune of Bégadan, Jean Guyon makes red wines that are sturdy and satisfying.

CHÂTEAU LA CARDONNE
In the Médoc commune of Blaignan, this château is under the same ownership as Château Lafite-Rothschild in Pauillac.

✴ AC Médoc.	Lestage-Simon, les Ormes-Sorbet, Patache d'Aux, Potensac, Ch Rollan de By, la Tour de By, la Tour-Haut-Caussan, la Tour St. Bonnet.
🍇 Red: Cabernet Sauvignon, Merlot, Cabernet Franc, Malbec, Petit Verdot.	
🍷 Full-bodied, often oak-aged reds with firm tannins.	🍴 Grilled entrecôte steak with a red wine and shallot sauce.
🍽 Ch Bellerive, Blaignan, Canteloup, la Cardonne, du Castéra, Greysac, Loudenne,	📅 1996, 1995, 1990, 1989.
	📉 5–10 years.

MOULIS

ONE THOUSAND TWO HUNDRED AND THIRTY FIVE ACRES (500 ha) of rolling countryside make up the Médoc *appellation* of Moulis. One of two *appellations* situated on the Atlantic rather than the Gironde side of the district, Moulis has traditionally been considered, together with its neighbor Listrac (see p.81), to be a "must try harder" *appellation*. In fact, the velvety red wines of Moulis are very different from the tougher, more tannic wines of Listrac, with ripe fruit and a rich blackcurrant perfume. The soil here is mixed clay, limestone, and gravel, which, taken together with variations in wine-making skill, makes for some very diverse wines. Many of the best come from vineyards around Grand Poujeaux, where several estates, including Château Chasse-Spleen and Château Poujeaux, produce excellent, long-lived, oak-matured wines.

CHÂTEAU POUJEAUX
This prestigious estate competes with Château Chasse-Spleen as the producer of the best wines of the appellation.

CHÂTEAU CHASSE-SPLEEN
This is an ambitious estate producing superb wines that have helped to create the modern reputation of Moulis.

✴ AC Moulis.	Grand-Poujeaux, Gressier-Grand-Poujeaux, Maucaillou, Mauvezin, Moulin-à-Vent, Poujeaux.
🍇 Red: Cabernet Sauvignon, Merlot.	
🍷 Supple, full-bodied reds aged in partially-new oak barrels.	🍴 Veal brisket with chard.
🍽 Ch Bel-Air Lagrave, Biston-Brillette, Branas-Grand-Poujeaux, Chasse-Spleen, Duplessis-Fabre, Dutruch-	📅 1998, 1996, 1995, 1990, 1989, 1988, 1986, 1985, 1983, 1982.
	📉 8–12 years.

PAUILLAC

IF ONE HAD TO CHOOSE a vinous example of the Gallic expression *embarras de richesses*, it would have to be this *commune*, which boasts three of the five 1855 red *premiers crus* and nearly a third of all of the *crus classés* in the Médoc. The wines produced here are among the most immediately attractive and long-lived in the world.

• Bordeaux

GRAND-PUY-LACOSTE
A popular wine with canny Bordeaux-lovers who appreciate its elegant flavors, and the fact that its price is more affordable than many of the wines from neighboring châteaux.

THE TOWN OF PAUILLAC has always struck me as having the atmosphere of a 19th-century vacation resort, with a river and a canal rather than the sea. There are terraced cafés, modest hotels, and even an oil refinery, now retired, but little to show that some of the world's greatest wines are produced in the vineyards nearby. Outside the town, however, on the land leading down to the river and on the road up to St. Estèphe (*see p.91*),

châteaux and vineyards dominate. Here are the *premiers crus* Latour, Lafite-Rothschild, and Mouton-Rothschild; and a pair of rival *deuxièmes crus*, Pichon-Longueville Comtesse de Lalande and Pichon-Longueville Baron de Longueville, glaring at each other across the road. Also present are Châteaux Lynch-Bages, Pontet-Canet, Clerc Milon, Grand-Puy-Lacoste, and d'Armailhac – all of which regularly stroll into the winners' circle in competitions between wines from throughout the world.

All of which begs the question, why is Pauillac so special? What can explain the intensity of blackcurrant and cigar-box flavors, the combination of velvet and discreetly hidden steel, or the longevity that allows the finest of these wines to taste fresh 50 years after the harvest? The answer lies in the combination of the Cabernet Sauvignon grape, the gravel soil, and the gentle hills on which the vines grow.

Pauillac has good proprietors, too. While Margaux (*see p.82*) has château owners who allow great vineyards to yield mediocre wines, here the Rothschild, Borie, Cazes, Tesseron, and de Lencquesaing families have all made the best of their land. Their wines have a suppleness that makes them easy to drink in their youth. But give them the time in the cellar they deserve, and they will develop layers of fruit and animal flavors unmatched anywhere else.

PICHON-LONGUEVILLE
COMTESSE DE LALANDE
Officially a deuxième cru in the 1855 classification, this château's rich, Merlot-influenced wines often compete on level terms with premiers crus wines in blind tastings.

HELD IN RESERVE
"Second wines" are those made from younger vines and slightly lesser vats, and are particularly worth buying in good vintages. This example is produced at Château Pichon-Longueville Comtesse de Lalande.

✴ AC Pauillac.	Lacoste, Haut-Bages-Averous, Haut-Bages-Libéral, Haut-Batailley, Lafite-Rothschild, Latour, Lynch-Bages, Mouton-Rothschild, Pedesclaux, Pibran, Pichon-Longueville Baron, Pichon-Longueville Lalande, Pontet-Canet, la Tour-Pibran.
❁ Red: Cabernet Sauvignon, Merlot, Cabernet Franc, Petit Verdot.	
🍷 Full-bodied red with a bouquet of blackcurrants and cigar-box cedar.	
🏰 Ch d'Armailhac, Batailley, Becasse, Clerc Milon, Colombier-Monpelou, la Couronne, Duhart-Milon-Rothschild, Fonbadet, Grand-Puy-Ducasse, Grand-Puy-	🍖 Rack of Pauillac lamb.
	🗓 1996, 1995, 1990, 1989, 1986, 1982, 1970, 1961.
	📈 10–25 years.

THE GREAT WINES OF PAUILLAC

CHÂTEAU LAFITE-ROTHSCHILD
Though far from the showiest of wines, Château Lafite-Rothschild remains one of the most stylish. It is also one of the wines most worth laying down in a cellar for a couple of decades, allowing it to develop its unique mixture of rich, complex flavors.

While the Bordeaux classification system now treated as holy writ was drawn up in 1855, the vineyards that produce the top wines of Pauillac were already being referred to as *premiers crus* by the 18th century.

Wines were being made from the vineyards of Château Latour in the 16th century – long before wine making began in most of the rest of the Médoc. By the 18th century these wines had already made their first appearance in the London auction houses. At that time, Château Latour was in the same hands as Château Lafite (later named Lafite-Rothschild) and the château that we now know as Mouton-Rothschild.

Château Latour's subsequent owners included the conglomerate that also owned the *Financial Times* and the multinational company Allied-Lyons, who unaccountably sold it in 1993 to a French businessman.

Latour can be a hard wine to judge in its youth, but with time, even in poor vintages, it develops wonderful sweet fruit. The "second wine," Les Forts de Latour, made from young vines and from the produce of lesser vineyards, offers an affordable taste of the Latour style.

While never as powerful as Château Latour, nor as showy as Mouton-Rothschild, Château Lafite-Rothschild is, for many, the finest and most elegant of all the wines of Bordeaux. The château was founded late in the 17th century. The quality of its output was recognized in the early 19th century, when the wines regularly fetched the highest price of all the wines in the Bordeaux region. The château was bought by the banker Baron James de Rothschild (hence the suffix to its name) in 1868, 13 years after the 1855 classification was issued. Its "second wine" is Les Carruades de Lafite.

Until the middle of the 18th century, the estate that we now know as Château Mouton-Rothschild was part of Château Lafite. Its wines were produced and sold separately, but for generations it failed to attain the prestige of either that château or Château Latour.

This may explain the decision in 1855 to rank Mouton as a *deuxième cru*. On the other hand, there are claims that anti-semitism may have been involved, for the estate had been bought by Nathaniel de Rothschild two years earlier. Whatever the explanation, the promotion to *premier cru* status that Baron Philippe de Rothschild was to achieve in 1973 after much lobbying was a major coup. No other change to the system of classification has ever taken place. Mouton-Rothschild's wines are bigger and richer and more immediately seductive than those of its neighbors, but as the historic vintages of 1945 and 1949 prove, they can age brilliantly.

TOWERING SUCCESS
The distinctive, domed tower of Château Latour is one of the landmarks of the Médoc.

CHÂTEAU MOUTON-ROTHSCHILD
This has the distinction of being the only château to succeed in challenging the 1855 classification, achieving promotion from deuxième to premier cru status.

PESSAC-LÉOGNAN

ONE OF THE YOUNGEST APPELLATIONS in France, Pessac-Léognan includes some of the finest red- and dry white-producing vineyards in the world. Just outside the modern city of Bordeaux, these vineyards produced the wines that first won prestige for the entire Bordeaux region, including a famous "Ho Bryan" enjoyed by Samuel Pepys in 1663.

CHÂTEAU CARBONNIEUX
Techniques at this Benedictine château, long known for its reliable whites, have improved dramatically in recent years, and wines here are now better than ever.

Despite a more sweetly fruity, mineral edge, the red wines of Pessac-Léognan are related in style to the wines of the gravelly Haut-Médoc to the north (*see p.81*). Even the best and slowest developing red wines, including those from Château Haut-Brion and La Mission Haut-Brion, are approachable in their youth, but take a decade to develop their complex flavors. Some estates, such as Domaine de Chevalier and Château Haut-Brion, have a long tradition of successful white wine making, using Sémillon and Sauvignon Blanc grapes. Others, such as Château Carbonnieux, have recently progressed by giant leaps, now making white wines that are complex and exciting.

UNTIL THE LATE 1980s, a cluster of illustrious estates, including Château Haut-Brion, Château Pape-Clément, Château Haut-Bailly, and Domaine de Chevalier, belonged to the *appellation* of Graves (*see p.80*), an area of gravelly vineyards extending nearly 40 miles (60 km) south from the city of Bordeaux. In 1987, however, it was decided to separate these northern vineyards from the lower-quality land further south, classifying them under the new *appellation* of Pessac-Léognan, named after the two *communes* of Pessac and Léognan.

This is not a large *appellation*, producing a total of just over nine million bottles each year, compared to the 22 million bottles of *appellation contrôlée* Graves. It is, however, perfect grape-growing land, with hilly, well-drained gravel vineyards that suit both the Sémillon and the Sauvignon Blanc grapes used to make dry white wines, and the Cabernet Sauvignon and the Merlot used in the supple reds.

CHÂTEAU SMITH-HAUT-LAFITTE
Recent investment at this estate has resulted in a great improvement in the quality of the wines made here.

DOMAINE DE CHEVALIER
Both red and white wines from this grand cru classé estate take up to 10 years to mature.

✱ AC Pessac-Léognan.	Larrivet-Haut-Brion, Latour, Laville-Haut-Brion, la Louvière, Ch Malartic-Lagravière, la Mission-Haut-Brion, Pape-Clément, Smith-Haut-Lafitte, la Tour-Haut-Brion.
🍇 Red: Cabernet Sauvignon, Merlot. White: Sémillon, Sauvignon Blanc.	
▪ Supple, earthy, tobacco-scented reds. Medium- to full-bodied whites.	🍴 Red: Roast lamb with garlic and rosemary.
▥ Ch Bouscaut, Carbonnieux, Dom de Chevalier, de Cruzeau, Ferrande, de Fieuzal, la Garde, Haut-Bailly, Haut-Brion, Haut-Gardère,	▦ 1996, 1995, 1990, 1988, 1986, 1985, 1983, 1982, 1970, 1961.
	▨ Red: 6–25 years. White: 3–15 years.

POMEROL

FLAT AND VISUALLY UNMEMORABLE, the Libournais *appellation* of Pomerol, on the eastern bank of the Dordogne, failed to receive even a mention under the Bordeaux Classification of 1855 *(see p.73)*. This has not prevented the best of the supple, velvety red wines of Pomerol from being among the most magnificent and expensive in the world.

SURPRISED BY SUCCESS
A newcomer to prosperity, the commune of Pomerol remains one of the sleepiest and most remote in Bordeaux. Lacking a village center, the area counts the church spire as its most important landmark.

ALTHOUGH THE area around Pomerol was first used for vine growing in the first century BC, it was not until the 1960s that its wines, now exclusively red, achieved international success. During the 18th century, the grapes grown in the flat, iron-rich clay vineyards of Pomerol were used to make mainly white wines. When the white grapes were eventually replaced with black, the quality of the wine they produced was not enhanced by the other food crops that were planted among the vines. For a long time the vineyards of the area were seen as being second best to those of St. Émilion *(see p.89)*, themselves considered decidedly second best to those of the Médoc *(see p.83)*. When George Saintsbury wrote his *Notes on a Cellar Book* in 1920, Pomerol did not even warrant a mention. The only markets for its wines were Belgium and northern France, and even there reputations were hard to build given the tiny annual production of most of the estates. There were, and are, no grand châteaux in Pomerol; even Château Pétrus, now the most famous estate in the *appellation*, producing some of the most expensive wines in the world, is no more than a modest country farmhouse making just 5000 cases of wine each year.

The credit for changing Pomerol's fortunes in the 1950s and 1960s must go to wine merchant and producer Jean-Pierre Moueix, who took charge of Château Pétrus, Château Lagrange, Château la Fleur-Pétrus, Château Latour, Château Pomerol, and Château Trotanoy. With his son Christian, Moueix introduced the wines of the region to the British and, more importantly, the Americans, who were seduced by their rich Dundee cake flavors, the softness of their tannins, and their characteristic hint of minerals. Most of the wines of Pomerol are made primarily from Merlot grapes, but estates such as Vieux Château Certan demonstrate the essential blending role played by the Cabernet Franc and Cabernet Sauvignon when they are planted on the appropriate soil.

CHÂTEAU PÉTRUS
The wines of Château Pétrus are some of the most sumptuous in the world.

VIEUX CHÂTEAU CERTAN
The traditional Merlot is skillfully blended with other grape varieties to produce exquisite wines here.

✳ AC Pomerol.	Gay, Gazin, Haut-Tropchaud, Lafleur, Lafleur-Gazin, Lagrange, Lagrave, Latour à Pomerol, Nénin, le Petit-Village, Ch Pétrus, le Pin, Clos René, Ch Rouget, Trotanoy, Vieux Château Certan.
🍇 Red: Merlot, Cabernet Franc, Cabernet Sauvignon.	
🍷 Deep-colored, full-bodied reds with supple tannins.	
🍴 Ch Beauregard, Bourgneuf-Vayron, Certan-Giraud, Certan de May, Clinet, Clos de Clocher, Ch la Conseillante, la Croix, la Croix de Gay, Clos de l'Église-Clinet, Ch l'Enclos, l'Évangile, Feytit-Clinet, la Fleur-Pétrus, le	🍴 Braised saddle of hare with cherries.
	🗓 1998, 1995, 1990, 1989, 1985, 1983, 1982, 1970,
	📈 5–25 years.

Premières Côtes de Bordeaux

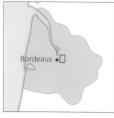

B Y AROUND 1000 AD, what is now known as AC Premières Côtes de Bordeaux was already an important wine-producing area. Part of the Entre-Deux-Mers district, the Premières Côtes is a narrow limestone ridge that runs south from Bordeaux for 37 miles (60 km) along the course of the Garonne, taking in 37 villages, each of which is entitled to add its name to the *appellation*.

Many sunshine hours and a clay and gravel soil help to produce fruity, Merlot-dominated reds that can make great drinking at around six years old.

Both sweet and dry whites are made here too, but dry whites must be sold under the general Bordeaux Blanc *appellation*. Meant to encourage the production of sweet white wines, which are mainly unexceptional here, the unfortunate effect of the rule is that there is little incentive to produce good dry white wines.

CHÂTEAU CARSIN
This recently developed, Finnish-owned estate uses modern wine-making techniques to get the best out of the Premières Côtes.

HILLSIDE VINES
Following a narrow limestone ridge along the north bank of the Garonne, the Premières Côtes de Bordeaux are hilly and picturesque, a marked contrast to the flatter land on the opposite bank.

✴ AC Premières Côtes de Bordeaux.	Fayau, du Grand Plantier, Haut Rian Matherau, Pascot, du Peyrat, de Plasson, Reynon, Sissan, Thieuley, Vieille Tour.
▣ Red: Merlot. White: Sémillon, Sauvignon Blanc, Muscadelle.	
▨ Medium-weight dry reds. Sweet whites.	▥ Entrecôte steak with shallots and wild mushrooms.
▥ Barreyre, Carignan, Carsin, Chaumont, de Chelivette,	▤ Red: 1998, 1996, 1995, 1990.
	▶ Red: 3–6 years. White: 5–10 years.

The Rising Stars of Bordeaux

Red wines from estates in a number of previously underperforming Bordeaux *appellations* have scored some startling recent successes. One of these *appellations* is the Premières Côtes de Bordeaux (*see above*), where the lead has been taken by two châteaux in particular. One is Château Reynon, where wines are produced by Professor Denis Dubourdieu of Bordeaux University. The other is the Finnish-owned Château Carsin, where wines are made by the Australian-born Mandy Jones using modern, Australian-designed equipment. Surprisingly, but justifiably, the price of wines from these châteaux is often higher than that of a St. Émilion Grand Cru (*see p.89*). Other rising star *appellations* include the Côtes de Francs (*see p.79*), and the Côtes de Bourg (*see p.78*), as well as various so-called satellite *appellations* of St. Émilion and Pomerol, such as St. Georges-St. Émilion (*see p.90*) and Lalande de Pomerol (*see p.81*). The vast improvement in these wines is due mainly to the application of better vine-growing and wine-making techniques, above all the careful selection of only healthy, ripe grapes. Also crucial is the fact that people are now prepared to pay high prices for good wines from what were often considered humble *appellations*.

CHÂTEAU REYNON
Denis Dubourdieu, an important influence on countless Bordeaux producers, produces his own wines at Château Reynon in the Premières Côtes.

St. Émilion

ALTHOUGH IT IS ONE OF THE MOST PRESTIGIOUS red wine *appellations* in the world, the wines of St. Émilion can be some of the most difficult to buy. The most sublime of all Bordeaux wines are made in the best parts of this *appellation*, but there are also plenty of very dull wines, sold at high prices thanks to the international prestige of their name.

THE ROOFS OF ST. ÉMILION
The small town of St. Émilion nestles comfortably on its high, limestone plateau, its warm terracotta roofs contrasting with the greens and browns of the priceless vines that surround it.

THE VINEYARDS OF ST. ÉMILION have been immortalized in Roman mosaics and praised by the Roman poet Ausonius. Despite its illustrious history, however, the lack of bridges across the Dordogne and the Garonne left St. Émilion isolated from the city of Bordeaux and its wine merchants, and as a consequence these wines were relatively little-known outside the region until the early 20th century.

Enjoying a huge postwar revival, the glorious fruitcake richness of St. Émilion's top wines now helps them to sell for some of the highest prices in Bordeaux. In 1958 the wines of St. Émilion were first officially classified under a complex and rather confusing system. The very best vineyards enjoy the status of *premiers grands crus classés* A and B, and are reevaluated every decade. Next come the, often quite ordinary, *grands crus classés* vineyards.

Finally, there is a third category, never re-evaluated, that includes more than 200 *grands crus* vineyards, most of which are even more ordinary than those labeled *grand cru classé*.

Both geographically and geologically there are at least four distinct parts to the St. Émilion *appellation*. Around and to the south of the town are the clay-limestone mixtures of both the St. Émilion plateau and the slopes of the Côtes St. Emilion, home to many, but not all, of the *premiers grands crus classés* vineyards. To the west of the Côtes is the gravel and sand area known as Graves-St. Émilion. Finally, further to the west is the large area of sandy soils, or *sables anciennes*, where many of St. Émilion's most ordinary wines are made. In the first three areas the Merlot grape is blended with as much as 65 percent Cabernet Franc, while on the *sables anciennes* wines are made with a much higher proportion of Merlot.

CHÂTEAU L'ANGÉLUS
One of St. Émilion's rising stars, the wines produced on this estate have been growing ever more impressive since the 1980s.

CHÂTEAU TROPLONG-MONDOT
Not the most famous perhaps, but even in difficult years, like 1994, this has been one of the most carefully made and most reliable of all St. Émilion's wines.

✱ AC St. Émilion, AC St. Émilion Grand Cru, AC St. Émilion Grand Cru Classé, AC St. Émilion Premier Grand Cru Classé A and B.	Dassault, la Dominique, Faugères, Fourtet, Figeac, Fombrauge, Fonplégade, Fonroque, Franc Mayn, des Jacobins, Larmande, Magdelaine, la Mondotte, de l'Oratoire, Troplong-Mondot, de Valandraud.
🍇 Red: Merlot, Cabernet Franc.	
🍷 Soft medium-bodied and deep-colored, full-bodied reds.	
🍽 Angélus, Ausone, Beauséjour, Beauséjour-Bécot, Belair, Canon, Canon la Gaffelière, Cap de Mourlin, Cheval Blanc,	🍴 Lamprey stewed in a red wine sauce.
	📅 1998, 1995, 1990, 1989, 1986, 1985, 1983, 1982.
	🍷 Red: 5–25 years.

ST. ÉMILION SATELLITES

WITH THE ESTABLISHMENT IN 1935 of the *appellation contrôlée* system, the villages close to St. Émilion were given their own *appellations*, enabling them to sell their wines under their own names rather than that of St. Émilion. Little known, but carefully made, they sometimes offer far better value than many of the wines of St. Émilion itself.

MONTAGNE-ST. ÉMILION
Like the rest of the Libournais, this is Merlot country, producing wines that are rich and velvety with luscious plum flavors.

T HE VILLAGES OF LUSSAC, Montagne, Puisseguin and St. Georges are situated to the north and to the east of the town of St. Émilion, giving their names to its four so-called satellite *appellations*. With a mixture of clay-limestone and gravel soil similar to that of St. Émilion, all four *appellations* grow the St. Émilion combination of Merlot and Cabernet Franc grapes, but with an even greater emphasis on the rich and spicy Merlot variety.

RUGGED CHARM
Robust, earthy, and rugged are words often used to describe the wines of the St. Émilion satellites. The same could be said of the region's architecture, such as this church in Montagne-St. Émilion.

"Most agreeable, early-developing claret" was the faint praise of British authority, Edmund Penning-Rowsell, writing in the 1970s about the wines of the St. Émilion satellites. He proposed that the wines of all four villages be classed together in a single *appellation* as St. Émilion-Villages. Wine writer Hugh Johnson, on the other hand, has more recently expressed the view that "these wines make up in satisfying solidity what they lack in finesse". Far worse than this could very often be said of the wines of St. Émilion, which sell at much higher prices.

My own opinion is that whatever the failings of the St. Émilion satellite *appellations*, they are due largely to the limited wine-making ambitions of the local *coopératives* and châteaux, made worse by a tendency for growers to opt for high grape yields at the expense of quality. The exciting results of improved wine-making techniques can be seen in the superb wines made recently at both Château St. Georges in St. Georges-St. Émilion and at Château Faizeau in Montagne-St. Émilion. Until more such talented wine makers come to work in this area, it is impossible to guess which of the four *appellations* has the greatest potential. At the moment, however, it is the wines of St. Georges-St. Émilion that age the best, and those of Puisseguin-St. Émilion that are the simplest and most one-dimensional.

CHÂTEAU CORBIN
Part of a growing group of innovative wine makers based in Montagne-St. Émilion, producers at Château Corbin make wines with more finesse than those of many of their neighbors.

❋ AC Puisseguin-St. Émilion, AC Lussac-St. Émilion, AC Montagne-St. Émilion, AC St Georges-St. Émilion	d'Arvouet, Beauséjour, Bonfort, Calon, Corbin, Faizeau, Fauconnerie, Vieux Château Calon.
❈ Red: Merlot, Cabernet Franc.	*Puisseguin-St. Émilion:* Bel-Air, Branda, Haut St.-Clair, Rigaud.
◿ Soft, round, fruity reds.	*St. Georges-St Émilion:* La Croix-St. Georges, Haut St. Georges, St. Georges.
⦀ *Lussac-St. Émilion:* Barbe Blanche, Bellevue, les Couzins, de la Grenière, Haut-Milon, Lyonnat, Moulin Noir, Trocard, Vieux Château Chambeau.	
	𝍖 Grilled lamb or pork.
Montagne-St. Émilion:	▤ 1998, 1996, 1995, 1990.
	⚘ 5–10 years.

ST. ESTÈPHE

FOR TRADITIONAL CLARET DRINKERS, the tannic, slow-maturing style of St Estèphe was everything a Bordeaux ought to be. As international taste in wine has swung increasingly toward more supple reds, this northern-most *commune* in the Médoc has often seemed unfashionable. However, recent vintages have seen a move toward fruitier, more supple wines.

WHEN THE CLASSIFICATION of the vineyards of Bordeaux took place in 1855, it was agreed that the wines of St. Estèphe were not the best in the Médoc, and the *commune* was awarded only five *crus classés*, as compared to 18 in Pauillac and 21 in Margaux (*see p.82*). Forty vineyards, however, were classified as *crus bourgeois*, below a *cinquième cru*, but better than an average unclassified *cru*.

Tough and deeply colored, with a lot of tannin and acidity, the traditional style of St Estèphe's wines is the very opposite of the juicy Merlot rich wines of nearby Pomerol (*see p.87*). More surprising is the fact that the wines of St. Estèphe are also very different from those of its neighbor, Pauillac, despite the fact that both the *appellations* share a gravel soil, and both have traditionally grown mainly Cabernet Sauvignon grapes. The soil of St. Estèphe, however, contains a lot of clay as well as gravel, which, in combination with the Cabernet Sauvignon, produces wines that may be a little rough if not extensively matured. The style can sometimes

work well, as shown by Château Montrose and Château Cos d'Estournel, where the wines are rich, spicy, and stylish.

A wine-making revolution began in St. Estèphe in the late 1980s, when a number of dynamic producers realized that, by growing more Merlot grapes, which suit the clay-rich soil here, and by harvesting them later, it was possible to make wines that are gentler and more supple than traditional St. Estèphe. Despite this, a high proportion of wines here are still made in bulk at the local *coopérative*, proof that St. Estèphe is still far from being a truly fashionable *appellation*. However, a trend is emerging, one that has proved unstoppable, for the best of these rich, berry-flavored wines to join company with some of the most sought after in the Médoc.

CHÂTEAU COS D'ESTOURNEL
With carved oak doors from the East African island of Zanzibar, the various non-European influences, which can be seen in the design of this unusual, purpose-built winery, give a strong indication of the exotic, spicy flavor of the wines within.

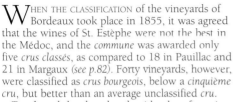

CHÂTEAU HAUT-MARBUZET
Henri Duboscq uses 50 percent Merlot grapes to make wines that are fruitier and less tannic than traditional St. Estèphe.

CHÂTEAU MONTROSE
One of St. Estèphe's two deuxième cru classé châteaux, Montrose makes classic, long-maturing wines using mainly Cabernet Sauvignon grapes.

❋	AC St Estèphe.	Lilian Ladouys, Marbuzet, Meyney, Montrose, les Ormes-de-Pez, Petit-Bocq, de-Pez, Phélan-Ségur, Picard, Tour de Pez, Tronquoy-Lalande.
❋	Red: Cabernet Sauvignon, Merlot, Cabernet Franc, Petit Verdot.	
❖	Full-bodied, deep-colored, tannic, slow-maturing reds.	
		🍴 Quails sautéed with artichoke hearts, onions and red Bordeaux.
▥	Andron Blanquet, Calon-Ségur, Chambert-Marbuzet, Cos d'Estournel, Cos-Labory, Le Crock, Haut-Beauséjour, Haut-Marbuzet, Lafon-Rochet, Lavillotte,	
		🍷 1996, 1995, 1990, 1989, 1986, 1983, 1982, 1970, 1961.
		⏳ 5–30 years.

ST. JULIEN

Bordeaux

OF ALL THE *APPELLATIONS* IN BORDEAUX, none offers a higher proportion of really fine red wine than St. Julien. There may be no *premiers crus* châteaux here, but the combination of gravelly soil and ambitious wine makers has resulted in the production of St. Julien wines that regularly challenge some of the biggest names in the Bordeaux region.

CHÂTEAU
GRUAUD LAROSE
The elegant style of the wines of Château Gruaud Larose sometimes prevents them from being fashionable, but in great vintages these are among the finest of all Bordeaux wines.

As ANYONE WHO HAS driven northward through the Médoc will know, St. Julien is a long way from Margaux *(see p.82)*, but a very short distance from Pauillac *(see p.84)*. In fact, the boundary between St. Julien and Pauillac is defined only by the Juillac stream. On one side stands Château Léoville-Lascases, and on the other its rival, Château Pichon-Longueville-Comtesse-Lalande,

and the *premier cru* Château Latour. In blind tastings, it is often hard to predict which will be the winner, as this trio share gravelly soil and use a similar, Cabernet-dominated, blend of grapes.

The combination of cedary, cigar box and fresh, blackcurrant flavors defines the character of St. Julien, whose wines are a touch less powerful than Pauillac, less austere than St. Estèphe *(see p.91)*, but more structured than Margaux. Château Léoville-Lascases' wines sell for prices close to those of the *premiers crus* of Pauillac, while its neighbor, the more affordable Château Léoville-Barton, often produces one of the best wines of the vintage. Other high-flyers among the 11 *crus classés* include Châteaux Branaire, Ducru-Beaucaillou, Lagrange, Léoville-Poyferré and Talbot, while *crus bourgeois* such as Châteaux Gloria, Moulin de la Rose, and St. Pierre produce wines that are better than some *crus classés* in other *communes*. The quality of the wine making here makes "second wines," such as Château Léoville-Lascases' Clos du Marquis and Château Lagrange's les Fiefs de Lagrange, well worth buying. The vineyards at the south of this *commune*, including both Beychevelle and Gruaud-Larose, produce plumper wines than those around St. Julien itself.

Modern St. Julien can be drunk quite young, but in good vintages it can take 10 years for the wines to take on more of the cigar box and lose the blackcurrant character of their youth.

CHÂTEAU LAGRANGE
Although not everyone was happy when Japanese buyers took over this château, it has since been restored to its former glory and the wines produced here have regained their former status.

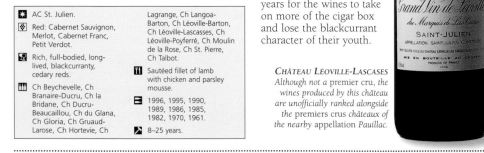

CHÂTEAU LÉOVILLE-LASCASES
Although not a premier cru, the wines produced by this château are unofficially ranked alongside the premiers crus châteaux of the nearby appellation Pauillac.

✱ AC St. Julien.	Lagrange, Ch Langoa-Barton, Ch Léoville-Barton, Ch Léoville-Lascasses, Ch Léoville-Poyferré, Ch Moulin de la Rose, Ch St. Pierre, Ch Talbot.	
🏵 Red: Cabernet Sauvignon, Merlot, Cabernet Franc, Petit Verdot.		
🍷 Rich, full-bodied, long-lived, blackcurranty, cedary reds.		
	🍴 Sautéed fillet of lamb with chicken and parsley mousse.	
Ⅲ Ch Beychevelle, Ch Branaire-Ducru, Ch la Bridane, Ch Ducru-Beaucaillou, Ch du Glana, Ch Gloria, Ch Gruaud-Larose, Ch Hortevie, Ch	▤ 1996, 1995, 1990, 1989, 1986, 1985, 1982, 1970, 1961.	
	🔺 8–25 years.	

STE. CROIX-DU-MONT

FOR THOSE WHO BELIEVE THAT VINES need to be grown on hills, Ste. Croix-du-Mont, on the right bank of the Garonne to the south of Loupiac (see p.81), might seem like a more promising place to produce sweet wines than the flatlands of Sauternes (see p.94) and Barsac (see p.76). The soil here is good and the vineyards face southward across the river, with morning mists encouraging the development of botrytis. In fact, the wines can have the full, honeyed character associated with good botrytized wines and are often better buys than many of the wines sold under more famous *appellations* like Sauternes and Barsac. Like Loupiac, Ste. Croix-du-Mont tends to be lighter in color and body than top Sauternes. This may be due to the fact that its producers can not afford to pick nobly rotten grapes in numerous pickings, and instead do so in one harvest.

CHÂTEAU LOUBENS
One of the most reliable producers of Ste. Croix-du-Mont, this château makes wines that are both luscious and subtle.

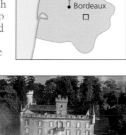

Bordeaux

CHÂTEAU CROIX-DU-MONT
The wines of Ste. Croix du-Mont might not be as prestigious as those of Sauternes, but the region does have some truly spectacular châteaux.

✴ AC Ste. Croix-du-Mont.	Grand Plantier, Lamarque, Lescure, Loubens, Lousteau-Vieil, Ch la Rame,
❀ White: Sémillon, Sauvignon Blanc, Muscadelle.	
🍷 Sweet whites, partially made from botrytized grapes.	🍴 Strawberry tart with a Ste. Croix-du-Mont sauce.
🍽 Ch de Beaucastel, Ch Bel Air, Ch des Coulinats, Crabitan-Bellevue, Ch Croix-du-Mont,	📅 1996, 1995, 1990, 1989, 1988, 1986, 1985, 1983, 1982.
	📌 5–10 years.

NOBLE ROT

The challenge facing the grape growers of Ste. Croix-du-Mont, like that confronting the producers of unfortified wines everywhere else, lies in managing the benign fungus known as *Botrytis cinerea* or noble rot. While the makers of dry wines simply wait for their grapes to ripen, dessert wine makers are entirely reliant on the the warm, humid weather conditions in which the botrytis develops. *Appellations* like Sauternes (see p.94), Barsac (see p.76), Loupiac (see p.81) and Ste. Croix-du-Mont in Bordeaux, Monbazillac (see p.228) and Jurançon (see p.226) in the southwest, and Vouvray (see p.190), Bonnezeaux (see p.178) and Quarts-de-Chaume (see p.185) in the Loire, all favor these conditions, with the quality of each vintage ultimately reliant

A STRANGE BEAUTY
Grapes affected by Botrytis cinerea are far from pretty, but they are essential to the production of great sweet wines.

on the weather from year to year. For example, the weather of 1982 was perfect for red Bordeaux, but less than great for Sauternes. Yields per vine are far smaller for botrytized wines than for dry wines, and this, coupled with the risk of poor weather destroying the crop, tends to discourage most producers from taking the risks required to harvest in successive pickings. Money has a part to play too, however, because makers of sweet wines rarely receive the financial rewards their efforts and risks deserve. For example, in 1997, even Château Climens, one of the most famous châteaux in Sauternes and a producer of botrytized wines, charged the same price per bottle as châteaux in the Médoc that produced twice as much wine per acre.

PAINSTAKING HARVEST
Picking nobly rotten grapes is a demanding task, and a far cry from the mechanized harvesting process often used for dry wines.

1994

Château Loubens

GRAND CRU

SAINTE-CROIX-DU-MONT

SAUTERNES

NO OTHER SWEET WINE HAS EVER come close to achieving the prestige accorded to the produce of this privileged corner of Bordeaux, and indeed the quality of the best of the white wines here has improved noticeably in recent years. Despite this, however, the presence of the word Sauternes on a label is no promise of any kind of quality.

CHÂTEAU RIEUSSEC
This property is one of the richest wine estates in the Sauternes region. It has an ideal situation for the production of good wines, on top of a low hill lying close to the little river Ciron.

THE FIRST WINES of the Sauternes were almost certainly dry and red. Whites have been made since the 17th century, and the earliest of these were dry. They were also so light that the Dutch merchants who bought them felt the need to fortify them with brandy. In 1787 US president Thomas Jefferson bought some Château d'Yquem and was so impressed that he wrote that Sauternes provided France's best whites – that is, after Champagne (*see pp.142–55*) and Hermitage (*see p.214*). No one is quite certain when the Sauternais began to make sweet wines. At Yquem it is said that a late harvest in 1859 resulted in the grapes being attacked by noble rot. Others fix the date 23 years earlier when a German grower named Focke imported a knowledge of botrytis from the Rhine. In

CHÂTEAU D'YQUEM
The high price of wines of Château d'Yquem is justified by the extreme care taken in vineyard and storage.

any case, the sweet 1859 Yquem was a hit when drunk at the Russian court, and since then the top wines of Sauternes have never looked back. The best châteaux, Yquem, Rieussec, and Suduiraut, are set atop small hills close to the Ciron river, whose mists help to create the perfect conditions for botrytis. Not only does Yquem enjoy the best site, it has traditionally taken the greatest care over its wines, painstakingly harvesting in successive pickings and even declining to release a vintage when the quality is thought insufficient.

The Sauternes *appellation* is allowed to include Barsac (*see p.76*), and on average its quality has improved in recent years: excess use of sulphur dioxide is more rare than it used to be. Even so, generic Sauternes is a label to be avoided and many smaller châteaux make disappointing wines in all but the best vintages.

The explanation for this may lie in legislation that denies Sauternes producers an entitlement granted to their neighbors in Cérons (*see p.95*). The latter are allowed to "declassify" their less impressive wines and sell them as Graves (*see p.80*). The Sauternais have two options: Sauternes and Bordeaux Blanc – the *appellation* under which they sell their (generally overpriced) dry whites.

CHÂTEAU GILETTE
This wine is something of an oddity: it is aged for many years in concrete vats before being released, and so keeps its freshness into old age.

✳ AC Sauternes (can also include wine from Barsac). Dry wine is sold as AC Bordeaux Blanc.	Justices, Lafaurie-Peyraguey, Lamothe, Lamothe-Guignard, de Malle, Rabaud-Promis, Raymond-Lafon, Rayne-Vigneau, Rieussec, Romer de Hayot, St. Amand, Sigalas-Rabaud, Suau, Suduiraut, la Tour Blanche, d'Yquem.
🍇 Sémillon, Sauvignon Blanc, Muscadelle.	
🍷 Powerful, lusciously sweet, dessert wine.	🍴 Foie gras.
🏰 d'Arche, Barréjats, Bastor-Lamontagne, Clos Haut-Peyraguey, Doisy-Védrines, de Fargues, Filhot, Gilette, Guiraud, Haut-Bergeron, les	🗓 1998, 1997, 1996, 1995, 1990, 1989, 1988, 1986, 1983, 1976.
	⏳ 5–30 years.

OTHERS

BORDEAUX IS USUALLY THOUGHT OF as a region that makes exclusively red and white wines, but it also produces rosés and sparkling wines. Bordeaux includes several small *appellations* whose wines are rarely seen anywhere outside the region. As wine making improves, these can be well worth seeking out for the excellent value they represent.

CARVED STONE
The wine from Château de Cérons is a good buy for anyone who seeks quality at a lower price. Shown here is a detail of the stone carving on the château's south façade.

AS RED BORDEAUX HAS BECOME richer and deeper in color and flavor, a number of producers have revived rosé and *clairet* (the style that falls between red and rosé). In fact, there is a direct connection between these wines and the darker reds: in many cases they are the same, but drawn from the vat when still only partly fermented.

Invented in 1990, the *appellation* of Crémant de Bordeaux is beginning to prove a source of small quantities – that is, around one million bottles per year – of good-value sparkling white and rosé wine. The principal grape is the Sémillon, usually with the addition of the Muscadelle, Sauvignon, Colombard and some Cabernet Franc.

The little-known wines of Cérons are produced from vineyards close to Barsac (*see p.76*). Like the wines of that *appellation*, they tend to be light and delicate in style and – in the case of the Grand Enclos du Château de Cérons – first-class alternatives to other, higher-priced sweet Bordeaux. Curiously, and sensibly, Cérons producers have

the option of selling their wine as Graves, unlike their neighbors in Sauternes and Barsac, who can only use their own *appellations* and Bordeaux Blanc.

Quite unrelated to the Graves *appellation*, the reds and whites of Graves de Vayres come from a small area of gravelly soil on the left bank of the Dordogne. Their individuality was appreciated in the 19th century, when their color was mostly white. Today the best examples, such as the wines of Châteaux la Chapelle-Bellevue, Lesparre, and Canteloup, are Merlot dominated reds.

Ste. Foy de Bordeaux, to the east of Entre-Deux-Mers (*see p.79*), is another white wine region that has switched to making reds. Among the most successful wines are the ones now being produced at 18th-century châteaux such as des Chapelains, du Petit Montibeau, and l'Enclos.

The wines of two *appellations*, Bordeaux-Haut-Benauge and Entre-Deux-Mers-Haut-Benauge, both come from the same nine *communes*, which lie to the west of Entre-Deux-Mers. The second of this pair is a dry wine that can include Ugni Blanc, Colombard, and Mauzac. It is similar in style to Entre-Deux-Mers.

Bordeaux-Haut-Benauge, on the other hand, can be medium-sweet or sweet, and is produced from the Sémillon, Sauvignon Blanc, and Muscadelle, which have to be used at a higher degree of ripeness. The result is more interesting than the semi-sweet wine of Côtes de Bordeaux-St. Macaire, a lesser-known *appellation* to the south.

STE. FOY DE BORDEAUX
Reds now dominate in this region because the market for sweet whites is uncertain. Producers still need to make a living, even when there is no noble rot – crucial for making fine sweet whites.

CHÂTEAU DE CÉRONS
The grapes are the same as in Sauternes; prices, however, are lower for reasons of prestige.

THE FOOD OF BORDEAUX

This region is renowned for producing some of the world's greatest red and sweet white wines, and its name is often featured on restaurant menus in the form of the Bordelaise wine sauce that is traditionally served with entrecôte steak. However, as visitors to Bordeaux soon discover, many other dishes are also enjoyed in this region, which encompasses fields, rivers, and the sea.

DUCK WITH CÈPES
Cèpe mushrooms are used instead of vegetables in this casserole, made from a confit of duck. Ham, onions, and herbs are added to make a richer sauce.

WHEN I WAS ONCE AT A competition to find the best *sommelier* in the world, an entrant lost points because he failed to propose Pauillac as the ideal wine to drink with lamb. While Mouton Rothschild has nothing to do with mutton or lamb (the *mouton* in this instance refers to a small hill), there is no question that the milk-fed baby lambs of this part of the Médoc produce some of the most tender and tastiest meat.

Despite the increasingly acknowledged fact that beef and Bordeaux are often not an ideal match, as the meat can make a tannic wine seem quite tough, the Bordelaise sauce, made with red wine and marrowbone, undeniably adds something to a steak. Even so,

FOIE GRAS
This pâté is a festive treat in Bordeaux, due to its high price and rich flavor. It is made from duck liver marinated in brandy and served with Sauternes wine.

PAUILLAC LAMB À LA PERSILLADE
The finest milk-fed baby lamb comes from the region of Pauillac. It is best as a rack of lamb cooked with a thick parsley crust and served as chops.

OYSTERS
Both wild and cultivated oysters are available in Bordeaux. They are usually eaten raw with bread and lemon juice and served with dry white Bordeaux.

if I had to recommend a traditional dish to enjoy with a bottle of Médoc, or Graves, I'd probably opt for a grilled wood pigeon sautéed *à la bordelaise,* with artichokes, onions, and potatoes and flambéed with a little fine Bordeaux brandy. Alternatively, I might choose a *confit d'oie* (preserved goose), possibly with a sorrel purée.

Just as the Burgundians surprise visitors by poaching

trout in red wine, chefs in Bordeaux use red wine to cook lampreys, the river fish that, like baby eels, are a delicacy fished in huge nets from the banks of the Gironde River. At one time, there was an industry for Gironde caviar, but sturgeon haven't been seen in the river for at least 10 years. Another treat, rarely associated with Bordeaux, are *cèpes,* the brown-capped, fat-stemmed wild mushrooms that are sold at the roadside and prepared *à la viande* with garlic, ham, parsley, and breadcrumbs. Local truffles are also relished in the form of a ragout stew with red wine, ham, leeks, carrots, celery, and onions. Like the truffles, now brought in from producers further inland, *foie gras* is also enjoyed here as a perfect partner for a glass of Sauternes.

The wines of Bordeaux are inevitably used to make a

MUSHROOMS
Cèpe mushrooms are served as vegetables in stews and casseroles with a variety of meats or poultry, or on their own with chopped garlic and parsley. Rich black truffles are enjoyed with Sauternes.

number of desserts, such as *granité,* a sorbet made with red wine, or with a sweet white such as Sauternes or Cérons. For those who prefer simple desserts, there are *poires au St. Émilion,* pears poached in red wine with orange juice and cinnamon.

REGIONAL CHEESES

Cheeses are produced throughout France, wherever there are cows, sheep, or goats. The farmers of Bordeaux, however, have been too busy tending vines to develop a reputation for the quality of their cheeses. Most of the cheese you will see at the markets and in restaurants is likely to have come from the neighboring regions of the southwest. Périgord, Limousin, and Quercy continue to produce great cheeses, including the wonderful goat's milk Cabécou and Rocamadour, and delicious ewe's milk Fourmes from Limousin

ABBAYE DE BELLOC
Actually produced in the Pays Basque, this cheese is made from the milk of red-nosed Manech ewes. It has a strong, lingering, well cooked flavor.

TOMME DE CHÈVRE FERMIER
Variations of this salty goat's cheese can be found all over France. Often produced in the southwest, it is enjoyed by many in Bordeaux.

BURGUNDY

THIS IS THE LAND OF TINY ESTATES, YIELDING

SIMILARLY TINY QUANTITIES OF OFTEN SUBLIME

AND EXTRAORDINARY RED AND WHITE WINES.

Burgundy region

IRST, A CONFESSION. I cannot begin to be as level-headed about Burgundy as I would like. This is the region and these are the wines with which I fell most passionately in love. I lived among the vineyards in the heart of Burgundy for nearly six years, and I have spent, and misspent, more money on the wines made here than on those produced anywhere else in the world. The relationship has been a tempestuous one. The greatest bottles, some of which have come from the region's most humble *appellations*, have been packed with wild fruit, perfume, and indescribable animal appeal. The lesser ones, far too many of which have carried prestigious labels and been undeniably expensive, have been variously dull, watery, acidic, and grubby. The problem is that, without pulling the cork, there is no way to be sure of what you are going to find.

There are several reasons for this notorious unpredictability. First, even the most southerly parts of Burgundy lie too far north to ripen grapes reliably every year. Second, while producers in Bordeaux (*see pp.70–97*), for example, have the flexibility by law to blend grape varieties to produce their best wines, in Burgundy many wines must be made from a single grape variety. In addition, an average Bordeaux château, producing 200–300,000 bottles of wine per harvest, enjoys economies of scale denied to the typically tiny Burgundy estate producing only 30,000 bottles.

A final, and crucial, factor is the optimistic readiness of wine drinkers to place their trust in the name of an *appellation*, hoping blindly that any bottle labeled Chablis (*see pp.112–13*), Beaujolais (*see pp.106–7*), Chassagne-Montrachet (*see p.115*) or Pouilly-Fuissé (*see p.132*), is going to live up to their expectations.

So why persevere against all the odds? Because the tiny vineyards in each of Burgundy's five wine-producing regions, from Chablis in the north to Beaujolais in the south, can produce wines that, at their best, are unequalled anywhere else. There are, for example, many delicious

🏔	111,000 acres (45,000 ha); 390 million bottles.	▨	Varied, ranging from limestone in Chablis and the Côte d'Or, where there is also marl and flinty clay, to granite in Beaujolais.
🌡	Generally continental with cool temperatures in the Chablis, to the substantially warmer Mâconnais region further south. Temperatures in individual vineyards are also influenced by altitude.		
		🍇	Red: Pinot Noir, Gamay, César. White: Chardonnay, Aligoté, Pinot Blanc, Pinot Gris.

GRAND DESIGN
Much of the new wine produced in Burgundy is still bought by négociant firms such as Louis Jadot, owner of these cellars. Often, wines from a number of different producers are skillfully blended before maturation begins.

ALL DIVIDED UP

Some of the most fragmented in France, the estates of Burgundy form a huge patchwork with an average size of only 10 acres (four ha). Each grower's vines are often further divided into several parcels, and the human factor contributes, inevitably, to the unpredictability of the wines

0 km 25

0 miles 25

HEART OF GOLD

A rich and fruitful plain, the province of Burgundy has long been famous both for its wines and its food. At its heart are the Côte de Nuits and Côte de Beaune regions, also known collectively as the Côte d'Or, or Golden Slope.

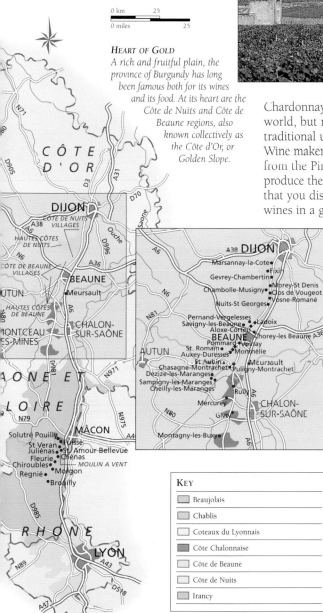

Chardonnays to be found throughout the world, but none that could be mistaken for a traditional unoaked or lightly oaked Chablis. Wine makers elsewhere make good red wines from the Pinot Noir grape, but none can produce the subtle light and shade of flavors that you discover when you taste the red wines in a good Côte d'Or cellar. Likewise, the Beaujolais region is often justly criticized for producing overpriced and disappointing wines, but, at its best, the combination of the Gamay grape, a granite soil, and the traditional wine-making techniques used here produces cherry and bitter chocolate flavors that are unlike those of any other wine. So, for me at least, the love affair continues; but I now look for producers whose names I know, such as those listed on the following pages, or buy from a wine merchant I trust.

KEY	
▢ Beaujolais	▢ Mâconnais
▢ Chablis	▨ Pouilly
▢ Coteaux du Lyonnais	▢ St. Véran
▨ Côte Chalonnaise	▨ Sauvignon
▢ Côte de Beaune	— *Département* boundary
▢ Côte de Nuits	━ Delimited AOC Region of Burgundy
▨ Irancy	

THE HISTORY OF BURGUNDY

The Burgundians have never forgotten the days when the Duke of Burgundy controlled land stretching as far north as Holland, negotiated with foreign rulers (including the sale of Joan of Arc to the English for 10,000 gold crowns), raised taxes, and oversaw the development of wealthy towns like Beaune and Dijon.

CHRONIQUES DES ROIS DE FRANCE
The Burgundian realm was one of the most important in 15th-century France. This manuscript shows a representative of Gontran, the 6th-century King of Burgundy, and his entourage arriving in the papal city of Avignon.

BURGUNDY'S PERIOD OF semi-nationhood provided the region with a strong sense of identity that still endures to this day. It also laid the foundations for a major wine industry in the area. The first evidence of wine production in Burgundy comes from Roman times. The Côte d'Or, or Golden Slope, which lies to the south of the present-day town of Dijon, was being used by wine makers by the fourth century. In the early days, however, vine growing there was probably not as rewarding as it is today. According to local legend, the Roman Emperor Constantine was informed in the year 312 that the inhabitants of the area were unable to pay their taxes – the vineyards were full of decrepit vines, and were barely accessible by horse and cart because of the large number of potholes in the roads. Today, the valuable Côte d'Or vineyards produce some of the very best wines in Burgundy.

A TRADITION OF QUALITY

The proper development of these vineyards came with the Church. In 587, the King of Burgundy, Gontran, donated land to a local abbey, as did Emperor Charlemagne 200 years later. Specific Côte d'Or vineyards were already being isolated for their quality and, according to local legend, it was the emperor himself who ordered that vines be planted on one particular hillside, having noticed that the snows always melted earlier there. This, he said, indicated that the slope in question benefited from more sunshine. The hill was the *grand cru* Corton, and the vineyard was what is now known as Corton Charlemagne. In Burgundian patois, the region's smallest plots of land, the named vineyards within every *commune*, are still known as *climats*

CHARITY BEGINS AT THE HOSPITAL
The Hospices de Beaune was founded as a charitable hospital in the 14th century. Today, money raised from the annual auction of its vineyards' wines is spent on the upkeep of a new hospital.

A FAMILY AFFAIR
This image of harvesters in the village of Meursault at the beginning of the 20th century illustrates that then, as now, grape picking involved every member of the family.

after their quirky microclimates. By the early 18th century, maps were being drawn up of the Côte d'Or indicating places such as Volnet (now Volnay), Puligny Morachet (now Puligny-Montrachet), Nuys (now Nuits-St. Georges) and Chambertin (now Gevrey-Chambertin), where the best wines were made. By this time, it was known that the Pinot Noir was the ideal grape variety for this northern region's reds, and that the Chardonnay was best for its whites. In fact, as early as 1395, the first edict was issued to ban the planting of the Gamay, the Pinot Noir's easier-to-grow relative.

The French Revolution of 1789 led to the breaking up of the monarchy and aristocratic estates, which were less cohesive units than their counterparts in Bordeaux. In 1790 this redistribution of land was accelerated with the introduction of the Code Napoléon, a law that specified equal inheritance among children, regardless of age and sex.

MARRIAGES OF CONVENIENCE

The result of the Code Napoléon law is visible throughout Burgundy. The patchwork of vines shows the effect of carving up pieces of land between the children of deceased wine growers. Look at the range of wines on offer in any Burgundian cellar and you will see the effect of the marriages between one grower's son and his neighbor's daughter. This can also be seen in the hyphenated names of estates like Coche-Boulicault and Coche-Dury.

Exploiting and marketing tiny quantities of several different wines was difficult, especially in a region that was prone to bad weather and poor harvests, so the first wine merchants were already buying, blending, and maturing wines by the early 18th century. For the next 200 years, these merchants more or less controlled the Burgundy wine market. It was not until the late 20th century that the owners of estates with an average size of only 15 acres (six ha), began handling their own wine from grape to bottle, making the most of the "small is beautiful" trend of the 1970s and 1980s. Loss of control by the merchants, combined with the introduction of *appellation contrôlée* legislation, did away with the most obvious falsifications of the Burgundy wine trade, but it also exposed the challenges of small-scale wine making in what can be a tricky climate. The established hierarchy of *grand cru, premier cru*, village, and regional wines will give you an idea of where to find the best bottles, but in reality a well-made village wine in a good year is often far better than a poorly made *grand cru* wine that sells at several times the price.

CHEVALIERS DU TASTEVIN
Burgundy's medieval image has been successfully promoted by the Confrèrie, the brotherhood of the Chevaliers du Tastevin, which literally means the "knights of the tasting cup." Founded in 1934, the group now holds banquets for members and their guests at Clos de Vougeot and at overseas "chapters."

A DRIVING TOUR OF BURGUNDY

This tour covers most of the significant wine-producing villages of the Côte de Beaune as well as the little-known Hautes-Côtes de Beaune. Also included is the hugely ornate Château de la Rochepot, which will delight those with a taste for fairy-tale architecture as well as for wine.

BEAUNE

The medieval town of Beaune ① is home to most of Burgundy's best-known wine merchants, a well-stocked *musée du vin,* and the world-famous Hôtel Dieu, a magnificent hospital built during the 15th century and financed through the sale of wine from its vineyards.

BEAUNE TO MEURSAULT

Take the Chalon-sur-Saône road out of town, forking right at the Cave Coopérative des Hautes-Côtes, toward Pommard ②. The cellars of the Château de Pommard are worth a visit, if only because the wine made here is sold nowhere else. Volnay ③ is a slightly larger village, set high enough to allow a panoramic view of the patchwork of individual vineyards below. There are plenty of excellent producers here, but one of the best is Michel Lafarge. Follow the road toward Auxey-Duresses, passing the village of Monthélie ④ and its château on your right. Like Monthélie, Auxey-Duresses ⑤ is a good source of underrated, and consequently affordable, red and white wines. The church here is also worth a visit for its triptych showing the Life of the Virgin. Meursault ⑥ is more of a town than a village; its main square, imposing church, and well-kept wine growers' homes and cellars reflect the success that Meursault's wines enjoy around the world. The Château de Meursault is where the wine makers Paulée hold a day-long lunch in November.

CHÂTEAU DE POMMARD
Visitors to the cellars of this château can buy fine, distinctive wines unavailable elsewhere.

LE MONTRACHET
Gates like this often indicate the name of the owner of a particular section of vineyard.

Burgundy ☐ Tour

To Auxerre

BOUZE-LÈS-BEAUNE

MALVILLY-MANDELOT 🍷

MELOISEY 🍷

⑯ ST. ROMAIN 🍷

Orches 🌿
⑮ 🍷

To Auxerre

MONTHÉLIE ④
🍷 🌿

AUXEY-DURESSES
⑤ 🍷

MEURSAULT ⑥
🍴 ★ 🍷 ℹ

CORMOT-LE-GRAND

🌿

LA ROCHEPOT   Gamay   Blagny
★   ⑭   ⑧ 🍷   🍷 🌿

⑬ NOLAY   ST. AUBIN ⑨ 🍷   ⑦
★   LE MONTRACHET ⑩   PULIGNY-
                                        MONTRACHET
                                        🍷 ℹ

                    CHASSAGNE- ⑪
CHANGE ●   MONTRACHET
                    🍷 ℹ

PARIS-L'HÔPITAL   SANTENAY   To Chalon-
                        ⑫ 🍷   sur-Saône

              DEZIZE-LÈS-MARANGES
              🍷 🌿

KEY

🍷	Tasting possible
🍴	Places to eat
★	Site of interest
ℹ	Tourist information
▬	Tour route
🌿	Viewpoint

0 km   2.5
0 miles   2.5

La Rochepot
The brightly-tiled roof of the medieval château rivals that of the Hôtel Dieu in Beaune (see p.99). It recalls the prosperous days when the Duchy of Burgundy stretched as far as Flanders.

Hill of Corton
The vineyards of the hill of Corton produce some of the best wines in Burgundy.

Puligny-Montrachet to Chassagne-Montrachet

Compared to Meursault, Puligny-Montrachet ⑦ is so quiet that it seems almost comatose. Merchant Olivier Leflaive offers a good range of white wines and a restaurant where they can be tasted with local dishes. There is little of note about Gamay ⑧, except for the fact that this is where the grape from which Beaujolais is made was supposedly first planted in Burgundy. St. Aubin ⑨ is a good source of fairly priced white wines, from estates like the Domaine Roux. The wine growers' track from St. Aubin to Chassagne-Montrachet passes the world-famous Le Montrachet ⑩ vineyard, whose stone gateways offer a fine photo-opportunity for visiting wine lovers. Sleepy but charming, Chassagne-Montrachet ⑪ is also worth a visit.

Santenay to La Rochepot

Santenay ⑫ offers a spa bath, an attractive main square, a casino, and some good-value red and white wines. Nolay ⑬, on the other hand, has no wine, but does boast a quaint 14th-century market hall. Wooded and hilly, the countryside here makes a spectacular backdrop for the Château de la Rochepot ⑭; its vibrantly colored roof is similar to that of the Hôtel Dieu in Beaune.

La Rochepot to Savigny-lès-Beaune.

You are now in the rugged hills of the Hautes-Côtes de Beaune. Pause at the top of the cliffs at Orches ⑮, where you may see hawks and other wild birds, before continuing on to the village of St. Romain ⑯, where producer Alain Gras makes and sells some great-value white wines.

Savigny-lès-Beaune to Beaune

The road to Savigny-lès-Beaune ⑰ offers a good view of the Château de Savigny, home to a motorcycle museum. Drive on to Aloxe-Corton ⑱ in the shadow of the hill of Corton, site of some of the best *grands crus* vineyards in the Côte de Beaune. Some of the best wines are made in Pernand-Vergelesses ⑲. At Chorey-lès-Beaune ⑳ the Domaine Tollot-Beaut and the Château de Chorey both make stunning red wines.

ALOXE-CORTON

AT THE NORTHERN END of the Côte de Beaune is the *appellation* of Aloxe-Corton, home to the famous red and white *grands crus* Corton vineyards. The rest of the *appellation* produces almost entirely red wines and has more in common with the red wine-producing Côte de Nuits to the north than with some of its more white-oriented neighbors to the south.

CHÂTEAU CORTON-ANDRÉ
With few small estates, the appellation of Aloxe-Corton remains very much the province of big-business merchant firms such as La Reine Pédauque, owner of this spectacular château.

LOCAL LEGEND SUGGESTS that not only did comedian Charlie Chaplin consider buying a plot of vines in the *commune* of Aloxe-Corton, but that more than a thousand years ago the wines here were a favorite of the Roman Emperor Charlemagne, who has given his name to the white wine-producing *grand cru* vineyard of Corton-Charlemagne.

Red wines make up 99 percent of the vintage in Aloxe-Corton, made, like almost all red Burgundy, from the powerful, tannic Pinot Noir grape. Wines are produced here that are among the longest-lived and slowest to develop of all the wines of Burgundy. As a result of this early impenetrability, many of the village and *premiers crus* wines of Aloxe-Corton are less popular than the softer, fruitier, and more immediately appealing wines of neighboring Beaune (*see p.108*) and Savigny-lès-Beaune (*see p.136*). After five to 15 years in the bottle, however, these wines develop a rich, meaty

fruitiness and offer excellent value. If drunk young, the similarly austere red and white *grands crus* wines of the *commune* also tend to compare badly with top-quality wines from nearby *appellations* such as Puligny-Montrachet (*see p.133*) and Chassagne-Montrachet (*see p.115*) to the south. After around 10 years, however, the red wines are smooth, with deliciously gamey flavors, while the whites are richly concentrated, with sumptuous flavors of butter, cinnamon, and honey.

The attention of many wine buyers has long been focused on Louis Latour and La Reine Pédauque, two long-established producer-merchant firms with cellars in the town of Aloxe-Corton. Neither of these, unfortunately, produces particularly exciting reds. More recently, however, investment by producers and *négociants* from all over Burgundy, including such illustrious names as Tollot-Beaut in Chorey-lès-Beaune, Bonneau du Martray in Pernand-Vergelesses, and Antonin Guyon in Savigny-lès-Beaune, has resulted in some innovatively made wines with a less rugged character than is traditional here.

LES COUTIÈRES
Wines from premiers crus vineyards like Les Coutières reach their peak after as many as 15 years in the cellar.

DOMAINE LATOUR
The négociant firm of Louis Latour owns vineyards in Aloxe-Corton and makes a speciality of the wines produced from them.

✳ AC Aloxe-Corton, AC Aloxe-Corton Premier Cru, AC Charlemagne Grand Cru, AC Corton Grand Cru, AC Corton-Charlemagne Grand Cru.	Colin et Fils, Joseph Drouhin, François Gay, Génot-Boulanger, Camille Giroud, Antonin Guyon, Louis Latour, Prince de Mérode, Antonin Rodet, Comte Sénard, Tollot-Beaut, Michel Voarick.
⬗ Red: Pinot Noir. White: Chardonnay, Pinot Beurot.	
◪ Rich, meaty, deep-colored, reds. Some full-bodied, slow-developing whites.	🍴 Roast pheasant stuffed with thyme and lemon in a red wine sauce.
▥ Arnoux, Bouchard Père et Fils, Denis Boussey, Champy, Marc	▤ 1997, 1996, 1995, 1993, 1990, 1989, 1988, 1985, 1978.
	▸ Red: 5–15 years.

GRANDS CRUS VINEYARDS OF THE MONTAGNE DE CORTON

Covering 445 acres (180 ha) of land on the slopes of the Montagne de Corton are the vineyards of Corton Grand Cru and Corton-Charlemagne Grand Cru. Extending into the three *appellations* of Aloxe-Corton (*see p.104*), Pernand-Vergelesses (*see p.130*), and Ladoix (*see p.122*), this is the largest area of *grand cru* land in Burgundy. Chardonnay vines grown on the highest slopes are classified under the Corton-Charlemagne *appellation,* producing 300,000 bottles of white wine each year. Below them are the Pinot Noir vines that make up the red wine *appellation* of Corton Grand Cru. Half a million bottles of red wine are made from these vines each year, some labeled as Corton Grand Cru, others specifying the *climat,* or named area, in which the grapes were grown. Tiny amounts of white wine, including some well-made examples by Louis Jadot, are sold as Corton Grand Cru *blanc.* The varied regions of this *appellation* produce wines of mixed quality, so look carefully at the label before buying. Wines from the Corton-Bressandes and Corton Clos de Roi *climats* are worth looking out for, as are those from the excellent Corton-Pougets, Corton-Perrières, Corton-Grèves, and Corton-Renardes. Both red and white wines are best matured for 10 years or so before drinking.

SET IN STONE
Plots within the Corton-Charlemagne vineyard are often identified with traditional stone signs.

FIELD OF DREAMS
Chardonnay vines in the Corton-Charlemagne grand cru vineyard produce some of the greatest white Burgundies of all.

AUXEY-DURESSES

BETWEEN MONTHÉLIE (*see p.126*) and Meursault (*see p.125*) in the valley of the river Dheune is the beautiful village of Auxey-Duresses. Two thirds of the wine produced here is red, much of it sold as Côte de Beaune-Villages. Maturing early, these are faintly rustic wines with a tendency toward tartness in all but the warmest years. That said, in good years they represent a real bargain. Generally speaking, the white wines of the *appellation* are better than the reds, comparing well with many humbler efforts from neighboring Meursault. Well-made examples of red and white wines from the south-facing *premiers crus* vineyards of Les Duresses and Climat du Val are worth paying more for, as are wines from the area's best producers, including Olivier Leflaive, Jean-Pierre Diconne, and Jean-François Coche-Dury.

HIDDEN TREASURE
Overshadowed by its more famous neighbors, Auxey-Duresses is the little-known source of some great-value wines, both red and white.

CHRISTOPHE BUISSON
Well-made wines like this one from producer Christophe Buisson are full of fresh raspberry fruit flavors.

❋ AC Auxey-Duresses, AC Auxey-Duresses Premier Cru.	Creusefond, Jean-Pierre Diconne, Joseph Drouhin, Louis Jadot, Jaffelin, Olivier Leflaive, Jean-Pierre Prunier, Pascal Prunier, Vincent Prunier, Roy.
❉ Red: Pinot Noir. White: Chardonnay.	
⬛ Soft, plump, slightly rustic reds. Early-maturing, medium-weight oaked whites.	🍴 Red: *coq au vin.*
▥ Comte Armand, D'Auvenay, Bouzereau, Coche-Dury, Alain	▤ Red: 1997, 1996, 1995, 1990.
	▧ Red: 3–10 years. White: 2–6 years.

BEAUJOLAIS

IN AN INCREASINGLY FASHION-CONSCIOUS WORLD, where even wines can be seen to be conforming to worryingly similar styles, Beaujolais still stands apart. And so it should. At its finest, Beaujolais is a refreshing antidote to all the richest, oakiest red wines in the world and is a great companion for all sorts of food, ranging from traditional French to spicy Asian.

GAMAY AT ITS BEST
The Gamay grape is grown outside Beaujolais, but it is here, on the granite soil of this region and in the warm but not overly warm climate, that it produces its characteristic banana, cherry, and hard-candy flavors.

THERE IS SOMETHING DELICIOUSLY androgynous about Beaujolais that somehow sets it between red and white wine, with the color of the former and the easy drinkability of the latter. The region's unique *ménage à trois* of the Gamay grape (a variety that never performs as well elsewhere), granite soil, and the *macération carbonique* process, whole-berry fermentation that is used by most

producers here, combines to produce wines with vibrant fruit and almost no perceptible tannin.

For most of its history, however, Beaujolais was little more than a jug wine. A century and a half after Thomas Jefferson's initials were inscribed on bottles of Château Lafite, Beaujolais was still being served in cafés directly from the cask and from pitchers, in the way of good ale. In the late 1950s and 1960s, Beaujolais found its way into bottles, but all too often the wine sold under this name overseas had more to do with North Africa than southern Burgundy.

The man who came to the region's rescue was a young, local grower called Georges Duboeuf, who in the 1960s lauched a *négociant* business that sold only genuine Beaujolais and also packaged and marketed the fresh, cherryish wine in a way that was noticed throughout the world. Duboeuf's most obvious contribution was his enthusiastic promotion of Beaujolais Nouveau or Beaujolais Primeur, which helped to increase sales of the newly-made wine from less than two million bottles in the late 1950s to a current figure of some 90 million bottles a year.

Copied by producers throughout the world, Beaujolais Nouveau is often dismissed by snobs as being a mere gimmick. They say that the hoopla surrounding the new red wine every November has nothing to do with "real" wine, but they are wrong. In fact, the annual bedlam

ROLLING HILLS
The charm of Beaujolais' landscape, with its gently rolling hills, is increased by the knowledge that every turn in the road could lead to yet another pretty village that is home to a wine maker.

▨ AC Beaujolais, AC Beaujolais Primeur, AC Beaujolais Supérieur, AC Beaujolais (village name), AC Beaujolais-Villages.	Jacques, Jacky Janodet, Pardon et Fils, Frédéric Pérol, Dominique Piron, Jean-Charles Pivot, Ch de Pizay, Plateau de Bel-Air, des Terres Dorés, Michel Tête, Ch Thivin, Frédéric Trichard, Maison des Vignerons.
▧ Red: Gamay.	
▨ Soft, fruity reds that generally mature early.	
▥ Aucoeur, Paul Beaudet, Berrod, Pierre-Marie Chermette, André Colonge, Joseph Drouhin, Georges Duboeuf, Henry Fessy, Ch des	▯ Chicken cooked with bamboo shoots.
	▤ 1998, 1997, 1996, 1995.
	▨ 1–3 years. Crus: 2–8 years.

JEAN-PAUL BRUN
Today, while most Beaujolais is made light and fruity for easy drinking, Jean-Paul Brun makes more traditional wines.

TERRES DORÉES

CUVÉE
À L'ANCIENNE

Beaujolais
APPELLATION BEAUJOLAIS CONTRÔLÉE
1997
Mise en domaine
JEAN-PAUL BRUN
Vigneron à CHARNAY-EN-BEAUJOLAIS F 69380
750 ML   PRODUCT OF FRANCE   11% VOL.

IN FULL FERMENT
The uncrushed Gamay grapes from Beaujolais ferment to provide zingy flavors that are rarely found outside this region

in wine bars across the globe has more to do with the history of wine than cellars full of old claret. For centuries, and certainly before the invention of the cork, the arrival of casks of fresh red wine would have been welcomed wherever it was drunk. Of course, popularization comes with a price tag. Now that these wines are rushed to every corner of the world in order to be uncorked in the middle of November, it is hardly surprising that most Beaujolais Nouveau is hastily made in order to be hastily sold. The existence of this style of Beaujolais, and the rapid and uncritical way in which it is drunk, has helped Beaujolais to dispose of much of its less impressive wine. However, the

basic Beaujolais sold during the rest of the year is a pretty mixed bag. Good individual estates and merchants, like Duboeuf and Loron, make decent wines, but the bottles from unfamiliar producers that are sold in supermarkets should be treated with suspicion. Wines labeled Beaujolais Supérieur should be made from ripe grapes, but this is an *appellation* that is only used for some 13 million bottles out of a potential total production of around 175 million. Head instead for the 38 *communes* whose harvest is sold under the Beaujolais Villages *appellation* or under the name of Beaujolais Villages plus the name of the village (as in Beaujolais Villages Lantignié and Beaujolais Villages Blacé).

Alternatively, take a further step up the ladder of quality and opt instead for one of the 10 Beaujolais *crus* of Brouilly, Chénas, Chiroubles, Côte de Brouilly, Fleurie, Juliénas, Morgon, Moulin-à-Vent, Régnié, and St. Amour. Today, rosé and white Beaujolais are rare, with much of the latter now being sold as St. Véran.

WHAT'S NEW?
Beaujolais Nouveau is no longer a novelty, but it still offers the first taste of the most recent vintage.

AGING BEAUJOLAIS

Sooner or later when visiting wine makers in Beaujolais, if you're lucky and they like you and think that you know a thing or two about wine, one of them will no doubt pull out an obviously old bottle of Beaujolais and challenge you to guess its age. Don't worry about getting the age wrong; some of the most experienced wine tasters have missed the target by as much as a couple of decades. The point the wine maker is striving to make is that, despite its reputation as being a wine that must be drunk young, good Beaujolais can actually mature and survive in the bottle for a surprisingly long time. Good bottles of Morgon and Moulin-à-Vent (*see p.128*) can develop complexity with age, but most other wines simply

turn into pleasant, but rather anonymous, old red wines that could easily be mistaken for mature, but not very good, red Burgundies. More important, the rich flavor they develop with time is gained at the expense of the vibrant character that gives Beaujolais its unique appeal.

WORTH LAYING DOWN
Morgon, from the village of Villié Morgon, is one of the few examples of Beaujolais that can benefit from aging for five years or longer.

BEAUNE

UNOFFICIAL CAPITAL OF BURGUNDY and one of the greatest of the world's wine towns, Beaune is home to many of the region's best wine merchants, including such famous names as Joseph Drouhin, Bouchard Père et Fils, and Louis Jadot. Often undervalued, the *appellation* of Beaune is the source of some of the most delicately appealing of red Burgundies.

BOUCHARD PÈRE ET FILS
Poetically but appropriately named, the Vigne de l'Enfant Jésus is a small patch of vines within the large Grèves vineyard to the west of the town, and is the source of some of the most delicious wines of the appellation.

ONE OF THE BEST WAYS to see the medieval city of Beaune is from one of the hot air balloons that float, full of tourists, above the town every day throughout the summer. From the sky it is clear that the shape of the city has changed little in the last few hundred years, with even the ring-road that surrounds it hugging the old fortified walls. Wander through the city on a Saturday, as traders compete to sell food, clothes, and other goods, and you will see that Beaune today is still very much the market town that it always has been. Underneath the streets, the cellars in which the city's wine merchants have traditionally stored their stock form a vast network of tunnels. Wine selling has long been a major occupation

HAND ON THE TILLER
Like Bouchard Père et Fils, owners of this château, many wine merchants are also talented producers, making some of their best wines themselves.

in the city, with merchants traditionally selling wines from throughout the Côte d'Or and further afield. Today's wine merchants do the same, but all will also offer local wines from the vineyards that surround the town on three sides. There are no *grands crus* here, but three quarters of the vineyards of the *appellation* have been granted *premier cru* status. The best of these are Les Avaux, Les Boucherottes, Les Bressandes, Les Cents Vignes, Clos du Roi, Le Clos des Mouches, les Epenottes, Les Grèves, Les Marconnets, Les Teurons, and Les Vignes-Franches. While there are still a number of individually-owned estates here, much of the best land is owned by large merchant firms such as Drouhin, Jadot, and Bouchard Père et Fils. By promoting more expensive wines from other *appellations,* the merchants of the city have, ironically, contributed to a general underestimation of the wines of Beaune. Known for their softness and their aromas of wild fruit and flowers, some of the great old wines of Beaune smell just like faded roses. As a general rule, a wine from a merchant's own Beaune vineyards will be some of his best, and some, like those from Drouhin's Clos des Mouches and Bouchard Père et Fils' Vigne de l'Enfant Jésus, can be great by any standards. White Beaune is a rarity, but can be as good as many of the wines of Chassagne-Montrachet (see p.115).

JOSEPH DROUHIN
Another great wine, delicate but with beautifully concentrated fruit flavors, this one comes from the Clos des Mouches vineyard and is made by merchant Joseph Drouhin.

✴ AC Beaune, AC Beaune Premier Cru.	Germain (Ch de Chorey), Camille Giroud, Louis Jadot, Michel Lafarge, Daniel Largeot, Laurent, Maillard Père et Fils, Albert Morot, Mussy, Jaques Prieur, Rapet Père et Fils, Thomas-Moillard, Tollot-Beaut.
✦ Red/ rosé: Pinot Noir White: Chardonnay.	
▣ Succulent, approachable, extremely delicate reds. Intense, fragrant whites.	
▥ Robert Ampeau, Arnoux Père et Fils, Bitouzet-Prieur, Bouchard Père et Fils, Pascal Bouley, Champy, Ch de la Tour, Joseph Drouhin, Dubois, Génot-Boulanger,	▥ Millefeuille of snails with cep mushrooms.
	▤ 1996, 1995, 1993, 1990, 1988, 1985, 1978.
	▨ Red: 3–12 years.

HOSPICES DE BEAUNE

A major date on the international wine calendar, the sale of wines from the Hospices de Beaune vineyards takes place each year on the third Sunday in November, and is the biggest charity wine auction in the world. In 1443, anxious to secure a place in heaven, tax collector Nicolas Rolin built a hospital, or *hôtel-Dieu*, providing free treatment for the poor of Beaune. He also gave vineyards for the upkeep of the hospital, and these, together with subsequent gifts of land from all over the Côte d'Or, are used to make more than a quarter of a million bottles of wine each year, the proceeds of which are still used to finance charitable works in the town.

In 1859 it was decided to sell the wines at an annual charity auction. Although made by a wine maker employed by the Hospices, the young wines are sold in the cask, and are matured and bottled by the buyer. Some of the 37 cuvées come from individual vineyards, while others are blends from different plots within the same *appellation*. Initially, each *cuvée* bore the name of the grower who tended the vines, but this was

COLORFUL GLORY
Now a major tourist attraction, the Hospices de Beaune functioned as a hospital until 1971.

later replaced by the name of the donor. The prices paid at auction have traditionally been thought to set the tone for the year's wines as a whole, but auction hysteria has in fact often led to the payment of overinflated prices. Wine making at the Hospices is a high-profile job, and wine-making techniques here are often the subject of heated controversy. In one famous incident, an entire *cuvée* was spoiled by the use of bad casks, resulting in the use of exclusively new oak barrels and risking over-oaking all but the most concentrated wines.

Almost as important as the vineyard and the wine making, however, is the way in which the wine is matured. At one memorable blind tasting, experts found little resemblance between various wines, all from the same *cuvée*, but bottled by different buyers. One thing that all the wines do have in common is an unusually high price tag, justified, naturally, by thoughts of the contribution you are making to a very worthy cause.

WHAT AM I BID?
The annual wine auction at the Hospices de Beaune is the centerpiece of a weekend of serious tasting and partying. Visitors come from all over the world to attend.

THE CUVÉES

Reds
Auxey-Duresses Boillot
Beaune Brunet
Beaune Clos de la Roche Georges Kritter
Beaune Clos des Avaux
Beaune Cyrot-Chaudron
Beaune Dames Hospitalières
Beaune Guigone de Salins
Beaune Hugues et Louis Bétault
Beaune Maurice Drouhin
Beaune Nicolas Rolin
Beaune Rousseau-Deslandes
Clos de la Roche Cyrot-Chaudron
Corton Charlotte Dumay
Corton Docteur Peste
Mazis-Chambertin Madeleine Collignon
Monthélie Lebelin
Pernand-Vergelesses Rameau-Lamarosse
Pommard Billardet
Pommard Dames de la Charité
Pommard Raymond Cyrot
Pommard Suzanne Chaudron
Savigny-lès-Beaune Forneret
Savigny-lès-Beaune Fouquerand
Volnay Blondeau
Volnay Général Muteau
Volnay-Santenots Gauvain

Whites
Bâtard-Montrachet Dames de Flandres
Corton-Charlemagne François de Salins
Corton-Vergennes Paul Chanson
Meursault-Charmes Albert Grivault
Meursault-Charmes de Bahèzre de Lanlay
Meursault-Genevrières Baudot
Meursault-Genevrières Philippe le Bon
Meursault Goureau
Meursault Humblot
Meursault Loppin
Pouilly-Fuissé Françoise Poisard

BOURGOGNE

UNLIKE BOTTLES OF GENERIC BORDEAUX or Claret, which can be found on the shelves of almost every supermarket, generic Bourgogne, or Burgundy, tends to be more difficult to find. And, because of the small size of the region and the often uncertain climate that prevails here, buying good examples at inexpensive prices can be very tricky indeed.

CÔTE CHALONNAISE
The vineyards of this somewhat unfashionable district, to the south of the better known Côte d'Or, produce some of the best of the red and white wines sold under the generic Burgundy appellation.

THE PROBLEM WITH BURGUNDY is that, unless you are a student of Burgundian geography and have memorized the names and addresses of the best producers, there is no way to predict the quality or style of wine in a bottle. The same word, Bourgogne or Burgundy, could appear on the label of an uninspiring wine from a merchant who has legally blended Pinot Noir from a combination of undistinguished vineyards, and on a brilliant bottle made in tiny quantities by one of the finest grape growers in the region. To complicate matters further, while most books quite fairly imply that red Burgundy is made exclusively from Pinot Noir grapes, you might come across a bottle bearing this label that legally has no characteristics of this grape whatsoever. In fact, you could even find that the grapes from which it was produced were not even grown on "Burgundy" soil and that they are instead Gamay grapes imported from a Beaujolais *cru* village.

Plain red and white Burgundy can come from vineyards almost anywhere in the *appellation*. The least promising regions, in all but the best vintages, are the cool Hautes-Côtes de Nuits and the Hautes-Côtes de Beaune, where grapes often fail to ripen fully. Vines grown on the flatter parts of the Côte d'Or produce riper grapes, but they rarely make wine of memorable quality. Some of the best basic Burgundy comes from the hillside vineyards of the Côte Chalonnaise and the Côte d'Or.

While red Burgundy made by top producers will be worth holding on to for five years or so, most examples are at their best within three or four years of production. Over time they will develop a more gamey character, but this will often develop at the expense of the rich, vibrant, raspberryish flavor that makes the Pinot Noir so seductive in its youth. Only the very best of white Burgundy will improve beyond three or four years.

BUXY
This small town in the south of the region produces reliable red and white Burgundy.

LES VIGNERONS D'IGÉ
Much of the generic Burgundy on offer in supermarkets is made by coopératives like this one.

❋	AC Bourgogne.	Giroud, Les Vignerons d'Igé, Louis Jadot, Patrick Javiller, Pierre Labet, Olivier Leflaive, Cave de Lugny, Ch de Meursault, Pierre Morey, Antonin Rodet, Tollot-Beaut, Henry de Vézelay.
⚘	Red: Pinot Noir. White: Chardonnay, Pinot Beurot, Pinot Blanc, Sacy.	
🍷	Light-medium reds. Dry whites that may be oaked.	
▥	Bertrand Amboise, Bertagna, Boisset, Bouchard Père et Fils, Alain Burguet, Cave de Vignerons de Buxy, La Chablisienne, Henri Clerc, Joseph Drouhin, Camille	🍽 Red: Snails cooked in garlic sauce.
		▤ Red: 1998, 1997, 1996, 1995.
		▧ Red: 3–4 years. White: 2–3 years.

OTHER STYLES OF BURGUNDY

Disposing first of Bourgogne Ordinaire and Grand Ordinaire, these all-too-honestly named wines are generally best avoided and are, in any case, rarely found outside the region and a few supermarket chains. The reds are mainly Gamay or substandard Pinot, while the whites tend to be a dull blend of poor Chardonnay and Aligoté, and even some Melon de Bourgogne. Bourgogne Clairet and Bourgogne Clairet Grand Ordinaire are even rarer *appellations* for pale reds that are almost never seen outside the region.

Far more interesting are the regional Burgundies, such as Bourgognes Moutrecul, that are made in the Côte d'Or and the Yonne.

Of the numerous regional red Burgundies from vine-yards close to Chablis, the

ones to watch out for are Bourgogne Irancy (soon to be known simply as Irancy), Bourgogne Epineuil's rosés, Bourgogne Côtes d'Auxerre, and Bourgogne Coulanges-la-Vineuse. In this last region, as in Bourgogne Chitry, Bourgogne Côtes d'Auxerre, Bourgogne-St. Bris, and Bourgogne Vézelay, the Pinot Noir is often blended with the local César, also known as the "Romain" and the "Gros Monsieur."

IRANCY VILLAGE
Although this small commune in the north of Burgundy is not well known, it does make good, fruity, raspberryish reds.

BROUILLY AND CÔTE DE BROUILLY

THIS IS RARELY AMONG THE FIRST of the Beaujolais *crus* to spring to mind. While the other *crus* are all restricted to the use of the Gamay grape in the production of their wines, the wine makers of Brouilly and the Côte de Brouilly may legally use a range of grape varieties. Brouilly's list of permitted varieties includes Aligoté, Melon de Bourgogne, and Chardonnay, while in the Côte de Brouilly the Pinot Noir and Pinot Gris are used. The Côte de Brouilly's vines are grown on the granite and schist slopes of Mont Brouilly, while Brouilly's vines have been planted on the foothills. This means that the wines of the Côte de Brouilly have more concentrated flavors and more structure, and last longer, than those of Brouilly. Even so, good Brouilly can be worth keeping for a few years.

CHÂTEAU THIVIN
Château Thivin produces some of the Côte de Brouilly's most complex wines.

MONT DE BROUILLY
Vines planted on the slopes of this hill produce the Côte de Brouilly's best wines. Brouilly is made from vines grown on much flatter land.

✱ AC Brouilly, AC Côte de Brouilly.	Ch de Tours. *Côte de Brouilly:* Jacques Depagneux, Georges Duboeuf, Ch du Grand Vernay, J C Pivot, Ch Thivin, la Voute des Crozes.
🍇 Red: Gamay.	
🍷 Full-bodied, fruity rich reds.	
🎚 *Brouilly:* Henry Fessy, Lafond, Laurent Martray, Plateau de Bel-Air, Jean-Paul Ruet, Thorin,	🍴 Black pudding. 📅 1997, 1996, 1995, 1994. ⏳ 5–8 years.

CHABLIS

PART OF A SMALL ISLAND of vines at the northern tip of Burgundy, the Chardonnay-growing *appellation* of Chablis is known worldwide for its classic dry white wines. Only 60 miles (100 km) from Paris, frost can ruin vintages in these cool vineyards. A good year, however, produces wines that are a unique combination of freshness and complexity.

IF IMITATION IS THE sincerest form of flattery, then the wines of Chablis are surely some of the most sincerely flattered in the world. Local imposters made the most of the town's prestigious name as early as the 19th century, using it to sell wine made all over the surrounding *département* of Yonne, planted at the time with more than 123,550 acres (50,000 ha) of vines. More recently, wines labeled as Chablis have been produced in locations as far apart as New York State, California, and Australia's Hunter Valley. The imitation stops with the name, however, as just about the only thing these wines have in common is that none of them tastes remotely like the wines made in and around the sleepy Burgundy town of Chablis.

Despite its well-deserved reputation as a source of great white wines, the 7415-acre (3000-ha) *appellation* of Chablis is by no means easy vine-growing land. While the area is officially part of the province of Burgundy, the cool, unpredictable viticultural conditions of Chablis have, in fact, much more in common, both geographically and climatically, with those of Champagne (*see p.142*), less than 30 miles (50 km) to the northeast, than with those of the rest of Burgundy to the south. Frost is a constant risk here and has, on occasion, been severe enough to wipe out the vineyards completely. One old grape grower I met can remember times in his childhood when he and his friends were able to toboggan down what are now some of top *grands crus* vineyards of the *appellation*. Today the grapes are protected by windmills, sprinkler systems, and oil burners, lined up every winter at either end of each row of vines. Even these measures, however, are not always sufficient to guarantee their survival in the event of a really cold snap.

Despite these difficult conditions, the international white Burgundy boom of the 1970s and 1980s, and the consequent pressures to increase production, led to a relaxation of the *appellation contrôlée* rules. The size of

NATURAL SELECTION
Now only a small appellation *far to the north of the major vineyards of Burgundy, Chablis was once at the center of a vast wine-producing region, covering most of the* département *of Yonne.*

✳ AC Petit Chablis, AC Chablis, AC Chablis Premier Cru, AC Chablis Grand Cru.	Durup, Corinne et Jean-Pierre Grossot, Laroche, Long-Depaquit, de la Maladière, des Maronniers, Louis Michel, Sylvain Mosnier, Gilbert Picq, Pinson, Raveneau, Simmonet-Fèbvre, Verget, Vocoret.	
❋ White: Chardonnay.		
🍷 Crisp, dry whites. *Grands crus* wines may be matured in oak.		
▥ Christian Adine, Barat, Billaud-Simon, Pascal Bouchard, Jean-Marc Brocard, La Chablisienne, Jean Collet, Jean Dauvissat, René et Vincent Dauvissat, Defaix, J-P Droin, Joseph Drouhin, Duplessis, Jean	🍴 Salmon grilled with lemon juice, parsley, and fennel.	
	🍇 1997, 1996, 1995, 1994, 1990.	
	▶ Village wines: 2–5 years. *Premiers crus* wines: 4–8 years. *Grands crus* wines: 6–12 years.	

DOMAINE LONG-DEPAQUIT
Modern techniques are used here to produce excellent wines, like this one from the premier cru *vineyard of Les Vaucopins.*

DOMAINE FRANÇOIS RAVENEAU
Probably the most famous estate in Chablis, the wines produced here are some of the finest and most long-lived of the appellation.

DOMAINE SIMONNET
As well as buying grape juice from other growers, the long-established négociant business of Simonnet-Febvre owns a small number of its own vineyards in Chablis.

the *appellation* was increased to include a number of previously abandoned vineyards. Some land previously classified as only village Chablis was promoted to *premier cru* status, and the *"petit"* traditionally used to identify the poorer vineyards of the *appellation* was removed from a large chunk of the area previously known as Petit Chablis. This expansion has led to some vigorous argument in the quiet town of Chablis, with traditionalists claiming that the soil of the newer vineyards does not produce the flinty, mineral flavors for which the best Chablis is famous. These purists believe that the special character of the wines is a result of a very particular type of chalk, known as Kimmeridgian, found beneath the best vineyards of the *appellation*. In contrast, much of the surrounding land is made up of Portlandian chalk, which is geologically similar, but not identical, to the Kimmeridgian variety. In the past the *appellation* laws have supported this view, either entirely excluding the Portlandian vineyards from the *appellation*, or classifying them as Petit Chablis.

LES PREUSES
Grapes grown in this steep grand cru vineyard make some of the most full-bodied wines in Chablis.

Currently, plenty of dull white Burgundy is now sold under the Chablis *appellation*, a trend that changes to the *appellation* rules have only exacerbated. Equally significant is commercial pressure to produce big, buttery wines, qualities that have little to do with the traditional, steely wines of Chablis. My advice is to tread very carefully when buying wines here. Some of the best buys are the intensely flavored wines

from the seven south- and west-facing *grands crus* vineyards, and the stylish but somewhat more variable wines from the more numerous *premiers crus* vineyards. A good producer is essential and some of the best in the area are listed in the box *(see p.112)*. Each of the *grands crus* vineyards of Chablis produces wines with their own particular character, but all need several years in the bottle to achieve the rich, dry combination of butter, nuts, and minerals that sets the wines of Chablis apart from all of the other Chardonnay wines in the world.

QUIET LIFE
A tributary of the larger Yonne, the Serein river flows slowly through the sleepy town of Chablis.

In addition to the argument over where the grapes should be grown, there is another controversy raging in the bars of Chablis. Should the wines be fermented and matured in new oak? A number of producers say yes, arguing that many of today's wine drinkers expect and enjoy at least a hint of oaky vanilla in their Burgundy. Others, however, disagree. Putting the wine in oak barrels, they believe, robs it of its unique, steely purity, reducing it to nothing more than an alternative to the wines of Meursault *(see p.125)*. Drinking an unoaked wine from a good producer such as Laroche, and comparing it with over-oaked lesser wines almost unrecognizable as Chablis, I sympathize with the unoaked school of producers. Then someone will hand me a glass of delicious, buttery, oak barrel-fermented *grand cru* Chablis from producer Jean-Paul Droin, and my reservations about the oak will fly straight out of the window.

THE VAUDEVEY VINEYARD
Together with six other plots, the Vaudevey, or Vau de Vey, vineyard was promoted to premier cru status in 1986, part of a recent relaxation of the appellation contrôlée rules here.

CHAMBOLLE-MUSIGNY

TOGETHER WITH ITS NEIGHBOR, VOUGEOT, Chambolle-Musigny was one of the first parts of the Côte de Nuits to be planted with vines. The wines produced here are famous for their delicacy, often described as "feminine," and their luscious depth of flavor, a fabulous combination of qualities that has made this one of the richest villages in Burgundy.

CHÂTEAU DE CHAMBOLLE-MUSIGNY Jacques-Frédéric Mugnier makes wonderfully aromatic wines from his vines in the AC Musigny Grand Cru vineyard.

THE WINES OF THE *COMMUNE* of Chambolle-Musigny, which includes the two *grands crus* vineyards of Musigny and Bonnes Mares, as well as the *appellations* of Chambolle-Musigny and Chambolle-Musigny Premier Cru, have long been seen as quite distinct from those made in the surrounding villages of the Côte de Nuits. For one 19th-century observer, a Dr. Lavalle, these were the "most delicate wines in the Côte de Nuits." One possible explanation for the delicacy of Chambolle's wines lies in the high proportion of limestone in the soil. Another theory credits the traditional use of both Pinot Blanc, used elsewhere as a white wine grape, and the more famous Pinot Noir in the red wines made here. The practice of combining grapes continues today, though the permitted white variety is now the Pinot Gris rather than the Pinot Blanc, still used in combination with the Pinot Noir.

AC CHAMBOLLE-MUSIGNY Although simpler in style and without the aging-potential of the Musigny Grand Cru wines, many village wines, such as this one from the Château de Chambolle-Musigny, are still magnificent examples of red Burgundy.

Paradoxically, despite the presence of the Pinot Gris in the vineyards, the only white wine that can now legally be made in Chambolle-Musigny uses Chardonnay grapes grown on Musigny Grand Cru land. Only tiny quantities of the highly-prized Musigny blanc are produced each year, all at Domaine Comte Georges de Vogüé.

There has, in the past, been an unfortunate tendency for the producers of Chambolle-Musigny to treat the terms "delicate" and "dilute" as though they were synonymous. Proof, however, that an entire *appellation* can improve the quality of its wines came in the early 1990s when the growers of Chambolle-Musigny decided to tighten the criteria required for a bottle to carry the village name. The result is consistently fine wines that are delicate but full of substance, with lingering perfumed flavors. As well as the Musigny and Bonnes Mares Grands Crus, there are also some extremely good *premiers crus* vineyards. A number of these, most notably Les Amoureuses, often produce wines of a quality to match those of *grand cru* status.

RURAL CALM Tucked away behind the route nationale, the village of Chambolle-Musigny is one of the quietest and most charming in the Côte d'Or.

✱ AC Chambolle-Musigny, AC Chambolle-Musigny Premier Cru, AC Bonnes Mares Grand Cru, AC Musigny Grand Cru.	Robert Groffier, Anne et François Gros, Hudelot-Noëllat, Louis Jadot, Dominique Laurent, Philippe Lecheneault, Leroy, Hubert Lignier, Denis Mortet, Mugneret-Gibourg, Henri Perrot-Minot, Georges Roumier, Bernard Serveau, de Vogüé.
🍷 Red: Pinot Noir. White: Chardonnay.	
🔖 Elegant, silky, refined, long-lived reds.	
🍴 Barthod-Noëllat, Bertagna, Ch de Chambolle-Musigny, Bruno Clair, Confuron-Cotetidot, Joseph Drouhin, Faiveley, Geantet-Pansiot,	🍽 Suckling wild boar.
	📅 1996, 1995, 1993, 1990, 1988, 1985.
	🍷 Red: 5–20 years.

CHASSAGNE-MONTRACHET

CHASSAGNE-MONTRACHET PRODUCES some of the world's finest white wines. Traditionally, however, the wines produced here have been red. As recently as 1985, despite the international reputation of white Chassagne, well over half of the vintage was red. By 1997, thanks to the worldwide popularity of the Chardonnay grape, 60 percent of the year's wines were white.

FRUITFUL ESTATES.
The growers of Chassagne-Montrachet, many of whom have built their homes among the vines, have no difficulty in selling the Chardonnay grapes from their sometimes tiny plots.

UNTIL FAIRLY RECENTLY the majority of wines produced in the *commune* of Chassagne-Montrachet were red. The traditional grapes here were the Gamay for the poorer land and the Pinot Noir in areas with richer soil. The Montrachet Grand Cru vineyard, however, shared with the neighboring commune of Puligny-Montrachet (see p.133), is one of the few vineyards in Chassagne-Montrachet that has traditionally been used to grow white grapes. Alongside the neighboring *grands crus* vineyards of Bâtard-Montrachet (also shared with Puligny) and Criots-Bâtard-Montrachet, it is now considered by many people to produce some of the finest dry white wine in the world. The best *premiers crus* vineyards include Morgeot, Chenevottes, Ruchottes, En Maltroye, and En Cailleret. Wines from Chassagne are generally fuller-bodied and with a slightly more mineral character than those from neighboring Puligny, often developing especially interesting flavors after a decade or so stored in the cellar.

Despite the recent huge popularity of Chassagne's white wines, there will always be red wine made here. This is simply because much of the soil, similar to the limestone marl of the Côte de Nuits, is better suited to the Pinot Noir grape than to the Chardonnay that is fast replacing it. Unfortunately, however, while a few producers do make fine red Chassagne, most of Chassagne's red wine has more in common with the simple, fresh wines of Santenay to the south-west (see p.136) than with the delicate wines of Volnay (see p.137) or Beaune (see p.108). Selling their red wines is rarely a problem for the wine growers here, however. The technique seems to be simply to force it onto customers who come in search of the world-famous white.

GAGNARD-DELAGRANGE
In producing their sublime wines, the wine makers of this estate use grapes that are grown in one of the least known of Chassagne's premiers crus vineyards.

DOMAINE RAMONET
With an estate including premiers crus and Montrachet Grand Cru vineyards, André Ramonet remains one of the very best producers in the area.

✱	AC Chassagne-Montrachet, AC Chassagne-Montrachet Premier Cru, AC Criots-Bâtard Grand Cru, AC Montrachet Grand Cru, AC Bâtard-Montrachet Grand Cru.
❦	Red: Pinot Noir. White: Chardonnay.
▨	Full-bodied fruity reds. Spicy, full-flavoured whites.
▥	Guy Amiot, Bernard, Chartron et Trebuchet, Marc Colin, Michel Colin-Deléger, Delagrange-Bachelet, Joseph Drouhin (de Laguiche), Henri Germain, Louis Jadot, Louis Latour, Olivier Leflaive Frères, Maltroye, Michel Niellon, Ch de Puligny Montrachet, Ramonet, Rodet, Roux, Verget.
▯	Grilled trout.
▤	1997, 1996, 1995, 1992, 1990, 1989, 1988, 1986, 1985.
▸	Red: 3–10 years. White: 3–20 years.

GAGNARD-DELAGRANGE
VIN DE BOURGOGNE
Chassagne-Montrachet
1ᵉʳ CRU "LA BOUDRIOTTE"
APPELLATION CONTROLÉE
GAGNARD-DELAGRANGE
Propriétaire-Récoltant à Chassagne-Montrachet (Côte-d'Or) France
PRODUCE OF FRANCE

RAMONET
1994
CHASSAGNE-MONTRACHET
Premier Cru "Morgeot"
APPELLATION CONTROLÉE
S.C.E. DOMAINE RAMONET
VITICULTEUR A CHASSAGNE-MONTRACHET
13,5% vol. CÔTE-D'OR, FRANCE

CHÉNAS

THE SMALLEST OF THE Beaujolais *crus*, the flat, silty soils of Chénas have kept it way behind the better-known *cru* villages such as St. Amour (*see p.134*), Morgon (*see p.128*) and Fleurie (*see p.119*). It is tempting to suppose that when the *appellation* boundaries were drawn up, Chénas was short-changed. Steep granite slopes in the west of the *appellation* produce the best Chénas wines, which are medium-bodied with a hint of oak. The Château de Chénas *coopérative* produces 45 percent of Chénas wines, and its medieval cellars are well worth a visit.

✴	AC Chénas.
🏵	Red: Gamay.
🍷	Medium weight, soft, fruity red.
▥	Louis Champagnon, Château de Chénas, Georges Duboeuf, Hubert Lapierre, Bernard Santé.
🍴	Chicken stewed with truffles.
▤	1997, 1996, 1995, 1994.
🕐	Red: 3–5 years.

CHÂTEAU DE CHÉNAS
Producer of almost half the wine in Chénas, this coopérative is one of the best in France.

CHIROUBLES

THIS IS THE *COMMUNE* that is said to make the most fragrant wines of all the Beaujolais *cru*. It is also the highest above sea level, forming a natural amphitheatre 1300 ft (400 m) above the Beaujolais plain. The soil is a light, thin, granite-sand that gives these wines a delicate, violet-perfumed character which, for many, represents the very essence of the wines of the Beaujolais region. Refreshing and fruity, these reds are delicious drunk young, accompanied by a wide variety of *charcuterie*, ranging from *andouillettes* to *saucisson*.

✴	AC Chiroubles.
🏵	Gamay.
🍷	Elegant, light, refreshing red.
▥	Émile Cheysson, Georges Duboeuf, Hubert Lapierre, Alain Passot, Ch de Raousset.
🍴	Andouillettes with mustard.
▤	1997, 1996, 1995, 1994.
🕐	2–4 years.

CHÂTEAU DE RAOUSSET
Light, fragrant Chiroubles is delicious when drunk young, but really good wines, like this one, often improve as they age.

CHOREY-LÈS-BEAUNE

THE VILLAGE OF Chorey-lès-Beaune lies on the flat plain to the north of the city of Beaune, its vineyards extending over both sides of the N74, bordering Savigny-lès-Beaune (*see p.136*) to the west, and Aloxe-Corton (*see p.104*) to the north. Chorey's best wines have more in common with the fruity, raspberry-jam reds of Beaune (*see p.108*) and Savigny-lès-Beaune than with the tough, tannic reds of Aloxe-Corton. Fruity and soft, these wines are best drunk within three years of the harvest. In the past, much of the wine produced in Chorey-lès-Beaune has been sold as the generic *appellation contrôlée* Côte de Beaune-Villages, but the recent success of local producers such as the Château de Chorey has encouraged both growers and *négociants* to print the name of the *commune* proudly on the label.

TOLLOT-BEAUT
Rich and oaky, many wines made at the Tollot-Beaut estate are as fine as more expensive wines from nearby Beaune.

CHÂTEAU DE CHOREY
Sister château to the Château de Savigny, the Château de Chorey offers good wine, as well as a place to stay for visitors to the region.

✴	AC Chorey-lès-Beaune, AC Côte de Beaune-Villages.
🏵	Red: Pinot Noir.
🍷	Soft, plump, fruity red for early drinking.
▥	Charles Allexant, Arnoux Père et Fils, Ch de Chorey (François Germain),

Doudet-Naudin, Joseph Drouhin, Drouhin-Laroze, François Gay, Guyon, Daniel Largeot, Maillard Père et Fils, Tollot-Beaut.

🍴	Terrine of ham with parsley.
▤	1996, 1995, 1993.
🕐	Red: 2–5 years.

CLOS DE VOUGEOT AND VOUGEOT

BEGUN AS A FEW VINES PLANTED by Cistercian monks in the 12th century, the Clos de Vougeot is now the largest, and arguably the most famous, *grand cru* in Burgundy. This walled vineyard is also a wonderful, living illustration of the origins of the region's wine industry and of the many changes that took place as a result of the French Revolution of 1789.

CHÂTEAU DU CLOS DE VOUGEOT
Set like a ship in an ocean of vines, the château-monastery is now one of the most famous tourist attractions in Burgundy. Inside are medieval wooden presses and a grand banqueting hall.

CISTERCIAN MONKS PLANTED a few vines here on the slopes close to their monastery during the 12th century. By the early 14th century, donations of land had swollen the estate to its current size of 125 acres (50 ha), and stone walls, the *clos*, had been constructed around it. More than two centuries later, following the Revolution of 1789, the vineyard was bought as individual holdings by six merchants. Each holding has been further split over the years, and the vineyard is now shared between more than 80 individuals.

There are several problems caused by the parcelling-up of the vineyard. First, there is the question of unequal land quality. The plots at the top of the *clos* are unquestionably finer than the ones in the middle, which in turn are better than the frequently waterlogged clay soils at the bottom. The monks solved this problem by bottling the wines from each section separately. Today, however, every bottle of Clos de Vougeot is eligible for precisely the same *grand cru* status. Even more significant, however, is the tiny scale of the plots and the wine-making constraints this places on their owners. Average production per owner is just 200 cases, with a third of the *vignerons* producing fewer than 75 cases of wine each year. In the absence of specialized micro-vinification equipment, it is very difficult to crush, ferment, and press such a trifling quantity of grapes. Both these points are worth bearing in mind if you encounter a disappointing wine. The château is the headquarters of the *Confrérie des Chevaliers du Tastevin*, a fraternity of wine makers established in 1934. Banquets and an annual wine tasting are held here.

Beyond the walled vineyard, there are 30 acres (12 ha) of vines, producing 70,000 bottles of red and 10,000 bottles of white Vougeot and Vougeot Premier Cru annually. These are rarities that often offer better value than Clos de Vougeot.

1994

CLOS·VOUGEOT
Grand Cru

GEORGES MUGNERET
Several members of the talented Mugneret family make good examples of Clos de Vougeot. Like many local people, Georges Mugneret refers to the appellation as Clos-Vougeot.

Jaffelin
CLOS DE VOUGEOT
GRAND CRU
APPELLATION CONTRÔLÉE
13 % vol.
75 cl   France

JAFFELIN
Like many of Burgundy's best négociants, or wine merchants, the firm of Jaffelin owns its own vineyards, including some in Clos de Vougeot.

✱	AC Clos de Vougeot Grand Cru, AC Vougeot Premier Cru, AC Vougeot.
❂	Red: Pinot Noir.
🍷	Plump, full-bodied, spicy red with flavors of red summer fruits, chocolate and licorice.
⫼	Amiot-Servelle, Robert Arnoux, Bertagna, Bouchard Père et Fils, Champy, Chanson Père et Fils, Jean-Jacques Confuron, Joseph Drouhin-Laroze, René Engel, Faiveley,

Genot-Boulanger, Anne et François Gros, Jean Grivot, Louis Jadot, Jaffelin, Méo-Camuzet, Leroy, Denis Mortet, Mugneret-Gibourg, Jacques Prieur, Prieuré Roch, Raphet, Henri Rebourseau, Daniel Rion, Ch de la Tour.

🍴	Oxtail stewed in red wine.
🗄	1996, 1995, 1993. 1990, 1985.
🍇	10–15 years.

CÔTE DE BEAUNE AND CÔTE DE BEAUNE-VILLAGES

THESE TWO SIMILARLY named *appellations* are in fact quite separate, with the Côte de Beaune label covering only a tiny area close to the town of Beaune itself. More confusion is sometimes caused by the fact that the Côte de Beaune-Villages *appellation* is generally thought to be the southern counterpart of Côte de Nuits-Villages (*see below*), when in fact the two *appellations* operate quite differently. The latter applies only to a very limited area, while most of the red wines produced in those parts of the Côte de Beaune entitled to their own *appellation* may also be sold as Côte de Beaune-Villages. The *appellations* of St. Romain (*see p.135*), Chorey-lès-Beaune (*see p.116*), Pernand-Vergelesses (*see p.130*) and Auxey-Duresses (*see p.105*) all sell many of what are often their less successful red wines as Côte de Beaune-Villages.

1996

CÔTE DE BEAUNE VILLAGES

BOUCHARD PÈRE & FILS

BOUCHARD PÈRE ET FILS
This established merchant specializes in making Côte de Beaune-Villages wines.

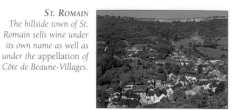

ST. ROMAIN
The hillside town of St. Romain sells wine under its own name as well as under the appellation *of Côte de Beaune-Villages.*

✴ AC Côte de Beaune, AC Côte de Beaune-Villages.	Père et Fils, Maurice Chenu, Coron Père et Fils, Edouard Delaunay, Jaffelin, Lequin-Roussot, Naigeon-Chauveau.
▥ Red: Pinot Noir.	
▨ Light, soft, fruity reds.	
▥ *Côte de Beaune:* Jean Allexant, Cauvard, Joseph Drouhin. *Côte de Beaune-Villages:* Bernard Bachelet, Bouchard	▯ Snails cooked Beaune style, served with garlic and parsley butter.
	▤ 1996, 1995.
	▧ 2–5 years.

CÔTE DE NUITS-VILLAGES

BURGUNDIANS HAVE ALWAYS associated quarries with good vine-growing land. Any wine from a vineyard called "Perrière" will have been grown on the site of a former quarry. The villages of Prissey, Comblanchien, and Corgoloin, whose limestone workings produced the coffee-colored marble used at Orly airport, are therefore, in theory at least, well placed to make good wine. They are, however, too small to warrant a single *appellation* and instead label their wines as the Côte de Nuits-Villages. The same designation is also used for some wines from Fixin (*see p.119*) and Brochon, at the northern end of the Côte de Nuits-Villages. Although it would be legal to blend the wines of the two extremes of the Côte de Nuits-Villages, in practice this is rare. Similarly, while the *appellation* permits white wine, very little is made.

1994

Côte de Nuits-Villages

APPELLATION CONTRÔLÉE

S.C.E.A. JAYER-GILLES

JAYER-GILES
This estate is one of the few to take the Côte de Nuits-Villages label seriously and to produce long-lived wines under it.

WOOD FROM THE TREES
Both red and white wines are aged here in barrels. However, they are seldom rich and complex enough to warrant more than a small amount of new oak.

✴ AC Côte de Nuits-Villages.	Drouhin, Michel Esmonin, Fougeray de Beauclair, Louis Jadot, Jayer-Giles, Henri Naudin-Ferrand, de la Paulette, Quillardet.
▥ Red: Pinot Noir. White: Chardonnay (very little is produced).	
▨ Medium- to full-bodied, simple, fruity reds.	▯ Duck roasted with bay leaves and cherries.
▥ De l'Arlot, Daniel Chopin-Groffier, Jean-Jacques Confuron, Maison Joseph	▤ Red: 1996, 1995, 1993.
	▧ Red: 3–6 years.

FIXIN

AT FIRST GLANCE the vineyards that form a square around the village of Fixin, with the best *premiers crus* located at the end closest to Gevrey-Chambertin (*see p.120*), look as though they might be a northern continuation of Gevrey-Chambertin. However, the microclimate here is quite different and the grapes ripen over a week later. Fixin's soil is different, too, with more clay in the flatter land on which the village wines are made. These conditions tend to make for rustic, tannic wines that take years to evolve into rustic, softer ones. It is not surprising, therefore, that much of the wine has been sold as Côte de Nuits-Villages (*see p.118*). Recently, better wine-making skills have resulted in more approachable wines and a greater incentive to print the village name on the label. White Fixin is rare, but Bruno Clair's is worth trying.

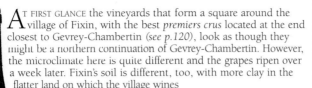

THE HARD EDGE
The cool microclimate of the small village of Fixin has traditionally led to wines that tend to be tannic and unripe.

DOMAINE ANDRÉ GEOFFREY
The wines of Fixin can be tough and fruitless, but those produced on this estate are stylish and drinkable.

✴	AC Fixin, AC Fixin Premier Cru.	Gelin, André Geoffrey, Jean-Pierre Guyard, Philippe Joillet, Armell et Jean-Michel Molin, Denis Philibert, Charles Vienot.
🍇	Red: Pinot Noir.	
🍷	Medium-bodied reds that tend to be rustic.	
🍴		🍴 Hare cooked in an earthenware pot.
🏛	Vincent Berthaut, Bruno Clair, Michel Defrance, Derey Frères, Doudet-Naudin, Fougeray de Beauclair, Pierre	📅 1996, 1995, 1993, 1990.
		🕐 5–12 years.

FLEURIE

IF THIS BEAUJOLAIS *CRU*, located between Moulin à Vent and Chiroubles, were called something completely different, its wines would probably still be associated with fields of spring flowers, because that is exactly what good examples smell like. This, the third largest and often the priciest of the Beaujolais *crus*, should be the very essence of classic Beaujolais, with its Gamay grapes, grown on large-crystal granite, being made into fresh, light red wines packed with summery flavors. For a panoramic view over this varied *commune*, climb to the top of the La Madonne chapel. The best, longest-lived wines might well come from the La Madonne and the Point du Jour vineyards, but there are other plots that could stake a reasonable claim to *premier cru* status if it were ever introduced for Beaujolais.

MADONNA AND VINES
The sloping vineyard of La Madonne produces some of the finest wines in Fleurie.

DOMAINE BERROD
The wines produced by Domaine Berrod have the floral character with which Fleurie is associated.

✴	AC Fleurie.	Duboeuf (des Quatre Vents, Ch des Deduits), Pierre Ferraud, Yves Métras, André Métrat (la Roilette), Albert Morel, Tête, Thorin, de la Treille.
🍇	Red: Gamay.	
🍷	Medium-bodied, floral, fragrant reds.	
🏛	Paul Beaudet, Berrod, Michel Chignard, Guy Depardon (du Point du Jour), Jean-Marc Déprés, Joseph Drouhin, Georges	🍴 Andouillettes.
		📅 1998, 1997, 1996, 1995.
		🕐 2–8 years.

GEVREY-CHAMBERTIN

APPRECIATED BY EMPEROR NAPOLÉON BONAPARTE in the 19th century, the red wines produced around Gevrey-Chambertin have continued to enjoy great popularity to this day, making it one of the richest villages in the region. The *appellation* is the largest in the Côtes de Nuits, producing wines that range, predictably, from the truly sublime to the very average.

LIMESTONE EXPOSURE
This unusually-situated vineyard offers a rare chance to see the limestone rock which underlies the appellation *of Gevrey-Chambertin, normally hidden beneath the topsoil and the vines.*

Monks from the Abbaye de Bèze planted vines here in the seventh century, quickly followed by an astute peasant named Bertin. Today, both the monks' walled Clos de Bèze and Bertin's field, or Champ Bertin, produce some of the finest red wines in Burgundy. At the northern end of the Côte de Nuits, the *appellation* of Gevrey-Chambertin includes nine *grands crus* and 27 *premiers crus* vineyards. The

very best of the *grands crus* are the neighboring Clos de Bèze and Chambertin vineyards at the center of a slope of *grands crus* vineyards to the south of the village. Now divided among 25 owners, the best wines made from these grapes are sublime and long lived, combining the flavors of plums and cherries, with a hint of spice. Of the remaining *grands crus*, the best are Griottes-Chambertin, Latricières-Chambertin, Ruchottes-Chambertin, and Mazis-Chambertin. More variable are Chapelle-Chambertin and Charmes-Chambertin, often producing wines that are less impressive than those from the best *premiers crus* vineyards such as Clos St. Jacques and Les Cazetiers. Village wines are of variable quality too, made from vines extending right down the hillside onto the flat land on the other side of the main road. That said, however, this is an *appellation* where the skill of the producer is just as crucial as the position of the vineyard, and where well-made village wines often outclass carelessly made wines from supposedly superior land.

CLOS ST. JACQUES
Although of supposedly humbler quality than the grands crus *vineyards nearby, the* premier cru Clos St. Jacques *vineyard is nevertheless capable of producing some truly superlative wines.*

LATRICIÈRES-CHAMBERTIN
A stone gateway marks out one proud owner's vines in this famous grand cru *vineyard.*

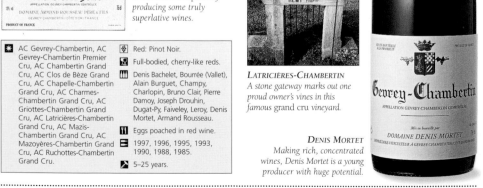

✱	AC Gevrey-Chambertin, AC Gevrey-Chambertin Premier Cru, AC Chambertin Grand Cru, AC Clos de Bèze Grand Cru, AC Chapelle-Chambertin Grand Cru, AC Charmes-Chambertin Grand Cru, AC Griottes-Chambertin Grand Cru, AC Latricières-Chambertin Grand Cru, AC Mazis-Chambertin Grand Cru, AC Mazoyères-Chambertin Grand Cru, AC Ruchottes-Chambertin Grand Cru.
▦	Red: Pinot Noir.
▧	Full-bodied, cherry-like reds.
▥	Denis Bachelet, Bourrée (Vallet), Alain Burguet, Champy, Charlopin, Bruno Clair, Pierre Damoy, Joseph Drouhin, Dugat-Py, Faiveley, Leroy, Denis Mortet, Armand Rousseau.
▯	Eggs poached in red wine.
▤	1997, 1996, 1995, 1993, 1990, 1988, 1985.
▨	5–25 years.

DENIS MORTET
Making rich, concentrated wines, Denis Mortet is a young producer with huge potential.

GIVRY

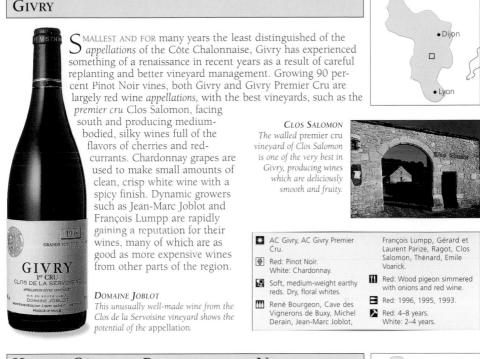

SMALLEST AND FOR many years the least distinguished of the *appellations* of the Côte Chalonnaise, Givry has experienced something of a renaissance in recent years as a result of careful replanting and better vineyard management. Growing 90 percent Pinot Noir vines, both Givry and Givry Premier Cru are largely red wine *appellations,* with the best vineyards, such as the *premier cru* Clos Salomon, facing south and producing medium-bodied, silky wines full of the flavors of cherries and red-currants. Chardonnay grapes are used to make small amounts of clean, crisp white wine with a spicy finish. Dynamic growers such as Jean-Marc Joblot and François Lumpp are rapidly gaining a reputation for their wines, many of which are as good as more expensive wines from other parts of the region.

CLOS SALOMON
The walled premier cru vineyard of Clos Salomon is one of the very best in Givry, producing wines which are deliciously smooth and fruity.

DOMAINE JOBLOT
This unusually well-made wine from the Clos de la Servoisine vineyard shows the potential of the appellation.

❈ AC Givry, AC Givry Premier Cru.		François Lumpp, Gérard et Laurent Parize, Ragot, Clos Salomon, Thénard, Emile Voarick.
🍇 Red: Pinot Noir. White: Chardonnay.		
🍷 Soft, medium-weight earthy reds. Dry, floral whites.		🍴 Red: Wood pigeon simmered with onions and red wine.
🏛 René Bourgeon, Cave des Vignerons de Buxy, Michel Derain, Jean-Marc Joblot,		📅 Red: 1996, 1995, 1993.
		⏳ Red: 4–8 years. White: 2–4 years.

HAUTES-CÔTES DE BEAUNE AND DE NUITS

RISING TO 1310 FT (400 m) above the western edge of the Côte de Nuits (*see p.118*) and the Côte de Beaune (*see p.118*) are the two mainly red *appellations* of the Hautes-Côtes de Nuits and the Hautes-Côtes de Beaune. Woodland and pasture among the vines make this some of the most beautiful landscape in Burgundy, but vineyards here are cool and exposed, giving the wines a noticeably unripe character in all but the very warmest years. In the 1960s, only 1235 acres (500 ha) were under vine here, but thanks to some dedicated producers, the rapidly improving wines of the area are currently enjoying a revival. Vineyards have been carefully replanted, and many growers are now embracing a more traditional approach to vineyard management. At their best, these light wines are supple and fruity and offer good.

SUN WORSHIPPERS
Many growers train their vines high in the exposed, high-altitude vineyards of the Hautes-Côtes, allowing the grapes to catch every drop of the sunshine they need for proper ripening.

DOMAINE DU BOIS GUILLAUME
Fresh and bone dry, this white wine is produced in only small amounts in the cool vineyards of the Hautes-Côtes de Beaune.

❈ AC Bourgogne Hautes-Côtes de Nuits, AC Bourgogne Hautes-Côtes de Beaune.		Naudin-Ferrand, Claude Nouveau, Lucien Rateau. *Hautes-Côtes de Nuits:* Chopin- Groffier, Gerbet, Michel Gros, Cave des Hautes-Côtes, Lechenaut.
🍇 Red: Pinot Noir. White: Chardonnay.		
🍷 Light reds. Dry whites.		🍴 Red: Spicy tripe sausages.
🏛 *Hautes-Côtes de Beaune:* Du Bois Guillaume, Henri Delagrange, Philippe Germain,		📅 Red: 1996, 1995.
		⏳ Red: 2–6 years.

JULIÉNAS

O NE OF THE MOST NORTHERLY of the 10 Beaujolais *cru* villages, the land around Juliénas was allegedly some of the first in Beaujolais to be planted with vines. Today the *appellation* includes four *communes*, with well-drained granite soils to the west, and ancient alluvial soils, laid down by the river Saône, to the east. When young, the wines of Juliénas are often underrated, passed over in favor of wines from better known *cru appellations* such as Fleurie (*see p.119*) and Moulin-à-Vent (*see p.128*). At their best, however, these are lively wines with powerful, fruity aromas, often developing unusual complexity after a few years in the bottle. One ceremony not to be missed is held here every November, when an artist or writer, deemed best taster of the new vintage, is awarded his or her weight in wine!

FROSTY VINES
Winter temperatures can be very low in hilly Juliénas, despite its southerly location a few kilometers beyond the town of Mâcon.

PASCAL GRANGER
Wines from this talented producer offer a delightful mouthful of fresh cherry and chocolate flavors.

✳	AC Juliénas.	Pascal Granger, Ch de Juliénas, Henri Lespinasse, René Monnet, de la Petite Croix, Bernard Santé, Michel Tête, Raymond Trichard.
🍷	Red: Gamay.	
🍷	Medium-bodied, spicy reds.	
🍴	Ernest Aujas, Jean Benon, du Bois de la Salle, Bernard Broyer, François Condemine, Gérard Descombes, Thierry Descombes, Georges Duboeuf, Pierre Ferraud,	🍴 Pike and veal dumplings with a cheese sauce .
		🍷 1997, 1996, 1995, 1994.
		⬆ 2–5 years.

LADOIX

T HE MOST NORTHERLY *appellation* in the Côte de Beaune and one of the least well known, Ladoix ends, confusingly, halfway through its namesake village of Ladoix-Serrigny. Despite some promising whites, this is mainly a red *appellation*, producing an unusually wide range of wines. Rugged village wines from the flatter and less well-exposed vineyards are sold mainly as Côte de Beaune-Villages (*see p.118*), while richer, smoother wines are made from grapes grown in the two *grands crus* and seven *premiers crus* vineyards to the north of the village. Four of the *premiers crus* vineyards of the *appellation* lie on the slopes of the Montagne de Corton, as do the famous *grands crus* vineyards of Corton and Corton-Charlemagne, shared with neighboring *appellations* Aloxe-Corton (*see p.104*) and Pernand-Vergelesses (*see p.130*).

SITTING PRETTY
The village of Ladoix-Serrigny is seen at its best from the hillside vineyards to the west, rather than from the busy route nationale that runs through its center.

CLAUDE MARÉCHAL
While many Ladoix village wines are fairly rustic, and sold as Côte de Beaune-Villages, this one is an exception to the rule.

✳	AC Ladoix, AC Aloxe-Corton Premier Cru, AC Corton Grand Cru, AC Corton-Charlemagne Grand Cru.	Cornu, François Gay, Claude Maréchal, André et Jean-René Nudant, Michel Tête.
🍷	Red: Pinot Noir. White: Chardonnay.	🍴 Year-old lamb stewed with spring vegetables, red wine, garlic, and thyme.
🍷	Soft, plump, rustic reds. Light-to medium-weight dry whites.	🍷 Red: 1996, 1995, 1993.
🍴	Chevalier Père et Fils, Edmond	⬆ Red: 4–6 years. White: 2–3 years.

MÂCON AND MÂCON-VILLAGES

DESPITE THE GREATER PRESTIGE enjoyed by the white wine-producing villages of the Côte d'Or and Chablis, the Mâconnais is the true engine room of white wine production in Burgundy. Varying in quality from workaday to excellent, a huge quantity of Chardonnay wine, sold as *appellations contrôlées* Mâcon and Mâcon-Villages, is made here every year.

CHARDONNAY COUNTRY
The Chardonnay is the grape of the Mâconnais region, flourishing in its limestone soils and ripening well in the almost Mediterranean sunshine.

SOMEWHERE IN THE ancient wine-producing district of the Mâconnais is the meeting point of northern and southern France. Suddenly, both the climate and the attitude of the people have more to do with the Mediterranean than with the English Channel. The grape harvest here takes place two weeks before that of the more northerly Côte d'Or, producing wines with richer, riper flavors. Despite a long tradition of red wine production, the Mâconnais today makes three times as much white wine as the rest of Burgundy put together. Light and dry, these fairly affordable wines vary from pleasant, undemanding bottles for drinking young, to château-bottled wines that are as good as those from Côte de Beaune *appellations* such as Meursault (*see p.125*). In theory, only wines made from grapes grown in the district's best vineyards can be sold as *appellation contrôlée* Mâcon-Villages. In practice, the label is used to sell more than 90 percent of the white wines made here. Better wines come from the vineyards surrounding 42 named villages, each one entitled to add its name to the Mâcon-Villages classification. Some of the best include Charmes, Prissé, Clessé, and Pierreclos. Best of all are the wines made by individual producers including Jean Thevenet in Clessé, who have proved decisively that top-quality wines can be made here, despite the more limited ambitions of the wine making *coopératives* responsible for 75 percent of Mâconnais wine production.

Light, fruity, and unmemorable, only a quarter of the district's wines are red. Made from either Pinot Noir or Gamay grapes, these are sold under the generic *appellation contrôlée* Bourgogne (*see p.110*), or as *appellations contrôlées* Mâcon or Mâcon Supérieur.

MÂCON-LUGNY
From the village of Lugny, this wine is sold by the prominent négociant firm of Louis Latour.

DOMAINE DE LA BONGRAN
Talented and innovative, producer Jean Thevenet makes delicious but controversial late-harvest wines.

✳️ AC Mâcon, AC Mâcon Supérieur, AC Mâcon-Villages or AC Mâcon-village name (white only), AC Mâcon-village name (red only).	Vignerons de Buxy, Cordier, des Deux Roches, Georges Duboeuf, de la Feuillarde, Fichet, Guffens-Heynen, Cave de Lugny, Roger Luquet, Mommessin, de Ruère, Saumaize-Michelin, Roger Thevenet, Valette, Cave de Viré.
🍇 Red: Gamay, Pinot Noir. White: Chardonnay.	
🍷 Light, fruity reds. Light, dry whites.	🍴 White: Deep-fried whitebait.
🏛 Daniel et Martine Barraud, Paul Beaudet, le Berceau du Chardonnay, de la Bongran, André Bonhomme, Cave des	🗓 White: 1998, 1997, 1996, 1995.
	⏳ White: 2–4 years. Red: 2–5 years.

MARANGES

THIS LITTLE-KNOWN and often overlooked *appellation*, to the southwest of Santenay, is the result of the amalgamation in 1989 of the even less well-known *appellations* of Cheilly-lès-Maranges, Dezize-lès-Maranges and Sampigny-lès-Maranges. Wines from these *appellations* were sold mainly as Côte de Beaune-Villages. Talented producers such as Vincent Girardin are working hard to create an identity for Maranges, and their wines often offer unusually good value. Even so, in less skilled hands Maranges wines still tend to be pretty rustic.

AC Maranges, AC Maranges Premier Cru.

Red: Pinot Noir.

Medium to full-bodied earthy, rustic reds.

Bernard Bachelet, Pierre Bresson, Fernand Chevrot, Vincent Girardin, Claude Nouveau.

Eggs poached in red wine.

1997, 1996, 1995, 1994.

Red: 4–6 years.

VINCENT GIRARDIN
A name to look out for, Girardin is one of several producers dedicated to raising the profile of Maranges.

MARSANNAY

AT THE NORTHERNMOST END of the Côte de Nuits, Marsannay enjoys the distinction of being one of the few *appellations* in Burgundy to produce excellent, raspberryish *rosé*. This is some of the best *rosé* in France, and very little of it is exported. Marsannay is also developing a reputation for its red wines, which are fruity but fairly tannic, offering good value when well made. The tiny quantities of white wine produced in Marsannay often represent the best buy of all, with buttery and mineral flavors similar to those of white Meursault *(see p.125)*.

AC Marsannay, AC Marsannay Rosé.

Red and rosé: Pinot Noir. White: Chardonnay.

Light to medium-bodied red. Medium-bodied dry rosé. Light, dry white.

Bruno Clair, Charlopin, Fougeray de Beauclair.

Ham and parsley terrine.

Red: 1998, 1997, 1996.

Rosé: 1–3 years.

BRUNO CLAIR
Marsannay was recently granted appellation *status, due in part to the excellent wines made by Bruno Clair.*

MERCUREY

THE BIGGEST *APPELLATION* in the Côte Chalonnaise, the region around the village of Mercurey is named after a local Gallo-Roman temple to Mercury, the messenger of the gods. While local *négociants* have long appreciated Mercurey's affordable red, and more recently white, wines, the harvest from such a large *appellation* is inevitably of varying quality. Wines from less well-situated vineyards have a tendency to be thin, while in a good year wines from the top *premiers crus* vineyards are similar to the best wines of Pommard *(see p.131)*. The number of *premiers crus* here has increased dramatically in the last decade, from five covering 40 acres (15 ha), to 30 with a total area of over 250 acres (100 ha). As a result, it is especially important to choose a good producer when buying wine here.

MICHEL JUILLOT
A talented producer of top-class Mercurey, Michel Juillot is also one of Burgundy's best vinous experimenters.

GENTLE SLOPES
Like the rest of the Côte Chalonnaise, the commune of Mercurey is made up of a series of small hills, with vineyards planted on many of the region's gentler slopes.

AC Mercurey Premier Cru, AC Mercurey.

Red: Pinot Noir. White: Chardonnay.

Medium to full-bodied reds. Medium-bodied, possibly oak-aged, whites.

Brintet, de Chamirey, Dureil-Janthial, Faiveley, Genot-Boulanger, Emile Juillot, Michel Juillot, Lorenzon, Meix-Foulot, Jean Raquillet, Antonin Rodet, de Suremain, Emile Voarick.

St. Florentin cheese.

Red: 1997, 1996, 1995, 1993

Red: 5–10 years. White: 4–6 years.

MEURSAULT

FOR HUNDREDS OF YEARS THE CHARDONNAY has been the primary grape of Meursault, where it flourishes in the poor, rocky soil. While the crown for the finest white Burgundy goes to Corton-Charlemagne or the *grands crus* of Chassagne-Montrachet, the wines of Meursault are deliciously dry and rich, full of the flavors of butter, nuts, and spices.

HIDDEN BLAGNY
Tucked away in the hills behind the village of Meursault, the tiny hamlet of Blagny produces delicious, long-lived white wines, sold either as AC Meursault-Blagny or as AC Meursault Premier Cru.

A S MUCH AS ONE THIRD of all the white wine from the Côte d'Or, (the *département* covering both the Côte de Nuits and the Côte de Beaune), comes from the *commune* of Meursault. In contrast to many white wine-producing Burgundy *communes*, such as Chassagne-Montrachet (*see p.115*), where white wines are a fairly recent phenomenon, Meursault has long been linked to the white Chardonnay grape. During the 18th century, former president Thomas Jefferson visited the region and noted that, "at Meursault only white wines are made, because there is too much stone for the red."

Considerably cheaper than the white wines of Corton-Charlemagne and Chassagne-Montrachet, the hazelnut and melted butter flavors of white Meursault are popular all over the world and are eagerly copied by California wine makers.

The wines of Meursault fall into a number of categories. First, there are the plain AC Meursault wines, which can be very plain indeed. Next come wines from good, named but non-*premiers crus* vineyards such as Les Clos de la Barre. Finally, there are many impressive *premiers crus* vineyards, of which Les Perrières produces some of the finest wines, long-lived though somewhat slow to develop. More easily accessible are wines from the well-named vineyard, Les Charmes. The best of these come from Les Charmes-Dessus. Also an excellent choice are wines from Les Genevrières and Les Gouttes d'Or. From La Pièce-sous-le-Bois in the nearby village of Blagny come fine whites, some sold as AC Meursault-Blagny and others as AC Meursault Premier Cru.

Red wines from Blagny are sold under their own *appellation*, the tiny AC Blagny Premier Cru. Reds from Meursault are produced in small quantities each year and are light and fruity, and best drunk young.

J-F COCHE-DURY
Wines from the Perrières vineyard tend to be long-lived. This one is made by Jean-François Coche-Dury, one of the best wine makers in Meursault.

DOMAINE DES COMTES LAFON
In the hands of brilliant wine maker Dominique Lafon of the Domaine des Comtes Lafon, the vineyard Le Clos de la Barre produces fabulous wines of almost premier cru quality.

❋	AC Meursault, AC Meursault Premier Cru, AC Meursault-Blagny Premier Cru, AC Meursault Côte de Beaune, AC Meursault-Santenots.	Boulanger, Henri Germain, Albert Grivault, Patrick Javillier, François Jobard, Rémi Jobard, des Comtes Lafon, Latour-Giuraud, Olivier Leflaive, Matrot, de Meu, de Meursault, Michelot, Pierre Morey, Jacques Prieur, Prieur-Brunet, de Puligny-Montrachet, Roult, Roux, Verget.
🍇	White: Chardonnay. Red: Pinot Noir.	
🍴	Broad, buttery whites with mineral overtones.	
🏛	Robert Ampeau, d'Auvenay, Bitouzet-Prieur, Bouzereau, Coche-Debord, Coche-Dury, Jean-Pierre Diconne, Jean-Philippe Fichet, Genot-	🍴 Crayfish.
		🗄 White: 1997, 1996, 1995.
		🗓 White: 3–20 years.

MONTAGNY

LYING AT THE SOUTHERN TIP of the Côte Chalonnaise, Montagny is one of the many strange anomalies in the *appellation* system. For no explicable reason, *premier cru* status is given to all the wines produced here, as long as their natural alcohol content is at least 11.5 percent. Even odder, another rule states that wines made in Montagny-lès-Buxy, Buxy, St. Vallerin, and Jully-lès-Buxy can be labelled as *appellation contrôlée* Montagny, but only wines from the *commune* of Montagny-lès-Buxy itself may have a vineyard name printed on the label. When well made, the rich white wines of Montagny are full of hazelnut and gun-flint flavors. In warm years, however, they tend to flabbiness. Some of the best wines are produced by the Cave de Buxy *coopérative*, which makes some excellent examples, both oaked and unoaked.

ROOFS OF MONTAGNY
Only wines made from grapes grown in the quiet commune of Montagny-lès-Buxy itself may have a vineyard named on the label.

LES LOGES
A quirk of the appellation *system, any* Montagny *wine with at least 11.5 percent alcohol can be labeled as premier cru.*

✺ AC Montagny, AC Montagny Premier Cru.	Joseph Faiveley, Louis Latour, Bernard Michel, Moillard, Antonin Rodet, Ch de la Saule, Jean Vachet.
🍷 White: Chardonnay.	
🍇 Medium- to full-bodied dry whites, increasingly often aged in oak barrels.	🍴 Choux pastry puffs, made with Gruyère or Franche-Comté cheese.
🍇 Maurice Bertrand et François Juillot, Coopérative des Caves de Buxy, Ch de Davenay,	🗓 1998, 1997, 1996, 1995.
	🔀 4–7 years.

MONTHÉLIE

DRIVING THROUGH THE small village of Monthélie toward St. Romain gives you a panoramic view of the vineyards, some of which face due south, while others face northeast. Most of the 11 *premiers crus* vineyards of the *appellation* are situated on the same limestone hillside as those of neighboring Volnay (*see p.137*), producing red wines that, when well made, are rich and ripe with a firm structure and a lingering, silky finish. Although generally considered not as good than those of Volnay, wines from top Monthélie producers, such as Monthélie-Douhairet, often disprove this theory. Village wines, however, are made from grapes grown on the flatter land below, and can be dilute and rustic. Fine white wines from the *premier cru* Les Champs-Fuillot are made by Paul Garaudet and Denis Boussey.

MONTHÉLIE VINEYARDS
The best of the Monthélie vineyards lie on the hillside to the east of the village. Flatter vineyards like these produce more ordinary wines.

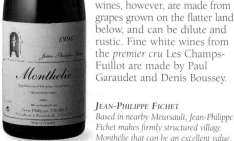

JEAN-PHILIPPE FICHET
Based in nearby Meursault, Jean-Philippe Fichet makes firmly structured village Monthélie that can be an excellent value.

✺ AC Monthélie, AC Monthélie Premier Cru.	Deschamps, Dupont-Fahn, J-P Fichet, Paul Garaudet, Jehan Changarnier, Ch de Monthélie, Monthélie-Douhairet, Pierre Morey.
🍷 Red/ rosé: Pinot Noir. White: Chardonnay	
🍇 Medium-weight, elegant, fruity reds. Medium-weight whites.	🍴 Eggs poached in red wine served with butter-fried bread.
🍇 Denis Boussey, Coche-Dury, Comtes Lafon, Maurice	🗓 1996, 1995, 1993.
	🔀 Red: 3–7 years.

MOREY-ST. DENIS

OFTEN OVERSHADOWED BY THE flair of nearby Vosne-Romanée *(see p.138)* and the opulence of neighboring Gevrey-Chambertin *(see p.120)* and Chambolle-Musigny *(see p 114)*, the Côte de Nuits village of Morey-St. Denis boasts a range of brilliant vineyards and some excellent producers who make some of the most reliable red wines in Burgundy.

GOLDEN HILLSIDE
The five grands crus vineyards of Morey-St. Denis sit between those of Chambolle-Musigny and Gevrey-Chambertin.

THE WINE-MAKING history of Morey-St. Denis is every bit as impressive as that of its illustrious neighbors, Gevrey Chambertin, Chambolle-Musigny, and Vosne-Romanée. Walled vineyards were planted here by monks, and were well regarded as early as the 12th century. Despite this, and despite the presence of several excellent *grands crus* vineyards, the wines of Morey-St. Denis often miss being included among the very best in Burgundy. Until 1927, when the *commune* of Morey took the name of one of its vineyards, the wines made here were often sold under the names of Gevrey-Chambertin or Chambolle-Musigny.

Probably the finest of the *grands crus* vineyards is the large, 42-acre (17-ha) Clos de la Roche. The other *grands crus* vineyards of the *appellation* are Clos de Tart, owned exclusively by the recently-improved merchant firm of Mommessin; Clos des Lambrays, newly promoted to *grand cru* status; Clos St. Denis; and a tiny 4.5-acre (1.84-ha) slice of the Bonnes-Mares vineyard lying mainly in Chambolle-Musigny. The best *premiers crus* vineyards are Clos Sorbé, Les Sorbés, Aux Charmes, Clos des Ormes, La Bussière, and Les Fremières. Outstanding village wines are made by producers including Ponsot, Dujac, Lignier, and Groffier, and all are as good as less well-made *grands crus* wines elsewhere.

Wine writers have always struggled to find the right words to describe the difference between the wines of Morey-St. Denis and its neighbors, often falling back on words like "feminine" and "elegant": for my part, I prefer to describe them as fine late-developers. Much of the unique character of these wines is due to the shallow soil here, which forces the vines to push their roots deep into the limestone beneath.

White wines are a true rarity in Morey-St. Denis, but those made from grapes grown in the stony soil of the *grand cru* Monts Luisants vineyard have unusual, wonderfully mineral flavors and are well worth buying.

CLOS DES LAMBRAYS VINEYARD
This vineyard has recently been elevated to grand cru status, but it remains to be seen whether the wines will justify its promotion.

CHAMPY PÈRE ET CIE
Bottled by the long-established Beaune négociant firm of Champy, this wine comes from the premier cru Clos des Ormes vineyard.

✳️ AC Morey-St. Denis, AC Morey-St. Denis Premier Cru, AC Clos St. Denis Grand Cru, AC Clos de la Roche Grand Cru, AC Bonnes Mares Grand Cru, AC Clos des Lambrays Grand Cru, AC Clos de Tart Grand Cru.	Dujac, Alain Hudelot-Noëllat, des Lambrays, Philippe et Vincent Lecheneaut, Hubert Lignier, Henri Perrot-Minot, Jean-Marie Ponsot, Georges Roumier, Armand Rousseau, Clos de Tart, Ch de la Tour, Tortochot.
🍷 Red: Pinot Noir.	🍴 Entrecôte steak sautéed with butter and mushrooms.
🍂 Earthy reds, tending to rusticity.	📅 1996, 1995, 1993, 1990, 1988, 1985.
🍇 Pierre Amiot, Bertagna, Bryczek et Fils, Champy,	⏲️ Red: 5–20 years.

MORGON

ONE OF THE LARGEST and best-known of the 10 Beaujolais *crus* (*see p.106*), the vineyards of Morgon cover an area centered on the village of Villié-Morgon. Dominating the area is the Mont du Py, which rises to 985 ft (300 m) above the village and is the source of the finest wines of the *appellation*. Made up of thin layers of easily split rock rich in manganese, ferric oxide, and pyrites, or fool's gold, the unique soils of the slopes are known locally as *terre pourrie*, or rotting earth, because of the rapid disintegration of the rock. The grapes grown here produce tightly structured wines with a bouquet of cherries and apricots that often matures perfectly for up to two decades. The flatter vineyards of the *appellation* produce more typical Beaujolais, which, though good, lacks the structure and longevity of wines from the Mont du Py.

CHÂTEAU DE FONCRONNE
This modern stained glass window in the Château de Foncronne shows the wine-growing history of the area.

MARCEL LAPIERRE
With vineyards on the slopes of the Mont du Py, Marcel Lapierre makes wines that are delightfully sturdy and long-lived.

✴ AC Morgon.	Jean Foillard, Gauthier, Dominique Jambon, Marcel Lapierre, Piron, Ch de Raousset, Pierre Savoye, Jacques Trichard.
🍷 Red: Gamay.	
🍇 Some of the most full-bodied, long-lived reds in Beaujolais.	
🍴 Aucoeur, Gerard Brisson, François Calot, de la Chanaise, Louis-Claude Desvignes, Georges Duboeuf (Jean Descombes), Henri Fessy,	🍽 Rib of veal with Dijon mustard, cream and shallots.
	▤ 1997, 1996, 1995, 1994.
	⧖ 4–20 years.

MOULIN-À-VENT

THE APPELLATION OF MOULIN-À-VENT is known as the "King of Beaujolais," thanks to the combination of its age, its size, and the concentrated flavors and the longevity of its wines. Granted *cru* status as early as 1936, Moulin-à-Vent covers more than 1660 acres (670 ha) of acidic, manganese-rich land in the northern part of the Beaujolais district. The manganese in the soil is often credited with giving the wines their rich flavors and deep color, as well as a powerful aroma of flowers and ripe fruits and an unusual capacity for development in the cellar, up to 20 years for the best wines. With a long history of wine making in the area, local rituals are still in evidence, especially after the grape harvest, when the new wine is blessed in the church of Romanèche-Thorins and carried around the town.

MOULIN-À-VENT
The derelict windmill, from which this appellation *takes its name, is one of the most famous landmarks of the region.*

CHÂTEAU DU MOULIN-À-VENT
Classically dark and long-lived wines are produced by the Bloud family at the imposing Château du Moulin-à-Vent.

✴ AC Moulin-à-Vent.	Ch du Moulin-à-Vent, des Perelles, de la Pierre, Benoît Trichard.
🍷 Gamay.	
🍇 Concentrated, deep-colored reds.	🍽 Charcoal-grilled woodcock with a raspberry and blackcurrant sauce.
🍴 Berrod, Jean Briday, Michel Brugne, Georges Duboeuf, Gay-Coperet, Guérin, Ch des Jacques, Paul Janin, Hubert Lapierre, du Matinal,	▤ 1998, 1997, 1996, 1995, 1993.
	⧖ 4–8 years.

NUITS-ST. GEORGES

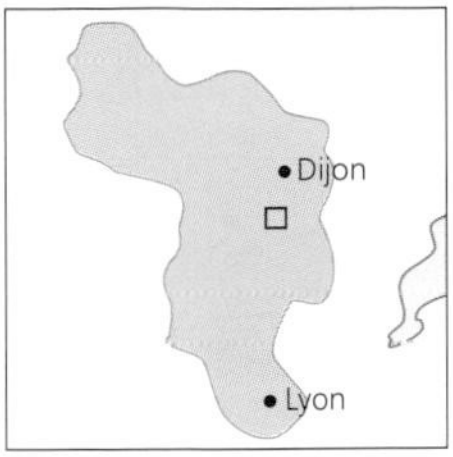

TOUGH AND TANNIC WHEN first made, the magnificent red wines of Nuits-St. Georges are some of the most misunderstood in Burgundy. More austere when young than the wines of neighboring *appellations* such as Vosne-Romanée *(see p.138)*, the sumptuous blackcurrant and game flavors of these wines often take as long as 20 years to reach their peak.

CHÂTEAU GRIS
Overlooking its namesake vineyard, one of the best in Nuits-St. Georges, Château Gris can be clearly seen from the autoroute *running below and is a well-known landmark of the* appellation.

SITE OF A GALLO-ROMAN villa and home during the Middle Ages to a monastic winery, the attractive town of Nuits-St.Georges lies at the heart of this *appellation*, toward the southern tip of the Côte de Nuits. Sandwiched between the larger centers of Beaune and Dijon, sleepy Nuits-St. Georges feels very much like a place that is driven around and not through. Despite this, several of the region's most successful *négociants*, including Boisset, Faiveley, and Labouré-Roi, have their cellars and headquarters here.

As in Beaune to the north *(see pp.108–9)*, there are, surprisingly, no *grands crus* vineyards in Nuits-St. Georges. The *appellation* does, however, boast more than 30 excellent *premiers crus* vineyards, many of which produce exciting wines that regularly outclass those from *grands crus* vineyards nearby. Reflecting the various different soil types of the *appellation*, the character of a *premier cru* wine from Nuits-St. Georges depends very much on the location of its vineyard. The stony soils to the south of the town are home to *premiers crus* vineyards including Les Cailles, Les St. Georges and Les Vaucrains, all of which produce classic, full-bodied wines with lots of tannin. To the south, around the village of Prémeaux-Prissey on the edge of the *appellation*, are the vineyards of Clos de la Maréchale and Clos Arlot, whose perfectly made wines are the richest in Nuits-St. Georges. Softer and more immediately seductive are wines from *premiers crus* vineyards to the north of the *appellation* such as Aux Boudots and Aux Murgers on the boundary with Vosne-Romanée *(see p.138)*.

While arguing over their favorite vineyards, devotees agree that the best wines here share a tight structure and deep, gamey blackcurrant flavors. Although softening beautifully after a few years in the cellar, these wines can be austere in their youth, when they are often mixed with flavorings, including the local blackcurrant liqueur.

HOSPICES DE NUITS
The charitable Hospices de Nuits raises money by auctioning the wines from its estate. Sold young, wines can be aged by the buyer.

DOMAINE DE L'ARLOT
Recently created, this estate in the south of the appellation *produces wines that are rich, modern, and impeccably made.*

- AC Nuits-St Georges, AC Nuits-St Georges Premier Cru.
- Red: Pinot Noir. White: Chardonnay.
- Full-bodied, even chunky reds.
- De l'Arlot, Robert Arnoux, Bertagna, Lucien Boillot, Robert Chevillon, Georges Chicotot, A Chopin, Jean-Jacques Confuron, R Dubois, Faiveley, Forey, Henri Gouges, Jean Grivot, Jayer-Gilles, Laurent, Philippe et Vincent Lecheneaut, Machard de Gramont, Alain Michelot, Mugneret-Gibourg, Leroy, des Perdrix, Pernin Rossin, Prieuré Roch, Henri et Gilles Remoriquet, Daniel Rion, Thomas-Moillard, Fabrice Vigot.
- Saddle of hare cooked with red wine and wild mushrooms.
- 1996, 1995, 1993, 1990, 1988, 1985.
- Red: 5–20 years.

PERNAND-VERGELESSES

WHAT'S IN A NAME? If the *grand cru* vineyard of Corton-Charlemagne, shared between the *appellations* of Aloxe-Corton (*see p.104*), Ladoix-Serrigny (*see p.122*), and Pernand-Vergelesses, were called Pernand-Charlemagne, I suspect the other wines of this picturesque hillside *commune* might be better known and more expensive. How many of the wines would justify their higher prices is less certain. The reds are pleasant and softly jammy, but often short of finesse and complexity. The whites, despite a tendency to thinness in cooler years, are better than the reds, with crisp, well-defined fruit and delicate flavors. Wines from the *premiers crus* vineyards of Les Vergelesses, Île des Vergelesses, and Les Fichots are a good buy, and worth cellaring for five years or so before drinking.

ROLLIN PÈRE ET FILS
This village white from reliable producer Rollin Père et Fils is likely to offer very good value.

ÎLE DES VERGELESSES
Although relatively little-known, this premier cru vineyard has given its name to both the village and the appellation.

✳	AC Pernand-Vergelesses, AC Pernand-Vergelesses Premier Cru.	Chandon de Briailles, Delarche, Joseph Drouhin, Dubreuil-Fontaine, Germain, Antonin Guyon, Laleure-Piot, Louis Latour, Pavelot, Rapet, Rollin.
🍇	Red: Pinot Noir. White: Chardonnay.	
🍷	Medium-weight, elegant reds. Crisp, appley, herbal whites.	🍴 Smoked goose fillets.
🍴	Arnoux, Bonneau de Martray, Camille-Giroud, Champy,	📅 1996, 1995, 1993.
		🕐 Red: 4–8 years. White: 2–5 years.

THE DOUBLE-BARRELED NAMES OF THE CÔTE D'OR

Many of the villages of the Côte de Beaune and the Côte de Nuits carry names that are "double-barreled." The fashion for hyphenated names swept the area during the 1860s, as canny producers realized that, while wines from named vineyards such as Le Corton, Le Chambertin, Le Musigny, and Le Montrachet were famous and easy to sell, those from neighboring vineyards were not. As a result, many villages, including Gevrey, Aloxe, Chambolle, Puligny, Pernand, and Chassagne, simply adopted the name of their best-known vineyards, giving them names such as Gevrey-Chambertin, Aloxe-Corton, and Chambolle-Musigny. Some already-famous *communes*, including Beaune, Volnay, Pommard, and Meursault, needed no such help, while others, like Fixin and Monthélie, had no

WRIT LARGE
Few wine drinkers can now forget that Musigny is the best vineyard in the commune of Chambolle.

famous vineyard to call on. The *communes* of Chorey and Savigny cleverly added the words "lès Beaune" (near Beaune) to their names. The name game has worked well for most but not all. The village of Ladoix (*see p.122*), for example, has arguably gained little by adding the Serrigny vineyard to its name.

Like their villages, the producers of the Côte d'Or often sport double-barreled names, such as Coche-Dury, Coche-Débord, and Millaut-Battault, a result of the laws of equal inheritance that became part of French law in the early 19th century. If, for example, Jean Dupont and his sister Marie were to marry their neighbors Hélène and Jacques Durand, their newly combined estates would be called Domaine Dupont-Durand and Domaine Durand-Dupont.

PERNAND-VERGELESSES
The successful marketing ploy of joining a prestigious vineyard to the original village name is a popular Côte d'Or phenomenon.

POMMARD

DESPITE POMMARD'S POSITION, between Beaune (*see p.108*) and Volnay (*see p.137*), its wines bear little resemblance to the light, delicate wines of either of those two *appellations*. Instead, these powerful red offerings are among the richest and most tannic in Burgundy. Although inaccessible in their youth, these wines are definitely worth waiting for.

DOMAINE MUSSY
Typical of the appellation, the powerful premiers crus wines of Domaine Mussy need at least five years to soften in the bottle before drinking.

A FEW KILOMETERS TO the south of Beaune, the small village of Pommard has a long history of prosperity and international fame, selling its wines on both sides of the Atlantic Ocean since the 18th century. In recent years, a combination of fame and easy pronunciation has helped to make the wines of Pommard some of the most saleable in the Côte d'Or, especially in the United States. Perhaps inevitably, laziness and greed have taken their toll here, too, often prompting growers and merchants to collude in turning a blind eye to poor wine making and fraud of all sorts. One of the most notorious malpractices has been the regular use of grapes grown in humble *appellation contrôlée* Bourgogne vineyards to make wines sold as *appellation contrôlée* Pommard. A partial explanation for the frequent adulteration here lies in the character of the wines themselves. As Lalou Bize-Leroy, possessor of one of the keenest palates in Burgundy, once famously said, the wines of Pommard are rather like its church: solid, square and, on first impression, less than inviting. Like the wines of nearby Aloxe-Corton (*see p.104*), these are wines with significant amounts of tannin, and definitely need cellaring. Adding so-called inferior grapes to the mixture has often made Pommard much easier to sell young.

Recent years have seen great improvements here, and good Pommard, although still not as drinkable in its youth as the wines of Volnay or Beaune, is as good when mature as the best of both those *communes*. Without doubt, the top vineyard here is Les Rugiens, but look out too for fine wines from Les Fremiers, Les Arvelets, En Largillière, Les Epenots, and Les Chanlins.

TENDING THE VINES
The early spring task of pruning is taking place here in the vineyards of the attractive Château de Pommard, a 50-acre (20-ha) walled estate on flat land to the southeast of the village.

JEAN LOUIS LAPLANCHE
Velvety and lush, the wines of the Château de Pommard are only sold at the estate.

COMTE ARMAND
Fine village and premiers crus wines are made on this renowned estate.

✴	AC Pommard, AC Pommard Premier Cru
▥	Red: Pinot Noir
▨	Full-bodied, broad wines with prominent black cherry flavors.
▥	Albert-Grivault, Ampeau, Comte Armand, J-M Boillot, Pascal Bouley, Champy, Coste-Caumartin, de Courcel, Paul Garaudet, Michel Gaunoux, Germain Père et Fils, Vincent Girardin, Bernard & Louis Glantenay,

Raymond Launay, Olivier Leflaive, Lejeune, Leroy, Aleth Leroyer-Girardin, de Montille, Pierre Morey, Mussy, Parent, Ch de Pommard, Pothier-Rieusset, Pousse d'Or, Rebourgeon Mure, Virely-Rougeot.

🍴 Wild boar with a red wine and cherry sauce.

🗓 1996, 1995, 1993, 1990, 1988, 1985.

⏳ 5–15 years.

POUILLY-FUISSÉ AND ITS SATELLITES

PART OF THE HUGE white wine-producing district of the Mâconnais, the *appellation* of Pouilly-Fuissé produces six million bottles of white wine every year. Made entirely with the Chardonnay grape and varying in quality from the basic to the sublime, the wines of Pouilly-Fuissé are undoubtedly some of the most famous white Burgundies in the world.

PREHISTORIC HUNTING GROUND
Land around the base of the Rock of Solutré, which towers over the tiny hamlet of Pouilly, is littered with the bones of prehistoric animals.

SURROUNDED BY CHARDONNAY vines at the base of the ancient Rock of Solutré, is the hamlet of Pouilly, which, together with the village of Fuissé to the east, gives its name to the *appellation* of Pouilly-Fuissé. A large *appellation* extending over four *communes,* the wines sold as Pouilly-Fuissé fall into two camps. First, there is the fresh, light but frankly dull Pouilly-Fuissé on offer in supermarkets and liquor stores around the world, which is practically indistinguishable from the far less expensive Mâcon-Villages (*see p.123*) produced to the north of Pouilly-Fuissé. Second, and much more important, there is the gloriously complex and long-lived Pouilly-Fuissé made by talented producers such as Vincent et Fils of Château Fuissé, J A Ferret, and Jean-Marie Guffens, which regularly puts to shame many a wine from other Burgundy *appellations,* such as Meursault (*see p.125*) and Puligny-Montrachet (*see p.133*).

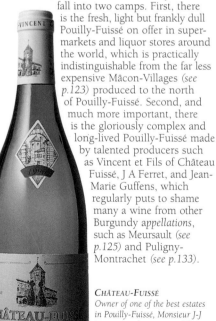

CHÂTEAU-FUISSÉ
Owner of one of the best estates in Pouilly-Fuissé, Monsieur J-J Vincent produces some of the very best of the area's wines. His vieilles vignes cuvée is as good as many of the greatest white wines in Burgundy.

Differing soils obviously have a part to play in the variable quality of the wines of Pouilly-Fuissé, with the fullest-flavored wines coming from the vineyards around the villages of Vergisson to the northwest and Fuissé to the southeast, in contrast to more complex wines made from grapes grown in the area around Pouilly in the center of the *appellation*. Much more significant than variations in the soil, however, is the care and skill of the wine growers, and of the producers at the large wine-making *coopératives* that make a high proportion of the wine here. For this reason it is essential to buy your Pouilly-Fuissé from a good producer or *négociant*. Failing this, it is not worth buying at all.

The *commune* of Pouilly adds its name to two small satellite *appellations* to the east of Pouilly-Fuissé, Pouilly-Vinzelles and Pouilly-Loché. The wines produced here are said to be lighter and simpler than those of Pouilly-Fuissé, though considering the featherweight character of many examples of Pouilly-Fuissé, this seems an unlikely claim. Wines produced at the Cave des Grands Crus Blanc in Vinzelles, however, are proof of just how good these wines can be.

VILLAGE CHURCH AT FUISSÉ
Two separate villages, Pouilly and Fuissé, give their names to the appellation of Pouilly-Fuissé. Most of the producers' cellars are to be found in the larger village of Fuissé.

* ✴ AC Pouilly-Fuissé, AC Mâcon-Chaintre, AC Mâcon-Fuissé, AC Mâcon-Solutré, AC Mâcon-Vergisson.

* 🍇 White: Chardonnay.

* 🍷 Medium- to full-bodied dry whites, some of which are aged in oak barrels.

* 🏛 Auvigue, Daniel et Martine Barraud, Cordier, Corsin, Michel Delorme, Joseph Drouhin, Georges Duboeuf, Dupond d'Halluin, Ferret, Ch de Fuissé, des Gerbeaux, René Guérin, Guffens-Heynen, Louis Jadot, Roger Lassarat, Noblet, Robert-Denogent, Jacques et Nathalie Saumaize, Saumaize-Michelin, Simonin, La Soufrandise, Valette, Verget.

* 🍴 Skate wings baked in the oven with cheese, lemon juice, and breadcrumbs.

* 🗄 1997, 1996, 1995.

* ⏳ White: 3–6 years.

PULIGNY-MONTRACHET

OF ALL THE WHITE WINES in Burgundy, none are more sought after than those of Puligny-Montrachet in the Côte de Beaune. Flourishing in the pebbly limestone soils of Puligny-Montrachet, the Chardonnay vine is king here and this small *appellation* of gently sloping vineyards is home to four of the greatest dry white *grands crus* in the world.

VALUABLE VINES
The Chardonnay vineyards of Puligny-Montrachet are some of the most valuable in the world. Often, the entire vintage is sold in advance, even before the grapes are harvested.

DESPITE THE FACT THAT this was one of the first parts of Burgundy to be planted with vines, the potential of Puligny-Montrachet's finest *terroir* was not recognized until relatively recently. Records show that, early in the 17th century, part of Le Montrachet, now considered the very best of Puligny's *grands crus* vineyards, was sold for an unusually low price, since at this time the wines of Le Montrachet enjoyed only a lowly reputation.

LOUIS CARILLON
Making good, but not too excessive, use of new oak barrels, Louis Carillon is one of the rising talents of Puligny-Montrachet.

Confusion often arises over the differences between the wines of Puligny-Montrachet and those of its neighbor, Chassagne-Montrachet *(see p.115)* to the south. Even though the two *appellations* share some of their best *grand cru* land, many of the respective wines they produce are, in fact, quite different. The primary difference is that only a tiny proportion of the wine produced in Puligny-Montrachet is red, as compared to nearly half of that from Chassagne-Montrachet. Both the white village wines and the white *premiers crus* wines of Puligny-Montrachet are considered, at their best, to be finer than the white wines of Chassagne-Montrachet, with the best parts of the shared *grands crus* vineyards of Bâtard-Montrachet and Le Montrachet falling in Puligny.

A number of France's greatest growers, *négociants*, and producers own vines and wineries in Puligny-Montrachet, including Olivier Leflaive at Domaine Leflaive and Louis Jadot at the Domaine du Duc de Magenta. Despite this, enormous international demand has encouraged the sale of substandard and overpriced wine. Wines from Puligny's four *grands crus* vineyards, however, are generally a good buy, especially when made by a recommended producer, as are wines from many of the *premiers crus* vineyards, including Le Cailleret, Champ Canet, Les Pucelles, and Les Chalumeaux.

DOMAINE LEFLAIVE
Pioneering the use of bio-dynamic wine-making methods on this prestigious estate, Vincent Leflaive's daughter, Anne, now produces even better wine than her famous father.

✳ AC Puligny-Montrachet, AC Puligny-Montrachet Côte de Beaune, AC Puligny-Montrachet Premier Cru, AC Bâtard-Montrachet Grand Cru, Bienvenues-Bâtard-Montrachet Grand Cru, AC Chevalier-Montrachet Grand Cru, AC Montrachet Grand Cru.	Chartron et Trébuchet, Henri Clerc, Coche-Dury, Joseph Drouhin, Louis Jadot, Louis Latour, Leflaive, Olivier Leflaive, Duc de Magenta, Maraslovac-Leger, Matrot, Marc Morey, Pascal, Jacques Prieur, Ch de Puligny-Montrachet, Sauzet.
🌷 White: Chardonnay.	🍴 Pan-fried salmon steaks.
🥂 Elegant, steely whites.	🗄 1996, 1995, 1992, 1990, 1989, 1988, 1986, 1985.
🍶 Guy Amiot, D'Auvenay, J-M Boillot, Louis Carillon,	🥂 White: 4–14 years.

RÉGNIÉ

THE *COMMUNE* OF RÉGNIÉ, or Régnié-Durette to give it its full name, became the 10th of the Beaujolais *crus* in December 1988. There are two styles of wine made here, one light and fragrant, the other full-bodied and well-structured. Most common, though, are wines for early drinking with vibrant, well-defined fruit flavors. After a slightly shaky start, when questions were asked about how deserving it was of promotion, this *appellation* is now building a good reputation for itself, thanks to the efforts of a number of committed producers.

* AC Régnié.
* Red: Gamay.
* Light- to medium-weight, fruity reds.
* Noël Aucoeur, René Desplace, Dominique Piron, de Ponchon, Joël Rochette, Georges et Gilles Roux.
* Honey-roast ham.
* 1998, 1997, 1996, 1995.
* 2–4 years.

DOMAINE AUCOEUR
Based in neighboring Villié-Morgon, Noël Aucoeur makes Régnié wines that are supple and richly flavored.

RULLY

MOST NORTHERLY of the Côte Chalonnaise *appellations*, the red wines of Rully often remind me of those from Côte de Beaune *appellations* such as Volnay (*see p.137*). Sparkling white wines are sold under the Crémant de Bourgogne *appellation*, and can be some of the best in Burgundy. Still white wines are fresh, and appley, while reds are medium-bodied, with wild raspberry and violet aromas. Twenty five *premiers crus* vineyards produce red and white wines with greater complexity and aging potential than the village wines.

* AC Rully, AC Rully Premier Cru.
* Red: Pinot Noir. White: Chardonnay.
* Elegant, well-structured reds. Oak-aged dry whites.
* Delorme, Joseph Drouhin, Dureuil-Janthial, Dury.
* Red: Eggs poached in wine.
* Red: 1997, 1996, 1995.
* Red: 3–5 years. White: 2–5 years.

JACQUES DURY
This producer makes classic, appley white Burgundy that competes with Côte d'Or wines.

ST. AMOUR

DESPITE THE POPULARITY of this wine on St. Valentine's Day, the *"amour"* in question is in fact St. Amator, a martyred Roman soldier turned Christian, whose statue now stands in the village of St. Amour-Bellevue. The most northerly of the Beaujolais *crus*, St. Amour, geologically speaking, is an area of transition, straddling the granite of Beaujolais to the south and the limestone of the Mâconnais to the north. As a result of the mixed limestone and granite-based gravel soils, the wines of St. Amour include some of the lightest and most supple reds of the region, many of them more in the style of the Mâconnais (*see p.123*) than the rest of Beaujolais. For a taste of the landscape as well as the wines, the hillside hamlet of Plâtre-Durand, with a tasting room in the Caveau du Cru St. Amour, is worth a visit.

ANDRÉ POITEVIN
A fine, juicy example with the perfumed, yet far from lightweight, character typical of the best of St. Amour's wines.

LOVELY SPOT
The unique combination of subsoils beneath the vines here is responsible for the delicate style of the best wines of this commune.

* AC St. Amour.
* Red: Gamay.
* Soft, plump, fruity reds, usually best for early drinking.
* Des Billards, Georges Duboeuf, Jean-Paul Ducoté, des Ducs, Henry Fessy, Janin, Patissier, du Plateau de Bel-Air, André Poitevin, Revillon, Michel Tête, Georges Trichard.
* Traditionally made coarse-cut pork sausage stewed with Beaujolais, garlic, onions, shallots, and wild mushrooms.
* 1998, 1996, 1995, 1993.
* Red: 2–4 years.

St. Aubin

NORTH OF THE RED AND WHITE wine-producing *appellation* of Chassagne-Montrachet (*see p.115*), and east of the world-famous white wine vineyards of Puligny-Montrachet (*see p.133*), is the Côte de Beaune *commune* of St. Aubin. There are 570 acres (230 ha) of vineyards here, just over half of which are planted with Chardonnay and Pinot Blanc vines. Many of the 29 *premiers crus* vineyards of the *appellation* also produce whites, with the best including Les Murgers des Dents de Chien and En Remilly. At their best, these hazelnut-tinged wines easily outclass many of the wines of Puligny-Montrachet. With ripe, wild strawberry fruit and a little more complexity than the village wines, *premier cru* red wines can offer good value here; but, unlike the whites, they rarely shake off their essentially rustic character.

HIDDEN TREASURE
Tucked away in the hills, St. Aubin is often unjustly overlooked by visitors drawn by the fame of the nearby villages of Puligny-Montrachet and Meursault.

ROUX PÈRE ET FILS
This is a rich, buttery, nutty wine that is every bit as good as many pricier ones from nearby Puligny-Montrachet

✴ AC St. Aubin, AC St. Aubin Premier Cru.	Lamy-Monnot, Olivier Leflaive, Henri Prudhon, Ch de Puligny-Montrachet, Roux Père et Fils, Thomas.
🍷 Red: Pinot Noir. White: Chardonnay, Pinot Blanc.	
🍽 Medium-weight, supple reds. Crisp medium-weight whites, some of which are aged in oak.	🍴 White: Puffs of flaky pastry filled with snails, garlic, and cep mushrooms.
🍇 Jean-Claude Bachelet, Champy, Marc Colin, Hubert	▤ White: 1996, 1995, 1993.
	⚡ White: 3–8 years.

St. Romain

AT AN ALTITUDE of around 1150 ft (350 m), St. Romain is almost Hautes-Côtes de Beaune territory (*see p.121*), with cool conditions that are often unfavorable for ripening grapes. Red wines here are pleasant but rustic. Whites, however, are fresh, minerally, and unoaked, perfect for those who wish to avoid the modern oaky style popular in *appellations* such as nearby Puligny-Montrachet (*see p.133*). In an ironic twist, thanks to the legendary cooper Jean François, St. Romain is best known as the exporter of some of the best oak barrels in the world!

✴ AC St. Romain.	**CHRISTOPHE BUISSON**
🍷 Red: Pinot Noir. White: Chardonnay.	*This is refreshing, minerally wine with a hazelnut richness.*
🍽 Light, soft, fruity reds. Crisp, racy whites.	
🍇 Christophe Buisson, Chassorney, Germain et Fils, Alain Gras, Thevenin-Monthélie.	
🍴 White: Frogs' legs.	
▤ White: 1998, 1997, 1995.	
⚡ White: 3–5 years.	

St. Véran

CREATED IN 1971, this *appellation* lies in both Beaujolais and the Mâconnais, covering white wines from the seven villages of Davayé and Prissé to the north of Pouilly-Fuissé (*see p.132*), and Chânes, Chasselas, Leynes, St. Amour, and St. Vérand to the south. The soil here is limestone and the grape variety is the Chardonnay, producing wines that combine richness with a slight mineral edge. A number of talented and ambitious producers with estates here means that the wines of St. Véran can often offer some of the best value in the region.

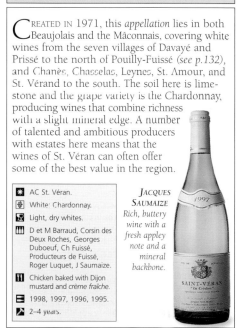

✴ AC St. Véran.	**JACQUES SAUMAIZE**
🍷 White: Chardonnay.	*Rich, buttery wine with a fresh appley note and a mineral backbone.*
🍽 Light, dry whites.	
🍇 D et M Barraud, Corsin des Deux Roches, Georges Duboeuf, Ch Fuissé, Producteurs de Fuissé, Roger Luquet, J Saumaize.	
🍴 Chicken baked with Dijon mustard and *crème fraîche*.	
▤ 1998, 1997, 1996, 1995.	
⚡ 2–4 years.	

SANTENAY

FAMOUS SINCE ROMAN times for its lithium-rich spa waters, Santenay is one of the most southerly wine villages in the Côte de Beaune. White Santenay is worth buying if you come across it, but all but two percent of the wines made here are red, falling into two basic styles. Wines from AC Santenay vineyards around and to the south of the village are full-bodied and earthy, while those from the 14 *premiers crus* vineyards at the northern end of the *appellation* are light and elegant, similar in style to the wines of Beaune (*see pp.108–9*).

✳	AC Santenay, AC Santenay Premier Cru.
⬡	Red: Pinot Noir.
🍷	Earthy, rustic reds.
⫿	Adrien Belland, Fernand Chevrot, Marc Colin, Vincent Girardin, Olivier Leflaive, Nouveau, Pousse d'Or, Prieur-Brunet.
🍴	Shoulder of Lamb.
▤	Red: 1996, 1995, 1993.
⏲	Red: 3–12 years.

ADRIEN BELLAND Producer of elegant wines, the grapes used here come from some of the finest vineyards in Santenay.

SAUVIGNON DE ST. BRIS

ONE OF THE MYSTERIES of the world of French wine is why these characterful white wines from the north of Burgundy are entitled to no more than the *VDQS* classification. The 150 acres (60 ha) of vines lie in the *département* of Yonne, to the southwest of the town of Chablis (*see pp.112–13*). Producers here use the Sauvignon grape, rather than the Chardonnay of Chablis, to make crisp, dry wines with herbaceous, smoky flavors similar to those of Sancerre, a further 60 miles (100 km) to the southwest.

✳	VDQS Sauvignon de St Bris.
⬡	Sauvignon Blanc.
🍷	Light, crisp, fruity dry whites.
⫿	Jean-Marc Brocard, la Chablisienne, Joel et David Griffe, St Prix, Sorin-Defrance.
🍴	Crayfish
▤	1998, 1997, 1996.
⏲	1–3 years.

JEAN-MARC BROCARD Despite their lowly VDQS status, J-M Brocard's wines are very often compared to those of Sancerre.

SAVIGNY-LÈS-BEAUNE

TUCKED AWAY IN THE VALLEY of the tiny Rhoin river, the *appellation* of Savigny-lès-Beaune includes 950 acres (385 ha) of vines, centered around the village of Savigny-lès-Beaune. From the east of the *appellation* come wines that are well structured but slightly rustic, while wines from vineyards to the north, closer to Pernand-Vergelesses (*see p.130*), are softer, with creamy fruit flavors. Hillside vineyards in this area make up the *appellation's* 22 *premiers crus*, while AC Savigny-lès-Beaune wines come from the flatter land in between. Around 90 percent of the wine produced here is red, but some white is also made, often, unusually in the Chardonnay-loving Côte de Beaune, using a proportion of the Pinot Blanc grape with its easily recognizable flavors of cream and brazil nuts.

SIMON BIZE This estate produces wines that are unusually long-lived, aging them in its cellars opposite the Château de Savigny.

VARIED VINEYARDS The vineyards of Savigny-lès-Beaune are among the most varied in the region. The best, which include Aux Vergelesses and Les Lavières, are as good as many premiers crus in neighboring Beaune.

✳	AC Savigny-lès-Beaune, AC Savigny-lès-Beaune Premier Cru.
⬡	Red: Pinot Noir. White: Pinot Blanc, Chardonnay.
🍷	Elegant, medium-weight reds. Light, spicy whites.
⫿	Arnoux, Bitouzet, Bize, Champy, Chandon de Briailles, Bruno Clair, Girard-Voillot, Joseph Drouhin, Dubreuil-Fontaine, Maurice Ecard, Pavelot, Tollot-Beaut.
🍴	Fillet of duck
▤	Red: 1998, 1996, 1995, 1993.
⏲	Red: 6 years. White: 2–3 years.

VOLNAY

Every lover of the wines of Burgundy has a favorite red wine from the region. Many would probably choose one of the prestigious names of the Côte de Nuits; but my own *appellation* of choice is Volnay, whose uniquely-perfumed blend of violets, raspberries, and ripe plums has always struck me as both ethereal and utterly seductive.

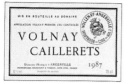

MARQUIS D'ANGERVILLE
Rich and cherry-flavored, this wine was produced by the Marquis d'Angerville, whose father was one of the founders of the appellation contrôlée *system.*

S ITUATED BETWEEN POMMARD and Meursault, the prosperous hillside village of Volnay was famous as early as the 17th century for a pale and delicate red wine known as *vin paillé* or "strawed wine." The wine was made from grapes pressed between straw lattices and fermented with very little maceration (contact between the fermenting juice and the grape skins). According to the cleric-author of *La Situation de la Bourgogne*, writing in 1728, "the grapes of this *terroir* can be left only a short time in the fermenting vat. If they are left there a

moment longer than necessary, the wine will lose its delicacy...". Modern Volnay is longer-lived than I would imagine the briefly-macerated earlier wines to have been, but much of it remains delicate and gloriously approachable in its youth.

During the early part of the 20th century, the Volnay name was regularly used by unscrupulous merchants to sell wines made from grapes grown as far away as southern France and Algeria. One Volnay estate-owner, the Marquis d'Angerville, responded by helping to lay the foundations of the *appellation contrôlée* system, leading, in 1932, to the establishment of the *Institut National des Appellations d'Origine*.

Appropriately, the talents of a number of excellent producers, including the son of the Marquis d'Angerville mentioned above, have now helped to make Volnay one of the most reliable *appellations* in the region. Other factors contributing to the reliability of Volnay's wines, as well as their smoothness and fragrance, include the shallow, chalky soil and the southeastern exposure of the vineyards. Although there are no *grands crus* here, more than half of the vineyards are *premiers crus*, the most impressive of which include Taille Pieds, Les Caillerets, Clos des Ducs, Clos des Chênes and Bousse d'Or. Volnay is predominantly a red wine *appellation* and the tiny amount of white wine produced here is sold as AC Meursault (*see p.125*).

MICHEL LAFARGE
A superb Volnay producer, Michel Lafarge makes wines that manage to combine richness, perfume, and purity.

SLEEPY STREETS
Tucked away high in the hills above the route nationale *and looking down over* premiers crus *vineyards, the picturesque village of Volnay has a quiet but distinctly prosperous air.*

✱	AC Volnay, AC Volnay Premier Cru.
🍷	Red: Pinot Noir.
🍇	Elegant, velvet-textured wines with red berry flavors.
▥	Marquis d'Angerville, Roger Bellend, Boigelot, J-M Boillot, Lucien Boillot, Bouchard Père et Fils, Pascal Bouley, Caillot, Camille Giroud, Champy, Coche-Dury, Joseph Drouhin, Génot-Boulanger, Vincent

Girardin, Jaffelin, Michel Lafarge, Comtes Lafon, Olivier Leflaive, Leroy, de Montille, Fernand et Laurent Pillot, Prieur-Brunet, Pousse d'Or, Rebourgeon Mure, Régis Rossignol-Changarnier, Vaudoisey, Voillot.

🍖 Roast saddle of hare.

⊟ 1998, 1997, 1996, 1995, 1993, 1990, 1988, 1985.

🍷 Red: 3–18 years.

VOSNE-ROMANÉE

THE ENTIRE CÔTE D'OR REGION can be compared to a golden crown full of precious jewels; but if one village is to be chosen as the most exotic of all its gems, then it has to be Vosne-Romanée. The most southerly of the Côte de Nuits villages, Vosne-Romanée is home to some of the most prestigious vineyards in Burgundy and produces stylish red wines.

CLOS DES RÉAS
The premier cru Clos des Réas vineyard is owned by a branch of the famous wine-making Gros family, producing rich, perfumed wines that represent an excellent value.

ONE 18TH-CENTURY source states that the village of Vosne-Romanée produced *"pas de vin commun,"* or "no wine of ordinary quality." Today, this *appellation* is still unusual in producing red wines of almost uniformly high quality, and you are far less likely to be disappointed by even the most basic wines of Vosne-Romanée than by corresponding wines from more variable Côte de Nuits *appellations* such as Gevrey-Chambertin *(see p.120)* or Nuits-St. Georges *(see p.129).*

The *appellation* of Vosne-Romanée includes a range of brilliant *premiers crus* and *grands crus* vineyards. The finest, or at least the most expensive, of the *grands crus* is the 4.4 acre- (1.8 ha-) plot known as La Romanée-Conti. Taking its name from Roman remains unearthed here and from its 18th-century owner, the Prince de Conti, La Romanée-Conti is now part of the world-famous Domaine de la Romanée-Conti (known to initiates as the DRC), which also includes the neighboring La Tâche vineyard. The wines produced here are extraordinarily rich, stuffed with plums and with more than a hint of spice. Other great *grands crus* vineyards here include La Romanée, owned by the *négociant*-producer firm Bouchard Père et Fils, Romanée-St. Vivant, Richebourg, and the recently

promoted but so far disappointing La Grande Rue.

Among the best of the 17 *premiers crus* vineyards of the *appellation* are Les Beaux Monts, Les Brûlées, Les Chaumes, Aux Malconsorts, Les Suchots, Clos des Réas, and Cros-Parantoux. In an area blessed with more than its fair share of excellent producers, those at the Domaine de la Romanée-Conti compete with other great wine makers including Lalou Bize-Leroy of Domaine Leroy, René Engel, Anne Gros, and Jean-Nicolas Méo of Domaine Méo-Camuzet.

Just beyond the northern boundary of the *appellation* are the *grands crus* vineyards of Echézeaux and Les Grands Echézeaux. Belonging to the nearby village of Flagey-Echézeaux, the wines here are similar to some of the best wines of Vosne-Romanée, though rarely quite as rich and complex.

DIVINE INTERVENTION
This much-visited crucifix stands close to the tiny grand cru vineyard of La Romanée-Conti, the source of some of the best, and most expensive, red wines in Burgundy.

LALOU BIZE-LEROY
Once a partner in the Domaine de la Romanée-Conti, Lalou Bize-Leroy now makes impeccable wines from her own organic vineyards nearby.

✳️	AC Vosne-Romanée, AC Vosne-Romanée Premier Cru, AC Richebourg Grand Cru, AC La Romanée Grand Cru, AC La Tâche Grand Cru, AC Romanée-St Vivant Grand Cru, AC Romanée-Conti Grand Cru, AC La Grande Rue Grand Cru.
🍇	Red: Pinot Noir.
🍷	Elegant, velvety reds.
🏛	Arnoux, Bouchard Père et Fils, Cacheux, Confuron-Cotédiot, Joseph Drouhin, Engel, Faiveley,
	Forey, François Gerbet, Jean Grivot, Anne Gros, Jayer-Gilles, Leroy, Méo-Camuzet, Mongeard-Mugneret, Mugneret-Gibourg, des Perdrix, Pernin-Rossin, Jaques Prieur, Prieuré-Roch, Rion, Romanée-Conti, Romaneé-St Vivant, Rouget, Jean Tardy, Thomas-Moillard.
🍴	Coq au vin.
📅	1996, 1995, 1993, 1990, 1988, 1985.
🍷	Red: 5–20 years.

OTHERS

ALONGSIDE THE CLASSIC PINOT NOIR and Chardonnay wines of Burgundy, a surprisingly wide range of lesser-known wine is also produced. Rarely seen at present outside their area of origin, many of these wines deserve to be much better known. One such is the distinctive Bourgogne Aligoté Bouzeron, made around the Côte Chalonnaise village of Bouzeron.

UNUSUAL IRANCY
Light, with raspberry fruit flavors, the little-known red wines of Irancy are made from a mixture of Pinot Noir and César grapes, and can be deliciously refreshing.

MENTION THE ALIGOTÉ grape to a wine enthusiast and he or she will probably think of Kir, the blend of white wine and blackcurrant liqueur invented by Canon Kir, one-time mayor of Dijon. Taste most Aligoté wines in their unadulterated form and you will have no difficulty in understanding why the good cleric decided to sweeten his. Although attractively fresh and appley at their best, these wines are very often savagely acidic. Notable exceptions to the tooth-stripping Aligoté rule are wines made from grapes grown around the village of Bouzeron in the Côte Chalonnaise. Here the grape performs well enough to have been awarded its own *appellation*, Bourgogne Aligoté Bouzeron, soon to be renamed more simply as *appellation contrôlée* Bouzeron.

Passetoutgrains was once the name of the most popular everyday red wine in Burgundy, made, as the name suggests, from a mixture of any grape varieties at hand. Its successor, the Bourgogne

Passetoutgrains *appellation*, has now evolved into a traditional blend of Gamay and Pinot Noir grapes. The officially sanctioned grape ratio is two parts Gamay to one part Pinot Noir, though many producers quietly admit that they prefer to use rather more of the Pinot Noir. Good examples of Bourgogne Passetoutgrains are produced at a surprising number of top estates and, full of interesting cherry and raspberry flavors, can be drunk as alternatives to cru Beaujolais (see pp.106–7).

Crémant de Bourgogne is Burgundy's generic white and rosé sparkling wine *appellation*. An increase in permitted grape varieties to include the Pinot Noir, the Chardonnay, and the Pinot Blanc, as well as the more traditional Aligoté and Gamay, has resulted in these wines improving dramatically in recent years. Today, examples made from the Chardonnay make a good alternative to Champagne Blanc de Blancs, while Crémant de Bourgogne Blanc de Noirs offers attractively pure Pinot Noir flavors.

One almost extinct red wine worth looking out for is made from the traditional César grape, grown in the Irancy area, close to Chablis. The legality of naming the César on bottles from the various *appellations* of the area is not clear, but these wines have a fascinating flavor that falls somewhere between that of red Burgundy (*see p.110*) made from the Pinot Noir grape and of red Anjou wines (*see p.178*) made from the Cabernet Franc.

JEAN-FRANÇOIS COCHE-DURY
The Aligoté grape variety tends to produce meanly acidic flavors, but may also be made into rich and unusual whites like this.

LIVING HISTORY
Vineyards around the Yonne village of St. Bris-le-Vineux are used to grow both the Sauvignon Blanc and the local César grape, varieties no longer popular in more southern parts of Burgundy.

THE FOOD OF BURGUNDY

The gastronomic tradition and reputation of Burgundy is almost as long-established as that of its wines. The great classics of Burgundian cooking are dishes that we associate with France as a whole. This is hearty, robust food of the sort that would be welcomed after a long day in the vineyard, not refined *haute cuisine*, and is the perfect accompaniment to a good bottle of Burgundy.

POULET DE BRESSE
This appellation contrôlée *chicken is cooked in a delicious white Burgundy and cream sauce, with wild morel mushrooms.*

BURGUNDY IS RICH in terms of ingredients of the highest possible quality. The town of Bresse claims to produce some of the world's best poultry, while the famous Charolais beef cattle are prized by chefs all over the world. The Morvan, with its many rivers, produces some of the finest freshwater fish in France, and its forests are home to a variety of game. There is also an abundance of delicate mushrooms, fat, gray snails, and luscious, ripe vegetables and fruit. On top of all that are the wines of Burgundy, which not only complement and enhance the food when drunk with it, but also play a major part in the preparation of

many great Burgundy dishes. Red wine forms the basis of casseroles such as the classic *boeuf bourguignon*, and of sauces for egg and fish dishes. White Burgundy plays a similar role in chicken and rabbit dishes. The fiery *marc de Bourgogne*, a spirit distilled from the residue of grapes, is used to wash the rinds of the local cheeses.

Traditionalists used to suggest that the same wine be used for the dish as would be served with it. Nowadays, however, the cost of a bottle of Grand Cru Chambertin, for example, is such that only a true purist, or a millionaire, would be prepared to pour half a bottle or more of this great red into

ESCARGOTS À LA BOURGUIGNONNE
The Romans brought their large eating-snails to France, where they were quickly adopted as a classic.

REGIONAL CHEESES

While Burgundy is not nearly as famous for its dairy products as it is for its wine, lush pastures and picture-book Charolais cattle make for rich, creamy cheeses that complement the region's wines perfectly. Even the smallest, most humble restaurants will usually offer a choice of perfectly-ripened, local cheeses. The distinction of many of the cheeses in this region, though, is the strength of the flavors, which often go far more successfully with the delicate local Pinot Noir grape variety than one might expect.

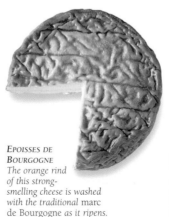

EPOISSES DE BOURGOGNE
The orange rind of this strong-smelling cheese is washed with the traditional marc de Bourgogne *as it ripens.*

BLEU DE BRESSE
This rich, creamy cheese, a classic of southern France, has a soft pâté that is peppered with patches of blue mould. When the cheese has ripened, a white rind forms.

OEUFS EN MEURETTE
This potent Burgundian dish is made with poached eggs and a rich sauce of bacon, vegetables, fresh herbs, good red Burgundy, and a dash of brandy.

The town of Dijon is famous for its mustard, in which eggs are cooked in the dish *oeufs à la dijonnaise*, and also for its blackcurrants, used as the basis of the delicious liqueur *crème de cassis*. This liqueur is used to make *kir,* a white-wine aperitif.

Burgundy is also known for a wide range of baked goods, including *pain d'épices* (spiced bread). One baked savory treat that is traditionally served at wine tastings is the very moreish *gougère,* a *choux* pastry made with cheese. It is eaten either cold or lukewarm and can be served plain, or garnished with mushrooms or vegetables.

CHARCUTERIE
As elsewhere in France, pork meats, including ham, pâté, sausage, and brawn, play a major role in the cuisine of Burgundy. On special occasions, the ham is often served whole.

the pot. Most modern chefs resort to a good, full-bodied red Burgundy instead.

Cream is used frequently in Burgundian dishes, often with mushrooms or ham. Ham, which was once the traditional dish at Easter, may also be braised in wine or set in a green parsley jelly – this is known as *jambon persillé*. Other *charcuterie* (pork products), such as *sansiot* (brawn), *saucisson* (salami-like sausage), *andouillettes,* and *pâtés,* are made throughout Burgundy.

BOEUF BOURGUIGNON
In this classic stew, cuts of beef are marinated, then slowly cooked in Beaujolais or Burgundy wine, to which cubed bacon, onions, and mushrooms are added.

CHAMPAGNE

MUCH MORE THAN A WINE, CHAMPAGNE IS NOW
SYNONYMOUS THROUGHOUT THE GLOBE WITH
THE NOTIONS OF QUALITY AND CELEBRATION.

UNCORK A GREAT CHAMPAGNE and you
might find yourself drinking something that seems to be much more than
a wine. At its best, Champagne can be
the most extraordinary drink: dry, yet
with some honeyed sweetness; rich, yet
fresh; delicate, yet mouth-filling; easy
to drink, yet offering layers of different
flavors ranging from fruits to nuts and
even dark chocolate. Some or all
of this is what I hope to find
when I hear the pop of the
cork. Experience, however,
has taught me that, despite
the fortune that this region
has spent on protecting its name,
the mere presence of the word
"Champagne" on the label of a wine
bottle gives me no reason to expect
anything very special at all. So, why are
some Champagnes so sublime, while
others can taste sourly acidic, sugary,

WATERY SAFEGUARD
Water is sprayed over the vines to protect them against frost, which can be a major hazard in this northern region.

🏔 74,000 acres (30,000 ha): 270 million bottles.

🌡 Marginal and highly variable, and subject to the effects of the northern latitude and the Atlantic Ocean. Summers can be very cool and vines are often threatened by frost in the spring.

▦ Chalk is the main distinguishing component of this region, extending down as much as 980 ft (300 m). The topsoil includes chalk rubble, clay, sand, lignite, marl, and loam.

▦ White/ rosé: Chardonnay, Pinot Noir, Pinot Meunier.

PALATE PLEASER
Unlike other regions, where wines are produced in individual villages, Champagne tends to offer a blend of grapes that have been grown in various parts of the appellation.

Champagne region

Reims
PARIS

or simply dull? The answer lies largely in the geography of this region. Champagne may have had the historic advantage of its close proximity to Paris and the wine drinkers of neighboring countries to the east, but it has always been a cold, northerly region. Grapes in these temperatures find it impossible to ripen sufficiently to produce still red and white wines that are good enough to compete with the wines of vineyards further south. Not that this handicap deterred the 16th-century Champenois, who dyed their wine with elderberry juice in an attempt to mimic the richer color of red Burgundy.

Champagne's success as a wine region came with a series of human interventions. Dom Pérignon, the 17th-century abbot of Hautvillers, is the man erroneously credited with putting the bubbles into what were still wines. In fact, fizziness was a phenomenon that he actually strove to avoid, if only because of the tendency at this time for many bottles of Champagne to explode. Dom Pérignon's greatest contribution to wine making was in fact the care he took in developing the art of blending wines from various parts of the Champagne region, rather than

INTO THE WINE
These vineyards near Cramant are exclusively planted with Chardonnay grapes that produce fine blanc de blanc *wines.*

following the example of his Burgundian counterparts in keeping them separate.

The combination of better wine, which still tended to fizz, and newly developed, stronger, non-exploding bottles was a great success, first in London, then in Paris. Ever since, most Champagne has been blended – a blend of grapes, of vineyards, and of vintages. And, as Dom Pérignon understood, the quality of the wines that go into that blend is far more important than the bubbles that have given Champagne its worldwide fame.

DOM PÉRIGNON
Credited with inventing Champagne, the famous abbot's greatest legacy lies in the art of blending.

KEY

▫ Aube Vineyards	▫ Vallée de la Marne
▫ Côte des Blancs	— *Département* boundary
▫ Côte de Sézanne	— Delimited AOC Region of Champagne
▫ Montagne de Reims	

(Map of the Champagne region shown at left, with labels: STE-MENEHOULD, SUIPPES, REVIGNY-SUR-ORNAIN, VITRY-LE FRANÇOIS, ST DIZIER, HAUTE MARNE, BRIENNE-LE-CHÂTEAU, BAR-SUR-AUBE, CHÂTILLON-SUR-SEINE, and various roads: D987, RD394, Saulx, RD395, N4, Voire, D400, D960, Aube, Ource; scale: 0 km 25, 0 miles 12.5)

THE HISTORY OF CHAMPAGNE

A glass of the finest Champagne, such as Bollinger, would be as recognizable to a Champagne enthusiast as a Chanel dress or a Guerlain eau de toilette would be to someone interested in clothes or fragrances. It is no coincidence that so many Champagne companies now come under the same ownership as couturiers and perfumiers.

CHAMPAGNE FLIES WONDERFULLY in the face of the philosophy of most French wines. Elsewhere, at the very core of the *appellation côntrolée* system, lies the notion that wine should express the character of the specific vineyard in which its grapes were grown. Even the finest Champagne, however, is mostly a blend of wines from different sites. While there are individual vineyard wines, the most illustrious Champagnes, such as Dom Pérignon and Roederer Cristal *(see p.151)*, are blends whose success lies in the way they embody the individual house style of their producers. Richard Geoffroy, the man responsible for making the wine named after Dom Pérignon, says that his focus is on "style, style, style."

Within those house styles, Champagne comes in a number of different colors and flavors. Its color ranges from white to shades of rosé, which can be made either by blending red and white wine or by allowing the skins of the black grapes to tint the juice rather than removing them before they do so. Next there is sweetness, which extends from aggressively bone-dry Brut Sauvage, Ultra Brut, or Brut Zéro to lusciously sweet Doux. In fact, these

VEUVE CLICQUOT FAN
The widow Clicquot, who invented the process of disgorging wine, had a strong promotional style – as this fan shows.

wines, at the far ends of the scale, are rarely made these days. The driest Champagne you are likely to find is Brut, which contains up to 0.5 oz (15 g) of sugar per liter of wine. For the sweeter-toothed, there is the oddly-named Extra Sec or Extra-Dry, which has 0.4–0.65 oz (12–20 g), the even more misleading Sec or Dry, which has 0.55–1.1 oz (17–35 g), and Demi Sec or Rich, with 1.1–1.6 oz (35–50 g). Slightly sweeter Champagnes can be far better than the cheap dry examples on offer in supermarkets.

CHÂTEAU CHANDON
The modern Champagne industry was a 19th-century success story, and the producers soon adopted their lifestyles to match. Moët & Chandon is now part of a group that produces perfume and fashion accessories.

PRESSING GRAPES
Some of the biggest presses used in wine making are used for the production of Champagne. The largest can take up to four tons of grapes at a time.

A MATTER OF STYLE

The style of any wine is determined by the grape variety from which it is made. Most Champagnes, including rosés, are blends of Pinot Noir, Pinot Meunier, and Chardonnay, but there are also pure Chardonnays (Blancs de Blancs) and wines made with no white grapes at all (Blancs de Noirs). Finally, there are vintage Champagnes, made from the fruit of a single harvest and judged by the producer not to require improvement by the addition of older wines, and the far more numerous nonvintage blends. To complicate matters even further, there are oddities like "recently disgorged" vintage Champagnes that develop fresh, yet rich, characters of their own through having been left on their yeast for several years longer than usual. And, subject to no rules at all, there are the so-called *prestige cuvées* that command the highest prices. Any Champagne producer can come up with a fancy name, bottle, and cost for one of his vintage or non-vintage wines, but there is no guarantee that the stuff that goes into that bottle is as special as its attractive, upmarket packaging.

Any or all of these styles may be produced by Champagne's individual estates, *coopératives,* and merchants. Historically, it was merchants such as Moët & Chandon (*see p.150*), Krug (*see p.149*), Roederer, and Bollinger who did the job best. The money they made from their sales across the world gave them numerous advantages. They had the greatest access to good grapes, both from their own vines and from their own choice of *grands crus* vineyards. They had the financial means to keep "reserve" wine from previous years to use in their non-

vintage wine, and they had the best wine-making equipment and blending skills.

Coopératives, by contrast, were thought to have the disadvantage of having to rely on grapes grown by their members in the vicinity of the winery. In other words, they had a far smaller palette to blend from. Also, the fact that most of their wines were sold cheaply under various customers' names did little to encourage them to focus on quality. Small estates, with only limited funds and their own grapes to work with, were believed to suffer from an even greater handicap. More recently, however, the picture has changed as critics have acknowledged the poor quality of some big-name Champagnes. Mumm's efforts have, for example, been unfavorably compared with the same company's Californian wines. *Coopératives* have launched own brands that sometimes compete on level terms with those of the merchants; and a small number of sophisticated, well-sited, top-quality estates have proved that they can defy expectations by making some of the best Champagne of all. As Champagne enters the 21st century, the well-known names face a growing number of challenges. There are new markets opening up around the world and new competitors are appearing both in Champagne itself and in other regions. With luck, the winners will be the Champagne drinkers, who will get an even better wine at a fairer price.

DRINK OF PRINCES...AND PRINCESSES ·
The major Champagne houses have traditionally used imagery associated with the royal families of Europe.

A DRIVING TOUR OF CHAMPAGNE

Despite the international fame of wines made by large producers from a mixture of grapes grown in various parts of the region, Champagne comprises many individual towns and villages. This tour, beginning and ending in the city of Reims, takes in some of them.

Champagne ▢ Tour

MONTAGNE DE REIMS
The lower slopes of the "mountain of Reims" are famed for their Pinot Noir.

REIMS TO BOUZY

Reims ①, the unofficial capital of this region, is the place to take advantage of the guided cellar tours offered by Champagne houses such as Louis Roederer, Lanson, Ruinart, Taittinger, Pommery, and Charles Heidsieck, whose cellars have been carved out of the chalk beneath the city. Make sure, though, that you take a break from wine to visit the magnificent cathedral here, where Joan of Arc watched the coronation of Charles VII in 1429. After Sillery ②, you drive past the so-called Montagne de Reims, a low hill covered by top-class Pinot Noir vines. A century or so ago, Sillery's wines were, in fact, sold under the name of this hill. In Mailly-Champagne ③, you could pause to stock up on a few bottles from the *coopérative*, one of the best in the region. The villages of Verzenay ④, Verzy ⑤, Ambonnay ⑥, and Bouzy ⑦ are all sources of good Pinot Noir, both in the form of Champagne and Bouzy Rouge Coteaux Champenois. For a fine example, visit Paul Bara in Bouzy or Egly-Ouriet in Ambonnay.

LOUVOIS TO AY

In Louvois ⑧ there is a château whose garden is said to have been modeled on that of Versailles. Your next stop, Mareuil-sur-Ay ⑨, is home to Billecart-Salmon, one of the region's finest firms. In Ay ⑩, you could visit Ayala, Bollinger, Deutz, and Gosset, as well as the Musée Champenois, which displays old wine-making implements.

ÉPERNAY TO VERTUS

Épernay ⑪ is most notable for the Avenue de Champagne, where Champagne houses such as Mercier and Moët & Chandon are based. Other firms here include Pol Roger, de Castellane, and Perrier Jouët. In Chavot ⑫, stop to take some

CHÂTILLON-SUR-MARNE
⑳ ★

⑲ DORMANS
★

● Vente

Dame

★
⑰ MAREUIL-EN-BRIE

⑱
ORBAIS-
L'ABBAYE

⑯ ★
MONTMORT

Etoges ●

A SLOW PROCESS
Traditional methods are still used all over Champagne. In a process called remuage, bottles of Champagne are gradually rotated in order to loosen the sediment and remove it.

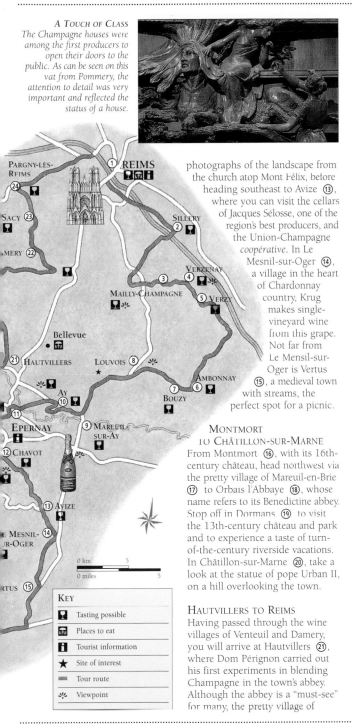

photographs of the landscape from the church atop Mont Félix, before heading southeast to Avize ⑬, where you can visit the cellars of Jacques Sélosse, one of the region's best producers, and the Union-Champagne *coopérative*. In Le Mesnil-sur-Oger ⑭, a village in the heart of Chardonnay country, Krug makes single-vineyard wine from this grape. Not far from Le Mesnil-sur-Oger is Vertus ⑮, a medieval town with streams, the perfect spot for a picnic.

MONTMORT TO CHÂTILLON-SUR-MARNE

From Montmort ⑯, with its 16th-century château, head northwest via the pretty village of Mareuil-en-Brie ⑰ to Orbais l'Abbaye ⑱, whose name refers to its Benedictine abbey. Stop off in Dormans ⑲ to visit the 13th-century château and park and to experience a taste of turn-of-the-century riverside vacations. In Châtillon-sur-Marne ⑳, take a look at the statue of pope Urban II, on a hill overlooking the town.

HAUTVILLERS TO REIMS

Having passed through the wine villages of Venteuil and Damery, you will arrive at Hautvillers ㉑, where Dom Pérignon carried out his first experiments in blending Champagne in the town's abbey. Although the abbey is a "must-see" for many, the pretty village of

KEY

🍷	Tasting possible
🏠	Places to eat
ℹ	Tourist information
★	Site of interest
▬	Tour route
⋇	Viewpoint

Hautvillers is worth exploring in its own right. From here, you could head east to the Royal Champagne in Bellevue, one of France's finest country hotels. The final stretch of your journey takes you through the vines and the villages of Chamery ㉒, Sacy ㉓, and Pargny-lès-Reims ㉔, each offering plenty of opportunities to taste Champagne made by growers, as opposed to those produced by the bigger companies in the towns.

BILLECART-SALMON

NO CHAMPAGNE has given me such consistent pleasure as the wine from this small family firm. The style is generally lighter and more delicate than most, and this is as apparent in the nonvintage as in the individual *cuvées*. These are the Elisabeth Salmon, the Nicolas-François Billecart, the Blanc de Blancs, and the Grande Cuvée. Billecart-Salmon also produces what, for many critics, is the finest, most reliable rosé in all of Champagne. The company has been producing rosé since 1830 and this style nowadays accounts for almost 20 percent of its annual sales.

🔲 Pinot Noir, Chardonnay, Pinot Meunier.	*CUVÉE ELISABETH SALMON*
🍷 Stylish, ultra-reliable Champagnes of all styles, with especially good rosé.	*The very epitome of*
🎬 Cuvée Nicolas-François, Cuvée Elisabeth Salmon Rosé, Blanc de Blancs, Grande Cuvée.	*pink Champagne, this fine cuvée has lovely*
🍴 None.	*raspberry*
🗄 1990, 1989, 1988, 1985, 1982.	*flavors.*

BOLLINGER

THE CHAMPAGNE OF James Bond – in the movies at least, for in the novels he favors another brand – is also a favorite with wine makers. The key to this firm's success lies in owning over 350 acres (140 ha) of top-quality vineyards and in pursuing a style that repays aging and serving with meals. Others offer RD ("recently disgorged") wines (*see p.29*), but Bollinger's RD is the classic. Its Vieilles Vignes Françaises ("native French vines") offer a chance to taste the fruit of some of the only vines in France not grafted onto American rootstock.

🔲 Pinot Noir, Chardonnay, Pinot Meunier.	*BOLLINGER 1990*
🍷 Rich, complex, full-flavored, mouth-fillingly yeasty wines across the board.	*Vintage Bollinger provides the*
🎬 Grande Année, RD (Récemment Dégorgé), Vieilles Vignes Françaises.	*quintessence of this*
🍴 None.	*house's*
🗄 1990, 1989, 1988, 1985, 1982.	*rich style.*

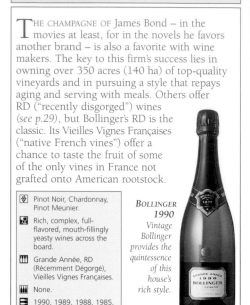

GOSSET

FOUNDED IN 1584, this is one of the oldest wine companies in the world. Indeed, it remained in the hands of the same family for over four centuries until it was bought recently by Beatrice Cointreau. The Gosset style is decidedly traditional, with a focus on barrel fermentation and a high proportion of black grapes. All the wines here are of high quality, ranging from the non-vintage Excellence to the top wine, the vintage Célébris. Gosset fans, however, tend to favor the non-vintage Grande Réserve, which is a Champagne to drink with food.

🔲 Pinot Noir, Chardonnay, Pinot Meunier.	*CÉLÉBRIS A top class*
🍷 Slow-developing Champagne with more biscuity flavor than is often fashionable nowadays.	*prestige cuvée with a lot of Chardonnay*
🎬 Grande Excellence, Grand Rosé, Grande Millésime, Célébris.	*character, Célébris*
🍴 None.	*is worth*
🗄 1990, 1989, 1988, 1985.	*cellaring.*

ALFRED GRATIEN

UNDER THE SAME OWNERSHIP as the Loire sparkling-wine producer Gratien & Meyer, this is one of the most traditional Champagne houses. Wines are fermented in (old) barrels and given unusually lengthy periods of contact with the yeast used to kick off the second fermentation. There is no malolactic fermentation (*see p.24*). This method gives the Champagnes a mixture of richness and freshness associated with "recently disgorged" (*see p.29*) wines. Mature when sold, these are wines that improve with keeping and go particularly well with food.

🔲 Pinot Noir, Chardonnay, Pinot Meunier.	*CUVÉE PARADIS*
🍷 One of the most distinctive, richly old-fashioned, full-flavored, biscuity Champagnes.	*This cuvée represents the quint-*
🎬 Cuvée Paradis, Vintage Brut.	*essence of the rich,*
🍴 Gratien & Meyer (Saumur).	*yeasty Gratien*
🗄 1990, 1989, 1988, 1987, 1985, 1983.	*style.*

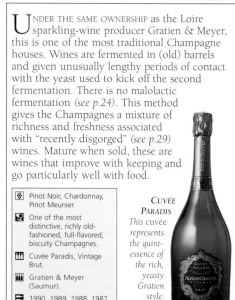

CHARLES HEIDSIECK

THIS FIRM DEMONSTRATES the importance to a Champagne house of a skilled wine maker, commitment to quality, and investment. In the 1970s, wines from Charles Heidsieck were sold in supermarkets, made to the standards that this implies. Under the management of Daniel Thibault, however, the quality of the wines has made quantum leaps. In 1998 he launched a set of nonvintage wines whose labels revealed the year when the *cuvée* was blended. It was one of these that beat the big-name vintage Champagnes in the London and Tokyo International Wine Challenges.

🍇 Pinot Noir, Chardonnay, Pinot Meunier.	**BRUT RÉSERVE MISE EN CAVE 1992**
🍷 Recently much improved, impeccably made wines that are richly flavored enough to drink with food.	*This is a revolutionary nonvintage wine with the quality and character of*
🍾 Mis en Cave Non-vintage, Cuvée des Millénaires.	*a vintage Champagne.*
🍾🍾 Piper Heidsieck.	
🥂 1990, 1989, 1985.	

HENRIOT

REVERSING THE TREND that has been prevalent elsewhere in Champagne, this firm recently went back from corporate status to being owned by the original family. The wines are still made by the makers of Veuve Clicquot (the firm with which Henriot used to share owners) but the style of the Henriot wines is distinctively its own. Chardonnay is the favored variety here – in the vintage Brut Souverain and in the rich but elegant vintage Blanc de Blancs. Joseph Henriot now owns the Burgundy *négociant* Bouchard Père et Fils, and has revolutionized quality there, too.

🍇 Pinot Noir, Chardonnay, Pinot Meunier.	**BLANC DE BLANCS**
🍷 Much improved producer with rich, toasty Champagnes and particularly good Blanc de Blancs.	*This is one of the best examples of pure Chardonnay produced in all Champagne.*
🍾 Souverain Brut, Blanc de Blancs, Enchantelleurs.	
🍾🍾 Bouchard Père et Fils Burgundy.	
🥂 1990, 1989, 1988, 1985.	

JACQUESSON

THIS FAMILY FIRM PROUDLY claims the Emperor Napoléon as one of its most distinguished customers and presents its Champagnes with gorgeous, instantly recognizable labels. The contents of the bottles are even more impressive: creamy rich wines, ranging from the non-vintage (which modestly describes itself as "Perfection") to the vintage Blanc de Blancs (arguably the best wine) and the vintage Brut. The "late-disgorged" style (known as *dégorgement tardif*) is Jacquesson's convincing answer to Bollinger's RD (*see p.29*): a gloriously mature, yet fresh wine.

🍇 Pinot Noir, Chardonnay, Pinot Meunier	**PERFECTION**
🍷 Rich, complex, and stylish wines that – especially the Blancs de Blancs – deserve to be far better known.	*This small firm's Champagnes are among the richest on the market*
🍾 Signature Brut, Blanc de Blancs, Dégorgement Tardif.	*and the most interestingly produced.*
🍾🍾 None.	
🥂 1990, 1989, 1988, 1985, 1983.	

KRUG

THE ROLLS-ROYCE OF CHAMPAGNE, Krug stands apart in the style of its Champagne, which is arguably the most like wine of all sparkling wines. By this I mean that it would be a choice Champagne to drink at dinner, but not one that I would choose purely for refreshment. Produced here is a long-lived vintage wine and a single-vineyard *blanc de blancs* called Clos de Mesnil; but for many lovers of fine Champagne, none of the wines can top Krug's nonvintage and nonvintage rosé, both of which contain an unusually high proportion of mature wine.

🍇 Pinot Noir, Chardonnay, Pinot Meunier.	**GRANDE CUVÉE**
🍷 Rich, mouth-filling wines, including dazzling non-vintage.	*This could well be the greatest of*
🍾 Grande Cuvée, Rosé, Vintage, Clos du Mesnil.	*all non-vintage Champagnes.*
🍾🍾 Pommery, Moët & Chandon, Krug, Dom Ruinart, Veuve Clicquot, Mercier.	
🥂 1990, 1989, 1988, 1985.	

LANSON

LANSON'S NAME, BUT NOT its vineyards, was bought in 1991 by Marne et Champagne, the second biggest producer in Champagne, which sells under its own and its customers' labels. It is too early to analyze the full impact on the Lanson name of not passing on the land on which the grapes were grown; the grapes were used for all of the long-lived vintage Champagnes so far released, but the nonvintage wines have kept their standard, and the same wine maker is still at the helm. Lanson's top wine, the Noble Cuvée, is highly recommendable, as is the recently revived Demi-Sec.

❀	Pinot Noir, Chardonnay, Pinot Meunier.
🍷	Full-flavored wines that repay patience.
🍶	Noble Cuvée, Blanc de Blancs.
🍾	Massé, Marne et Champagne brands including Besserat de Bellefon and Alfred Rothschild.
🥂	1993, 1990, 1988.

LANSON
The gold label denotes a vintage Champagne; Lanson's vintage wines are unusually long-lived.

LAURENT-PERRIER

A LARGE AND AMBITIOUS family-owned firm, producing over twice as much wine as Roederer, Laurent-Perrier owns a number of other Champagne houses, including Salon and de Castellane and half of the previously unconnected Joseph Perrier. Despite the volume of wine produced, the quality of the richly flavored, heavily Pinot Noir-influenced nonvintage is remarkably consistent. Also produced here is a set of more ambitious nonvintage Champagnes entitled Grand Siècle, including a *blanc de blancs*, a rosé, and the excellent La Cuvée.

❀	Pinot Noir, Chardonnay, Pinot Meunier.
🍷	Very elegant dry (including ultra-dry) white Champagne, plus serious rosé and rich "La Cuvée" blends.
🍶	Grand Siècle (especially Cuvée Alexandre).
🍾	de Castellane, Delamotte, Joseph Perrier, Salon
🥂	1990, 1988, 1985.

GRAND SIÈCLE
This highly unusual blend is made up of three different vintages.

MOËT & CHANDON

THIS IS THE ONE CHAMPAGNE that everyone has heard of, which is hardly surprising when you consider that over 20 million bottles are sold every year and the contents of large bottles are regularly sprayed around by winners at sporting events. Despite occasional hitches in the past, the style and quality are now highly reliable and the vintage Brut and vintage Rosé are among the best in the region. The generally brilliant *prestige cuvée* Dom Pérignon, which is also produced in surprising volumes, is worth leaving in the cellar for a decade after its release.

❀	Pinot Noir, Chardonnay, Pinot Meunier.
🍷	Lovely toasty wines that – including the nonvintage – improve with keeping.
🍶	Vintage Brut Impérial, Dom Pérignon (white and rosé).
🍾	Mercier, Pommery, Veuve Clicquot, Krug, Ruinart, Canard Duchêne.
🥂	1992, 1990, 1989, 1988, 1985.

1993 BRUT IMPÉRIAL
Often overshadowed by nonvintage wines, this is great, nutty-toasty wine.

POL ROGER

THE WINES MADE BY this family-owned firm are highly popular with traditional wine merchants and with others who like delicate, finely-structured, nonvintage and vintage Champagne. Unlike some houses that tend to favor one grape variety over the others, Pol Roger likes to use the region's three varieties equally. The strongest overseas link is with the UK, where Pol Roger's first exports were sent, and where Sir Winston Churchill was one of its greatest fans. He is commemorated by the black border around the label of the Cuvée Sir Winston Churchill.

❀	Pinot Noir, Chardonnay, Pinot Meunier.
🍷	Stylish, mostly Pinot Noir-influenced wines that last brilliantly.
🍶	Brut Chardonnay, Cuvée PR Réserve Spéciale, Cuvée Sir Winston Churchill.
🍾	None
🥂	1990, 1989, 1988, 1985, 1983.

EXTRA DRY
This is one of the finest, most delicate Champagnes; the opposite of the rich Bollinger style.

POMMERY

POMMERY BOASTS CELLARS named after the cities to which the biggest shipments were sent in the last century, as well as no fewer than 450 acres (300 ha) of great vineyards. Despite joining the LVMH group along with Moët & Chandon, Ruinart, and Veuve Clicquot, Pommery has kept its light, delicate style, thanks to the efforts of Prince Alain de Polignac, who still runs what was once the family firm. The Cuvée Spéciale Louise Pommery wines, named after the daughter of the founder (and Alain de Polignac's ancestor) are among the best of all the *prestige cuvée* wines.

		LOUISE
🍇	Pinot Noir, Chardonnay, Pinot Meunier.	*A lovely, rich, and classily complex wine, Louise will certainly improve with time.*
📷	Fast improving, subtle nonvintage wines, Chardonnay-influenced Royal Apanage, rich Cuvée Louise.	
▥	Louise, Royal Apanage.	
▥	Krug, Mercier, Moët & Chandon, Ruinart, Veuve Clicquot.	
▤	1991, 1990, 1989, 1988.	

ROEDERER

ONE OF THE BIG family-owned Champagne houses, Roederer is also quietly one of the most dynamic, having taken over Deutz Champagne and made investments in vintage port, the Rhône, and Bordeaux, not to mention a winery producing top-class sparkling wine in California. Roederer's flagship is its Cristal, whose reputation – and clear glass bottle – date back to the days when the Czar of Russia was a customer. The Brut Premier and Vintage are equally recommendable, and share the distinction of being worth leaving in a cellar for 5–10 years.

		CRISTAL BRUT
🍇	Pinot Noir, Chardonnay, Pinot Meunier.	*This is an ultra rich, Pinot Noir-influenced wine. The rare Cristal Rosé is great too.*
📷	Richly approachable when young, this house's non vintage wines develop great complexity with time. Also a frequent success in unfashionable vintages.	
▥	Blanc de Blancs, Cristal.	
▥	Deutz, Roederer Estate/ Quartet (California).	
▤	1991, 1990, 1989, 1988.	

RUINART

THE OLDEST CHAMPAGNE house, Ruinart was founded in 1729 by a priest called Dom Ruinart. It has grown enormously since it was bought in the 1960s by Moët & Chandon. Unlike some subsidiaries of the Louis-Vuitton-Moët-Hennessy concern, this firm continues to give the impression of independence. The style of the wines is full-flavored and old-fashioned, and the emphasis is on Chardonnay, much of which comes from Ruinart's vineyards. The Blanc de Blancs (grown on the Montagne de Reims as well as the Côte des Blancs) is especially recommendable.

		BRUT
🍇	Pinot Noir, Chardonnay, Pinot Meunier	*This is a first-class Champagne with rich nutty, appley flavor, revealing the influence of Chardonnay.*
📷	Full-bodied but stylish Champagnes.	
▥	Blancs de Blancs, R de Ruinart, Dom Ruinart Rosé.	
▥	Moët & Chandon, Mercier, Pommery, Veuve Clicquot, Canard Duchêne, Krug.	
▤	1993, 1992, 1990, 1988.	

SALON

THE ADJECTIVE "UNIQUE" is far too easily used these days, but it genuinely does apply to this subsidiary of Laurent-Perrier that sells only one wine: a vintage *cuvée* that is made only in years when the climate has been good enough. Slightly less unusually, Salon normally chooses not to allow its wine to go through malolactic fermentation (*see p.24*). The resulting leanness leads to the Champagne being released several years after other houses' wines of the same vintages have sold out. Buy Salon's wines when you see them: they are among the finest Champagne of all.

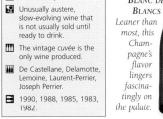

		BLANC DE BLANCS
🍇	Chardonnay.	*Leaner than most, this Champagne's flavor lingers fascinatingly on the palate.*
📷	Unusually austere, slow-evolving wine that is not usually sold until ready to drink.	
▥	The vintage *cuvée* is the only wine produced.	
▥	De Castellane, Delamotte, Lemoine, Laurent-Perrier, Joseph Perrier.	
▤	1990, 1988, 1985, 1983, 1982.	

TAITTINGER

WITH MORE THAN 620 acres (250 ha) of top-class vines, Taittinger is one of the biggest producers of Champagne. The light, creamy style of Taittinger's wines can be explained by the firm's preference for Chardonnay, of which it has a fine selection of vineyards in the Côte des Blancs. The nonvintage is generally unremarkable, but the vintage is usually beautifully biscuity. However, Taittinger's star wine is without doubt the Comtes de Champagne *prestige cuvée* that, for some wine tasters, is the best *blanc de blancs* (meaning "white of whites") Champagne of them all.

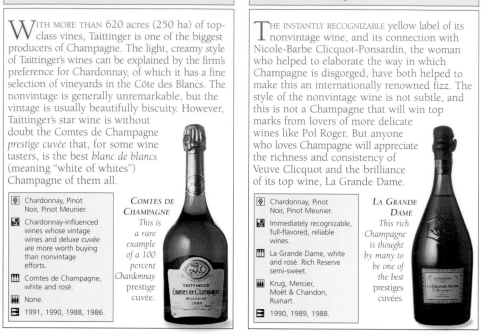

🍇	Chardonnay, Pinot Noir, Pinot Meunier.
📋	Chardonnay-influenced wines whose vintage wines and deluxe *cuvée* are more worth buying than nonvintage efforts.
🍾	Comtes de Champagne, white and rosé.
🍶	None.
📦	1991, 1990, 1988, 1986.

COMTES DE CHAMPAGNE
This is a rare example of a 100 percent Chardonnay prestige cuvée.

VEUVE CLICQUOT

THE INSTANTLY RECOGNIZABLE yellow label of its nonvintage wine, and its connection with Nicole-Barbe Clicquot-Ponsardin, the woman who helped to elaborate the way in which Champagne is disgorged, have both helped to make this an internationally renowned fizz. The style of the nonvintage wine is not subtle, and this is not a Champagne that will win top marks from lovers of more delicate wines like Pol Roger. But anyone who loves Champagne will appreciate the richness and consistency of Veuve Clicquot and the brilliance of its top wine, La Grande Dame.

🍇	Chardonnay, Pinot Noir, Pinot Meunier.
📋	Immediately recognizable, full-flavored, reliable wines.
🍾	La Grande Dame, white and rosé. Rich Reserve semi-sweet.
🍶	Krug, Mercier, Moët & Chandon, Ruinart.
📦	1990, 1989, 1988.

LA GRANDE DAME
This rich Champagne is thought by many to be one of the best prestiges cuvées.

THE STILL WINES OF CHAMPAGNE

For most people, apart from those who like to use a swizzle-stick to remove the bubbles from their Champagne, this region's wines will always be sparkling whites or rosés. Bubble-free red, rosé, and white wine is, however, what this region used to produce, and is still the style of wine obstinately being made by some small estates and bigger companies under the labels of Bouzy Rouge, Rosé des Riceys, and Coteaux

SEEING RED
The village of Bouzy provides Pinot Noir grapes for top-quality Champagne, and for still red wine.

Champenois. The two things these wines have in common are their generally high prices and the fact that they are only worth buying in warmer vintages. Bouzy Rouge from a cool year, for example, tastes like the most aggressively unripe red Burgundy, while Coteaux Champenois made in cool conditions is more like extra-green Chablis. Unfortunately, a

LES RICEYS
Some producers in Les Riceys still use barrels like these for their old-fashioned rosé wines.

good vintage rarely occurs in the same village more than once in 10 years. Those who are curious to taste these wines should seek out a white wine from Lilbert-Fils and Egly-Ouriet, who also make an excellent red, and Alexandre Bonnet's Rosé des Riceys. An interesting trend, championed by producers like Maurice Vesselle and Herbert Beaufort, is still *blanc de noirs*, a still white wine that is made in a similar way to Champagne, but from black grapes.

OTHERS

WHILE A SMALL NUMBER of "big name," or Grande Marque, Champagne houses generally tend to hog the limelight, the Champagne region boasts a plethora of other producers, ranging from big *coopératives* to tiny family estates. The quality of their wines varies enormously, ranging from acidic and dull examples to subtle and sublime ones.

DE VENOGE
In recent years, the wines produced by this traditional firm, including this rosé, have improved a great deal.

EAGLE-EYED READERS SCANNING the alphabetically organized entries of the previous pages will have noticed the absence of a number of well-known Champagne houses. Where, they might wonder, are Mumm or Mercier or Perrier-Jouet, to name but three brands whose names are widely seen in glossy advertisements prior to New Year's Eve. I make no apology for consigning these, and several other big names, to the "Others" category, for the simple reason that, in my and many other critics' opinion, their Champagnes, though in some cases recently much improved, are just not as good as those of the producers I have covered in individual detail. Nor, significantly, are they better than some of the *coopératives* and smaller producers that I felt it was appropriate to include in this section.

Among the firms worth mentioning here is Marne & Champagne, a company that is often left out of wine books because its Champagne is sold under hundreds of different labels. Not only does Marne & Champagne own Lanson and the generally decent Besserat de Bellefon, it also sells Champagne under the Alfred Rothschild label, which is rarely seen outside France. Another firm that has swallowed other Champagne houses is Vranken, which now produces wines under its own name and others', including Heidsieck Monopole and Demoiselle. Bruno Paillard is an up-and-coming merchant worth watching, both for its own wines and for those made by its subsidiaries Delbeck and Boizel. Ayala and de Cazanove are older firms that have improved the quality of their wines recently, as have De Venoge and Canard Duchêne, which is a subsidiary of Veuve Clicquot.

De Castellane and Deutz belong respectively to Laurent-Perrier and Roederer and make reliable, good value wines, as do some of the smaller firms such as Charles Ellner, Delamotte, Duval-Leroy, Drappier, Forget-Brimont, Hamm, Harlin, Joseph Perrier, Alexandre, and Bonnet. *Coopératives* that I'd recommend include the *cuvée* Orpale wines from the Union Champagne and wines sold under their own names by Beaumont de Crayères, Jacquart, Mailly Grand Cru, Pannier, Palmer, and Nicolas Feuillatte. As for smaller estates, the ones I'd choose include Paul Bara, Jacques Beaufort, Chartogne-Taillet, Egly-Ouriet, Gimonnet, Margaine, Pierre Moncuit, Jacques Selosse, Jean Vesselle, and Vilmart.

MAKING HISTORY
Champagne Demoiselle, the firm whose wines are stored in this cellar, is a relatively recent creation. Its wines, however, are already competing with some of the big names of the past.

DUVAL-LEROY
The Champagne made by this company is often sold under the labels of its customers – from supermarkets to luxury hotels.

THE FOOD OF CHAMPAGNE

The region that has given us the world's most famous sparkling wine can claim surprisingly few traditional dishes that are specifically its own. The inhabitants of this cool, fertile farming region have been blessed with fine raw materials and have always eaten well, but, borrowing extensively from neighboring regions, they have not proved to be particularly inventive cooks.

POTAGE ST. GERMAIN
Fresh green peas, grown in the rich market gardens of Champagne, are used to make this creamy soup finished with pieces of smoked ham.

ONE UNUSUAL FEATURE of the cuisine of the Champagne region is its limited use of beef. Where beef is used, it is usually as part of a mixture of meats, most memorably in a local version of the Burgundian *pot au feu,* known here as *potée champenoise* or as *potée des vendangeurs* (grape pickers' stew). This hearty dish is made from five meats and five vegetables, often salt pork, shin of beef, silverside of beef, chicken, and spicy sausage, together with carrots, leeks, turnips, savoy cabbage, and onions. Another mixed-meat dish is *épaule d'agneau farcie à la champenoise,* in which a shoulder of lamb is stuffed with a mixture of chopped pork and tomatoes flavored with juniper and Champagne.

JAMBON DES ARDENNES
Hilly and densely forested, the Ardennes region is famous for its cold-smoked hams, eaten as an appetizer with pickles, and in many traditional local dishes.

TRUITE ARDENNAISE
Delicate brown trout are common in the many rivers that run through the entire Champagne region. In this simple but delicious dish, the fish are sautéed in butter before being finished off with a sauce of crème fraîche and Ardennes ham.

PÂTÉ EN CROÛTE
Pâtés of all sorts, including pork, goose, wild boar, goose liver, and more, are made in Champagne, often wrapped in a rich pastry shell and baked in the oven.

Pork is a staple meat in this region, and pigs, traditionally fattened on acorns, appear in dishes ranging from smoked Ardennes ham and pork chops grilled with sage leaves, to spicy tripe-filled sausages and *pieds de porc à la Ste.-Menehould*, pigs' feet simmered slowly in a rich stock until tender.

A variety of meats and fish are cooked with the sparkling or still white wines of the region, including pike, eels, ham, chicken, guinea fowl, pheasant, and *sanglier* (wild boar) from the extensive forests of the Ardennes. The local red wines are also used in cooking, and many restaurants offer *poulet sauté au Bouzy*, a variation on the Burgundian *coq au vin*. *Ouyettes* (goose pies) are a speciality here, as are tiny song thrushes, often stewed with juniper berries, *à l'ardennaise*. River fish are plentiful in the region and popular dishes include trout fried in butter with a ham and *crème fraîche* sauce, and pike with bacon and pickles. Accompaniments to these dishes include potatoes fried with onions and garlic or a salad of dandelion leaves and crisply fried bacon.

To finish the meal there might be a Genoese sponge cake filled with praline cream, or almond meringues also full of thick cream. My own favorites include a Champagne sorbet, red fruits with Champagne, or *fraises Eugénie*, fresh strawberries served with warm *sabayon*, a sweet dessert cream.

LAND OF PLENTY
A great variety of fruit and vegetables, including peas, onions, tomatoes, asparagus, plums, and cabbages, is grown in the rich farmland of Champagne and sold in shops and markets throughout the region.

REGIONAL CHEESES

In the year 1217, the Comtesse de Champagne sent 200 Brie de Meaux cheeses as a gift to the King of France. One of the oldest and finest of French cheeses, Brie from the village of Meaux was popular with the Emperor Charlemagne as early as the ninth century. Today, Brie is made in huge quantities on farms and in factories all over the Champagne region, and varies from the simple to the sublime. Langres à la Coupe and Chaource are two other regional specialities. Produced in smaller volumes, they are of far more consistent quality.

LANGRES À LA COUPE
This cylindrical cheese has a well in the middle into which Champagne or marc is poured. The rind is rubbed with brine and annato for color.

CHAOURCE
This mild cow's-milk cheese does not take long to mature. It quickly forms a tasty, edible white rind and develops a soft, oozingly creamy center.

JURA AND SAVOIE

TWO OF THE MOST OVERLOOKED WINE REGIONS
IN FRANCE, JURA AND SAVOIE OFFER UNIQUE
FLAVORS AND STYLES NOT FOUND ELSEWHERE.

☐ Jura and Savoie region

IN LES ROSIÈRES, JUST NORTH of the town of
Arbois, there is a vineyard that deserves a
place not only in the history of French wine,
but of wine in general. It was here, in the
late 19th century, that, in answer to a request
from Napoleon III, Louis Pasteur carried out
his experiments on why grape juice turned
into wine and, more specifically, why that
wine so often turned into vinegar. Pasteur
chose this region for the simple reason
that this is where he grew up. His interest
in yeast and bacteria must, however, have
been influenced by the way in which the
yeast that formed on the surface of the Jura
and Savoie's *vins jaunes* had the same effect
on them as it does on *fino* sherry. These
"yellow wines" take their name from the
color they develop after they have been pur-
posefully oxidized under a yeast *flor*.

CHÂTEAU D'ARLAY
This estate in Arbois
produces some of the
best vins de paille
to be found in the
Jura and Savoie.
These very sweet
"straw wines" are
made from grapes
that were traditionally
dried on straw mats.

🏔 8600 acres (3500 ha): 35 million bottles.	🪟 Clay and limestone.
🌦 The Jura and Savoie experiences a continental climate, with hot summers and cold winters. Its close proximity to mountain ranges can provoke sudden changes in the weather.	🍇 Red Jura: Pinot Noir, Poulsard, Trousseau. White Jura: Chardonnay, Savagnin. Red Savoie: Gamay, Pinot Noir, Mondeuse. White Savoie: Jacquère, Chasselas, Chardonnay.

CHÂTEAU CHALON
The commune of Château Chalon produces the
most famous vins jaunes made from 100 percent
Savagnin. Grapes here are picked as late as
possible, even when there is snow on the ground.

Today, while the Juraciens still tend to claim that *vin jaune* is their finest wine, I'd vote for the equally unusual *vin de paille*, a sweet white wine named after the ancient method of drying the grapes out on straw mats before fermenting their juice. Today, this wine is made in the same way as the Amarone of the Veneto in Italy, the bunches of grapes being either hung from the rafters of huts or laid out on racks.

The Jura now focuses on producing far greater quantities of red wine, which is made from the Pinot Noir and the local Trousseau and Poulsard grapes, and white wine, made mainly from the Savagnin and Chardonnay. However, the Jura vineyards now occupy just a fraction of the 50,000 acres (20,000 ha) that they covered before the arrival of phylloxera. As recently as the 1960s, this region, whose wines were praised more than 2000 years ago by Pliny, seemed in danger of giving up wine making altogether. Rescue came in the unlikely form of a clever marketeer called Henri Maire, whose firm now owns the vineyard where Pasteur conducted his experiments, and the launch of his highly successful Vin Fou (Crazy Wine). I am grateful to Monsieur Maire for having helped these wines to survive, although I personally prefer the other, more traditional styles of wine from the Jura.

If it weren't for the readiness of vacationers in nearby ski resorts such as Val d'Isère to pay over the odds for the wines of Savoie, it is quite possible that they might also have disappeared. These light, berryish reds and rosés, made from the Mondeuse, and fresh whites, which are largely produced from a variety confusingly known both as the Roussette and the Altesse, are ideal après-ski fare and go perfectly with local cheeses. They are generally quite short-lived, however, and outside Savoie have a hard time competing with fuller-flavored wines from other French wine regions.

Unlike most of the wines in France, there is very little variation in the quality produced in the Jura and Savoie from one vintage to the next. Your best bet is to buy a bottle from the very latest vintage, rather than one that is several years old.

MOUNTAINS OF GRAPES
Located close to the ski slopes of the French Alps, the vineyards of the Jura and Savoie are situated on the lower slopes of the Jura mountains. The climate here is continental, with warm summers and cold winters.

KEY

☐ Arbois	☐ Seyssel
☐ Château Chalon	☐ Vin du Bugey and Roussette du Bugey
☐ Côtes de Jura	☐ Vin du Savoie and Roussette du Savoie
☐ Crépy	– – International boundary
☐ L'Étoile	— *Département* boundary

ARBOIS

ONE OF THE BEST-KEPT SECRETS of the wine world, Arbois is a picturesque medieval market town that has hardly changed at all since Louis Pasteur lived here more than a century ago. Even compared to the other French regions that are still producing traditional wines, the white wines of Arbois seem to have been caught in a time warp all of their own.

A HIDDEN TREASURE
Tucked away in the hills, the small town of Arbois is surrounded by sloping vineyards. Grape varieties are grown here that are found almost nowhere else in France.

THIS ONCE-IMPORTANT wine-making region enjoys a climate of its own that is less sheltered than that of Alsace and more continental than that of nearby Burgundy, the region to which it was once attached. The summers and autumns here can be warm, but the winters are bitterly cold and grapes often have a tough time ripening. Wine making is also often much poorer than it ought to be, with heaviness and staleness being all too easy to find. While it is generally believed that the best wines of the region are to be found within the *appellations* of Château Chalon (*see p.159*) and L'Étoile (*see p.160*), similar wines made by good estates in Arbois can be of a very similar quality. The red and rosé wines that are made from the Pinot Noir grape variety compete with red Burgundy (*see p.111*), while those made from the local Poulsard and Trousseau grapes can, when allowed to maintain their

freshness, be quite berryish and spicy. White wines made from the Savagnin, a local grape variety that is both unrelated to and quite unlike the Sauvignon Blanc, come in three styles: the very sherrylike, intentionally oxidized *vin jaune*, the somewhat sherrylike, unintentionally oxidized white Arbois and the Reciotolike, raisiny *vin de paille* that is made from grapes that have been dried to concentrate their juice, before being aged for up to four years in wood. Wines from the village of Pupillin fall under Arbois' own supposedly, though often unconvincingly, superior Villages *appellation*. Good producers of Arbois, such as the Fruitière Vinicole d'Arbois and the Domaines Rolet and Puffeney, are leading a trend toward fresher-tasting reds and whites. However, there are plenty of bottles, including the large number on offer from the dynamic merchant Henri Maire, credited with rescuing this region from near extinction, which, unfortunately, show no such spark.

CHÂTEAU D'ARLAY
This estate is consistent in its production of some of the best raisiny, rich vins de pailles of the region.

✳ AC Arbois, AC Arbois Mousseux, AC Arbois Pupillin.	Maurice Chassot, Désiré Petit et Fils, Jacques Foret, Fruitière Vinicole d'Arbois, Pierre Overnoy, Jacques Puffeney, Rolet, du Sorbief, André et Mireille Tissot, Jacques Tissot.
🍇 Red/ rosé: Poulsard, Pinot Noir, Trousseau. White: Chardonnay, Savagnin. *Vin jaune:* Savagnin.	
	🍴 *Vin jaune:* Ragoût of goose with apples.
🍷 Light, quite floral reds. Light, dry rosés. Characterful, nutty *vins jaunes.*	🗓 1996, 1995, 1990.
	📅 Red: 3–5 years.
🏛 Lucien Aviet, Ch Béthanie,	White /rosé: 2–4 years. *Vin jaune:* 10–20 years.

FRUITIÈRE VINICOLE D'ARBOIS
This producer is a reliable source of red and white wine.

BUGEY

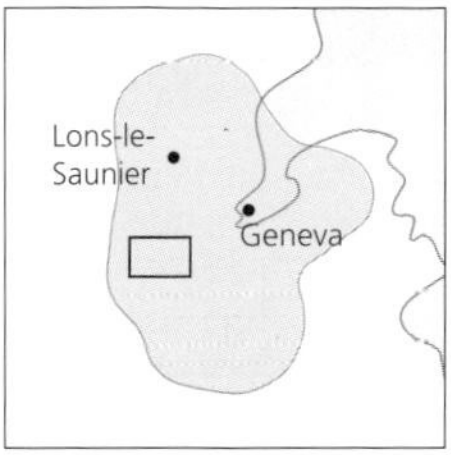

THE VINEYARDS OF BUGEY are scattered from Bourg-en-Bresse to Ambérieu, and along the eastern bank of the Rhône river from Seyssel to Lagnieu. The vines are planted on limestone soil, with red, white, and rosé wines being made under the Vin du Bugey *VDQS* or, in the case of Virieu-le-Grand, Manicle, Montagnieu, Machuraz, and Cerdon, with the name of the village. Of the varietal wines, the widely planted Gamay is used to produce vibrant, easy-going reds, while the Pinot Noir is used to make what is sometimes called "Junior Burgundy." The most interesting Bugey wines are the deeply colored, slightly bitter reds made from the Mondeuse grape. The rosés, made mainly from the Gamay or Pinot Noir, are light and fresh, while the whites are light, fresh, and off-dry. The *VDQS* can also be used for sparkling wines.

CHRISTIAN BEAULIEU
The red wines of Bugey can be light and feeble, but this example shows that rich, fruity wines can be produced here.

UNDERRATED VINEYARDS
The region of Bugey produces attractive, light VDQS *wines that can be better than* appellation contrôlée *wines from elsewhere.*

- VDQS Vins du Bugey (village names may be added).
- Red/ rosé: Poulsard, Gamay, Mondeuse, Pinot Noir. White: Roussette, Jacquère, Chardonnay, Pinot Gris, Aligoté.
- Light reds. Light, dry whites. Dry rosés.
- Christian Beaulieu, Caveau Bugiste, Caveau du Mont July, Cellier de Bel-Air, Eugène Monin.
- Partridge cooked with bacon and cheese and served with noodles.
- Red/ rosé: 1997, 1996.
- Red/ rosé: 1–3 years.

CHÂTEAU CHALON

NAMED AFTER THE HILLTOP village rather than an estate, as its name suggests, Château Chalon's *vins jaunes* are produced exclusively from Savagnin grapes that are grown on limestone and marl soil. Wines bearing the Château Chalon label must be aged for at least six years and three months in sealed, partially filled wooden casks, during which time they develop their famous yeasty flavor and take on a sherrylike character. Château Chalon is usually sold in a special 62 cl "clavelin" bottle that supposedly represents the amount of *vin jaune* produced from one liter of wine.

- AC Château Chalon.
- *Vin jaune:* Savagnin.
- Nutty-flavored *vins jaunes* that are golden in color.
- Berthet-Bondet, Jean Bourdy, Courbet, Durand-Perron, Jean Macle.
- Chicken breast cooked in *vin jaune*.
- 1990, 1989, 1985.
- 20 years.

JEAN BOURDY
This producer is one of the most reliable sources of dry, salty Château Chalon.

CÔTES DU JURA

THIS ISOLATED REGION has retained traditional grape varieties and methods of wine making in its use of the Poulsard, Trousseau, and Pinot Noir grapes for red wines and the Savagnin and Chardonnay for its whites. Styles include lightly fruity still reds and rosés, nutty dry whites, sparkling wines, and slowly-matured sherrylike *vins jaunes*. The most interesting wines are probably the lusciously sweet *vins de paille* that are made from grapes that have been dried to concentrate their juice, before being aged for up to four years in wood.

- AC Côtes du Jura.
- Red/ rosé: Poulsard. White: Chardonnay, Savagnin. *Vin jaune:* Savagnin.
- Light, pale reds. Light, dry whites. Dry rosés. Strong, nutty *vins jaunes*.
- Ch d'Arly, Jean Bourdy.
- *Vin jaune:* Cream cheese.
- Red: 1996, 1995, 1990.
- *Vin jaune:* 10–15 years.

JEAN BOURDY
This pale red wine is made from the plummy Poulsard grape.

CRÉPY

THE WINES OF CRÉPY have much in common with their neighbors in Switzerland: they are made from two varieties of the Chasselas grape, the Chasselas Roux and Vert; they are light, floral, and slightly spritzy; they are liked by skiers; and they carry price tags to match. There is much debate as to whether these wines should be allowed to go through malolactic fermentation (see p.24). Those that don't are dry, crisp, and fruity, with a slight spritz. Those that do are fuller-bodied and almondy, and can be kept for a year or two.

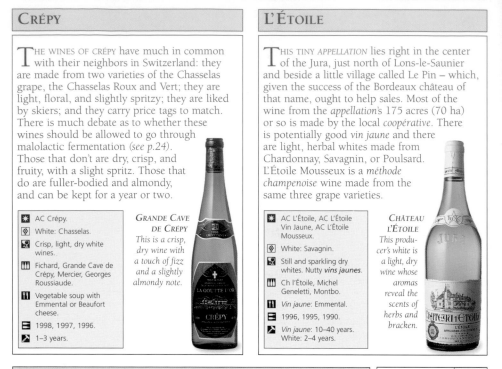

* AC Crépy.
* White: Chasselas.
* Crisp, light, dry white wines.
* Fichard, Grande Cave de Crépy, Mercier, Georges Roussiaude.
* Vegetable soup with Emmental or Beaufort cheese.
* 1998, 1997, 1996.
* 1–3 years.

GRANDE CAVE DE CRÉPY
This is a crisp, dry wine with a touch of fizz and a slightly almondy note.

L'ÉTOILE

THIS TINY APPELLATION lies right in the center of the Jura, just north of Lons-le-Saunier and beside a little village called Le Pin – which, given the success of the Bordeaux château of that name, ought to help sales. Most of the wine from the appellation's 175 acres (70 ha) or so is made by the local coopérative. There is potentially good vin jaune and there are light, herbal whites made from Chardonnay, Savagnin, or Poulsard. L'Étoile Mousseux is a méthode champenoise wine made from the same three grape varieties.

* AC L'Étoile, AC L'Étoile Vin Jaune, AC L'Étoile Mousseux.
* White: Savagnin.
* Still and sparkling dry whites. Nutty vins jaunes.
* Ch l'Étoile, Michel Geneletti, Montbo.
* Vin jaune: Emmental.
* 1996, 1995, 1990.
* Vin jaune: 10–40 years. White: 2–4 years.

CHÂTEAU L'ÉTOILE
This producer's white is a light, dry wine whose aromas reveal the scents of herbs and bracken.

VIN DE SAVOIE

THE VIN DE SAVOIE APPELLATION is made up of a diverse series of separate areas, mostly on scree slopes or glacial moraine. Some villages are allowed to add their name to the appellation for their red, white, or rosé wines, which can be made from a range of grapes. In general, whites whose labels don't refer to Roussette, Altesse, or Bergeron will be made from Jacquère, a late-ripening variety that makes Savoie's lightest wine. This does not apply to the villages of Marignan, Marin, and Ripaille, where the Chasselas is used. The Altesse is also known as the Roussette and used for its own appellation, Roussette de Savoie. The Mondeuse grape is used for reds in the communes of Chautagne, Cruet, Jongieux, and St. Jean de la Porte. The Vin de Savoie appellation can also be applied to a number of sparkling wines.

LOUIS MAGNIN
This Chignin Bergeron, made from the Jacquère grape, is one of the most refreshing light white wines in France.

MOUNTAIN FRESH
The light white wines produced in this vineyard next to the Lac St. André are ideal après-ski fare.

* AC Vin de Savoie, AC Vin de Savoie Mousseux, AC Vin de Savoie Pétillant, AC Roussette de Savoie.
* Red: Gamay, Pinot Noir, Mondeuse. White: Jacquère, Chasselas, Roussette, Chardonnay.
* Light reds. Crisp, dry whites.
* Dominique Allion, Louis Magnin, Claude Marendon, Michel Menetrey, Raymond Quénard, Trosset, Varicon et Clerc.
* White: Chicken braised with salt pork and vin jaune.
* White: 1998, 1997, 1996.
* White: 1–3 years.

SEYSSEL

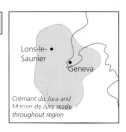

OF ALL THE SAVOIE *APPELLATIONS*, this is arguably the most interesting, offering quite different still and sparkling whites from vineyards between the villages of Anglefort and Chanay. The still wines are largely made from the Chasselas, but are given an extra floral character by the presence of at least 10 percent of the Roussette, whose origins are said to be in this area. The sparkling Seyssel is far better known than the still. The Chasselas and Roussette are used in these, too, but as supporting actors to the local Molette, which contributes to wines such as the vintage Royal Seyssel Cuvée Privée, which are at once elegant and biscuity, like fine Champagne with more flowers but less fruit. Both the sparkling and the still styles of Seyssel make excellent accompaniments to the local speciality, *Raclette*.

SOURCE OF BUBBLES
Many of the best grapes from these vineyards will probably be used for sparkling wine.

MAISON MOLLEX
A fresh example of the Roussette grape from one of the most reliable producers in the region.

⭐ AC Seyssel, AC Seyssel Mousseux	Molette, Royal Seyssel, Varichon et Clerc.
🍇 Still white: Chasselas, Roussette. Sparkling white: Molette, Chasselas, Roussette.	🍴 Still: Salad of fresh crayfish served with crusty bread and a sauce of melted buttter flavored with shallots, white wine vinegar, and parsley.
🍷 Light, dry whites. Often good-value sparkling whites.	📅 Still: 1998, 1997, 1996.
🏘 Maison Mollex, Clos de la	🕐 1-3 years.

OTHERS

THE CRÉMANT DU JURA SPARKLING WINE, made from a mixture of the Savagnin, Pinot Blanc, and Chardonnay, is potentially delicious and can be a good value if you pick a producer such as Grand Frères. The most distinctive "other" wine of the region has to be the Macvin de Jura, which stands firmly apart from all of France's red and white wines as an historic curiosity. It counts as a *vin doux naturel* like Muscat de Beaumes-de-Venise, Banyuls, and Rasteau, but lacks the rich, fruity appeal of those fortified wines. It offers a taste (an acquired taste, one might say) of the distant past. Its production process involves the cooking of the juice of Savagnin grapes until half or more of the liquid has evaporated. The boiled and unfermented juice is then fortified with local brandy and flavored with herbs and spices. The result, which is technically questionable as "wine" because of the lack of fermentation, is left to mature in a cask for six years. This truly original method is believed to have been devised by the nuns of the abbey of Château Chalon in the 9th century. The Domaine Bourdy, which makes the best examples of Macvin today, uses a recipe from 1579. Many French critics, and most wine writers outside France, dislike the stewed, medicinal character of Macvin, a wine that seems to have a lot more in common with Vermouth than with most of the wines that we drink today.

CHÂTEAU CHALON
It was at the abbey here that the curious technique for producing Macvin originated over a thousand years ago.

DOMAINE GRAND FRÈRES
Rich, sparkling Crémant du Jura like this is rarely seen outside the region, but is worth buying.

LANGUEDOC-ROUSSILLON

UNTIL RECENTLY THE SLEEPING GIANT OF THE

WINE WORLD, THIS REGION IS NOW PRODUCING

A WIDE RANGE OF WORLD-CLASS WINES.

Languedoc-Roussillon region

THE FIRST THING TO MENTION about this region is its size. The vineyards cover over 740,300 acres (300,000 ha), three times as as much as Bordeaux. This is the source of one in 10 bottles of the world's wine, and one in three bottles of French wine.

Until recently, however, this region was rarely mentioned in wine books. The explanation was simple: very little of the wine produced here carried the essential words *appellation contrôlée* on its labels. In fact, much of the annual harvest was either sold in returnable bottles or despatched directly to the subsidized European wine lake.

French and Euro-bureaucrats would gladly have seen most of the non-*appellation* vineyards being converted into orchards, but a few dynamic individuals had other plans. Men like Robert Skalli of

HEADING TO PORT
The Mas Amiel's rich, darkly luscious Maury is one of France's most impressive fortified wines, and one that easily stands up to comparisons with many vintage ports.

🅰 815,000 acres (330,000 ha): 290 million bottles.	▨ Very varied, with limestone in the hills and fertile alluvial soil on the plains.
🌡 The entire region is highly influenced by the proximity of the Mediterranean, but some areas, for example, the hills of the Minervois and Limoux, are cooler, thanks to their slightly higher altitudes.	🍇 Red: Grenache, Cabernet Sauvignon, Merlot, Cinsault, Carignan, Syrah, Mourvèdre. White: Clairette, Chardonnay, Ugni Blanc, Grenache Blanc, Muscat, Sauvignon, Viognier.

LAND OF PROMISE
After centuries of being regarded as a source of cheap bulk wine, to be served from jugs or blended with produce from other parts of France, Languedoc-Roussillon, the largest single wine region in the world, is finally beginning to develop its potential.

Fortant de France and an Englishman called James Herrick, who had made his fortune on wine in Australia, realized that Languedoc-Roussillon had a good climate and plentiful land. What it lacked were internationally-popular grape varieties and the skills required to turn them into commercial wines. So, thousands of acres of Chardonnay, Merlot, Sauvignon Blanc, Viognier, Syrah, and

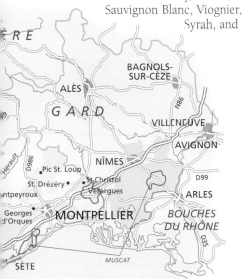

FRUIT AND NUTS
These Côtes du Roussillon vines are grown alongside almond trees and illustrate the tradition here of varied agriculture.

While the outsider Aimé Guibert of Mas de Daumas Gassac had the temerity to try to make a *Vin de Pays de l'Hérault* that would sell for the price of a good Bordeaux, many of his neighbors still fail to make the most of either their vines or their grapes.

Among the *appellations*, matters are just as confused. Some areas, like Banyuls, Collioure *(see p.164)*, Maury *(see p.168)*, Faugères *(see p.167)*, St. Chinian *(see p.170)*, and Pic-St. Loup in the Coteaux du Languedoc *(see p.166)*, have proven that they can make wines of great quality. Elsewhere, though, big *appellations* such as Corbières *(see p.165)* and Minervois *(see p.169)* cover land whose potential ranges from fine to decidedly ordinary. If Languedoc-Roussillon had received the same attention as, say, Bordeaux and Burgundy, the best sub regions would have been far more clearly identified a long time ago. As it is, you are far better off buying a *vin de pays* from a good producer than trusting an *appellation*.

Cabernet Sauvignon were planted, while overseas buyers sent wine makers into the *coopératives* to oversee the harvest and the fermentation process. The effect was superficially dramatic. Within a few years, the shelves were filled with varietal *vins de pays* that competed directly with their counterparts from the New World.

Unfortunately, while the best of these wines were good, far too many were unimpressive, lacking the fruity intensity of the New World and the complexity traditionally associated with France. The biggest handicap here probably lies in the limited aspirations of the region's wine growers, even some of the most important ones.

KEY TO REGIONS

- Collioure and Banyuls
- Corbières
- Costières de Nîmes
- Coteaux du Languedoc
- Roussillon (including Côtes du Roussillon and Côtes du Roussillon-Villages)
- Fitou
- Limoux
- Maury
- Minervois
- Other AOC regions (including Cabardès, Faugères, Muscat, St. Chinian)
- *Département* boundary

BANYULS

I F A PATRIOTIC FRENCHMAN is happy to drink Vin Jaune as a Gallic alternative to sherry, he can also enjoy Banyuls' fortified wine as an alternative to tawny port. The four *communes* of Banyuls-sur-Mer, Cerbère, Collioure, and Port Vendres form Banyuls, France's most southern *appellation*. The grape variety that grows best on the thin, acidic soil here is the Grenache, which must make up at least 75 percent of all Banyuls Grand Cru. Banyuls' red, white, rosé, and tawny wines are all *vins doux naturels*, with the reds being its most famous. Aged in oak for 30 months, red Banyuls has an aroma of raisins, coffee, stewed fruit, and almonds and can last for as long as 40 years. While some Banyuls take on an oxidized, *rancio* character, others, which do not make contact with air to preserve their fruitiness, are known as *rimages*.

SUNBATHING IN BANYULS
Like a number of the world's greatest fortified wines, Banyuls wine benefits from being warmed by the sun during production.

DOMAINE DU MAS BLANC
Domaine du Mas Blanc's Cuvée de la St. Martin is one of the finest examples of Banyuls' famous fortified wines.

✱	AC Banyuls, AC Banyuls Grand Cru.	l'Abbé Rous, du Mas Amiel, du Mas Blanc, L'Etoile, Clos des Paulilles, Cellier des Templiers, La Tour Vieille, Vial Magnères.
🍷	Red/ white/ rosé: Grenache Noir, Grenache Gris, Grenache Blanc, Macabéo, Malvoisie.	
🍷	Rich, red *vins doux naturels*. Medium-sweet, white and rosé *vins doux naturels*.	🧀 Red: Roquefort cheese.
🍽	De la Casa Blanca, Cave de	📅 Red: 1994, 1991, 1988, 1985, 1983.
		📊 Red: 2–25 years.

CABARDÈS

E VERY YEAR, MILLIONS of vacationers pass Cabardès' vineyards as they drive along the A61 highway north of Carcassonne. Since the Carignan and Aubun grape varieties, which tend to produce rather dull wines, were phased out here and replaced with more popular grapes like Cabernet Sauvignon, Merlot, Grenache, Syrah, Fer, and Cinsault, Cabardès has grown in popularity. Cabardès' wines, which are also sold as Côtes du Cabardès et de l'Orbiel, are red and rosé, with the lean reds being the more interesting of the two.

CHÂTEAU CONSTANCE
The quality of this wine is higher than that implied by Cabardès' VDQS status.

✱	VDQS Cabardès.
🍷	Red/ rosé: Grenache, Syrah, Cinsault, Cabernet Sauvignon, Cabernet Franc, Merlot, Malbec, Fer.
🍷	Light, fruity reds. Peppery rosés.
🍽	De Cabrol, Ch Constance, de Pennautier, Ventenac.
🍖	Red: Assorted pork meats.
📅	Red: 1998, 1996.
📊	Red: 2–5 years.

COLLIOURE

C OLLIOURE IS UNFORTIFIED Banyuls, or vice versa. These two *appellations* share the same steep, narrow terraces around the pretty seaside town and artists' colony of Collioure and the villages of Port-Vendres, Banyuls-sur-Mer, and Cerbère. Most Collioure is full-bodied red wine, made from the Grenache Noir and Mourvèdre, blended with the Carignan, Cinsault, and Syrah. As the Carignan is slowly phased out, the quality of Collioure is improving and some of the less well-situated vineyards are being replaced with peach orchards and scrubland.

DOMAINE LA TOUR VIEILLE
The Cuvée Puig Oriol from this estate is a powerful, long-lived red wine.

✱	AC Collioure.
🍷	Red/ rosé: Grenache Noir, Mourvèdre.
🍷	Heady, full-bodied reds. Flavorsome, dry rosés.
🍽	Du Mas Blanc, de Jau, Clos de Paulilles, de la Rectorie, des Templiers, la Tour Vieille, Vial Magnères.
🍖	Red: Meat and bean stew.
📅	Red: 1996, 1994.
📊	Red: 4–6 years.

CORBIÈRES

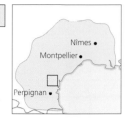

THIS *APPELLATION* WAS ONE OF THE biggest beneficiaries of the international wine boom of the 1970s and 1980s, with its red wines offering a good value before the emergence of East European, Southern French, and New World wines. Today, Corbières has plenty of competition from nearby Minervois (see p.169) and the Coteaux du Languedoc (see p.166).

A TASTE OF THE SEA
Parts of the Corbières appellation, like this area near Periac de Mer, are very close to the Mediterranean, which has a direct influence on the flavor of the wines that are produced here.

CORBIÈRES IS A HUGE AND enormously varied region to the southeast of Carcassonne. Due to its size and the diversity of its soils, altitudes, microclimates, and grape varieties, it is very difficult to generalize about the quality or style of the wines produced here. Any attempts to assess the potential of the *appellation* are further hampered by the poor quality of the wine making at many of the *coopératives* that handle the majority of Corbière's grapes, and the traditional reliance on the somewhat dull Carignan grape, which still covers over half of the vineyards and yields up to 60 percent of the wine in any bottle. In an attempt to make some sense of the region, 11 separate regions, unofficial vineyard zones, have been identified. It is likely that one day, at least, some of these will be officially recognized as

appellations. Unfortunately, even within these zones there can be huge variations in both altitude and climate. To date, some of the region's best wines have been produced in Lézignan and Alaric in the north of the region, Boutenac in the center, and on the hills of Termenes in the southwest. Sigean, located on the Mediterranean coast, also produces good wines, although this hilly area is probably the most varied of all the 11 regions.

Skilled producers, who focus on using the grapes from the Syrah and old Carignan vines planted on limestone soil (especially in Boutenac), make wines with rich, ripe, fruity flavors and enough structure to make them worth keeping for a few years. It has, however, been too easy to sell dull examples of Corbières to those who have not yet tasted the better Vins de Pays d'Oc (see p.233) from the same region. Today, over 90 percent of Corbières is red, but some of its dry whites, made from grapes including the Muscat, Vermentino, Marsanne, and the Roussanne, are worth trying.

CHÂTEAU D'AGUILHAR
The rugged countryside that surrounds Château d'Aguilhar has changed little over the years.

CHÂTEAU DE LASTOURS
This brilliant estate is also a home for mentally handicapped residents, who help to produce the château's wines.

✸ AC Corbières.	Caumont, Grand Moulin, Hélène, de Lastours, Vignerons de la Méditerranée. Meunier St. Louis, d'Ornaisons, les Palais, Pech-Latt, Producteurs de Mont Tauch, du Révérend, St. Auriol, St. Estève, Celliers St. Martin, Salvagnac, du Vieux Parc, Villemajou, la Voulte Gasparets.
⬘ Red/rosé: Carignan, Syrah, Mourvèdre, Grenache, Picpoul, Terret. White: Bourboulenc, Maccabeo, Grenache Blanc.	
⬗ Spicy, full-bodied, dry reds. Medium-bodied, dry rosés. Rare but refreshing, light, aromatic, dry whites.	
▥ Ch d'Aguilhar, Aiguilloux, Caraguilhes, des Chandelles, Etang des Colombes, Grand	🍴 Red: Game stew.
	🍷 Red: 1998, 1996, 1994.
	⬙ Red: 3–8 years.

COSTIÈRES DE NÎMES

WINES FROM THE PEBBLEY VINEYARDS OF Costières de Nîmes, located between the regions of the Rhône and Languedoc, have had a good reputation since Roman times. In this century, most of the area's predominantly Carignan grapes were used to make basic red wines. Then, in the 1980s, ambitious estate owners fought to attain promotion from *VDQS* to *appellation* status, and changed the name of the *appellation* from Costières du Gard to Costières de Nîmes. Today, Costières de Nîmes covers 24 *communes* from Beaucaire to Vauvert along the Rhône, and, although a token amount of white wine is made, most of the wines made here are red or rosé. Carignan still contributes up to 40 percent of the blend, but the Grenache and Syrah, which form at least 25 percent of the blend, are increasingly prevalent.

READY FOR THE HARVEST
Rain is fortunately not often a problem in this southern region of France, but it pays to be prepared.

MAS DES BRESSADES
Rich Costières de Nîmes wine like this is a good alternative to the pricier wines of the Rhône's Crozes-Hermitage and St. Joseph.

✴	AC Costières de Nîmes.	Campuget, Mas de Bressades, Ch Mourgues du Grès, de Nages, Tuilerie de Pazac, Valcombe.
🍷	Red: Grenache, Carignan, Syrah. White: Clairette, Grenache Blanc, Bourboulenc. Rosé: Carignan, Cinsault, Mourvèdre, Syrah.	🍴 Sausage, meat, and bean stew.
🗺	Medium- to full-bodied reds. Soft whites. Dry rosés.	🗓 1998, 1996.
🏛	Ch de l'Amarine, Ch de	📆 Red: 2–6 years. White/ rosé: 1–3 years.

COTEAUX DU LANGUEDOC

THESE VINEYARDS ON THE HILLS and the great plain of Languedoc had already been established by the Greeks by the time Julius Caesar conquered Gaul. In fact, wine makers back in Rome were so impressed by the wines of this area that they unsuccessfully attempted to curtail competition from them. In the 18th century, Languedoc's wines flourished once again, before being struck by phylloxera in the 1880s. Today, Languedoc is seen as one of the most exciting wine-making areas in France, with its whites and rosés, which rely on technical wine making, often providing better money than wines from Provence. One *commune* that is showing great potential is Pic de St. Loup, where wine makers like l'Hortus are making wines that outclass many a Châteauneuf-du-Pape *(see p.207)*.

ABBAYE DE VALMAGNE
As is the case in many other parts of France, a church has provided the ideal setting in which to mature red wine.

PRIEURÉ DE ST. JEAN-DE-BÉBIAN
Owned by the former editors of two French wine magazines, this is an impeccably made, richly flavored red.

✴	AC Coteaux du Languedoc.	Mas Bruguière, Mas Julien, Peyre-Rose, Prieuré de St. Jean-de-Bébian.
🍷	Red/ rosé: Carignan, Cinsault, Grenache, Syrah, Mourvèdre. White: Grenache, Bourboulenc, Clairette.	🍴 Red: Entrecôte steak grilled with garlic and thyme.
🗺	Full-bodied reds. Light, dry rosés. Light, dry whites.	🗓 1997, 1996.
🏛	D'Aupilhac, de l'Hortus,	📆 Red: 3–8 years. White/ rosé: 1–3 years.

FAUGÈRES

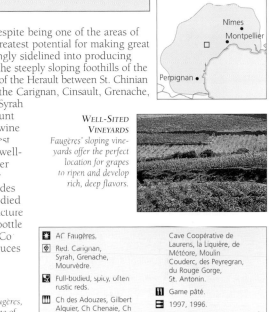

UNTIL ABOUT 20 YEARS AGO, despite being one of the areas of southern France with the greatest potential for making great red wine, Faugères was surprisingly sidelined into producing Muscats and *eaux-de-vie.* Today, the steeply sloping foothills of the Cévennes, a mountainous corner of the Herault between St. Chinian and Cabrières, are planted with the Carignan, Cinsault, Grenache, Lladoner Pelut, Mourvèdre, and Syrah vines. Apart from a small amount of dry rosé, almost all of the wine produced here is red. The best examples, like those of the well-established Domaine Alquier and the relative newcomer Michel Louison's Château des Estanilles, are rich, full-bodied and spicy, with enough structure to reward several years of bottle aging. Alternatively, Cave Coopérative de Laurens produces good, inexpensive wines.

WELL-SITED VINEYARDS
Faugères' sloping vineyards offer the perfect location for grapes to ripen and develop rich, deep flavors.

GILBERT ALQUIER
One of the pioneers of modern Faugères, the Domaine Alquier produces some of the finest reds of the appellation.

❇️ AC Faugères,	Cave Coopérative de Laurens, la Liquière, de Météore, Moulin Couderc, des Peyregran, du Rouge Gorge, St. Antonin.
🍷 Red: Carignan, Syrah, Grenache, Mourvèdre.	
🍇 Full-bodied, spicy, often rustic reds.	
	🍽️ Game pâté.
🍴 Ch des Adouzes, Gilbert Alquier, Ch Chenaie, Ch des Estanilles, Ch Grézan,	🗓️ 1997, 1996.
	⏳ 2–4 years.

FITOU

THE OLDEST *APPELLATION* IN Languedoc-Roussillon, Fitou is divided into two zones that border Corbières *(see p.165).* The smaller zone lies around the coastal town of Fitou, while the larger's vineyards dominate the land between Villeneuve-les-Corbières and Tuchan. Although the *communes* here can produce Rivesaltes *vins doux naturels,* most of the wines are reds, made mainly from Carignan blended with the Grenache, the Lladoner Pelut, and Syrah. However, the Carignan tends to produce dull wines unless the vines are old and yields are modest. Recently, wine production has been a problem here, with many producers coasting along on the success they enjoyed in the 1980s. These wines should be herb-flavored, taking on a wild, spicy character after four or five years; but Fitou that is worth aging is a rare find now.

MEDITERRANEAN VINES
Many of Fitou's vineyards are quite close to the sea, but the best wines are produced from the grapes grown further inland on hillside slopes.

CHÂTEAU L'ESPIGNE
This Fitou has an unusually rich flavor and a level of complexity that is seldom found in this appellation.

❇️ AC Fitou.	Corbières, Producteurs de Mont Tauch, de la Rochelierre, de Rolland, Val d'Orbieu (Vignerons de la Méditerranée).
🍷 Red: Carignan, Grenache, Mourvèdre, Syrah.	
🍇 Simple, medium- to full-bodied, rustic reds.	
	🍽️ Pigeon simmered with onions and Bayonne ham.
🍴 Ch l'Espigne, Lepaumier, Lerys, Ch de Nouvelles, Maîtres Vignerons de Cascastel, Cave Pilote de Villeneuve-les-	🗓️ 1997, 1996.
	⏳ 3–4 years.

LIMOUX

ACCORDING TO THE LIMOUXINS, Limoux has been making sparkling wine since 1531, long before Dom Pérignon began his experiments in Champagne. More recently, however, this medieval city close to Carcassonne has become the focus for another innovation. Until the early 1990s, the *coopérative* here concentrated on turning the Mauzac grape into sparkling Blanquette de Limoux. Today, that often less than aromatic variety has been blended with the Chenin Blanc, Pinot Noir, and Chardonnay. While the locals still enjoy their Crémant de Limoux, made from a stipulated minimum 90 percent Mauzac, modern Blanquette de Limoux may contain just 15 percent Mauzac. As well as making good sparkling wine, Limoux now has a separate *appellation* for its increasingly impressive Chardonnay.

LIMOUX CELLAR
The combination of chalky soil, a coolish climate, and a fermentation process that takes place in oak barrels like these gives Limoux Chardonnay a similar character to some Burgundian wines.

ST. LAURENT
This méthode champenoise sparkling wine benefits from the use of a wide range of grape varieties.

✱ AC Limoux, AC Blanquette Méthode Ancestrale, AC Blanquette de Limoux, AC Crémant de Limoux.	and Roger Antech, Collin, de Flassian, de Fourn, Guinot, les Caves du Sieur d'Arques, Vignobles Vergnes.
⬧ White: Mauzac, Chardonnay, Chenin Blanc.	🍴 Mussels marinated in lemon and garlic.
▣ Dry, sparkling whites. Barrel-fermented still whites.	📅 1996, 1994.
▥ De l'Aigle, Aimery, Georges	⏳ Sparkling: 5–6 years. Still: 3–4 years.

MAURY

UNLIKE BANYULS (*see p.164*), which appears on most French wine lists, the wines of Maury, to the south of Corbières (*see p.165*), remain fairly unknown. This is somewhat surprising given the prestige this town's wines enjoyed in the second century BC and the potential quality of its climate and soil. Perhaps one of the reasons for Maury's recent fall from grace is the reliance the *appellation* traditionally placed on the Macabéo and Carignan grapes, which tend to produce dull wines. This is likely to change, however, as regulations raise the proportion of a more flavorsome grape, the Grenache, to 75 percent in the year 2000. Like Banyuls, Maury can be fresh and light or in the form of tangy *rancio*, and may be drunk as an aperitif or with dessert. For a taste of fine Maury, try a really mature bottle from Mas Amiel.

A PERFECT SITUATION
Maury's hot climate and schistous soil provide the ideal conditions for the Grenache grape to ripen, and subsequently to be used in the production of unique, fortified wines.

MAS AMIEL
Mas Amiel leads the way in quality Maury, producing a range of rich, concentrated, plummy wines.

✱ AC Maury.	de Maury, Maurydoré, la Pléiade, Robert Ponderoux.
⬧ Red: Grenache Noir, Grenache Gris, Grenache Blanc.	🍴 Cheddar and/or parmesan cheese served with fresh grapes.
▥ Rich, fortified reds which compete with vintage and tawny port.	📅 Mainly non-vintage.
▦ Mas Amiel, Jean-Louis Lafage, les Vignerons	⏳ 5–25 years.

MINERVOIS

O FTEN SEEN AS CORBIÈRES' SIBLING, this region, which stretches across south-facing limestone hills between St. Chinian (*see p.171*) and Carcassonne, has a character all of its own. However, like Corbières (*see p.165*), Minervois has a range of environments and unofficial vineyard zones have been designated. In the cool, western area, rainfall is higher and the Syrah and Grenache grow well, while in the region's arid heart-land it is the Mourvèdre that excels.

The best Minervois is made in the northern zone of Minervois-la-Livinière, with the general quality of Minervois tending to be higher than that of Corbières. This may be due to the lower proportion of Carignan used and the excellent skills of its producers, such as Châteaux de Lastours and de Gourgazaud. Although 95 per-cent of Minervois is red, whites are made from Rhône and Mediterranean grape varieties.

GORGE DE LA CESSE
The landscape in this large region, ranging from hot, limestone slopes in the heartland to rugged mountains in the west, is among the most varied in southern France.

DOMAINE PICCININI
This estate has been one of the pioneers of the "la Livinière" region.

✴ AC Minervois.		de Gourgazaud, Ch de Lastours, Ch Maris, Ch les Ollieux, d'Oupia, Ch les Palais, Paraza, Piccinini, Ste. Eulalie, la Tour-Boisée, Ch Villerambert-Julien.
🍷 Red: Carignan, Grenache, Syrah, Mourvèdre. White/ rosé: Grenache Blanc, Bourboulenc, Macabéo.		
		🍴 Ragout of veal.
🍖 Full-bodied, dry reds.Dry whites. Dry, fruity rosés.		📅 1996, 1995, 1994.
🍶 Ch Domergue, Fabas, Ch		⏳ Red: 3–5 years. White/ rosé: 1 year.

MUSCAT APPELLATIONS

W HILE THE BEST-KNOWN French fortified wine for many people is the Rhône's Muscat de Beaumes-de-Venise, nine in 10 bottles of *vin doux naturel* come from Languedoc-Roussillon's five Muscat *appellations*. Of Frontignan and Mireval, coastal neighbors near Sète, Frontignan has the greater fame, thanks partly to legends citing Hercules and Thomas Jefferson as enjoying its *vins doux naturels* and *vins de liqueurs*. The

wines of Mireval, however, made from the Muscat Blanc à Petits Grains, are often more elegant, as are the rare Muscats de Lunel. More run-of-the-mill, Muscat de Rivesaltes, made from the Muscat Blanc à Petits Grains or Muscat d'Alexandrie, differs greatly from the blended wines of Rivesaltes. The appealing, apricoty character of Muscat de St. Jean-de-Minervois, an *appellation* within Mireval, has only just been "discovered."

MUSCAT
Fortified Muscat, such as this Muscat de Rivesaltes, should taste like a mixture of fresh grapes and marmalade.

CHÂTEAU DE LA PEYRADE
Most of France's fortified Muscats are made by coopératives, but some estates, like Château de la Peyrade, also produce top-class Muscat.

✴ AC Muscat de Frontignan, AC Muscat de St. Jean-de-Minervois, AC Muscat de Lunel, AC Muscat de Mireval, AC Muscat de Rivesaltes.		🍷 White *vins doux naturels*.
		🍴 Cazes, de Corneilla, Deltour-Grousset, Força Real, de Jau, Lacoste, Mas Liaro, Nouvelles, Ch de la Peyrade, Sarda-Malet.
🍶 White: Muscat Doré de Frontignan, Muscat Blanc à Petits Grains, Muscat Rosé à Petits Grains, Muscat d'Alexandrie.		🍴 Lemon and raisin cheesecake.
		📅 Mainly non-vintage.
		⏳ 1–3 years.

ROUSSILLON

BEST-KNOWN AS HALF OF Languedoc-Roussillon, despite the proven potential of some of its vineyards, this large area has yet to create an independent identity for itself. However, new grape varieties are being introduced, wine making is improving dramatically, and the quality of some individual *communes* is steadily being established.

CÔTES DU ROUSSILLON
Sheltered by mountain ranges on three sides, the vineyards of Côtes du Roussillon are planted in the sunniest region in France. This hilly landscape is home to a wide range of grape varieties.

WINE MAKING IN ROUSSILLON probably dates back to the 7th century BC, when vines were imported by Greeks who were attracted to the area by the minerals to be found on the Catalan coast. The vines continued to thrive during the Middle Ages, when the sweet wine they produced was known as "Vin d'Espagne." The high mountain ranges on three sides of the vineyards form a natural amphitheatre that shelters the vines. To the north there are Les Corbières, to the west Le Canigou and Les Albères, which form the frontier with Spain. With more than 2,550 hours of sunshine a year, this is France's sunniest region, and the ripening of grapes is not the problem it is elsewhere. Vintages of Roussillon rarely vary as the climate is generally fairly consistent. Although Roussillon's vine growers planted vines before neighboring Languedoc, they still seem to be striving for their own regional identity. The area's two main *appellations* for still,

dry wines are the Côtes du Roussillon and the Côtes du Roussillon-Villages. The Côtes du Roussillon covers an area of about 12,355 acres (5,000 ha) for red, white, and rosé wines, while the Côtes du Roussillon-Villages is limited to red wines from 25 villages located along the river Agly (of which Caramany and Latour-de-France are allowed to add their names to the wine's label). As is seen elsewhere in this area, while Carignan is still the dominant grape, quality has improved as the percentage of the Syrah and Mourvèdre varieties has been increased. Either of these grapes must now comprise 20 percent of the final blend. As for the Carignan, this often performs best when producers use the *macération carbonique* process to extract as much fruit as possible from this potentially dull grape. White wines are still forced by regulations to use a high percentage of the Maccabéo and Malvoisie varieties, while no more than 50 percent of the more flavorsome Grenache Blanc, Roussanne, Marsanne, or Vermentino may be used. Fortunately, wine makers sometimes find that their hands slip while they prepare the blends.

LES VIGNERONS CATALANS
This coopérative produces several excellent cuvées, including Cuvée du Presbytère from Caramany.

DOMAINE GAUBY
Domaine Gauby is an excellent estate whose wines prove that subtle, elegant wines can be produced in this region.

✱ AC Côtes du Roussillon, AC Côtes du Roussillon-Villages, AC Grand Roussillon	Gardiés, Gauby, Ch de Jau, Laporte, Lequerde, Maîtres Vignerons de Tauteval, de Rombeau, Mas Rous, St. François, Sarda-Malet, des Schistes, Cellier de Trouillas, les Vignerons Catalans, Vignerons de Pézilla.
▣ Red/ rosé: Carignan, Syrah, Grenache, Mourvèdre, Maccabéo. White: Maccabéo, Malvoisie.	
▣ Varied, but potentially spicy reds. Floral whites. Dry rosés.	❚ Roasted veal fillet with Madeira sauce.
▥ Caves de Baixas, Brial, de la Casenove, de Castelnou, Cazes, des Chênes, Mas Crémat, Fontanel, Força Réal,	▤ Red: 1998, 1996. ▸ Red: 2–6 years. White: 1–4 years.

ST. CHINIAN

ST. CHINIAN GAINED ITS *appellation* status in 1982, although its potential to produce great red wine was recognized as early as 1300. Located in the Hérault, north of Narbonne and northwest of Béziers, St. Chinian encompasses 20 villages. The high altitude here and the schistous and gravelly, chalky soil help to make St. Chinian wines lighter, more elegant, but often less interesting than the wines of neighboring Faugères (*see p.167*). However, some producers, like Domaine Canet-Valette, the châteaux Cazal-Viel and Coujan, and the *coopérative* at Roquebrun, are beginning to make interesting wines with cherryish flavors, while still managing to preserve the natural finesse of the wine. Both the red and rosé wines are made primarily from the Syrah, Carignan, Grenache, Cinsault, and Mourvèdre varieties.

AUTUMN GOLD
One of the best times to visit St. Chinian is in the few weeks following the harvest, when the vines' leaves have turned to shades of copper and gold.

CLOS BAGATELLE
This estate produces spicy wines that develop well after four or five years in the cellar.

▣ AC St. Chinian.	Coopérative de Roquebrun, Deslines, Ch Milhau-Lacugue, des Pradels, Soulie des Joncs, Ch des Villespassans, Viranel.
▣ Red/ rosé: Carignan, Syrah, Grenache, Mourvèdre, Cinsault.	
▣ Full-bodied, dry reds. Dry rosés.	▣ Potatoes cooked with onions, Bayonne ham, garlic, and parsley.
▣ Ch des Albières, de Astide Rousse, Clos Bagatelle, Canet-Valette, Ch Cazal-Viel, Coujan,	▣ Red: 1998, 1996, 1994.
	▣ Red: 2–5 years.

OTHERS

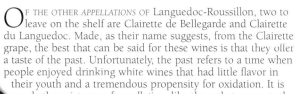

OF THE OTHER *APPELLATIONS* OF Languedoc-Roussillon, two to leave on the shelf are Clairette de Bellegarde and Clairette du Languedoc. Made, as their name suggests, from the Clairette grape, the best that can be said for these wines is that they offer a taste of the past. Unfortunately, the past refers to a time when people enjoyed drinking white wines that had little flavor in their youth and a tremendous propensity for oxidation. It is only the existence of *appellations* like these that prevents the Clairette from becoming an endangered species, but I can see no reason why anyone would actually choose to use it in the production of classic, dry white wines like Clairette de Bellegarde. The sweet, dry, fortified and unfortified Clairette du Languedoc *rancio* wines are much more interesting, in much the same way that the only way to make the Spanish Palomino grape into a wine worth drinking is to turn it into sherry.

Typically, while the dull white Clairettes have *appellation* status, the light but pleasantly flavored reds of the Côtes de la Malepère and the Côtes de Millau all still

CLAIRETTE DE BELLEGARDE
Coopératives such as this in Languedoc-Roussillon are happy to promote and sell their wines to residents, tourists, and passersby.

CHÂTEAU MALVIÈS
This château is one of the leaders in a move to produce more fruity Côtes de la Malepère wines.

have only *VDQS* status. Of these, the former taste like a cross between the wines of the Côtes du Rhône (*see pp.210–11*) and basic Bordeaux (*see p.77*), while the latter have a flavor more like a blend of Beaujolais (*see pp.106–7*) and the Côtes du Rhône.

THE LOIRE VALLEY

OF ALL THE WINE REGIONS IN FRANCE, NONE

OFFERS A WIDER VARIETY OF WINES TO ENJOY

ON A WARM SUMMER'S DAY THAN THE LOIRE.

Loire valley region

WHEN IT COMES TO marketing wine, a river can be very useful. Every year, thousands of tourists follow the Loire river as it stretches across France. As they stop for a meal and choose a local wine, though, unless they have a helpful *sommelier* at hand, they could find the choice a little confusing.

At the western, maritime end of the river, there are the dry, non-aromatic white wines of Muscadet *(see p.183)*. When well made, these crisply refreshing wines are the perfect partners to all kinds of seafood. Nowadays, however, wine drinkers tend to demand more flavor than the grapes used to make Muscadet are able to deliver.

Move eastward along the river and you reach Anjou *(see p.178)* and Saumur *(see p.187)*, names that are respectively associated with sugary rosé and inexpensive sparkling wine. But look at the wine lists in restaurants here and you will see that both come in a number of much more interesting, bubble-free styles. Haut-Poitou *(see p.181)* and Touraine *(see p.189)* offer the chance to taste a range of wines made from the Sauvignon Blanc, the variety with which the Loire valley is most often associated. At their best, these wines have the fresh, light appeal of gooseberries, blackcurrants, and crunchy raw vegetables. Too many, however, taste green and unripe. An excess of green flavors can also be a

WATCHING THE RIVER FLOW
As the Loire and its offshoots flow westward to the Atlantic, they pass through vineyards that produce an enormously varied range of dry, sweet, still, and sparkling wines.

| 0 km | | 25 |
| 0 miles | | 25 |

| 🔺 | 87,150 acres (35,000 ha): 390 million bottles. | ▦ | Varied, with granite in Muscadet, schist in Layon, sandy gravel in Chinon, tufa chalk in Vouvray, and gravelly limestone in Sancerre. |
| 🌡 | Atlantic to Continental. Muscadet, on the coast, is quite damp and frost is a problem, as it is elsewhere in this region. Heading east, the summers get warmer and the winters harsher. | 🍇 | Red: Cabernet Franc, Malbec, Gamay. White: Chenin Blanc, Sauvignon Blanc, Melon Blanc. |

SECRET DELIGHT
Far from being the best-known wine of the region, Jasnières does, however, produce some of the world's finest dry and sweet examples of wines made from the Chenin Blanc.

feature of the red wines of Chinon (*see p.180*), Bourgueil, and St. Nicolas de Bourgueil (*see p.179*). However, in ripe vintages and in the hands of skilled wine makers, these can offer a great counterpoint to red Bordeaux.

Vouvray (*see p.190*), which showcases the

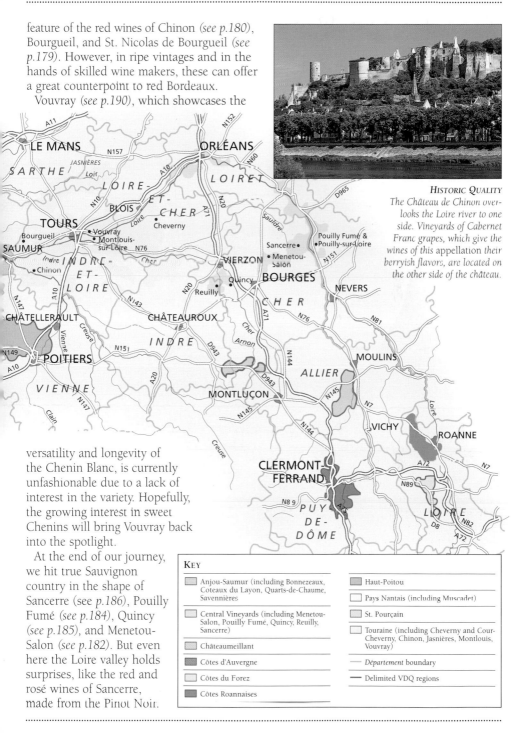

HISTORIC QUALITY
The Château de Chinon over-looks the Loire river to one side. Vineyards of Cabernet Franc grapes, which give the wines of this appellation their berryish flavors, are located on the other side of the château.

versatility and longevity of the Chenin Blanc, is currently unfashionable due to a lack of interest in the variety. Hopefully, the growing interest in sweet Chenins will bring Vouvray back into the spotlight.

At the end of our journey, we hit true Sauvignon country in the shape of Sancerre (see *p.186*), Pouilly Fumé (see *p.184*), Quincy (see *p.185*), and Menetou-Salon (see *p.182*). But even here the Loire valley holds surprises, like the red and rosé wines of Sancerre, made from the Pinot Noir.

KEY

- Anjou-Saumur (including Bonnezeaux, Coteaux du Layon, Quarts-de-Chaume, Savennières)
- Central Vineyards (including Menetou-Salon, Pouilly Fumé, Quincy, Reuilly, Sancerre)
- Châteaumeillant
- Côtes d'Auvergne
- Côtes du Forez
- Côtes Roannaises
- Haut-Poitou
- Pays Nantais (including Muscadet)
- St. Pourçain
- Touraine (including Cheverny and Cour-Cheverny, Chinon, Jasnières, Montlouis, Vouvray)

--- *Département* boundary
— Delimited VDQ regions

THE HISTORY OF THE LOIRE VALLEY

Built between the 13th and 16th centuries, the many magnificent châteaux of the Loire valley served as fortresses, and later as luxurious palaces, for the kings of France. With royal patronage and easy access to the foreign markets of England and the Netherlands, the region, and particularly towns such as Angers, grew rich on the profitable wine trade.

CHÂTEAU DE CHINON
Henry II, first of a long line of Anglo-Norman kings, died here at the now spectacularly ruined Château de Chinon in the early part of the 13th century.

No one knows for sure how wine making first began in the Loire valley, but it seems very likely that grape vines were brought here from the areas now known as Bordeaux to the south and Burgundy to the east. The Romans occupied the area for the first four centuries AD, leaving their mark in the form of place names such as Pouilly-sur-Loire (*see p.184*), derived from the words *Paulica villa*, or the villa of Paulus. Likewise, the red wine *appellation* of Saumur-Champigny (*see p.187*) may take its name from the Latin *campus ignis*, or the fiery field, while the Porte César in Sancerre (*see p.186*) is named after the Roman Emperor Julius Caesar. Evidence that the Romans brought their wine-making technology exists in the form of excavated kilns, used for firing terracotta wine amphorae, dating from the first century. By 591 AD, wine making was

sufficiently established here for Bishop Gregory of Tours, in his book, *The History of the Franks*, to describe a successful harvest and to complain that the marauding Bretons were occupying vineyards in the region we now know as Muscadet (*see p.183*). By the 12th century, the red wine of Anjou was being shipped to England by the merchants of Angers, while large quantities of red and white wines were also exported from various parts of the region to the prosperous independent principality of Flanders. A vigorous Loire valley wine trade continued until the middle of this century, boosted by the region's proximity to Paris, as well as to the Atlantic coast and overseas markets.

THE GRAPE VARIETIES OF THE LOIRE
Cabernet Franc and Sauvignon Blanc vines arrived in the Loire valley from Bordeaux between 1000 and 1500. The Sauvignon Blanc, however, was not widely planted here until the 16th century, when it was introduced to what are now the *appellations* of Pouilly-sur-Loire, Sancerre, Quincy, (*see p.185*) and Reuilly (*see p.185*). Despite its apparently invincible position in these *appellations* today, until the 18th century the Sauvignon Blanc lost out to the now almost-forgotten Chasselas grape, popular with growers who appreciated its higher yields. It was only after the vineyards were replanted

ILLUMINATED GRAPE HARVEST
This page, from the 15th-century illuminated manuscript, Les Très Riches Heures du Duc de Berry, shows the grape harvest at the Château de Saumur.

TUFA WINE CELLARS
A soft chalk boiled by volcanic action, tufa underlies many parts of the Loire valley and for centuries has been excavated to make both homes and wine cellars.

following their 19th-century devastation by phylloxera that the Sauvignon Blanc was established as the major grape of these *communes*. Also popular in the region is the Melon de Bourgogne, sometimes called the

RARE MUSCADET
These wines from Muscadet are made from the Melon de Bourgogne, first planted here during the 17th century.

Muscadet, which arrived in Anjou during the Middle Ages. By the 17th century, although banned in Burgundy, it was planted as a hardy white grape to replace existing black vines in what now corresponds to the *appellation* of Muscadet. With the exception of California, the Melon is now grown no-

where else. Just as closely linked with the Loire is the Chenin Blanc. Little-known elsewhere in Europe, no one is sure of its origins, though one theory, supported by Jancis Robinson in her book, *Grapes, Vines and Wines*, suggests that the Chenin Blanc is native to the Loire valley region. Whether this is true or not, it has been used to make wine here since the 15th century, and probably far longer.

INTO THE 21ST CENTURY

Until the middle of this century, the Loire valley stood out as one of the few places in the world where fresh white wines could be produced with any reliability. Since then, however, the invention of equipment to control temperature during transportation, and the planting of superior grape varieties in regions enjoying more favorable climates, have dealt the region a hefty body blow. Although the best wines of the Loire are improving in quality and attracting world-wide interest, a large proportion of the area's wines are poorly made from overcropped, underripe grapes. It makes little sense to buy a watery, acidic Loire Sauvignon Blanc when similarly priced, more flavorsome wines are made from the same grape in southern France, elsewhere in Europe, and in the New World. Those who have studied the recent history of the Loire valley know that its wine regions are liable to shrink as well as grow. The vines of the once-famous wine-producing Côtes d'Auvergne district, for example, now cover only one fiftieth of the 148,260 acres (60,000 ha) they occupied before the arrival of the phylloxera blight. It is a rare gambler who would bet on Loire valley *appellations* such as Muscadet retaining anything like their current size very far into the 21st century.

RENAISSANCE GLORY
Straddling the Cher river to the east of Tours is the Château de Chenonceaux. First built as a medieval fortress, the château was reconstructed in 1512 in the modern Renaissance style.

A DRIVING TOUR OF THE LOIRE

Beginning at the city of Tours, this route takes you along various tributaries of the middle reaches of the Loire, through Vouvray, famous for its rich Chenin Blanc wines, down to Azay-le-Rideau, with its elegant château, and through the red wine vineyards of Chinon and Bourgueil.

Loire Valley   □ Tour

TOURS

No wine lover's visit to the Loire valley is complete without a visit to the Musée des Vins de Touraine beneath the Église de St. Julien in Tours ①. Take the time, too, to explore the cathedral and to stroll around the narrow streets of the city center, which is full of well-preserved Renaissance buildings.

VOUVRAY TO CHINON

Home of the Chenin Blanc grape, Vouvray ② is, for many people, the quintessential town of Touraine. Here you can see many comfortable homes and well-equipped wine cellars dug by their troglodytic inhabitants from the chalk hills. Among many great producers here, I particularly recommend Philippe Foreau, Domaine Huët, and Domaine des Aubuisières. Take a break from wine to visit the extravagantly beautiful Renaissance château of Chenonceaux. Here you can imagine chivalrous interludes on the three-story bridge that straddles the river Cher, a tributary of the Loire, and ponder the unashamed acres of cellulite in the Rubens' paintings that hang inside. Rejoin the Loire at the richly historical town of Amboise ③, home to, among other things, the 18th-century Pagode de Chanteloup and a chapel said to be the final resting place of Leonardo

DIG FOR VICTORY
Like many buildings in Vouvray, this wine cellar is dug from the town's chalky rock.

da Vinci. Heading westward along the bank of the Loire, you will come to Montlouis-sur-Loire ④. For a taste of the dry, sweet, still, and sparkling wines made here, visit Jacky Blot's Domaine de la Taille aux Loups in

nearby Husseau. My choice for lunch or an overnight stay is the sleepy town of Chinon, which you can reach by following the road to Esvres, Saché ⑤, and Azay-le-Rideau ⑥, with its island château. From here the D757 leads to Chinon ⑦. The Domaine Couly-Dutheil is one of the largest estates in the region and its cellars here offer the chance to try wines from a variety of vineyards.

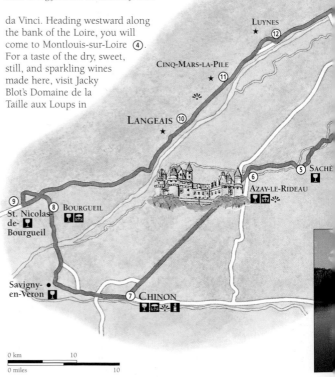

LUYNES
★ ⑫

CINQ-MARS-LA-PILE
★ ⑪

LANGEAIS ⑩
★

⑥
⑤ SACHÉ
AZAY-LE-RIDEAU

⑨
⑧ BOURGUEIL
St. Nicolas-
de-
Bourgueil

Savigny-
en-Veron

⑦ CHINON

KEY

![]	Tasting possible
![]	Places to eat
![]	Tourist information
★	Site of interest
▬	Tour route
☀	Viewpoint

0 km   10

0 miles   10

HISTORIC AMBOISE
The Pagode de Chanteloup in the town of Amboise is all that remains of an 18th-century château. An earlier château still stands in the town, complete with the hooks used to hang political prisoners.

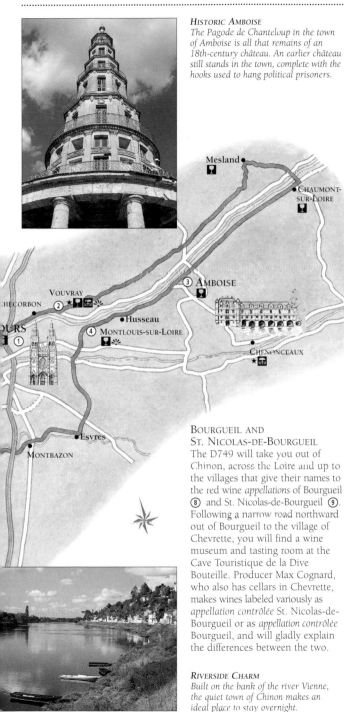

TOURING TIPS

INFORMATION: Office de Tourisme, 78 Rue Bernard-Palissy, **Tours** 📞 02 47 70 37 37. Maisons du Vin throughout the region offer information on wine, but for wine information on the area as a whole it is worth visiting the Comité Interprofessionel de Touraine at 19 Square Prosper-Mérimée, **Tours** 📞 02 47 05 40 01.

EVENTS: Every *appellation* in the Loire valley has an annual fair at which it shows off its wines. The Foire de la Loire in Angers, held every year during the first week of February, offers the chance to taste wines from the entire region.

RESTAURANTS:
Domaine des Hautes Roches, 86 Quai de la Loire, **Rochecorbon** 📞 02 47 52 88 88. Great food, great wine, and an unforgettable setting where the rooms are carved into the chalky rock.
Au Plaisir Gourmand, 2 Rue Parmentier, **Chinon** 📞 02 47 93 20 48. A lovely country restaurant in the heart of Chinon offering a wide range of wines from this *appellation*.

HOTELS:
Hostellerie Gargantua, 73 Rue Voltaire, **Chinon** 📞 02 47 93 04 71. In the heart of Chinon, with great views of the river, this quaintly-turreted hotel offers an ideal base from which to explore.
Hotel de l'Univers, 5 Boulevard Heurteloup, **Tours** 📞 02 47 05 37 12. A magnificent Belle Époque hotel, with furniture to match. Ask for the room in which Winston Churchill used to sleep.

BOURGUEIL AND ST. NICOLAS-DE-BOURGUEIL

The D749 will take you out of Chinon, across the Loire and up to the villages that give their names to the red wine *appellations* of Bourgueil ⑧ and St. Nicolas-de-Bourgueil ⑨. Following a narrow road northward out of Bourgueil to the village of Chevrette, you will find a wine museum and tasting room at the Cave Touristique de la Dive Bouteille. Producer Max Cognard, who also has cellars in Chevrette, makes wines labeled variously as *appellation contrôlée* St. Nicolas-de-Bourgueil or as *appellation contrôlée* Bourgueil, and will gladly explain the differences between the two.

RIVERSIDE CHARM
Built on the bank of the river Vienne, the quiet town of Chinon makes an ideal place to stay overnight.

LANGEAIS TO LUYNES
From Bourgueil, head east to Langeais ⑩, where there is an unspoiled 15th-century chateau. Then take the D57 out of the village for a kilometer or so to take advantage of a panoramic view over the river and vineyards of Bourgueil. In Cinq-Mars-la-Pile ⑪ is a ruined château and, at Luynes ⑫, the château that was once home to 17th-century churchman Cardinal Richelieu.

ANJOU

Rosé d'Anjou, the commercial wine sold cheaply in supermarkets throughout the world, may represent nearly half of the wine produced in Anjou, but it is not the wine by which the *appellation* should be judged. For fine examples of rosé wines, try the Cabernet d'Anjou, arguably the longest-lived rosé in the world, or the Rosé de Loire. Anjou's white wines are traditionally made from the Chenin Blanc, to which Chardonnay or Sauvignon Blanc may now be added. This blending, plus a little aging in new oak, has brought some welcome roundness to what, in cool years, can be green wines. Anjou Coteaux de la Loire can provide an affordable taste of late-harvest Chenin Blanc, with Anjou-Gamay being a generally feeble alternative to Beaujolais (*see pp.106–7*). For superior reds, try Anjou Villages, whose reds offer rich, blackcurrant flavors.

A TOUCH OF CEREMONY
The wine makers in this part of the Loire valley still make the most of every opportunity available to celebrate their traditions.

CHÂTEAU DE LA GENAISERIE
Yves Soulez, the producer of this wine, is one of the best wine makers in the Loire.

☀ AC Anjou, AC Anjou Coteaux de la Loire, AC Anjou Gamay, AC Anjou Mousseux, AC Anjou Pétillant, AC Cabernet D'Anjou.

⬡ Red/ rosé: Cabernet Franc, Cabernet Sauvignon, Grolleau. White: Chenin Blanc, Chardonnay, Sauvignon Blanc.

⬡ Light- to medium-bodied reds. Crisp, dry whites. Medium-sweet rosés.

▥ Arnault et Fils, Ch de Fesles, Gaudard, Genaiserie, Jean-Yves Lebreton.

🍴 Pike in butter and shallot sauce.

▤ Red: 1997, 1995.

⬿ Red: 3–8 years.

BONNEZEAUX

THOUARCÉ
This fine windmill, overlooking the vines of Thouarcé, is the most recognized landmark in this region of France.

The vineyards of this Coteaux du Layon *grand cru* face south on La Montagne, Beauregard, and des Fesles, three steep, schist slopes bordering the river Layon. The only grape variety grown here is the Chenin Blanc, which is often harvested in numerous pickings when botrytized. Yields here are low, with the minimum required ripeness for the grapes at harvest being higher than that of Sauternes (*see p.94*). In fact, grape growers here have been known to pick absurdly ripe grapes, with an alcoholic strength of up to 40 per-cent. At its best, Bonnezeaux is intensely sweet, with flavors of pineapple and licorice when young and a honeyed-vanilla complexity that develops with age. In recent years, many vines that were once abandoned have been replanted, expanding the *appellation* from 94 acres (38 ha) in 1979 to 198 acres (80 ha).

MARK ANGELI
Not only is this one of the richest, sweetest, and most luscious wines of the Loire, it is also one of the world's best white wines.

☀ AC Bonnezeaux Grand Cru.

⬡ White: Chenin Blanc.

⬡ Lusciously sweet, long-lived, and ideally botrytized whites.

▥ Mark Angeli, Ch de Fesles, Gilardeau, Godineau, des Grandes Vignes, la Petite Croix, des Petits Parts, du Petit Val, René Renou, Louis et Claude Robin, de Trompe-Tonneau, la Varière.

🍴 Grilled *foie gras* with truffles.

▤ 1997, 1995, 1990, 1989, 1986, 1985, 1979.

⬿ 5–15 years.

BOURGUEIL AND ST. NICOLAS-DE-BOURGUEIL

THE *APPELLATIONS* OF *BOURGUEIL* and St. Nicolas-de-Bourgueil, located between Tours and Saumur, both claim that their wines have individual qualities. Renowned as some of the finest Cabernet Franc-based reds in the Loire, the difference between the two is actually very hard to discern. Bourgueil's vines are grown on either a sand and gravel plateau or on clay and tufa slopes, and its wines have a fruity character.

On the higher slopes, the grapes ripen up to 10 days earlier than on the plateau, resulting in more complex wines. St. Nicolas-de-Bourgueil's soil is sandier than that of Bourgueil and although its wines are lighter, they are just as good. Even though a *coopérative* controls one third of the *communes* here, techniques do vary, with some producers placing greater reliance than others on aging in wood.

PIERRE-JACQUES DRUET
Pierre-Jacques Druet produces some of the best traditional wines of Bourgueil.

INGRANDES DE TOURAINE
As is the case almost everywhere in the Loire valley, Bourgueil has a wealth of prosperous châteaux and farms.

✴ AC Bourgueil, AC St. Nicolas-de-Bourgueil.	St. Nicolas-de-Bourgueil: Yanick Amirault, Max Cognard, Delauney Druet, Frédéric Mabileau.
🍇 Red/ rosé: Cabernet Franc, Cabernet Sauvignon.	
🍷 Fragrant, medium-bodied reds. Dry rosés.	🍴 Stuffed cabbage.
🍽 Bourgueil: Yanick Amirault, Max Cognard, Delauney Druet.	☰ Red: 1997, 1995, 1990, 1989.
	⮞ Bourgueil: 3–10 years. St. Nicolas-de-Bourgueil: 2–5 years.

CHÂTEAUMEILLANT

THIS AREA COVERS about 247 acres (100 ha) in the middle of France, around the town of Châteaumeillant and between St. Pourçain and Touraine. The soil here is volcanic, which explains why, as in Beaujolais (*see pp.106–7*), Gamay is the most widely planted vine and why white wine is no longer made here. Other grapes used in the production of red wines are the Pinot Noir and the Pinot Gris, with the same three used for rosé wines. The reds, though tannic, are fresh and best drunk young; but it is the light, fresh rosés that stand out.

✴ VDQS Châteaumeillant.	
🍇 Red/ rosé: Gamay, Pinot Noir, Pinot Gris.	
🍷 Dry, light, but firm reds. Dry, light rosés.	
🍽 Du Chaillot, Cave des Vins de Châteaumeillant, Cellier du Chêne-Combeau.	
🍴 Rosé: Cheese omelette.	
☰ Red: 1997, 1995.	
⮞ Red: 2–5 years.	

CAVE DES VINS DE CHÂTEAU-MEILLANT
This rosé is light, fresh, and berryish with a tannic backbone.

CHEVERNY AND COUR-CHEVERNY

THESE ARE TWO OF the first *appellation* vineyards you encounter when traveling west from Orléans to Blois. In 1993 the area was elevated from *VDQS* to *appellation* status, and Cour-Cheverny became a separate *appellation* for white wines made from the Romorantin grape, which produces light, dry wines with a delicate, floral aroma. Cheverny's white wines, on the other hand, are made from the Sauvignon grape and have lively fruit and good balance. Both the white and red wines, made mainly from the Gamay variety, are best drunk young.

✴ AC Cheverny, AC Cour-Cheverny.	
🍇 Red/ rosé: Gamay. White: Sauvignon Blanc, Romorantin.	
🍷 Light reds. Crisp, dry whites. Dry rosés.	
🍽 Les Caves Bellier, François Cazin, de la Gaudronnière.	
🍴 Cour-Cheverny: Pike.	
☰ White: 1997.	
⮞ White: 1–3 years.	

FRANÇOIS CAZIN
This wine offers the chance to taste the flavor of the floral Romorantin variety.

CHINON

THE TOWN AND FORTIFIED CASTLE of Chinon, and the vineyards that come up to its walls, lie within a triangle formed at the merging of the Loire and Vienne rivers. Although, historically, the wine produced here was quite often green and edgy with a rustic character, this *appellation* now produces some of the world's best examples of Cabernet Franc. Recently, better wine making skills have improved the average quality of Chinon's wines significantly, as has the gradual phasing out of the Cabernet Sauvignon grape variety, which can be hard to ripen. Most producers here age their wines in small barrels, although when over-oaked the blackcurrant flavor, for which they are best known, can be lost. Chinon's rosés, rarely found outside Chinon itself, are also worth trying, as are the similarly rare Chenin Blanc dry white wines.

CLOS DE L'ECHO
COULY-DUTHEIL
This vineyard, situated next door to the ruins of the Château de Chinon, produces some of the best wine in the appellation.

OLGA RAFFAULT
There are several members of the Raffault family living in Chinon. The two names to look out for are Olga and Jean-Maurice.

✳ AC Chinon.	Delaunay, Ch de la Grille, Charles Joguet, Logis de la Bouchardière, du Raffault, Olga Raffault.
🍇 Red/ rosé: Cabernet Franc. White: Chenin Blanc.	
🍷 Fragrant, medium-bodied reds. Dry, aromatic whites. Dry, light-bodied, fruity rosés.	🍴 Red: Veal casserole
	📦 Red: 1997, 1995, 1990, 1989.
🍴 Philippe Alliet, Bernard Baudry, Couly-Dutheil,	📅 Red: 5–10 years. White: 3–7 years.

COTEAUX DU LAYON

THE COTEAUX DU LAYON borders the river Layon from Neuil to Chalonnes and has been famous for its sweet white wines since the fourth century. While the Coteaux du Layon *appellation* covers white wines made in 25 *communes* that overlap Anjou, Coteaux de la Loire (*see p.178*), and Saumur (*see p.187*), the area's best wines are made to tight regulations in Beaulieu, Faye, Lambert, Rablay, Rochefort, St. Aubin, and St. Lambert, seven villages that make up the *appellation* of Coteaux du Layon-Villages. The wines made in these *communes* each have characters of their own, with Beaulieu making more delicate wines than Rablay's full-bodied whites. All Coteaux du Layon wines are produced from ultra-ripe grapes that are harvested in numerous pickings. The best wines are produced by the Coteaux du Layon-Chaume, a one-village *appellation*.

CHÂTEAU LA
GENAISERIE
With its numerous chateâux and grand hotels, the Coteaux du Layon is a beautiful region of France to visit.

DOMAINE DES FORGES
Claude Branchereau, the owner of this estate, is one of the most quality-conscious producers in the Coteaux du Layon.

✳ AC Coteaux du Layon, AC Coteaux du Layon-Chaume, AC Coteaux du Layon-Villages.	Ch Pierre Bise, Pithon, Ch la Plaisance, Ch des Rochettes, de la Roulerie, des Sablonnettes, Ch Soucherie, la Varière.
🍇 White: Chenin Blanc.	
🍷 Medium and sweet whites.	🍴 Sweet: Apple tart with crème fraiche.
🍴 Pierre Aguilas, Patrick Baudoin, des Baumard, du Breuil, Cady, Delesvaux, des Forges, Godineau, Ogereau,	📦 1997, 1995, 1990, 1989, 1985, 1976.
	📅 Sweet: 10–20 years.

HAUT-POITOU

I̲F THE *COOPÉRATIVE* AT NEUVILLE had not successfully promoted Diane de Poitiers, a *méthode champenoise* wine, this *VDQS* might be almost unknown. Haut-Poitou covers about 1,730 acres (700 ha) of vineyards scattered across a wide, flat plain stretching south of Saumur (*see p.187*), down to Poitiers itself. In this dry, hot *appellation*, vines grow on limestone and marl soil and produce wines that in warm years are often characterized by their fruity flavors.

Among the white wines produced here, the Sauvignon Blanc was the first to attract attention to the area. Today, its wines continue to be produced in the original floral style, with a light, crisp acidity. Haut-Poitou also makes red and rosé wines that are enterprisingly produced from varieties including the Pinot Noir, Gamay, Merlot, Malbec, and Cabernet Sauvignon.

MODERN TIMES
The traditional vineyards here have been adapted in order to enable modern equipment to be used to harvest the grapes.

CAVE DE HAUT-POITOU
One of the most dynamic coopératives in France, this winery single-handedly created Haut-Poitou's good reputation.

✱	VDQS Haut-Poitou.
🍇	Red/ rosé: Pinot Noir, Gamay, Merlot, Malbec, Cabernet Franc, Cabernet Sauvignon. White: Sauvignon Blanc, Chenin Blanc, Chardonnay.
🍷	Light reds. Light, crisp still whites. Dry sparkling whites.
⫴	Robert Champalou (Ch de Dizilay), Gérard Descoux, Cave du Haut-Poitou, Jacques Morgreau, de la Rôtisserie.
🍴	White. Port Salut (cheese)
▤	White: 1998, 1997, 1995.
▶	Red: 1–4 years. White: 1–3 years.

JASNIÈRES

L̲IKE SAVENNIÈRES (*see p.188*) and Vouvray (*see p.190*), this small, 119-acre (48-ha) *appellation* within the Coteaux du Loire provides the perfect example of how the Chenin Blanc grape can be affected by the marginal climate of the Loire. In cooler years, its dry white wines are acidic enough to threaten to remove the enamel from your teeth. However, when the climate allows, the flavor of Jasnières' dry white wine can be a combination of flowers, nuts, honey, and apples, but with a steely, acidic backbone. Since the early 1990s, the wine makers here have been making sweet, and even dry, botrytized wines in good years. These botrytized wines have a more instant appeal than more traditional Jasnières, and their success has helped to ensure the survival and the increasing prestige of this *appellation*.

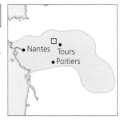

PRIME POSITION
As in other areas of France, Jasnières' vines are planted on slopes, while a variety of other crops are grown on the flatter land.

DOMAINE DE LA CHARRIÈRE
The "raisins nobles" referred to have been affected by the noble rot that gives Jasnières' white wines their character.

✱	AC Jasnières.
🍇	White: Chenin Blanc.
🍷	Steely, dry whites. Dry or sweet botrytized whites in exceptional years.
⫴	Claude Cartereau, de Cezin, de la Charrière, Joël Gigou, Jean-Jacques Maillet, Renard-Potaire, Bénédicte de Rycke, des Vaux du Loire.
🍴	Braised foreloin of pork with prunes.
▤	Sweet: 1997, 1996, 1995, 1994, 1993, 1990, 1989, 1985.
▶	Dry: 5–10 years. Sweet. 7–20 years.

MENETOU-SALON

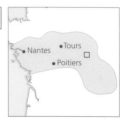

THE VINEYARDS OF Menetou-Salon lie between the city of Bourges and the vineyards of Sancerre (*see p.186*) to the east. In just 40 years, the grape growers of Menetou-Salon have expanded their vineyards from 50 acres (20 ha) in 1959 to 500 acres (200 ha) today. Menetou-Salon's wines (especially those from vineyards around Morogues) are often good alternatives to the average and lesser-quality wines of neighboring Sancerre. Most Menetou-Salon red wines are light, fruity, and best drunk young. Some of the best, however, are matured in oak barrels and age well. Menetou-Salon's white wines, on the other hand, are typical of the Sauvignon Blanc, but tend to lose their initial floral appeal quite quickly, replacing it with an earthiness that makes fine, delicate whites a rare find.

LIMESTONE SOIL
The Sauvignon Blanc and Pinot Noir grapes grown in Menetou-Salon, near Morogues, owe their flavor to the limestone soil that is found here.

DOMAINE JEAN TEILLER
Good Menetou-Salon like this competes directly with the better-known Sancerre and Pouilly Fumé.

✴	AC Menetou-Salon.		Gilbert, de Loye, Henry Pelle, Prieuré de St. Céols, la Tour St. Martin, Jean Teiller, Christopher and Guy Turpin.
🍷	Red/ rosé: Pinot Noir. White: Sauvignon Blanc.		
🍶	Light reds. Refreshing, crisp, dry whites. Dry rosés.	🍴	White: Stuffed sole.
		🍷	White: 1997, 1995.
🏛	De Beaurepaire, Roger Champault, Charet et Fils, de Chatenoy, Pierre Clement, de Coquin, Fournier, Jean-Paul	📈	Red: 2–5 years White: 1–2 years Rosé: 1 year

MONTLOUIS

MONTLOUIS LIES ON the west bank of the Loire, directly opposite the *appellation* of Vouvray (*see p.190*) and only a few kilometers east of the center of Tours. The vineyards of Montlouis slope south towards the Cher river and include the villages of Montlouis, Lussault, and St. Martin-le-Beau. Once sold under the name of Vouvray, the white wines of Montlouis can be dry, medium-dry, or sweet. The only grape variety used here is the Chenin Blanc, known as the Pineau de la Loire. In this area, the soils are rich in flinty clays and are quite sandy, resulting in light wines with mineral overtones. Like Vouvray, the best wines produced in Montlouis are the sweet wines that are sold as AC Montlouis Moelleux and the slightly sparkling wines that are sold as AC Montlouis Pétillant.

SMALL ESTATES
Unlike the good-quality wines produced in other appellations, most of Montlouis' best wines are made by small estates like this.

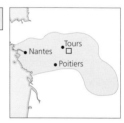

OLIVIER DELÉTANG
This producer makes some of the best examples of the subtly appealing Montlouis wines.

✴	AC Montlouis.		Christian Galliot, Levasseur, des Liards, Patrick Marne, de la Milletière, Dominique Moyer, Ch de Pintray, la Taille aux Loups, des Tourterelles.
🍷	White: Chenin Blanc.		
🍶	Dry, medium, and sweet whites.		
		🍴	Pike with butter sauce.
🏛	Claude Boureau, Patrice Benoit, des Chardonnerets, Francois Chidaine, de Cray, Laurent Chatenay, Olivier Delétang, Daniel Fisselle,	🍷	1997, 1995, 1990, 1989.
		📈	5–10 years.

MUSCADET

ONE OF THE BEST-KNOWN white wines in the world, Muscadet enters the 21st century confronting the very real prospect of being unfashionable and unwanted. Unlike wines such as the Chardonnays and Sauvignons that, for the moment, tend to occupy the spotlight, this is not a fruity or oaky white wine, but is instead fairly neutral in flavor.

SMALL IS BEAUTIFUL
While big merchants blend and sell much of the wine produced in the appellation of Muscadet, a growing number of small estates are now producing and bottling their own wines.

GOOD MUSCADET, LIKE THE OYSTERS with which I like to drink it, comes my way all too rarely. The producers in this frost-prone region make their wine from the Melon de Bourgogne, a relatively flavorless grape variety that bears none of the muskiness implied by the name Muscadet. This grape, of which the wine growers of Muscadet are so proud, is actually relatively new to the area. In the 17th century the wines made here would have been mostly thin, weedy, and acidic reds. However, when the vineyards were

CHERISHING TRADITION
Stained-glass windows like these celebrate the replanting of the region's vineyards after the harsh frosts of 1709.

almost wiped out by frost in 1709 the Dutch merchants, who were the grape growers' biggest customers, encouraged them to plant a second rate variety from Burgundy. Known as the Melon de Bourgogne, this variety could survive the cold weather. The neutral flavor of the wines made from the Melon de Bourgogne was of little concern to the producers. Initially, it was only ever going to be used to make cheap brandy.

Muscadet did, however, have one important distinction. The tradition of being bottled *sur lie*, while still in contact with its sediment, kept the wine fresh and gave it a slight spritz and yeasty roundness. In the mid-20th century, before the world became awash with good Chardonnay and Sauvignon, this tradition gave Muscadet a brief heyday of international popularity.

Today, Muscadet can be bought *sur lie* or not (not to be recommended) and under one of four *appellations*. Of these, basic Muscadet (not to be recommended either) represents less than a fifth of the total production; the Coteaux de la Loire's wines are generally green and unripe; and the Côte de Grandlieu, which was created in 1994, covers most of the wine that used to be sold as basic Muscadet. The one to look out for is Sèvre-et-Maine, but frankly, your best chance of getting a crisp, dry, lemony wine to drink with your oysters will be to trust one of the producers listed on the left.

**CHÂTEAU L'OISELINIÈRE
DE LA RAMÉE**
One of a range of excellent wines produced by Domaines Chéreau-Carré, this is a great example of how Muscadet should taste.

✹	AC Muscadet, AC Muscadet des Coteaux de la Loire, AC Muscadet Côtes de Grandlieu, AC Muscadet de Sèvre-et-Maine, AC Muscadet *sur lie*.
❊	White: Muscadet.
🍷	Steely, dry whites.
▥	Audouin, Donatieu Bahuand, de Beau-Lieu, de Beauregard, Gilbert Bossard, de la Botinerie, Chéreau-Carré, Ch du Cléray, de Contreaux, Gadais, Ch de

la Galissonnière, de la Garnière, de Goulaine, de l'Hyvernière, des Jardins de la Ménardière, Christian and Pascale Luncan, Michel Luncan, Métaireau, Clos du Moulin, Ch l'Oiselinière de la Rameé, de la Preuille, de la Ragotière, Dominique and Vincent Richard, Clos St. Vincent des Rongères, Sauvion.

🍴 Oysters on the shell.

🝪 1998, 1997.

🕐 0–2 years

POUILLY-FUMÉ AND POUILLY-SUR-LOIRE

FIRMLY IDENTIFIED WITH the Sauvignon Blanc grape, the *"fumé"* in Pouilly-Fumé describes the grape's somewhat elusive, smoky, gun-flint flavor, brought out by the flinty chalk of the best vineyards in the *appellation*. Wines sold under the less prestigious Pouilly-sur-Loire label are made from the Chasselas grape.

DIDIER DAGUENEAU
Implementing a number of innovations, including partial maturation in oak barrels, the hugely talented Didier Dagueneau has helped to revolutionize the wines of Pouilly-Fumé.

A N AREA OF GENTLY SLOPING vineyards situated on the eastern bank of the Loire, today the *appellation* of Pouilly-Fumé is most strongly associated with the Sauvignon Blanc grape. Surprisingly, however, it was not until the late 19th century, when widespread replanting of vines became necessary as a result of damage caused by the phylloxera louse, that the Sauvignon Blanc grape was grown here at all.

CHÂTEAU DU NOZET DE LADOUCETTE
The fairy-tale towers of the Château du Nozet de Ladoucette provide a dramatic contrast to the humble appearance of many other domaines in the appellation of Pouilly-Fumé.

Until then, the vineyards here were planted almost exclusively with Chasselas, a popular, sweet table grape traditionally considered to have a great affinity with the soils of the area. With floral aromas and low acidity, the still and sparkling wines made from these grapes are often tired and flabby, and as a result are fast becoming an endangered species. In 1997, only 300,000 bottles of Chasselas wine were produced here, compared to 7.75 million bottles made from the Sauvignon Blanc. Wines made here from the Chasselas are sold as *appellation contrôlée* Pouilly-sur-Loire, which covers the same geographical area as the exclusively Sauvignon Blanc *appellation* of Pouilly-Fumé.

The much-vaunted smoky flavor of the wines of Pouilly-Fumé is, in truth, a characteristic specifically associated with wines made from grapes grown in the flinty soil of the best vineyards of the *appellation*. Another arguable piece of received wisdom is that the best wines here have more depth and structure than those of Sancerre *(see p.186)* on the opposite bank of the Loire. This may occasionally be true, but more often the wines of the two *appellations* are hard to tell apart.

Some of Pouilly's best wines are made by the innovative producer Didier Dagueneau. By fermenting in new oak he produces crisp wines with a hint of vanilla, many of which age extremely well. His experimental, late-harvest sweet wines are also worth looking out for.

CHÂTEAU DE LADOUCETTE
This may not be the best wine in Pouilly-Fumé, but it is one of the most reliable and easiest to find.

💮	AC Pouilly-Fumé, AC Pouilly-sur-Loire.	Deschamps, Ch Favray, des Fines Caillottes, Pascal Jolivet, Masson-Blondelet, Joseph Mellot, Ch du Nozet, Roger Pabiot, Caves de Pouilly-sur-Loire, Raimbault-Pineau, Guy Saget, Yvon et Pascal Tabordet, Thibault, Ch de Tracy.
🍇	White: Sauvignon Blanc (AC Pouilly-Fumé only), Chasselas (AC Pouilly-sur-Loire only).	
🍷	Crisp, dry whites with smoky grape flavors.	
🏛	Des Berthiers, Bouchié-Chatellier, Henri Bourgeois, Cailbourdin, Chatelain, Patrick Coulbois, Didier Dagueneau, Jean-Claude Dagueneau, Marc	
		🍴 Trout grilled with lemon juice and toasted almonds.
		🍾 1998, 1997, 1995.
		⏲ 1–4 years.

QUARTS-DE-CHAUME

THE GREAT, SWEET WHITE wine *appellation* of Quarts-de-Chaume, on the banks of the Layon tributary, is a tiny plateau of vines in the middle of the much larger Coteaux-du-Layon *appellation* (*see p.180*). Occupying around 100 acres (40 ha) of gravelly clay slopes around the village of Chaume, only 100,000 bottles of Quarts-de-Chaume are produced here each year, from very ripe, mainly botrytized, Chenin Blanc grapes. The southerly aspect of the vineyards, combined with careful harvesting and a high proportion of old vines, produces low yields of extremely high quality. Lighter and slightly dryer than the wines of nearby Bonnezeaux (*see p.178*), the wines of Quarts-de-Chaume make attractive drinking when young, but after 10 years in the cellar they will develop inimitable and gloriously complex flavors of beeswax, honey, and spice.

WAITING GAME
Producers in Quarts-de-Chaume must wait patiently for the late-harvest, often botrytized, Chenin Blanc grapes that give their rich sweet flavors to the wines of the appellation.

CHÂTEAU BELLERIVE
This is a serious wine that is a pleasure to drink young, but will be even better after a decade of maturation in the cellar.

✖ AC Quarts de Chaume.		Ch Papin, du Petit Metris, Ch de Plaisance, Joseph Renou de la Roche Moreau, Ch de Suronde.
🍷 White: Chenin Blanc.		
🍇 Complex, long-lasting sweet whites, usually made from botrytized grapes.		🍴 Foie gras with a Quarts-de-Chaume sauce.
🍽 Des Baumard, Ch de Bellerive, de la Bergerie, Ch Pierre Bise, Ch de l'Echarderie, de Laffourcade, des Maurières,		📅 1997, 1995, 1990, 1989, 1985, 1976.
		⏳ 10–20 years.

QUINCY

UNLIKE ITS NEIGHBORS Reuilly (*see p.185*) and Menetou-Salon (*see p.182*), the vineyards of Quincy, on the western bank of the Auron tributary, are planted exclusively with Sauvignon Blanc vines. This is a white-only *appellation* and its wines can offer a good-value alternative to those of Sancerre (*see p.186*) or Pouilly-Fumé (*see p.184*). Despite promising, sandy, flint soils, limited wine-making techniques mean that wines here are often unpleasantly green and acidic. Lightly oaked wines, however, made from old, low-yielding vines, are well worth buying.

✖ AC Quincy.	***JEAN-MICHEL SORBE***
🍷 White: Sauvignon Blanc.	*This producer makes fresh, tangy wines, often similar to those of Sancerre, and just as good.*
🍇 Crisp, dry whites.	
🍽 Des Ballandors, Godinat, Mardon, Grand Rosières, Jacques Rouzé, Jean-Michel Sorbe.	
🍴 Omelette fried in butter with goat's cheese, fresh chives and tarragon.	
📅 1998.	
⏳ 1–3 years.	

REUILLY

ALL THREE STYLES of wine, red, white, and rosé, are produced from grapes grown on the 75 acres (30 ha) of limestone-rich soils that make up the *appellation* of Reuilly. White wines, made exclusively from the Sauvignon Blanc grape, are dry with flavors of grass and nettles. Rosés are distinctive and dry, made from the black Pinot Gris, while light, fruity reds are made from a blend of the Pinot Noir and the Pinot Gris. There are bargains here, especially among the reds and rosés, but many of these wines have a tendency toward the overly acidic.

✖ AC Reuilly.	***REUILLY***
🍷 Red/ rose: Pinot Noir. White: Sauvignon Blanc.	*Best drunk within a year or so of the harvest, white Reuilly is simple and refreshing.*
🍇 Light, fruity reds. Crisp, dry whites. Dry light-bodied rosés.	
🍽 Bigonneau, Lafond, Grandes Rosières, Jean-Michel Sorbe.	
🍴 Fresh oysters with lime.	
📅 White: 1998.	
⏳ White: 1–3 years.	

SANCERRE

SET HIGH ON A ROCKY outcrop, the ancient town of Sancerre keeps watch over the vineyards of the *appellation* below. Stretching along the western bank of the Loire to the north of its confluence with the Allier, Sancerre is now world-famous for its dry, aromatic white wines, but the area was well known for excellent red wines as early as the 12th century AD.

PERFECTLY SITUATED
In all but the coldest years, Sauvignon Blanc vines flourish in the limestone and gravel soils of the Sancerre hillsides, producing classic wines full of the flavors of gooseberries and flint.

WINE HAS BEEN MADE in the area around the town of Sancerre for many hundreds of years. One local legend suggests that when the church of St. Martin was rebuilt during a drought in 1040, the mortar was mixed with wine rather than water. By the 13th century, the wine of Sancerre was being praised in poetry as worthy of the royal table. Three hundred years later, King Henri IV declared that the wine of the village of Chavignol, a few kilometers northwest of Sancerre, was the best he had ever drunk and that its general consumption would bring an end to the currently raging religious wars. This method of pacification is sadly untestable today, however, as the Sancerre enjoyed by Henri IV was almost certainly a deeply colored red, made from a combination of Pinot Noir and Gamay grapes, very different from the much lighter red wines produced in Sancerre today. The first written reference to white Sancerre

appears as late as 1816, and the preferred grape for white wine at that time was the sweet-tasting but undistinguished Chasselas. Sancerre as we know it today, made from the Sauvignon Blanc, is a product of the *appellation contrôlée* system established in 1936. It was not until 1959 that red wines made from the Pinot Noir were included in the *appellation*.

Today the limestone and gravel vineyards of the *appellation* are used to produce some of the finest examples of Sauvignon Blanc in the world. Unfortunately, over-cropping and under-ripening also result in large amounts of thin, miserable white wine that is sold far too easily throughout the world. With 16 villages and 440 producers, sorting the good wines from the bad would be easier if Sancerre were to name its best villages and vineyards with a *crus classés* system similar to that in place in Beaujolais (*see pp.106–7*). As in the neighboring *appellation* of Pouilly-Fumé (*see p.184*), some interesting experiments have been made here with sweet, late-harvest white wines. Red and rosé Sancerre wines sell well, but rarely stand comparison with good examples of Pinot Noir produced elsewhere.

ANDRÉ DÉZAT
Producing elegant, aromatic wines, André Dézat represents the traditional face of Sancerre.

VINCENT PINARD
Reliable and innovative, producer Vincent Pinard offers individual cuvées of his Sancerre wines.

✱ AC Sancerre.	Alphonse Mellot, Thierry Merlin-Cherrier, Paul Mille-rioux, de Montigny, Roger Neveu, du Nozay, Vincent Pinard, Hippolyte Reverdy, Jean-Max Roger, de Saint-Romble, des Trois Noyers, Vacheron, André Vatan.	
✿ Red/ rosé: Pinot Noir. White: Sauvignon Blanc.		
🍷 Light reds with berry flavors. Racy, pungent, dry whites. Soft, dry rosés.		
🏛 Sylvain Bailly, Jean-Paul Balland, Henri Bourgeois, Cotat, Lucien Crochet, Vincent Delaporte, André Dezat, de la Garenne, Gitton, les Grands Groux, Pascal Jolivet, Serge Laporte,	🍴 White: Grilled salmon steaks with a sauce made from fish stock, cream, and crayfish.	
	▤ White: 1998, 1997.	
	▨ White: 1–4 years.	

SAUMUR

PART OF THE LARGER *appellation* of Anjou, Saumur, also known as the "pearl of Anjou," produces red, white and rosé wines, as well as sparkling whites, and rosés. Much less well known than sparkling Saumur, the red wines of the *appellation* range from light, fruity Saumur *rouge* to full-bodied, fragrant Saumur-Champigny, the hidden treasure of the *appellation*.

GRATIEN & MEYER
Creamy, appley, Cuvée Flamme is one of the best sparkling wines of the Loire valley.

THE CHALKY, TUFA SOILS to the south of the town of Saumur are home to Cabernet Franc and Cabernet Sauvignon vines. These are used to produce fresh, light, Beaujolais-style red wines rarely seen outside France, which are sold as red *appellation contrôlée* Saumur. To the east of the town, on the gravelly limestone soil around the confluence of the Loire and Vienne rivers, are the Cabernet Franc vineyards of the Saumur-Champigny *appellation*. These provide some of the Loire valley's best red wines, as good or better than the classic wines of nearby Chinon (*see p.180*), Bourgueil (*see p.179*), and St. Nicolas de Bourgueil (*see p.179*). The popularity of this wine has led recently to a huge increase in production, and also in price. There are now more than 10 million bottles of Saumur Champigny produced every year, and consequently the

KEEPING WARM
Oil burners are a necessary feature of the vineyards in Saumur, protecting the vines against hazardous frost.

concentration of flavor and general quality is very variable. For this reason it is wise to buy your wine from one of the scrupulous producers listed below, all of whom make excellent wines, including red Saumur or Saumur-Champigny.

The cool climate and chalky soils of the *appellation* make this ideal sparkling-wine territory, and the white and rosé sparkling wines of Saumur are far better known than the region's reds, and a popular alternative to more expensive Champagne. The wines of the two *appellations contrôlées*, Saumur Mousseux and Saumur Pétillant, are made largely from the Chenin Blanc, giving them an aromatic flavor of apples and nuts. This differs from the yeasty flavors of the Chardonnay-dominated wines of Champagne, though the recent addition of Chardonnay grapes to Saumur's sparkling wines has given them a more Champagne-like flavor. The popularity of both *appellations* is diminishing, however, as producers turn to making wines sold under the generic but more prestigious Crémant de Loire *appellation*.

Made, like the sparkling wines, from mainly Chenin Blanc grapes, the still whites of Saumur are often undistinguished, with a tendency to taste thin and acidic. A notable exception to this are the semi-sweet *appellation contrôlée* Coteaux de Saumur late-harvest wines. Full-bodied and deliciously rich, these wines are rare but well worth seeking out.

DOMAINE FILLIATREAU
The Vieilles Vignes, or old vines, of this estate produce wines that are gloriously rich and blackcurranty.

✳ AC Saumur, AC Saumur-Champigny, AC Cabernet de Saumur, AC Coteaux de Saumur, AC Saumur Mousseux, AC Saumur Pétillant	des Vignerons de Saumur, Clos des Cordeliers, Yves Drouineau, Filliatreau, de la Guilloterie, Hospices de Saumur, du Hureau, Joseph, Langlois Château, René-Noël Legrand, Roches Neuves, Clos Rougeard, Ch de Targé, Ch de Villeneuve.
🍇 Red: Cabernet Franc, Cabernet Sauvignon. White: Chenin Blanc, Chardonnay.	
🍷 Fruity light reds. Dry, still whites. Dry sparkling whites.	🍴 Red: Roast goose with chestnut stuffing.
	🍾 Red: 1998, 1997, 1996.
ⅢⅢ Ackerman, du Bois Mozé, de Bonneveaux, du Caillou, Cave	⌛ Red: 2–10 years. White: 1–3 years.

SAVENNIÈRES

FAMOUS SINCE THE 18th and 19th centuries, when it was a popular sweet white wine, Savennières is now one of the world's most extraordinary dry white wines. It is also one of the best examples of the ability of the Chenin Blanc grape to be both ripe and fiercely acidic at the same time. The vineyards of Savennières face southeast across the Loire river to Rochefort, just south of Angers. The mineral intensity of Savennières' wines is attributed to the volcanic debris that lies beneath the soil, while the concentration of their flavor is due to the low yield, one of the smallest of any *appellation*. When young, the combination of honey and tart cooking apples in Savennières puts off many modern drinkers, but drink it with creamy food after five years or so and it will live up to its reputation as the world's greatest Chenin Blanc.

COULÉE-DE-SERRANT
Nicolas Joly uses bio-dynamic methods (see below) to farm his vines in this beautiful, riverside site, where he produces some of the region's best wines.

DOMAINE DE CLOSEL
Dry Savennières is, for many, the ultimate expression of the appley, honeyed, nutty character of the Chenin Blanc grape.

✳ AC Savennières.	Laffourcade, aux Moines, Ch Pierre-Bise, de Plaisance, de la Roche-aux-Moines, Pierre Soulez, Ch de Varennes.
🏵 White: Chenin Blanc.	
🍷 Long-lived, acidic, dry whites.	
🍴 Des Barres, des Baumard, Benon, la Bizolière, de Chamboureau, Clos Rougeard, de Closel, Coulée-de-Serrant, Emile, d'Epire, la Franchaie,	🍽 Salmon in filo pastry with a *beurre blanc* sauce.
	📅 1997, 1995, 1990, 1989, 1985.
	⏰ 10–20 years.

SAVENNIÈRES GRANDS CRUS

THESE TWO SMALL *GRANDS CRUS* within the *appellation* of Savennières have attracted a cult following for lovers of the Chenin Blanc. The three producers all battle against naturally low yields that are further jeopardized by the risk of frost. Nicolas Joly, who owns Coulée-de-Serrant *(see above)* and vineyards in Roche-aux-Moines, is raising the odds by tending his vines and producing his wines according to the strictest bio-dynamic rules. The procedures, which include timing vineyard work in accordance to phases of the moon and treating the soil with small doses of manure that has been stored in a cow's horn, are, predictably, often mocked. However, this has not deterred Joly and his fellow believers, like Lalou Bize-Leroy of Domaine Leroy in Burgundy, whose wines are good enough to silence the mockery.

ROCHE-AUX-MOINES
The Chenin Blancs of Roche-aux-Moines and Coulée-de-Serrant are complex, honeyed, floral yet mineral wines that go brilliantly with rich fish dishes like salmon.

CHÂTEAU DE CHAMBOUREAU
At its finest, grand cru Savennières like this is one of the most complex, long-lived white wines in the world.

✳ AC Savennières Roche-aux-Moines, AC Savennières Coulée-de-Serrant.	Moines, Ch de la Roche-aux-Moines, Ch de Chamboureau.
🏵 White: Chenin Blanc.	🍽 Trout cooked in foil and served with new potatoes and garden peas.
🍷 Long-lived, bone-dry whites with great complexity.	📅 1997, 1995, 1990, 1989, 1985.
🍴 Coulée-de-Serrant, aux	⏰ 10–20 years.

TOURAINE

THE LOIRE REGION COVERS A WIDE RANGE of landscapes as it stretches west-ward to the sea, and the Touraine *appellation* lies at its heart. Within its borders are examples of most of the reds and the dry and sweet white wines that are produced in the Loire. Between tastings, the spectacular châteaux of this attractive *appellation* are well worth taking time out to visit.

LE *CHÂTEAU D'AZAY LE RIDEAU*
The grandeur and beauty of this famous château reflects the historic importance of this region and its prestige at the royal court. Azay le Rideau is one of France's most beautiful châteaux.

DESPITE THE PRESENCE OF all kinds of other agriculture competing for space, the Touraine *appellation* is huge, amounting to some 40 million bottles of red, white, and rosé wines. These are produced primarily from the Gamay, Sauvignon Blanc, and Chenin Blanc, but also from the Cabernet Franc and Cabernet Sauvignon, the Malbec and the Pinots Noir, Meunier and Gris, the Grolleau and Pineau d'Aunis. Chardonnay is also present, but its use has been restricted since 1994. Wines

A PATCHWORK LANDSCAPE
Vines share the land here with a wide range of other crops. The rolling land is flatter around the town of Tours, becoming hillier in the more remote areas of the appellation.

range from excellent Sauvignons and Cabernet Francs to dull Chenin Blancs and Gamays that taste as though they were lucky to make it into a bottle. The name of the producer here is crucial. *Coopératives* like Oisly et Thésée and the Cellier Léonard de Vinci in Limeray do well, as do a number of good merchants like Aimé Boucher and Bougrier.

Finer wines are supposedly produced under three separate Touraine *appellations*: Touraine-Mesland, Touraine-Amboise, and Touraine Azay-le-Rideau. In fact, everything here depends on the producer, but visitors will be so dazzled by the beauty of the châteaux and the region's landscape that they will probably forgive all kinds of faults.

Touraine Azay-le-Rideau produces light-dry and semi-sweet Chenin Blancs and good Malbec and Gamay-based rosés. For red wines head to Touraine-Mesland, where the reds are dominantly Cabernet Franc and have more character and body than those of Touraine-Amboise. The white wines of both these *appellations* are best avoided in all but the ripest vintages.

Other styles that are worth looking out for are Touraine Pétillant and Touraine Mousseux. The sparkling and semi-sparkling whites and rosés are a good value when well made, but the real curiosities are the blackcurrant Cabernet Francs, made in Chinon (*see p.180*), Bourgueil, and St. Nicolas de Bourgueil (*see p.179*).

DOMAINE BELLEVUE
Fresh, tangy Sauvignon has the refreshing bite of wine that is produced in a cool climate.

✴	AC Touraine, AC Touraine-Amboise, AC Touraine Azay-le-Rideau, AC Touraine-Mesland, AC Touraine Mousseux, AC Touraine Pétillant.
❀	Red/ rosé: Gamay, Cabernet Franc, Malbec, Pinot Noir, Pineau d'Aunis. White: Chenin Blanc, Sauvignon Blanc.
⬣	Light, often fruity reds. Light, dry whites. Dry or medium rosés. Sparkling reds, whites

and rosés.

⬛	Bellevue, de la Besnerie, Paul Buisse, la Chapelle de Cray, de la Briderie, les Corbillières, de la Gabillière, Henry Marionnet, Moncontour, Octavie, Oisly et Thésée, Oudin Frères.
🍴	White: St. Marcellin cheese
⬛	White: 1997, 1995.
⬛	Red: 3–8 years. White: 1–4 years. Rosé: 1–2 years.

VOUVRAY

IF ONE *APPELLATION* IN THE LOIRE had to be chosen to demonstrate the extraordinarily varied potential of the Chenin Blanc, it would be Vouvray. While better sweet, dry, or sparkling wines may be made in other parts of the Loire, only Vouvray can produce all three quite so well and, at the same time, demonstrate the aging potential of the Chenin Blanc.

PHILIPPE FOREAU
Philippe Foreau is, unarguably, one of Vouvray's top three wine makers. His estate, Domaine du Clos, is definitely a name to look out for.

FEW WINE REGIONS ANYWHERE have given me more, and less, pleasure than these vineyards on the northern bank of the Loire river. Vouvray has produced extraordinarily old sweet wines that have glorious flavors of apples, honey, and praline, as well as aggressive young wines that are packed full of surplus sulphur dioxide and tooth-stripping acidity. There is nothing new about the minefield character of Vouvray; as the British

author Roger Voss points out, Dutch merchants routinely blended other wine into Vouvray from the 15th to the 19th centuries, and during the early 20th century, the Loire grape growers casually used Vouvray's name on wines from vineyards scattered throughout other parts of Touraine.

In the 1960s and 1970s, Vouvray was consigned to the role of being the French semi-dry alternative to poor-quality German wines. Thankfully, in the 1990s, a run of good vintages and the success of quality-conscious producers like the Domaines Huët and des Aubuisières and Clos Naudin have led to a huge improvement in the quality of Vouvray. Most observers tend to focus on the sweet wines that, like any wines that are late-harvested, are the most seductive and long-lived of Vouvray's wines. However, I must confess to being more fascinated by the semi-dry and dry wines that walk the tightrope between richness and acidity. Fine examples of either style can be complex wines, full of floral and nutty flavors. Be warned when buying Vouvray that many of its wines make no mention on the label of their level of sweetness. As one wine maker explained to me, "customers prefer to drink semi-dry wine, but they like to fool themselves that it is dry." Although the quality of Vouvray Mousseux does vary, a well-made example is smooth and creamy.

WINTER IN THE CLOS BAUDOIN
The weather between harvesting the grapes for the late-picked, sweet wines and the budding of the next year's crop can be very tough on both the vines and the people who tend them.

DOMAINE HUËT
The sparkling and still wines of this estate are skillfully produced using strictly organic methods.

✱ AC Vouvray, AC Vouvray Mousseux, AC Vouvray Pétillant.	Huët, Daniel Jarry, Bernard Mabille, Francis Mabille, Vincent Peltier, Prince Poniatowski (Clos Baudoin), Pichot, Vaugondy.
🍇 White: Chenin Blanc, Arbois.	
🍷 Dry-sweet still whites. Dry sparkling whites. Dry-sweet semi-sparkling whites.	🍴 Chicken braised in milk and stock.
	▤ 1997, 1995, 1990, 1989, 1985.
▥ Des Aubuisières, Bourillon D'Orléans, Marc Brédif, Didier Champalou, Gagneux, Ch Gaudrelle,	▧ Still dry: 5–20 years. Still sweet: 7–30 years. Sparkling: 1–3 years. Semi-sparkling: 0–1 year.

OTHERS

AS WELL AS THE "BIG NAME" WINES covered on previous pages, the Loire also offers a large number of smaller *appellation* and *VDQS* wines that cover a wide range of styles. Often overlooked by people outside the region itself, these wines are discovered with much delight by visitors, who soon learn to appreciate their fresh, characterful flavors.

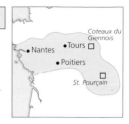

SMALL IS BEAUTIFUL
While there are many large estates in France, most of the vineyards in this region are quite small and are often tended by local farmers who have other crops.

O F THE OTHER WINES from the Loire, Gros Plant, made from a naturally acidic grape called the Folle Blanche, deserves a passing glance. Although this wine is perfectly acceptable on the Atlantic coast as an accompaniment to seafood dishes when it is well made, young and preferably bottled *sur lie*, it is not a wine that I would travel too far to drink.

Wines labeled as Rosé de Loire are dry and made from the Cabernet Franc or Sauvignon, the Pineau d'Aunis, the Grolleau, or Gamay grapes, grown anywhere within the *appellations* of Anjou (see p.178), Saumur (see p.187) or Touraine (see p.189). Not surprisingly, it varies in both style and quality and should be bought with care. Crémant de Loire comes from the same areas and Cheverny (see p.179). Wines that carry this label can be white or, sometimes, rosé and are made from grapes that include the Chenin Blanc, Chardonnay, Pinot Noir, Cabernet Franc, and Cabernet Sauvignon.

Mostly known for its light reds made from the Gamay grape, the Coteaux d'Ancenis is a small

COTEAUX DU VENDÔMOIS
An up-and-coming region, the Coteaux du Vendômois is the traditional home of the Pineau d'Aunis grape variety.

740 acres (300 ha) *VDQS* region that also makes inexpensive, and generally unmemorable, wines from the Chenin Blanc, Cabernet Franc, and the Pinot Gris, known here as the Malvoisie.

Elevated to *appellation contrôlée* status in 1998, the Coteaux du Giennois is a small but growing region of some 370 acres (150 ha) yielding Gamay, Sauvignon Blanc, and Pinot Noir grape varieties. The limestone and silex soil here results in the production of quite serious, if shortish-lived wines.

If a long history has any value, on the other hand, St. Pourçain ought to be an *appellation* wine rather than a *VDQS*. Grapes were, after all, first planted here by the Phoenicians in around 1100 BC. The red and the rosé wines are both juicy blends of the Gamay and Pinot Noir grapes, while the dry, grassy white wines are a combination of the local Tressalier and the Chardonnay and Sauvignon. I predict an elevation to *appellation contrôlée* status before too long.

Other light, Gamay-based wines worth drinking young, and while in the region, are those labelled Côtes du Forez, Châteaumeillant, Côtes d'Auvergne, and Côtes Roannaises. Also of interest are the red wines of the Coteaux du Vendômois. These reds show how wines made mainly from the Pineau d'Aunis grape can be strengthened by blending with the Gamay or Cabernet Franc grape varieties.

LES VIGNERONS FOREZIENS
This Côtes du Forez estate is one of the very few wine producers to concentrate on the Gamay grape.

THE FOOD OF THE LOIRE

Mention the Loire to any Frenchman and there is a strong chance that he will describe it as "la Douce France," the part of his country where life is sweet. This is the place where you will find fish from the river and the sea as well as game, pork, and every kind of dairy food, not to mention the wide range of fruit and vegetables that grow in abundance here.

THE FOODS THAT YOU will come across vary as you follow the Loire River toward the sea. At the eastern end of the river you will find pike stuffed with pork, and the goat's cheese that has been produced near Sancerre since the Moors introduced goats here in the eighth century.

In Touraine, as elsewhere in France, meat and fish are traditionally used together in ways that might surprise many modern diners. The *vol au vent d'Amboise,* for example, has little in common with the small mouthfuls bearing this name that are handed around at cocktail parties. This one measures 10 in (25 cm) across and is made with pike, scallops, veal sweetbread, morel mushrooms, truffles, cream, and eggs. Sweetbreads, which are a

RILLETTES
In this regional delicacy, the melted fat of pigs' kidneys and strips of pork are cooked together with herbs and spices. When cool, the mixture is served as pâté.

SAUMON AU BEURRE BLANC
Salmon is delicious served with a traditional, delicate butter sauce made with vinegar, dry white wine, preferably Muscadet, and shallots.

FRUITS DE MER
The Atlantic Ocean and the Loire River are perfect sources for a wide range of fresh shellfish. One of the best ways to serve them is simply piled high on a large platter with a slice of lemon and a glass of chilled Muscadet.

MOULES MARINIÈRES
This light, fresh-tasting mussel dish is popular everywhere. The mussels are cooked in a sauce of white wine, shallots, herbs and, for added richness, cream.

regional speciality, also feature in *la beauchelle*, a pie whose ingredients also include white wine and mushrooms. Veal, also popular, is mixed with cream and mushrooms to make stuffed artichokes.

Game is also popular, with partridge, pheasant, duck, and quail appearing on most menus. One of the tastiest game dishes, *magrets à la Clavelière*, involves cooking a fillet of duck with

shallots, grapes, Armagnac, and Muscadet. *Lièvre à la royale*, an even richer dish, unites hare with *foie gras*, red wine, and four cloves of garlic and four shallots per person.

Among the fish dishes that you might encounter in the Loire are bass grilled in a salt crust, shad cooked with sorrel, salmon in a *beurre blanc* or *beurre nantais* (butter, shallots, and wine) sauce, and carp stuffed with mushrooms. There could also be monkfish, sole meunière, whitebait (known here as *petite friture* or *buisson de goujon*), and *Chaudrée,* a soup that combines fish and garlic. Often treated as delicacies elsewhere, lobster, mussels, and oysters are featured on the menus of some quite humble restaurants in and around Nantes. The wine, parsley, and mussels all go into the same pot for *moules marinières*, while oysters are sometimes served hot with cream and leeks.

As an accompaniment to one of the Loire's sweet wines, you could try a *tarte tatin,* a caramelized, upside-down apple tart, a *tarte aux poires* (pear tart), a *gâteau nantais,* made with almonds and rum, or a *méli-mélo de fruits rouges,* a dessert that combines strawberries, raspberries, blackberries, blackcurrants, redcurrants, Muscadet, and sugar.

FISH IN ABUNDANCE
Salmon, trout, carp, and pike are all caught fresh from the Loire River. In addition, the Atlantic Ocean provides the locals with a range of other fish.

REGIONAL CHEESES

Historically, most of the cheese to be found in this region, especially around Anjou, was made from cow's milk. However, goat's cheeses such as the Crottin de Chavignol are found close to the border with Burgundy and can be traced back as far as 1573. During the maturing and ripening process, as different molds form and flavors strengthen, the surfaces of many of these cheeses become pungent rinds. Even today, cheese is sent to the market wrapped in hay or rolled in ash, as was the tradition 300 years ago.

CROTTIN DE CHAVIGNOL
When fresh, this goat's cheese has a white surface that hardens and blackens with age. When fully ripe, it is strong and has a meaty texture.

TOMME DE CHÈVRE
Varieties of this cheese can be found throughout France. In the Loire, during the ripening process it is rubbed with a cloth that has been soaked in Muscadet.

PROVENCE AND CORSICA

PROVENCE AND CORSICA HAVE THE POTENTIAL

TO PRODUCE A WEALTH OF WINES THAT ARE

PACKED WITH THE FLAVOR OF THE SUN.

Provence and Corsica regions

ORDER A BOTTLE OF PROVENÇAL rosé in a restaurant in Paris, and you are likely to be presented with a dull, copper-colored wine with about as much freshness as last week's newspaper. Provence does make good wines, but the problem is, people claim, that they just don't travel very well. In reality, as any experienced wine maker will tell you, a well-produced wine can be carried around the world without suffering any ill effects. Take, for example, all the Australian wines that are enjoyed in countries like Canada, thousands of miles away. The thing that does genuinely suffer from travel sickness and jet lag is our memory. Unexceptional wines that we enjoyed in a little café at the edge of the beach on a sunny, carefree day in Provence simply lose their allure when they are set in

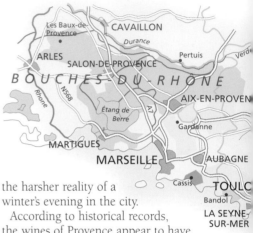

the harsher reality of a winter's evening in the city.

According to historical records, the wines of Provence appear to have traveled more successfully when the Romans carried them home in *amphorae*. However, those wines, like the region's best today, were almost certainly red. Provence's famous rosé is a relatively modern invention, most of which should be treated with the contempt that it deserves. If you want to enjoy wines that really exploit the full potential of this glorious region, head for *appellations* like Bandol *(see p.196)*, Cassis *(see p.197)*, Palette *(see p.198)* and Coteaux d'Aix-en-Provence *(see p.197)*, and the village of Les Baux-de-Provence, within that last *appellation*.

DOMAINE DE ROCHEBELLE
While coopératives and merchants have traditionally sold most of the wine in Provence, small estates like this are increasingly developing reputations for the quality and character of their wines.

KEY		
⬛ Ajaccio		◻ Côtes de Provence
⬛ Bandol		⬛ Muscadet du Cap Corse
⬛ Bellet		— Palette
⬛ Cassis		⬛ Patrimonio
⬛ Coteaux d'Aix-en-Provence		◻ Vin de Corse
◻ Coteaux Varois		— *Département* boundary

SEA VIEW
Corsica's wines might not be as famous as those from some other regions, but few could ask for better weather or more breath-taking views of the Mediterranean.

In wine making, as in so many other things, Corsica seems to be much further from the rest of France than the 105-miles (170-km) sea journey might lead one to expect. Towns with names like Ajaccio and Porto-Vecchio and estates called Catarelli and Torraccia reveal a strong Italian influence here that is also evident in the flavor of its wines. In many ways, Corsica seems to have more in common with the Italian islands of Sardinia and Sicily than with the French mainland. The Nielluccio, for example, the most widely planted grape variety in Corsica, is actually a close cousin of the Sangiovese of Chianti.

Until recently, tasting a range of the island's wines made almost laughable the generous way in which the *appellation contrôlée* authorities have handed out *appellation* status here. Most of the wines on offer could be said to have deserved little more than *vin de pays* status. Now, however, a growing number of estates are producing good, characterful wines that truly exploit the potential of Corsica's grape varieties.

🄰 54,000 acres (22,000 ha): 165 million bottles.		▦ Varied, including granite, sandstone, and occasional outcrops of limestone and flint.
🄰 Despite occasional variations caused by the proximity of the Mediterranean, the climate here is generally very warm in both summer and winter. Dry conditions can be a problem for the vines.		🄵 Red: Nielluccio, Syrah, Grenache, Mourvèdre, Cinsault, Carignan, Sciallero, Barbarossa. White: Ugni Blanc, Grenache.

Ajaccio

Aᴛ ғɪʀsᴛ ɢʟᴀɴᴄᴇ, ᴛʜɪs ʟᴀʀɢᴇ *appellation* on the west coast of Corsica would seem destined to produce thick wines with high alcohol levels. But the temperature here is actually cooler than one might expect, thanks to an altitude of over 330 ft (100 m) and to the moderating effect of the sea. Low temperatures in the spring help to reduce yields and aid in the production of wines with concentrated flavors.

The red wines are primarily made from the Sciacarello grape that does well on the granite soil here. Until recently, the flavor of the Ajaccio was often obscured by an excess of tannin and a lack of freshness. Improved winemaking skills and the efforts of ambitious producers have, however, exposed the peppery character of the Sciacarello and the more herby appeal of the local Vermentino grape that is used for white Ajaccio.

Worth the Detour
Corsica's popularity with tourists from both the French mainland and from further afield ensures that most of the wine is sold and drunk on the island.

Clos Capitoro
One of Corsica's best wines, this Ajaccio is fresh, fruity, and very characterful.

✳	AC Ajaccio.	🏛 Clos d'Alzeto, Clos Capitoro, Comte Peraldi.
🍇	Red/ rosé: Sciacarello, Barbarossa, Nielluccio, Vermentino, Grenache, Carignan, Cinsault. White: Ugni Blanc.	🍽 Red: Baked eggs with parmesan cheese, chard, and chervil.
🍷	Light-colored, peppery reds and rosés. Dry, fruity, if often quite acidic whites.	📅 Red: 1998, 1996, 1995. ⏳ Red: 3–5 years. White: 1–3 years. Rosé: 1–2 years.

Bandol

Oɴᴇ ᴏғ ᴛʜᴇ ʟᴏɴɢᴇsᴛ-ᴇsᴛᴀʙʟɪsʜᴇᴅ *appellations* in France, Bandol's full-bodied wines were popular at court in the 16th and 17th centuries and were supposedly credited by Louis XV, who said they provided him with "vital sap and wits." Like Bordeaux (*see p.77*), Bandol benefited from being a port, and at one point it no doubt shipped more wine under its name than was produced from its vines. Following replanting as a result of phylloxera, a group of producers fought to restrict the *appellation* to the natural amphitheater of terraced vines. Today, however, the main threat comes from the vacation homes that sell more easily than the wines. Bandol's red wine is made primarily from the Mourvèdre grape, which gives it an intense, spicy flavor. The peppery rosés are also good, but the whites are generally dull.

The Perfect Setting
The grapes that are produced by these vines ripen reliably in what is some of the finest sunshine in France.

Domaine Tempier
This estate has, almost single-handedly, established the growing, international reputation of the wines of this appellation.

✳	AC Bandol.	des Costes, la Noblesse, Pibarnon, Pradeaux, Romassan, de la Rouvière, Tempier, Terrebrune, la Tour de Bon, Vannières.
🍇	Red/ rosé: Mourvèdre, Grenache, Cinsault. White: Sauvignon Blanc.	
🍷	Dark, full-bodied reds. Simple, dry whites. Full-flavored, dry rosés.	🍽 Duck with olives. 📅 Red: 1995, 1994, 1990.
🏛	Barthes, Bastide Blanche, Bunan, de Frégate, Moulin	⏳ Red: 3–10 years. White/ rosé: 1–3 years.

LES BAUX DE PROVENCE

THIS SPECTACULAR HILLTOP medieval village, which is now France's second most popular tourist attraction after Mont St. Michel, has recently, and justifiably, gained the entitlement to add its village name to the vast *appellation* of the Coteaux d'Aix en Provence. Its best reds are deep, dark, chocolatey wines, with notes of plums and cherries, while the rosés can compete with the best of the Rhône. There are some excellent producers here, including a number who use a combination of traditional and organic methods in the vineyards.

✴	AC les Baux de Provence.
❧	Red/ rosé: Grenache, Cinsault, Mourvèdre, Syrah, Cabernet Sauvignon.
🔍	Full-bodied reds. Dry rosés
🏛	Terres Blanches, Mas de la Dame, Mas de Gourgonnier.
🍴	Cold beef salad.
☰	Red: 1998, 1995, 1994.
⏱	Red: 3–10 years. Rosé: 1–3 years.

MAS DE GOUR-GONNIER This rich, gamey wine has fruity, berryish flavors.

BELLET

ONE OF FRANCE'S SMALLEST *appellations*, Bellet is situated on the steep hills to the west of Nice. The cooling Alpine winds combine with sea breezes to give this area a surprisingly cool microclimate. The wines produced here use grape varieties that are found almost nowhere else. The fragrant reds are made from the Braquet (Italy's Brachetto) and the Fuella (Folle Noir), while the whites are made primarily from the Rolle, blended with the Ugni Blanc, Pignerol Muscadet, Mayorquin, Clairette, Bouboulenc, and the Chardonnay.

✴	AC Bellet.
❧	Red/ rosé: Braquet, Fuella, Cinsault. White: Rolle.
🔍	Full-bodied, earthy reds. Scented, full-bodied whites. Dry, full-bodied rosés.
🏛	Ch de Bellet, de Cremat.
🍴	Sea bass with fennel.
☰	Red: 1996, 1995, 1994.
⏱	Red: 3–10 years. White/ rosé: 1–3 years.

CHÂTEAU DE BELLET The Cuvée Baron G combines the flavors of the local grapes with the spice of new oak.

CASSIS

ONE OF FRANCE'S OLDEST *appellations*, this fishing village turned arty resort lies several miles east of Marseilles. Tourism and real estate are pushing the vineyards out, but the estates that remain take advantage of the prices their wines command. The rosés are pleasant, but unremarkable, and the dense and deep-colored reds are best drunk young. Cassis' white wine, made from the Ugni Blanc, Sauvignon Blanc, Clairette, Doucillon, Marsanne, and Pascal Blanc are more interesting and go perfectly with the local fish dishes.

✴	AC Cassis.
❧	Red/ rosé: Mourvèdre, Grenache, Cinsault. White: Clairette, Ugni Blanc, Marsanne.
🔍	Medium-bodied reds. Dry, perfumed, full-bodied whites. Dry rosés.
🏛	Du Bagnol, Ste. Magdeleine.
🍴	Pizza.
☰	White: 1998, 1996.
⏱	1–4 years.

CLOS STE. MAGDELEINE Examples of fine Cassis, like this, are among the world's most distinctive white wines.

COTEAUX D'AIX EN PROVENCE

THE COTEAUX D'AIX EN PROVENCE is a relatively new *appellation*, covering some 50 *communes* spread across Provence from Arles eastward to Rians and from the Durance river south to Marseilles. The area's traditional grape varieties have recently been enhanced by the addition of up to 30 percent of the Cabernet Sauvignon. This has improved the aging ability of many of the area's reds, but it is still too small a proportion to allow the inclusion within the *appellation* of the Cabernet-influenced wines of Domaine de Trevallon, the region's top estate.

✴	AC Coteaux d'Aix en Provence.
❧	Red/ rosé: Grenache, Cinsault, Mourvèdre.
🔍	Medium-bodied, fruity reds. Light, dry rosés.
🏛	De Beaulieu, Calissanne, Fonscolombe, Pigoudet.
🍴	Red: Lamb with garlic.
☰	Red: 1998, 1997, 1996.
⏱	Red: 2–5 years. White/ rosé: 1–3 years.

CHÂTEAU DE FONSCOLOMBE This large, 18th-century château is the producer of one of the best wines of the appellation.

COTEAUX VAROIS

THIS PART OF PROVENCE has for long been a vinous no-man's-land. Today, however, quality is improving, thanks to new rules prescribing an increase in the proportion of Mourvèdre, Syrah, or Grenache in red and rosé wines to 80 percent by the year 2000. Good, peppery, redcurranty examples of the rosé are often better than the ubiquitous Côtes de Provence *(see right)*. The reds can have a Rhônelike richness, while the rare whites are dry, aromatic, and good with local specialities such as *poulpe* (octopus) *à la Provençale.*

❀ AC Coteaux Varois.	*DOM DU*
✷ Red/ rosé: Grenache, Syrah, Mourvèdre. White: Vermentino.	*DEFFENDS CLOS DE LA TRUFFIÈRE*
⬛ Full-bodied reds. Light- to medium-bodied whites. Medium-bodied, dry rosés.	*This wine is a star feature in*
▦ Des Chaberts, du Deffends.	*any lineup*
❙❙ Red: *steak au poivre.*	*of reds from*
▤ Red: 1998, 1996, 1995.	*Provence.*
⬈ Red: 2–5 years. White/ rosé: 1–3 years.	

MUSCAT DU CAP CORSE

UNTIL 1993 THESE classic wines, produced in 17 villages in the rugged north of Corsica, had no *appellation* of their own and no means of finding their way to markets beyond Corsica. Thus they were rarely compared with such Muscats as Beaumes-de-Venise *(see p.215)* and Frontignan. The chalky soil and sea breezes seem to contribute to what can be some wonderful, ripe purity of fruit, with fresh, perfumed aromas. For sweet-wine fans, these Muscat Blanc à Petits Grains wines are among France's finest *vins doux naturels.*

❀ AC Muscat du Cap Corse.	*DOMAINE DE*
✷ White: Muscat Blanc à Petit Grains.	*CATARELLI De Catarelli*
⬛ Sweet *vins doux naturels.*	*produces a luscious,*
▦ Antoine Arena, de Catarelli, de Gaffory, Dominique Gentile, Leccia, Orenga de Gaffory, San Quilico.	*orange-scented wine that would*
❙❙ Chocolate cake.	*go well with*
▤ 1996.	*fruit salad*
⬈ 1–3 years.	*or chocolate.*

CÔTES DE PROVENCE

AROUND HALF OF FRANCE'S rosé wine is made in this, France's largest *appellation,* which covers some 45,000 acres (18,000 ha) of diverse countryside, with similarly diverse vines. Reds range in flavor from intense Syrah to light, peppery Grenache. Wine-making skills and aspirations vary, too. For dull, disappointing Provence wine, try picking up a rosé at random in a supermarket. But there are serious rosés to be had (including the highly priced wines from Domaine Ott), as well as a growing number of worthwhile reds and whites.

❀ AC Côtes de Provence.	*DOMAINE*
✷ Red/ rosé: Carignan, Syrah, Cabernet. White: Clairette.	*RICHEAUME The ideal weather*
⬛ Full-bodied reds. Crisp, dry whites and rosés.	*conditions of Provence*
▦ La Bernarde, de la Mireille, Richeaume.	*have enabled producers like*
❙❙ Red: *saucisson sec.*	*Domain*
▤ Red: 1998, 1996, 1995.	*Richeaume to*
⬈ Red: 2–4 years. White/ rosé: 1–3 years.	*start making organic wine.*

PALETTE

TODAY, THIS WINE comes from two producers, both taking advantage of the limestone soil and relatively cool climate of the north-facing slopes to the east of Aix. To give credit where it is due, however, the *appellation* (whose fans have included Kings René and Edward VII) owes its existence to the efforts of just one estate, Château Simone. Considering Palette's tiny size, the list of permitted grape varieties seems ludicrously long. But there is no doubting the quality of this small area's red wines, which can keep for up to 20 years.

❀ AC Palette.	*CHÂTEAU*
✷ Red/ rosé: Grenache, Mourvèdre, Cinsault, Syrah. White: Clairette, Muscat, Ugni Blanc, Sémillon.	*SIMONE A classic of southern France –*
⬛ Traditional rich reds and whites. Long-lived rosés.	*well worth keeping for a*
▦ Ch Cremade, Ch Simone.	*few years*
❙❙ Red: Braised calf's liver.	*before*
▤ Red: 1998, 1995, 1990.	*drinking.*
⬈ Red: 5–15 years. White/ rosé: 3–7 years.	

PATRIMONIO

Patrimonio is Corsica's oldest *appellation* and one of its best. It comprises seven *communes* and is situated just west of Bastia on the island's northern tip. The dominant grape for the reds, Nielluccio, is cited as a native grape, but is almost certainly the Sangiovese of Tuscany, and may be a fairly recent introduction in Corsica. The combination of this and other Italian and Italianate varieties with the local limestone soil contributes to the long-lived, meaty, herby style of some reds, such as Orenga de Gaffory's oak-aged Cuvée des Gouverneurs.

The rosés, made from varieties including Grenache, have a similar herby, peppery style to many rosés from Provence, but they are often better made and better value. The Patrimonio *appellation* also covers whites, which are now made solely from the local Vermentino.

SAVAGE COUNTRY
The northern part of the island of Corsica boasts some spectacularly rugged countryside.

ANTOINE ARENA
This is a perfect chance to try the herby flavors of the Vermentino grape, which gives Corsica's whites their character.

🔅 AC Patrimonio.		Antoine Arena, de Caterelli, Dominique Gentile, Leccia, Clos Marfisi, Orenga de Gaffory, Pastricciola.
❋ Red/ Rosé: Nielluccio, southern Rhône varieties. White: Vermentino.		
🍷 Deep-colored, full-bodied, often very peppery reds. Dry, peppery rosés. Mostly light, dry whites.	🍴 White: Fish soup.	
	📋 Red: 1996, 1995.	
📖 Dom Aliso-Rossi,	⏳ Red: 3–5 years. White, rosé: 1–3 years.	

VIN DE CORSE

This generic *appellation* applies to the whole island of Corsica and covers red, white, and rosé wines, many of which do not warrant *appellation* status. Production is centered mainly on the large *coopératives* on the east coast, but smaller estates do make interesting wines, often under the name of smaller *appellations*. For example, Domaine de Torraccia produces red and rosé wines of the Vin de Corse Porto Vecchio *appellation*. The pink is a full-bodied rosé, perfect with *bourride*, the local fish stew, while the red has flavors of berries, herbs, and tobacco. The Vin de Corse Figari *appellation* is close to Bonifacio in the south. Much of its wine is quaffing fare, but Domaine de Tanella and Poggio d'Oro are two quality-conscious names to watch. Other small *appellations* are Vin de Corse Calvi and Vin de Corse Sartène.

WINTER WONDERLAND
Corsica's snowy hills overlook these sloping vineyards on the east coast. Here, the vines are pictured "resting" before the growing season.

CLOS CULOMBU, CORSE CALVI
This cuvée prestige is one of the best examples of the kind of well-made wines that are now being produced here.

🔅 AC Vin de Corse Coteaux du Cap Corse.		Clos d'Alzeto, Dom de Tanella, Clos Culombu, Clos Landry, Maestracci, Poggio d'Oro, Clos Reginu, de Torracia.
❋ Red/ Rosé: Nielluccio, Sciacarello, Grenache, southern Rhône varieties; White: Vermentino.		
🍷 Full-bodied, herby reds. Dry rosés. Dry or sweet whites.	🍴 Rosé: Fish stew.	
	📋 Red: 1998, 1996.	
	⏳ Red: 2–4 years. White/ rosé: 1–3 years.	

THE RHÔNE VALLEY

OF ALL THE WINES PRODUCED IN FRANCE, NONE
OFFER MORE EXCITINGLY SPICY FLAVORS THAN
THOSE OF THE RHÔNE VALLEY.

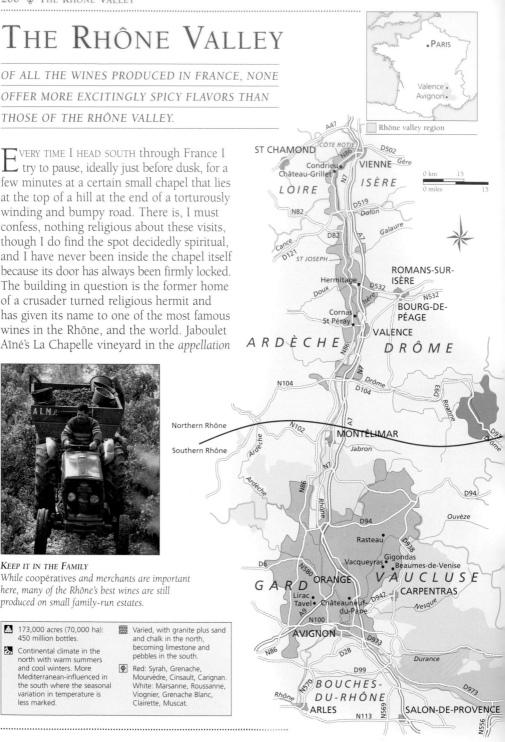

EVERY TIME I HEAD SOUTH through France I try to pause, ideally just before dusk, for a few minutes at a certain small chapel that lies at the top of a hill at the end of a torturously winding and bumpy road. There is, I must confess, nothing religious about these visits, though I do find the spot decidedly spiritual, and I have never been inside the chapel itself because its door has always been firmly locked. The building in question is the former home of a crusader turned religious hermit and has given its name to one of the most famous wines in the Rhône, and the world. Jaboulet Aîné's La Chapelle vineyard in the *appellation*

KEEP IT IN THE FAMILY
While coopératives and merchants are important here, many of the Rhône's best wines are still produced on small family-run estates.

🏔 173,000 acres (70,000 ha): 450 million bottles.

🌡 Continental climate in the north with warm summers and cool winters. More Mediterranean-influenced in the south where the seasonal variation in temperature is less marked.

▨ Varied, with granite plus sand and chalk in the north, becoming limestone and pebbles in the south.

🝖 Red: Syrah, Grenache, Mourvèdre, Cinsault, Carignan. White: Marsanne, Roussanne, Viognier, Grenache Blanc, Clairette, Muscat.

of Hermitage (see p.214) is not only one of the most famous, it is also one of the most gloriously situated I know. The view across the sinuous river below is spectacular enough, but it is the vertiginous slope of the terraced vineyard itself that always makes me reflect on the extraordinary human effort involved in planting, tending, and picking grapes here. An hour or so further south you will find another uninhabited building and another, very different, site of vinous pilgrimage. This is the château of Châteauneuf-du-Pape (see p.207), the ruined castle that was once the summer residence of the exiled Pope John XXII. There are no spectacular slopes here, but walking through the vineyards is still no easy matter because the ground is covered with an astonishing number of the large round pebbles that are more usually associated with particularly inhospitable beaches.

Both these vineyards produce mainly red, with a little white wine. In Hermitage at the northern end of the Rhône valley, and in the nearby appellations of Crozes-Hermitage (see p.213), St. Joseph (see p.216), Cornas (see p.209), and the Côte Rôtie (see p.212), the smoky, blackberry flavor of the reds comes exclusively from the Syrah grape. In Châteauneuf-du-Pape, Gigondas (see p.213), and in the villages making wines sold as Côtes du

LIFE AT THE TOP
The vineyards of the Rhône valley are far more often planted on steep slopes than those of Bordeaux or Burgundy.

Rhône (see pp.210–11), the flavors are more varied, depending on the proportions in which a cocktail of grape varieties are used. Although the Syrah still features here, the leading player is the Grenache. Wines from this variety vary enormously depending on how they are made, but they are all marked out by the instantly recognizable and deliciously incongruous smell and taste of freshly ground pepper.

For centuries, these Rhône reds were used to improve the appearance and color of weedy wines from Bordeaux (see pp.70–97) and Burgundy (see pp.98–141). At one time, the practice was so acceptable that higher prices were charged for Médoc wines (see p.216) that had been "hermitagé," that is, dosed with Hermitage. Today, rightly or wrongly, such mixtures are illegal, but in any case would be unlikely since wine drinkers are willing to pay as much for the sun-packed flavors of the finest wines of the Rhône as they do for the best wines of other regions.

ALL SPICED UP
From the vineyards stretching out from the Rhône valley come a range of sweet and dry red, white, and rosé wines whose common characteristic is their rich and often spicy flavors.

N85
Bléone
N85

ALPES-DE-
HAUTE-PROVENCE

N96
Durance
D11
Verdon
D554
D11

KEY	
🟦 Châtillon-en-Diois	Cornas, Côte Rôtie, Gigondas, Hermitage, Lirac, St. Joseph, St. Péray, Tavel, Vacqueras)
☐ Clairette de Die	
☐ Coteaux de Pierrevert	🟩 Côtes-du-Rhône-Villages (including Beaumes-de-Venise, Rasteau)
☐ Coteaux du Tricastin	☐ Côtes du Ventoux
☐ Côtes du Luberon	☐ Côtes du Vivrais
🟦 Côtes-du-Rhône (including Château Grillet, Châteauneuf-du-Pape, Condrieu,	— *Département* boundary

THE HISTORY OF THE RHÔNE VALLEY

The Rhône valley has inevitably played a huge role in the history of France, serving as a principal artery between the north and south. But it has also been a source of fine wine, from the vineyards that were established 2000 years ago in the northern part of the region, to those further south at Châteauneuf-du-Pape that gained their fame 1300 years later.

I N THE EARLY DAYS of the Roman Empire, no river in France was more important to traders than the Rhône. We know that, during the first century BC, wine from Rome and Provence was carried up the river valley and used as currency by the tribes who were struggling for supremacy in Gaul. Even before Julius Caesar and his troops arrived in Chalon-sur-Saône, in what is now part of southern Burgundy, the wine business was thriving enough for two enterprising Romans to have already set up shop as merchants.

The first quality wines said to have originated in the Rhône were the red wines that were made in the vineyards of Hermitage (*see p.214*) and the Côte Rôtie (*see p.212*) by a tribe called the Allobroges. These wines were evidently good enough for Pliny to note in

PAPAL POWER
In 1367 Pope Urban V tried to return the papal court from Avignon to Rome. The move happened 10 years later.

71 AD that the red wines of Vienne were sold at a premium. They were also considered fine enough to be exported to Rome and even across the Channel to the new colony of Britain. Historians still argue over whether the grape variety grown by the Allobroges was the Syrah or the Pinot Noir. The quality of these wines lay in the ripeness of their flavors, but the flavor of the grape may well have been hard to discern behind the pine resin that was used to preserve the wine on its travels. As elsewhere in France, monasteries in the Rhône grew vines and made wine in the 12th and 13th centuries, but none of the wines they made gained the reputation enjoyed by their counterparts further north in Burgundy. Recognition for the region's potential arrived in 1305, when Pope Clement V temporarily moved his palace from Rome to Avignon. Although the papal preference was apparently for Burgundy, most of the wine drunk at the papal court was from local vineyards. Pope John XXII, unknowingly, gave the name to the Rhône's most famous wine, Châteauneuf-du-Pape, when he built himself a summer home in a flattish, pebbled region near Avignon.

In the 15th and 16th centuries, the region began to prosper as Lyon became an important trading center for silk. Rivalry with the Burgundians, however, who banned all Rhône wines from passing through Dijon on the grounds that they were "*très petits et povres*"(very small and poor), prevented the wines from being sold in northern France,

CHÂTEAUNEUF-DU-PAPE
In the 14th century, Pope John XXII built a new castle, the Châteauneuf-du-Pape, and planted the vineyards that produce one of the most famous wines of the Rhône.

HOME AWAY FROM HOME
Paul Signac's painting of the Palais des Papes in Avignon evokes the mood of the castle in which the exiled popes established themselves when they decamped from Rome.

Britain, and the Low Countries. Rhône wines finally began to develop a following among wine drinkers in Paris and London in the 17th and 18th centuries, and among merchants, who used Hermitage to improve the quality of red Bordeaux.

Ironically, it was not long before the wines of another Rhône *commune* found themselves to be the focus of attention among blenders and vinous fraudsters. When the vineyards of Châteauneuf-du-Pape were replanted at the beginning of the 20th century, after being destroyed by phylloxera, unscrupulous merchants and vine growers used this famous name on wines that had nothing to do with its pebbled vineyards. In response to these threats to the prestige of their wines, a group of quality-conscious Châteauneuf-du-Pape producers, led by Baron le Roy (see p.35), the owner of the finest domaine in the region, drafted a set of laws that dictated the boundaries within which Châteauneuf-du-Pape could be made. These rules covered a range of stipulations, including vine varieties, pruning, training, and ripeness, and even the health of the grapes. Thus it was that Châteauneuf-du-Pape became the true birthplace of the *appellation contrôlée* system.

These efforts, and the wine-making success of the region's best growers and merchants,

helped to keep the key *appellations* of the Rhône firmly among France's more respected wines, but it was the rare exceptions, such as Jaboulet's Hermitage la Chapelle, that were ranked alongside the top reds of Bordeaux.

This changed in the 1980s and 1990s, with the arrival on the scene of the American wine guru Robert Parker. Like the Romans of 2000 years earlier, Parker relished the naturally ripe and "voluptuous" style of the region's top wines, and treated them as seriously as he did the classic wines of the Médoc (see p.83) and St. Émilion (see p.89). As wine makers throughout the world tasted recent vintages from the Rhône and wines made from the same grape varieties in Australia and California, they began to question whether they ought to be planting Syrah, Grenache, and Viognier grapes instead of Cabernet, Merlot, and Chardonnay. No French wine region enters the 21st century better placed than the Rhône valley.

THE RHÔNE
The banks of this 125-mile (200-km) river are lined with vineyards, from Valais in Switzerland to the Bouches-du-Rhône just west of Marseilles in the south of France.

A DRIVING TOUR OF THE RHÔNE

This short tour takes you southward past the Syrah-dominated vineyards of the northern part of the Rhône valley, through evocatively named and often spectacular *appellations* that include the Côte Rôtie, Hermitage, and Condrieu, famous for its unexpectedly exotic white wines.

CHÂTEAU GRILLET
This tiny appellation *uses the Viognier to make good but overpriced white wines.*

VIENNE TO AMPUIS

It is worth pausing in Vienne ① to visit some of the city's churches and its Roman monuments, including La Pyramide, a 82 ft (25 m) obelisk that, less than credibly, is said to mark the tomb of Pontius Pilate. Leaving Vienne, follow the Rhône southward for a few kilometers before crossing to the west bank, where you will find yourself in the heart of the small but illustrious *appellation* known as the Côte Rôtie or "roasted hillside." Pass through the village of Verenay ②, where local producers worth visiting include Clusel-Roch and Jean-Michel Gérin. Then turn left, following the steeply sloping vineyards toward Ampuis ③. This quiet town is just beginning to wake up to the recent explosion of interest in the wines of both the Côte Rôtie and neighboring Condrieu. The merchant firm of Marcel Guigal, maker of some of the finest and most expensive wines of the Côte Rôtie, has cellars here. Among Guigal's very best, single-estate wines is one named after the imposing Château d'Ampuis, visible in the distance, but which sadly is not open to visitors.

CONDRIEU TO ST. PIERRE-DE-BOEUF

Not far from Ampuis is the town of Condrieu ④, surrounded by the vineyards of its namesake white wine *appellation,* where the Viognier grape shows what it can do when used on its own. If you pass through Condrieu at harvest time, look out for actor Gérard Depardieu, who owns a vineyard here. Turning right onto the D34 at the village of Vérin, you will reach the spectacular punchbowl vineyard and château that make up the tiny *monopole* of Château Grillet ⑤. Although the setting is worth a look, no examples of this rather overpriced wine are sold at the château. Offering better value, Condrieu producers well worth visiting include André Perret and Yves Cuilleron at Verlieu ⑥, and Alain Paret, whose cellars are at St. Pierre-de-Boeuf ⑦.

ST. PIERRE-DE-BOEUF TO ST. DÉSIRAT

The red and white wines sold under the *appellation* of St. Joseph are produced in *communes* spread over 37 miles (60 km) between Condrieu and Hermitage. The best place to head for is the 16th-century village of Malleval ⑧. To get there, turn

off the N86 at St.-Pierre-de-Boeuf on the D503, through the Gorge de Malleval and past the Saut de Laurette waterfall, taking the D79 to Malleval. Its medieval salt market, the château, and the cellars of Pierre Gaillard are well worth visiting. Returning to the N86, some of the best-value wines in the area can be found at the *coopérative* of St. Désirat ⑨, one of the most highly regarded in France.

CROZES-HERMITAGE AND TAIN L'HERMITAGE

Cross the river at Sarras and follow the N7 before turning left onto the D163, which takes you up through the vineyards of Crozes-Hermitage ⑩. Michel Martin is a producer worth visiting in Crozes-Hermitage, and there are plenty of good estates in nearby villages, such as Chanos-Curson. Back on the N7, you will soon reach Tain l'Hermitage ⑪, which faces its twin town of Tournon-sur-Rhône on the opposite bank of the river, and takes its name from the single hillside that makes up the *appellation* of Hermitage. These great granite vineyards cover an area of 311 acres (126 ha) on the east bank of the river. All face due

HERMITAGE HILL
These famous hillside vineyards separate Crozes-Hermitage from the riverside town of Tain l'Hermitage.

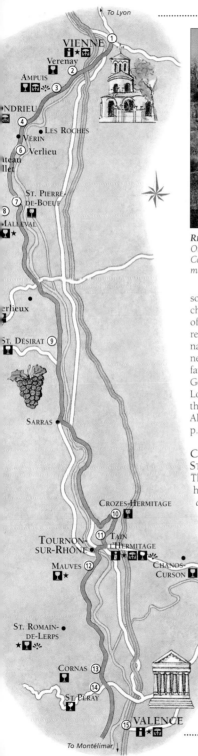

RIVERSIDE TERRACES
On the western bank of the Rhône, these Cornas vineyards produce wines that are magnificently dark and powerful.

south, overlooked by the famous chapel that stands in the vineyard of Hermitage La Chapelle. You can reach the chapel by following the narrow road that climbs the hill near the *cave coopérative*. My favorite producer of Hermitage is Gérard Chave of Domaine Jean-Louis Chave, who can be found in the nearby village of Mauves ⑫. All of the wine makers listed on p.214 are also worth a visit.

CORNAS TO ST. PÉRAY AND VALENCE

The village of Cornas ⑬ lies at the heart of the small and underrated *appellation* of Cornas. The vines here are sheltered from the mistral winds, producing unusually well-ripened grapes. For a fine

KEY	
🍷	Tasting possible
🏛	Places to eat
ℹ	Tourist information
★	Site of interest
▬	Tour route
❄	Viewpoint

0 km   5
0 miles   5

view of the vineyards and the river, head up the narrow road to St.-Romain-de-Lerps, returning to pick up the N86 that leads to the sparkling wine village of St. Péray ⑭ and on to the town of Valence ⑮, where the vineyards are increasingly being encroached upon by housing developments.

CHÂTEAU GRILLET

CHÂTEAU GRILLET
The brown bottle and distinctive label make it easy to recognize the wines of Château Grillet.

SURROUNDED BY THE *APPELLATION* of Condrieu (*see p.208*) the vineyards of this unusually tiny, single-estate *appellation* face southeast, providing perfect ripening conditions for the low-yielding Viognier vines. Extravagantly praised by 18th-century connoisseurs, the delicate white wines of Château Grillet have traditionally been considered some of the best in France. But vintages in the 1980s and early 1990s were disappointingly dull and over-sulphured.

More recent efforts have shown a marked improvement, and at their best these wines can develop remarkably with time. Prices are still very high and my advice for anyone looking for great apricot-scented Viognier wines is to consider the best wine of Condrieu, before indulging in the extravagance of the wines of Château Grillet with their extravagant price tags.

FADED GLORY
Gloomily imposing, the once great Château Grillet overlooks its vineyards, which nestle comfortably in a natural granite amphitheater.

✱ AC Château Grillet.	▮ Fresh black truffles baked in a puff-pastry case with *foie gras* and smoked bacon.
✿ White: Viognier.	
▨ Opulent, perfumed, dry whites.	▤ 1997, 1996, 1995, 1994.
⦀ Château Grillet.	⏣ 5–20 years.

THE VIOGNIER REVIVAL

The Chardonnay is the most widely planted, white-wine grape variety in the world, and its apparent ubiquity has prompted some of the more experimental wine makers to search for an alternative. Having dismissed the Riesling, the Sauvignon Blanc, the Sémillon, the Chenin Blanc and the Pinot Gris, a number of producers, including the prominent Beaujolais *négociant* Georges Duboeuf, have turned their attention to the Viognier. This fragrant but low-yielding grape was once widely planted along the northern part of the Rhône valley. Its tendency, however, to give small crops, and to make wines that go flabby a few years after bottling, led to a decline in its popularity. By 1968 there were just 35 acres (14 ha) of Viognier vines under cultivation. As part of the grape's recent revival, Georges Duboeuf has planted significant Viognier vineyards in the Ardèche, and

there are now more than 370 acres (150 ha) of Viognier vines further south in Languedoc-Roussillon. The variety's greatest success, however, is most evident in the vineyards of the recently rejuvenated *appellation* of Condrieu (*see p.208*). Often made with nearly 100 percent Viognier grapes, the exotically perfumed and perfectly balanced white wines made here are some of the most exciting in the Rhône valley.

CHALLENGING BUT REWARDING
Deliciously fragrant but temperamental and low-yielding, the Viognier is a difficult grape variety to grow.

CHÂTEAUNEUF-DU-PAPE

THE APPELLATION OF Châteauneuf-du-Pape is situated in the sun-baked southern reaches of the Rhône valley, where the Mediterranean climate allows a great number of grape varieties to flourish. These well known vineyards are famous as much for their unusual covering of glacier-scoured stones as for the spicy, long-lived red wines that they produce.

SHINGLE VINEYARDS
It is the pebbles in Châteauneuf-du-Pape that set its vineyards apart from wine-growing land elsewhere in France. At night, the stones give off heat that has been stored during the day.

DOMINATING ITS NAMESAKE village, the now-ruined 14th-century château at Châteauneuf-du-Pape was built for Pope Jean XXII as a summer retreat from the papal court in the nearby city of Avignon. By the second half of the 14th century, flourishing walled vineyards were established here, producing popular red and white wines sold throughout the region, until the later part of the 18th century, under the name of *vin d'Avignon.*

Classified under the rules of the *appellation contrôlée* system in 1936, the *terroir* of Châteauneuf-du-Pape is unusually varied, with soils ranging from sand through to gravel and alluvial deposits. As a result, producers here are entitled to combine 13 different grape varieties, from the Grenache and the Syrah to the Mourvèdre, the Terret Noir, and the white Bourboulenc. Despite this freedom, most wine makers use a mixture of only three or four grape varieties, with the Syrah, the Mourvedre, and the Grenache the most widely used. Another famously unusual feature of most parts of the *appellation* are the large, cream-colored pebbles that make the vineyards look like shingle beaches, storing heat during the day and reflecting it onto the vines at night.

The wide range of red wines produced here can be broadly classified as light and fruity for early drinking, or richly gamey and long-lived. White wines are often dull, though better use of the Roussanne grape is helping to make some intriguingly aromatic wines.

CHÂTEAU RAYAS
This is one of the very best estates in the appellation. Unusually for Châteauneuf-du-Pape, the wines here are made entirely from a single grape variety, the Grenache.

CHATEAU RAYAS
CHATEAUNEUF-DU-PAPE
APPELLATION CHÂTEAUNEUF-DU-PAPE CONTRÔLÉE
PROPRIETAIRE
J REYNAUD
750ml
CHÂTEAUNEUF DU PAPE
VAUCLUSE
FRANCE

PAPAL RUINS
Long-deserted, the papal château still exerts an air of authority over the surrounding vineyards.

✱	AC Châteauneuf-du-Pape.
🍷	Red: Grenache, Syrah, Mourvèdre, Cinsault. White: Grenache Blanc, Clairette, Bourboulenc.
🍾	Full-bodied dry reds. Small amounts of dry white.
🏛	Pierre André, Ch de Beaucastel, Beaurenard, Bosquet des Papes, Cabrières, les Caillous, Chapoutier, la Charbonnière, Clos du Mont Olivet, Clos des Pâpes, Delas, Font de

Michelle, Fortia la Gardine, Guigal, Jaboulet, Janasse, Mont-Redon, la Mordorée, Nalys, la Nerthe, du Pegaü, Ch Rayas, Réserve des Célestins, de la Solitude, Tardieu-Laurent, du Trignon, Vieux Télégraphe, de Villeneuve.

🍴 Red: leg of lamb in pastry.
🗓 Red: 1995, 1994, 1990, 1989.
⏳ Red: 5–20 years. White: 3–5 years.

CHÂTEAU DE BEAUCASTEL
Producing wines of wonderful character, this estate remains the favorite of many French critics.

CLAIRETTE DE DIE

HUGGING THE SLOPES OF the Drôme valley, about (40 km) 25 miles to the east of the Rhône, the sparkling white wine *appellation* of Clairette de Die is something of an anomaly in a region better known for full-bodied red wines from *appellations* such as Côte Rôtie (*see p.212*) and Crozes-Hermitage (*see p.213*). The area covered by the Clairette de Die *appellation* produces two contrasting styles of sparkling wine. The first is a dry, neutral-tasting wine made entirely from the Clairette grape and known, since a recent name change, as Crémant de Die. The second is the deliciously ripe and peachy Clairette de Die Méthode Dioise Ancestrale. Made from a mixture of Clairette and Muscat grapes, this unusual wine is bottled during its initial fermentation so that trapped carbon dioxide gives the wine its bubbles.

VINCENT ACHARD
This fine producer makes fruity, semi-sweet Méthode Dioise Ancestrale, sold until 1999 as Clairette de Die Tradition.

WINDSWEPT SLOPES
In contrast to the Rhône valley red wine appellations to the north, the bleak, windswept slopes of the Drôme valley are best suited to the production of white sparkling wines.

✳	AC Clairette de Die Méthode Dioise Ancestrale, AC Crémant de Die.	Cornillon, Magord, Jean-Claude Raspail, Union des Jeunes Viticulteurs (Chamberan).
🍇	White: Clairette, Muscat à Petits Grains.	
🍷	Dry and semi-sweet sparkling whites.	🍴 Clairette de Die Méthode Dioise Ancestrale: Raspberry and strawberry tart.
🍽	Vincent Achard, Cave Cooperative de Die, Didier	📆 1997, 1995.
		⏳ 1–2 years.

CONDRIEU

DRY AND RICHLY ALCOHOLIC, and with a wonderful and totally unexpected perfume of peach blossom, apricots, and violets, the white wines of Condrieu are the best in the Rhône valley and have recently acquired almost cult status. Originally planted during the first few centuries AD, the south-facing vineyards around the town of Condrieu in the eastern part of the *appellation* have long been used to to produce semi-sweet, often botrytized, late-harvest wines; a style that is being successfully revived today. Planted, as today, with the fragrant but tempera-mental Viognier grape (*see p.206*), by the 1960s the vineyards of Condrieu covered only 25 acres (10 ha). Today, however, thanks to a combination of the Rhône boom of the last 20 years, the recent popularity of the Viognier, and, most important, the arrival of many talented young producers, the area under vines has risen to 230 acres (93 ha).

YVES CUILLERON
This Condrieu producer makes fragrant, late-harvest sweet wines as well as more typical apricot-scented dry ones.

PICKING IN CONDRIEU
Yields are low and harvesting is hard in the steeply sloping vineyards of Condrieu, two explanations for the high prices paid for the hugely popular wines of the appellation.

✳	AC Condrieu.	Pierre Dumazet, Philippe Faury, Pierre Gaillard, Jean-Michel Gerin, Guigal, André Perret, Georges Vernay, François Villard.
🍇	White: Viognier.	
🍷	Full-bodied, highly-perfumed dry whites. Occasional sweet whites.	🍴 Crab bisque with a garnish of deep-fried sage.
🍽	Ch d'Ampuis, Patrick et Christophe Bonnefond, Louis Chèze, Gilbert Chirat, Clusel-Roche, Yves Cuileron, Delas,	📆 1997, 1996, 1995, 1994.
		⏳ 2–4 years.

CORNAS

A N AREA OF STEEPLY TERRACED, south-facing granite vineyards on the western bank of the Rhône, the tiny *appellation* of Cornas covered only 130 acres (53 ha) in 1975. Since then, however, the increasing international popularity of wines from the Rhône has given the full-bodied, somewhat rustic red wines of Cornas a new lease on life and the area under vines has now risen to 190 acres (76 ha). Improved vinicultural practices have increased grape yields, and new techniques, such as de-stemming the grapes before fermentation and the use of new oak barrels for maturation, have produced smoky wines that are fruitier and less tannic than the wines traditionally made here. Robust and meaty, wines made by old-school producers such as Auguste Clape can also offer excellent value, but they need time in the bottle to soften.

SUNTRAP SLOPES
The terraced south- and southeast-facing vineyards on the hillsides of the Cornas appellation are perfectly positioned to soak up every available ray of sunshine.

AUGUSTE CLAPE
Bucking the modern trend in Cornas toward a lighter, fruitier style, these more traditional wines are attractive and robust.

✴ AC Cornas.		Lionnet, Robert Michel, Rochepertuis, de Saint-Pierre, Tardieu-Laurent, Noël Verset, Alain Voge.
🍇 Red: Syrah.		
🍷 Full-bodied, deep-colored reds that are very tannic when young.		🍴 Partridges braised with green cabbage.
🍽 Thierry Allemand, Guy de Barjac, Chapoutier, Auguste Clape, Jean-Luc Colombo, Courbis, Jaboulet, Jean		📅 1995, 1994, 1990, 1989, 1988.
		📈 8–10 years.

COTEAUX DU TRICASTIN

S PREADING OUTWARD from the eastern bank of the Rhône just south of Montélimar, the little-known hillside vineyards of Tricastin were awarded *appellation contrôlée* status in 1973. Several grape varieties are grown here, but many of the red and rosé wines of the *appellation* are made from a blend of the peppery Syrah and the rich Grenache. Fruity and spicy, the red wines in particular can offer excellent value. White wines are increasingly made from a blend of Viognier, Marsanne, and Roussanne grapes, and are improving rapidly.

DOMAINE DE GRANGENEUVE
This light, fruity wine with spicy, peppercorn flavors offers good value and easy drinking.

✴ AC Coteaux du Tricastin.	
🍇 Red/ rosé: Grenache, Cinsault, Syrah, Carignan. White: Clairette, Viognier, Roussanne, Marsanne.	
🍷 Soft, spicy reds. Dry, crisp whites. Dry rosés.	
🍽 Grangeneuve, des Rozets, du Vieux Micoulier.	
🍴 Cold roast beef.	
📅 1998, 1997.	
📈 1–4 years.	

CÔTES DU VENTOUX

C LOSE TO THE POINT where the Rhône valley meets Provence is Mont Ventoux, venerated in local folklore as the source of the bitterly cold, high speed *mistral* wind that whips down the Rhône valley every winter. The limestone vineyards of the surrounding Côtes du Ventoux *appellation* are used to grow grape varieties including the Grenache, the Cinsault, the Mourvèdre, and the Syrah, producing light, early-drinking red wines that are fruity and easy-going. Smaller amounts of unmemorable white and rosé wine are also made here.

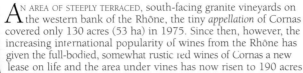

CHÂTEAU UNANG
In contrast to many Rhône valley wines, those of the Côtes du Ventoux are fresh and fragrant for early drinking.

✴ AC Côtes du Ventoux.	
🍇 Red/ rosé: Grenache, Syrah, Cinsault, Carignan. White: Clairette.	
🍷 Light, scented reds. Dry whites. Dry rosés.	
🍽 Des Anges, Michel Bernard, Jaboulet, Ch Pesquié.	
🍴 Roast partridge.	
📅 1998, 1997, 1996.	
📈 1–4 years.	

CÔTES DU RHÔNE

OF ALL THE LARGER, SO-CALLED generic *appellations* in France, it is the Côtes du Rhône, stretching along the banks of the river Rhône from Vienne to Pertuis, and the Côtes du Rhône-Villages with its 16 named villages, that would get my vote for the greatest improvement in wine making in recent years, offering some of the very best value.

DOMAINE DE LA CANTHARIDE
This wine from the village of Visan is deliciously peppery when young, and develops an extra richness with age.

OFFICIALLY, A BOTTLE of wine labelled *appellation contrôlée* Côtes du Rhône could come from any part of a large swathe of vineyards between Vienne and Pertuis, in other words, from anywhere along the Rhône valley. In practice, the geography of the region means that the contents of such bottles have almost certainly been crushed from grapes grown in the southern Rhône. Between them, 10,000 wine makers produce around 300 million

SPICE WORLD
A wide variety of grape varieties are grown in the hillside vineyards of the Côtes du Rhône, producing many excellent red wines, well known for their distinctively rich and spicy flavors.

bottles of *appellation contrôlée* Côtes du Rhône each year. Both the soils and the grape varieties grown here are diverse, with the dominant Grenache followed closely by the Syrah, the Mourvèdre, and the Cinsault. As for the whites, these include a mixture of varieties from the dull Clairette to the fragrant Roussanne. Further variety is guaranteed by the ways in which the wines are now made. Many of the reds are now made by the *macération carbonique* method (*see p.24*), which makes for light, juicy wines that are easy to sell within months of the harvest. At the same time, the trend among more ambitious producers is to use more traditional techniques to make wines with a firmer structure and greater longevity.

In theory, the finest wines of the Côtes du Rhône are found among the 20 million bottles labeled as Côtes du Rhône-Villages. Many of the best of these are produced in the villages listed on the right, each of which is named on the label (after Côtes du Rhône in the case of the first 16, before it in the case of Brézème). While *villages* wines quite justifiably command the highest prices, many good wines are also sold under the more basic Côtes du Rhône *appellation*, made by well-known *négociant* firms including Jaboulet Aîné and Guigal, and on estates throughout the southern Rhône valley such as Château Mont-Redon in Châteauneuf-du-Pape (*see p.207*).

DOMAINE DE LA GRANDE BELLANE
This is a really good single-estate wine from the village of Valréas, packed full of rich, spicy fruit flavors.

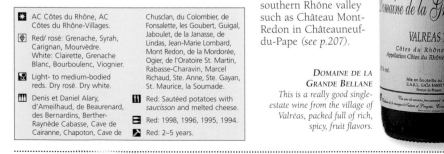

✱	AC Côtes du Rhône, AC Côtes du Rhône-Villages.
❀	Red/ rosé: Grenache, Syrah, Carignan, Mourvèdre. White: Clairette, Grenache Blanc, Bourboulenc, Viognier.
🍷	Light- to medium-bodied reds. Dry rosé. Dry white.
▥	Denis et Daniel Alary, d'Ameilhaud, de Beaurenard, des Bernardins, Berther-Raynède Cabasse, Cave de Cairanne, Chapoton, Cave de Chusclan, du Colombier, de Fonsalette, les Goubert, Guigal, Jaboulet, de la Janasse, de Lindas, Jean-Marie Lombard, Mont Redon, de la Mordorée, Ogier, de l'Oratoire St. Martin, Rabasse-Charavin, Marcel Richaud, Ste. Anne, Ste. Gayan, St. Maurice, la Soumade.
🍴	Red: Sautéed potatoes with *saucisson* and melted cheese.
▤	Red: 1998, 1996, 1995, 1994.
▧	Red: 2–5 years.

GREAT WINE VILLAGES OF THE RHÔNE VALLEY

The first 16 villages belong to the *appellation* Côtes du Rhône-Villages and print their name after the name Côtes du Rhône. Listed at the end is Brézème, which has its own *appellation*.

Beaumes-de-Venise *(see p.215)* Best known for its fortified wines made from the Muscat grape, this village also produces good, light but juicy, peppery reds. Best producers include Domaine de Fenouillet and Château Redortier.

Cairanne One of the star villages of the region, home to several ambitious producers making some seriously good spicy wines.

Chusclan The wines to buy here are the rosés, which can be better than those of nearby Tavel *(see p.217)*. The reds are attractive too, but they are less worth keeping.

Laudun Producers here make unusually good white wines, as well as some of the region's finest Grenache-dominant reds. The best wines will improve with a year or two in the bottle.

Rasteau *(see p.216)*.This village and Beaumes-de-Venise *(see above)* are noted as the only two *communes* in France that include both fortified *(vin doux naturel)* and unfortified wines.

Roaix The *commune* of Roaix shares a wine-making *coopérative* with the neighboring village of Séguret *(see below)*, producing intense reds that repay three or four years' aging.

Rochegude Although once famed for its whites, this *appellation* now covers only red wines, which are light and peppery.

Sablet Competing with Cairanne *(see above)*, and named for its sandy soil, this is a dynamic *commune* known for its light reds, but an increasing use of the Syrah grape is producing longer-lived wines.

St. Gervais This *commune* is increasingly well regarded, thanks partly to the efforts of producer Guy Steinmaier at Domaine Ste. Anne. The Mourvèdre and Syrah grapes both perform well in this

southern region, as does the Viognier, which contributes to some fine whites

SOUTHERN SUNSHINE
At the southern end of the Côtes du Rhônes-Villages appellation, Séguret overlooks vineyards full of sun-loving Grenache vines.

St. Maurice-sur-Eygues Most of the unexceptional wines here are produced by the local *coopérative*.

St. Pantaléon-les-Vignes and **Rousset-les-Vignes** The coolest climate in the Rhône explains the lightness of the wines made in these two neighboring villages.

Séguret Some of the most serious and tightly structured in the region, these are wines that deserve to be kept for four years or more before drinking.

Valréas This *commune* produces some of the most attractively fruity, floral reds in the Rhône.

Vinsobres This *commune* produces some varied reds that range from light and easy-drinking to slow-maturing and intense.

Visan Delicious when young, many of the wines from this *commune* also age well, and are worth keeping in the bottle for a few years.

Brézème Lying midway between the northern and southern Rhône and to the north of the Villages, Brézème labels its wines Brézème-Côtes du Rhône. The reds here are also distinguished in that they are made only from the Syrah grape.

INTENSE WINES
In the shadow of brooding hills, the Grenache vineyards of Vinsobres produce the varied range of red wines sold as Côtes du Rhône-Vinsobres

CÔTE RÔTIE

THE CÔTE RÔTIE, or the "roasted hillside," where the grapes are often literally roasted in the sun, produces red wines that live up to their evocative name, being deep-coloured, luscious, and powerful. Covering the steep slopes behind the village of Ampuis, the vineyards form a bridge between Burgundy to the north and the Rhône valley to the south.

CHÂTEAU D'AMPUIS
Many of the finest wines of the Côte Rôtie come from producer Marcel Guigal's collection of individually bottled vineyards, including his most recent acquisition, the Château d'Ampuis.

D ESPITE A VINICULTURAL history dating back nearly 2,000 years, a large proportion of the vineyards of the Côte Rôtie were not replanted following the devastating late 19th-century epidemic of vine louse, or phylloxera. Vines gave way to fruit trees and, for the first three quarters of the 20th century, the wines of the Côte Rôtie were almost forgotten. While a small number of wine makers have always persevered on the steep and challenging slopes here, credit for the rescue of the *appellation* has to go largely to the gifted producer and

négociant, Marcel Guigal. Not only is Guigal a tireless promoter of high-quality Côte Rôtie, he has also revealed the potential of several individual estates by producing and bottling their wines separately. Today, Guigal's single-estate wines, produced from grapes grown in the vineyards of La Landonne, La Mouline, La Turque, and the Château d'Ampuis, are undoubtedly the very best of the *appellation*, and command prices that are some of the highest in France. Guigal also produces a wine known as *Brune et Blonde*, made from a blend of grapes grown on two of the best-known slopes of the Côte Rôtie, the Côte Brune and the Côte Blonde. With differently colored soils, popular legend has it that the vineyards were named after the hair colour of the two beautiful daughters of the local landowner.

This is quintessential Syrah country, producing great wines with complex berry flavors and an unmistakable smoky note. Increasingly, producers are adding up to 20 percent white Viognier grapes to the Syrah, giving the wines an exotic violet and apricot perfume.

CÔTE BLONDE
Naming an individual vineyard is common practice in the varied Côte Rôtie. The chalky-sand soil of of the Côte Blonde produces fresh wines for early drinking.

PACKED WITH FLAVOUR
The arid slopes of the Côte Rôtie are home to low-yielding vines that produce flavorsome grapes.

LA LANDONNE
The single-vineyard wines of this estate have contributed to the prestige of the appellation.

✳ AC Côte Rôtie.	Robert Jasmin, la Landonne, Bernard Levet, Gabriel Meffre, les Moutonnes, Michel Ogier, René Rostaing, Georges Vernay, Vidal-Fleury, François Villard.
❀ Red: Syrah, Viognier.	
▨ Full-bodied reds with an opulent bouquet.	
▥ Ch d'Ampuis, Pierre Barge, Michel Bernard, de Boisseyt, Patrick et Christophe Bonnefond, Bernard Burgaud, Champet, Chapoutier, Clusel-Roch, Yves Cuilleron, Delas, Philippe Faury, Gaillard, Jean-Michel Gérin, Marcel Guigal, Jean-Paul et Jean-Luc Jamet,	⧈ Leg of lamb roasted with fresh rosemary and whole garlic cloves.
	⧉ 1997, 1996, 1995, 1994, 1991, 1990, 1989, 1988, 1985.
	⧗ 10–15 years.

CROZES-HERMITAGE

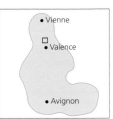

COVERING AN AREA OF 2470 acres (1,000 ha), this large *appellation* spreads out around 11 villages to the north and south of the town of Tain-l'Hermitage. Like the *terroir*, the wines of Crozes-Hermitage are very varied, but at their complex, full-bodied, fruity best, they are a fantastic value. The finest estates, including Les Chassis and Domaine de Thalabert, lie to the north of Tain-l'Hermitage on south-facing slopes along the banks of the Rhône.

Further east the land is flatter, yields are higher, and the wines are more ordinary. Ninety percent of the wines produced here are red, made mainly from Syrah grapes mixed with small amounts of the Roussanne and Marsanne varieties. White wines are made from the delicate Roussanne, either alone or mixed with the Marsanne, and are often fresh and elegant.

HIDDEN TREASURE
Some of the best vineyards in Crozes-Hermitage are tucked away just behind the slopes used to produce the more expensive wines of Hermitage (see p.214).

THE BROTHERS CHAPOUTIER
The largest landowners in Crozes-Hermitage, the Chapoutier brothers produce a variety of fine wines.

✳ AC Crozes-Hermitage	des Desmeure, Entrefaux, Alain Graillot, Jaboulet,
🍇 Red: Syrah, Roussanne, Marsanne. White: Roussanne, Marsanne.	Etienne Pochon, des Remizières, Marc Sorrel, Caves de Tain-l'Hermitage, Tardieu-Laurent, de Thalabert, Vidal-Fleury.
🍷 Full-bodied reds. Full-bodied, shorter-lived dry whites.	🍴 Chicken sautéed with basil.
🍽 Belle, Chapoutier, les Chassis, Chave, des Clairmonts, Colomber, Combier, Delas,	📅 1996, 1995, 1994.
	📈 5–8 years.

GIGONDAS

THE VILLAGE AND THE surrounding vineyards that make up the *appellation* of Gigondas are situated in the spectacular Dentelles de Montmirail mountains to the east of the small town of Orange. In the early 1950s, the *commune* was granted *appellation contrôlée* Côtes du Rhône-Villages status, and in 1971 its wines were promoted to the classification *appellation contrôlée* Gigondas. At their best, the red wines of Gigondas are plummy and rich, dominated by the mellow flavors of the Grenache, carefully combined with smaller amounts of the tannic Syrah and the aromatic Mourvèdre. A great alternative to the more expensive vintages of nearby Châteauneuf-du-Pape (*see p.207*), these wines will develop well for up to a decade. Dry, peppery rosé wines are also made here, and are well worth looking out for.

MOUNTAINS OF LACE
Small but poetically named, the "lacy" Dentelles de Montmirail mountain range forms a stunning backdrop to the vineyards of Gigondas.

DOMAINE DU CAYRON
Strangely underrated, the peppery, long-lived wines of Gigondas offer some of the best value in the region.

✳ AC Gigondas.	Marcel Guigal, Jaboulet, Ch de Montmirail, Piaugier,
🍇 Red/ rosé: Grenache, Syrah, Mourvèdre.	Raspail-Ay, St. Gayan, Ste. Anne, Santa Duc, Tardieu-Laurent, des Tourelles, Ch du Trignon, Vidal-Fleury.
🍷 Full-bodied, sometimes rustic reds. Dry, peppery rosés.	
🍽 Des Bosquets, Brusset, De Cabasse, du Cayron, Delas, des Espiers, les Goubert, du Gour de Chaule,	🍴 Ragout of lamb.
	📅 1997, 1995, 1994.
	📈 Red: 3–10 years.

HERMITAGE

THE VINEYARDS OF Hermitage lie deep in Syrah country on the steep slopes of the Rhône valley between the *appellations* of Crozes-Hermitage (*see p.213*) and St. Joseph (*see p.216*). Flourishing here as almost nowhere else in the world, the Syrah, with its spicy, smoky flavors, is the only grape variety used in the complex, long-lived red wines of the *appellation*.

WRIT LARGE
The stone walls that hold the steeply terraced vineyards of Hermitage in place are often used as billboards by négociants eager to publicize the locations from which they make some of their finest wines.

PRODUCING CLASSIC, inky-black wines, the unique vineyards of Hermitage have been famous for more than 500 years. By the 19th century, the wines of Hermitage were commanding higher prices than the wines of the best Bordeaux estates. Fanning out around the town of Tain-l'Hermitage, this is a hillside *appellation* of rocky vineyards, distinguished by a mushroom-shaped underlying granite outcrop and a due-south aspect, which allows the ripening grapes to catch every drop of sunshine.

Unlike most Syrah-based *appellations*, including nearby Crozes-Hermitage and St. Joseph, which use small amounts of various white grape varieties to add perfume and lightness to their wines, the reds of Hermitage include nothing except the richly tannic Syrah. Although packed with the flavors of raspberries, blackberries, pepper, and smoke, these wines can be somewhat tough and inaccessible in their youth. A decade or so in the cellar, however, gives them a wonderfully gamey complexity.

Extending over 380 acres (154 ha), the single south-facing slope that makes up the Hermitage *appellation* includes a number of subtly different environments, and wines here traditionally have been made from a blend of grapes selected from several sites. Increasingly, however, producers are choosing to make their wines from grapes grown on single, named plots of land. The best of these vineyards include Paul Jaboulet Aîné's well-known La Chapelle. Other excellent single-estate wines to look out for include Les Bessards and Les Greffieux.

The white wines of Hermitage, once as highly regarded as its reds, are now produced in only tiny quantities, but in two distinct styles. First, with its own *appellation*, but rarely produced, is the unusual wine known as *vin de paille*. Made by drying the grapes on straw before pressing, the best of these wines are crisp and honeyed. More common are rich, dry white wines made from a mixture of Marsanne and Roussanne grapes, which often improve for as long as 10 years in the bottle.

KEEPING FAITH
A well-known landmark, this tiny chapel stands in Paul Jaboulet's famous vineyard, La Chapelle.

JEAN-LOUIS CHAVE
The wines produced by Jean-Louis Chave are some of the very best of the appellation.

✴	AC Hermitage, AC Hermitage Vin de Paille.
❁	Red: Syrah. White: Marsanne, Roussanne.
▦	Powerful, tannic reds. Full-bodied, herb- and peach-scented whites.
▥	Albert Belle, Michel Bernard, Chapoutier, Bernard Chave, Jean-Louis Chave, Gérard Chave, du Colombier, Delas Frères (Marquise de la Tourette, les Bassards), Faurie, Ferraton, Grippat, E Guigal, Guyot, Paul Jaboulet Aîné, des Remizières, St. Jemms, Marc Sorrel, Cave de Tain l'Hermitage, Tardieu-Laurent, De Vallouit.
▦	Roast pheasant with a sauce of red wine, shallots, and wild mushrooms.
▤	1996, 1995, 1994, 1990, 1989, 1988, 1985.
▸	Red: 10–20 years. White: 8–15 years.

LIRAC

KNOWN UNTIL RECENTLY as an unsuccessful emulator of the rosé wines produced by its southern neighbor, Tavel (*see p.217*), today the *appellation* of Lirac is more famous as a producer of fast-improving red and white wines. Set on the west bank of the Rhône just north of Avignon, the producers of Lirac use a classically varied southern Rhône combination of the Grenache, Syrah, Mourvèdre, and Cinsault grape varieties to make red wines that are medium-bodied, smooth, and spicy. At their best, these represent excellent value. The dry white wines made here are losing their reputation for dullness and have been vastly improved by the inclusion in 1992 of the Marsanne, the Roussanne, and the fragrant Viognier on the list of permitted grape varieties. Many are now attractively floral.

GRENACHE VINES
Skilfully combined with other grape varieties, the mellow flavors of the Grenache are an important component in the red and rosé wines of Lirac.

DOMAINE PÉLAQUIÉ
Deliciously rich and peppery at their best, the little-known red wines of Lirac can offer excellent value.

AC Lirac.		Martine, la Fermade, Maby, de la Mordorée, Chapelle de Maillac, Pélaquié, St. Maurice, St. Roch, Ch de Ségriès.
Red/ rosé: Grenache, Carignan, Mourvèdre, Syrah. White: Clairette, Ugni Blanc, Marsanne, Roussanne, Viognier.		
Medium- to full-bodied reds. Dry whites. Dry rosés.	Red: Saddle of hare roasted with thyme and garlic.	
Ch d'Aquéria, des Causses et Saint-Eymes, de Devoye	1997, 1995, 1994.	
	Red: 2–5 years. White/ rosé : 1–3 years.	

MUSCAT DE BEAUMES-DE-VENISE

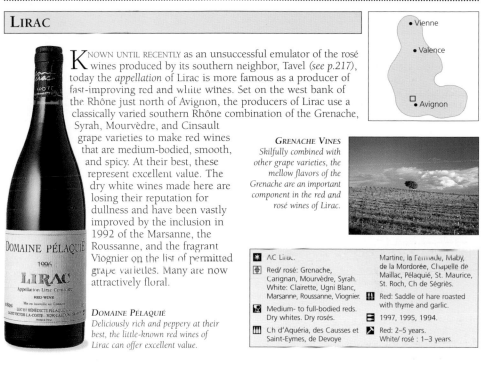

ALTHOUGH IT PRODUCES high-quality red wines that are sold under the Côtes du Rhône-Villages *appellation*, the village of Beaumes-de-Venise, to the east of the town of Orange, is more famous for its apricot-gold *vins doux naturels* (*see p.29*), made from the fragrant Muscat grape. Most of the Muscat wines here are made at the Coopérative des Vins et Muscats, famous due to its hugely successful 1970s marketing campaign, which sold the wine throughout northern Europe as a dessert wine to be enjoyed by the glass, thanks to its screw-top bottle. While the *coopérative*-made wines are of reasonable quality, they do not compare to the single-estate, cork-stopped vintage wines made by individual producers. The best wines of this rather overpriced *appellation* are rich and peachy, achieving a perfect balance of sweetness and acidity.

PROVENÇAL SUN
The sun baked vineyards around the village of Beaumes-de-Venise are used to grow two varieties of the Muscat grape, named for its distinctive musky fragrance.

DOMAINE DE DURBAN
The best wines here are made by individual producers like this one, rather than in the local coopérative

AC Muscat de Beaumes-de-Venise.		Venise, des Bernardins, Chapoutier, de Coyeux, de Durban, de Fenouillet, Paul Jaboulet Aîné, la Soumade, Vidal-Fleury
White: Muscat Blanc à Petits Grains, Muscat Rosé à Petits Grains.		
Fragrant *vins doux naturels*.	Three-chocolate mousse with bitter orange sauce.	
Beau Mistral, de Beaumalric, Cave Coopérative des Vignerons de Beaumes-de-	Mainly non-vintage.	
	1–5 years.	

RASTEAU

Vienne
Valence
Avignon

THIS CÔTES DU RHÔNE-VILLAGES *commune* offers both fortified and unfortified wines. The grapes are 90 percent Grenache (Noir, Gris, or Blanc) from the villages of Rasteau, Sablet, and Cairanne. Fortification is carried out by adding brandy during early development. The fortified wines are in *rancio* style – that is, they are purposely maderized by storing the wine in oak casks, which are later exposed to air and sunlight. The wines vary with the quality of grapes, the cleanliness of casks, and the degree of maderization. Some are like thick, sweet sherry; others have a delicate, Madeiralike quality. Rasteau's red table wines, though possibly less exciting, tend to be reliable, peppery Rhônes. The whites can be dull and are almost always best drunk young.

CAVE DES VIGNERONS
As in some other parts of the Rhône, the smaller coopératives here produce some of the best – and best-value – wines.

MARIE-FRANCE MASSON
This is a peppery-rich wine that could serve as a perfect illustration of the flavors of the southern Rhône.

✴ AC Rasteau, AC Rasteau Rancio.	des Girasols, de la Grangeneuve, Masson, de la Soumade, Francis Vache, Cave des Vignerons de Rasteau.
❀ Red/ White/ Rosé/ Tawny: Grenache Noir, Grenache Gris, Grenache Blanc.	
🍷 Peppery red wines and cask-aged sweet *vins doux naturels*.	🍴 *Vin doux naturel:* Chocolate tart.
▥ Des Coteaux des Travers,	▤ Red: 1998, 1996, 1995, 1993.
	⏳ 3–10 years.

ST. JOSEPH

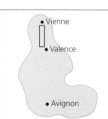

Vienne
Valence
Avignon

ONCE CALLED Vin de Mauves, after the *commune* of that name, St. Joseph became an *appellation* in 1956. It then grew to six times its former size, stretching south down the west bank of the Rhône to Valence. Many of the new plantings took little account of the character of the original vineyards, with the effect that buying St. Joseph today is a hit-or-miss business – wines range in style and quality from basic Côtes du Rhône (*see pp.210–11*) to junior Hermitage (*see p.214*). The best vineyards are on the sandy and gravelly granite slopes behind and around Tournon. Grapes ripen less well than they do in Hermitage, and wines are less intense. Even so, they can be first-class, blackberryish reds for relatively early drinking. Small quantities of Marsanne- and Roussanne-based whites are also produced.

MAUVES
The village that once gave its name to the entire region is now a quiet commune almost hidden among the vines.

JEAN-LOUIS GRIPPAT
Classy reds like this can sometimes age more successfully than feeble examples of supposedly classier Hermitage.

✴ AC St. Joseph.	Pierre Coursodon, Yves Cuilleron, Pierre Gaillard, Graillot, J-L. Grippat, Jaboulet, Perret, Georges Vernay, Villard.
❀ Red: Syrah. White: Marsanne, Roussanne.	
🍷 Soft, fruity, medium-bodied reds. Fragrant, richly flavored dry whites.	🍴 Red: Wood pigeon with onions, red wine, and ham.
▥ Cave de St. Désirat, Cave de Tain-l'Hermitage, Chapoutier, Chave, Chèze, Courbuis,	▤ Red: 1998, 1996, 1995, 1993.
	⏳ Red: 3–10 years. White: 1–3 years.

St. Péray

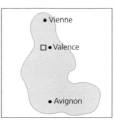

THIS *APPELLATION* IS SITUATED on the west bank of the Rhône, opposite and now almost within the sprawling outskirts of Valence. Fighting competition from developers is not made any easier by the undistinguished character of these light, often quite acidic wines. St. Péray's style makes it an anomaly in this area of rich, meaty Syrahs and full-bodied Viogniers. Conditions for grape growing are affected by a cooler climate and the richness of the soils. Most of the grape harvest goes to make rustic *méthode traditionelle* sparkling wines, which are jointly produced by the *caves coopératives* of Tain-l'Hermitage and St. Péray, and mostly sold within the region itself. For a taste of what this *appellation* can produce when given more individual care and attention, try the wines of Jean Lionnet and Marcel Juge.

THREATENED TERRITORY
Vines in St. Péray are giving way to houses and apartment blocks that will accommodate the growing population of nearby Valence.

JEAN LOUIS ET FRANÇOISE THIERS
Thiers offers an increasingly rare example of gently floral, dry sparkling wine made from traditional Rhône grape varieties.

❈	AC St. Péray, AC St. Péray Mousseux.	Jean Lionnet, Jean-Louis et Françoise Thiers, Alain Voge.
🌢	White and sparkling: Marsanne, Roussanne.	🍴 Still: Shoulder of veal cooked with white wine, leeks, onions, and capers.
🍷	Still, dry whites. Sparkling dry whites.	
🍴	Cave de Tain-l'Hermitage, J.-F. Chaboud, Auguste Clape, Bernard Gripa, Marcel Juge,	🗄 Still: 1998, 1997, 1996. ⧗ Sparkling: 1–3 years. Still: 1–4 years.

Tavel

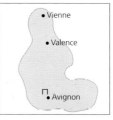

A FAVORITE WITH BOTH Louis XIV and the novelist Honoré de Balzac, this is the most famous rosé in France, and the only Rhône *appellation* to produce exclusively pink wine. Until recent times, despite the fact that it often tasted stale and dull, it was praised for its bronze color and lauded as the only rosé wine that improves with age. This reputation helped to swell the vineyards to nearly 2,500 acres (1,000 ha).

There is no disputing the potential of the Grenache, Syrah, and Mourvèdre to make good wine on Tavel's sandy, clay-alluvial, and pebbly soils, and modern wine growers and critics respectively produce and praise much fresher, more violet-hued wine. Good Tavel should be both fragrant and fruity, yet full-bodied and bone-dry. It is an excellent food wine that can accompany *charcuterie*, fish in sauce, or white meats.

ROSÉ PROSPECTS
Better wine making and vine growing is improving the prospects for the vineyards of Tavel.

DOMAINE DE VALÉRY
Despite its traditional bronze color, this is an example of Tavel whose rich, peppery flavors will not displease modern drinkers.

❈	AC Tavel.	Trinquevedel, de Valéry, Vieux Moulin de Tavel, du Vieux Relais.
🌢	Rosé: Grenache, Cinsault.	
🍷	Potentially refreshing, peppery, dry rosé.	🍴 Squid stuffed with onions and garlic, stewed in squid ink and white Côtes du Rhône wine.
🍴	Ch d'Aquéria, de la Forcadière, de la Genestière, Guigal, Jaboulet Aîné, de la Mordorée, Prieuré de Montezargues, Ch de	🗄 Rosé: 1998, 1997, 1996. ⧗ 2–5 years.

VACQUEYRAS

CHÂTEAU DES TOURS

Serious examples of Vacqueyras like this réserve can compete well with – and outlive – Châteauneuf-du-Pape.

EIGHTEEN YEARS AFTER GIGONDAS (*see p.213*) became the first of the named Côtes du Rhône-Villages (*see p.211*) to get its own *appellation*, this village achieved similar recognition in 1990. Its best reds rarely match good examples of Gigondas and do not always outclass wines from Côtes du Rhône-Villages *communes* such as Cairanne. The reds contain Grenache (a minimum of 50 percent) plus Syrah, Mourvèdre, and Cinsault. At their best, they are deep-colored, spicy wines; though after three or four years in the bottle they lose some of their rustic character and gain complexity. The rosés are good; whites are less so, partly because of their high content of the Grenache Blanc, Clairette, and Bourboulenc. An increased proportion of the Marsanne, Roussanne, and Viognier would improve them dramatically.

VACQUEYRAS VINEYARD
The Grenache from vineyards such as this produces some of the most peppery red wines in the Rhône region.

✺ AC Vacqueyras.	Montvac, Sang des Cailloux, Tardieu-Laurent, Ch des Tours.
🍇 Grenache, Syrah, Mourvèdre, Cinsault.	🍴 Roast lamb with garlic, herbs, zucchini, and tomatoes.
🍷 Rustic, full-bodied red. Small quantities of less impressive white and rosé.	▣ Red: 1998, 1997, 1995.
🏚 Dom des Amouriers, Burle, Clos de Cazaux, la Fourmone, Jaboulet, de Montmirail, de	▨ Red: 2–10 years. White: 1–4 years. Rosé: 1–3 years.

GRAPE VARIETIES OF THE RHÔNE

Four varieties are well known for the role they play in the wines of the Rhône valley. First there is the leading player, the Syrah, from which are made the rich, dark, smoky, blackberryish red wines of Hermitage (*see p.214*), Côte Rôtie (*see p.212*), Cornas (*see p.209*), St. Joseph (*see p.216*), and Crozes Hermitage (*see p.213*) in the northern Rhône. Second is the Grenache, the mainstay of the strawberry-cherryish, peppery-red Côtes du Rhône (*see pp.210–11*) and Châteauneuf-du-Pape (*see p.207*) of the southern Rhône. Third is the Muscat, which produces the unashamedly grapey wines of Beaumes-de-Venise (*see p.215*), and fourth is the newly fashionable Viognier, found in the perfumed

MARSANNE
Often underestimated, this variety is the mainstay of many Rhône whites, with its distinctive combination of spicy and floral aromas and flavors.

white wines of Condrieu (*see p.208*) and Château Grillet (*see p.206*). The Rhône is also the traditional home of a large range of other less well-known grapes. Some, such as the Grenache Blanc, the Bourboulenc, and the Clairette, are decidedly dull and depend on good wine making to produce white wines with any degree of flavor. Then there are the far more characterful Roussanne and Marsanne, which are used to make some of the world's most fascinatingly floral dry whites. The spicy Mourvèdre and Cinsault, though usually better in blends than as soloists, can contribute quite significantly to the flavor of red Châteauneuf-du-Pape and a range of other red wines.

MOURVÈDRE
One of the unsung heroes of the Rhône, this spicy variety is a component of many Châteauneuf-du-Pape wines.

OTHERS

AMONG THE OTHER WINES of the Rhône, some are dull and old-fashioned, while others offer some of the best value in France. Among those most worth seeking out are light, juicy reds that compete well with Beaujolais, spicy, fuller-bodied Côtes du Rhône-style reds, and the extraordinary sweet whites that are now being made from partially dried grapes.

CÔTES DU VIVARAIS
While this region is best known for its fairly-priced wines, its orchards are also the source of a wide variety of fruits that, like the grapes, ripen well in the climate here.

ONE RHÔNE WINE I WOULD dispose of quickly is Coteaux de Die, which gained an *appellation* in 1993 as part of the redefinition of the sparkling wines previously called Clairette de Die. Under the new arrangements, less of Die's *appellation* bubbly is now made from the dull Clairette grape; instead of consigning the now redundant Clairette grapes to *vin de pays* blends, the authorities generously encourage producers to turn them into a still wine that they can sell under this *appellation*.

Similar generosity was shown in 1998 when the Coteaux de Pierrevert were promoted from *VDQS* to *appellation contrôlée*.

Châtillon-en-Diois is a small *appellation* that celebrated its 25th birthday in 1999. The white is made from two Burgundy grape varieties, the

PLUS ÇA CHANGE
The view from the old château in Cadenet, over village roofs, is typical of much of this part of the Côtes du Lubéron.

Chardonnay and Aligoté, while the red is made from the Gamay with some Pinot Noir and Syrah.

Côtes du Lubéron owes its *appellation* status to the efforts of Jean-Louis Chancel, who, during the 1970s and 1980s, invested part of a fortune made from vegetable oil in relandscaping and planting 400 acres (160 ha) of pebbly vineyards and in building his showcase Val Joanis wine estate. The quality of the Val Joanis Grenache-Syrah reds has not always justified the creation of the *appellation*, and the whites have been downright dull, but the rosés have been good and a number of other producers, such as la Vieille Ferme, Châteaux de l'Isolette, Canorgue, and the Domaines de la Citadelle and de Fontenille, make attractive, fairly lightweight wines in all three styles.

One region that can offer good-value reds is Côtes du Vivarais. Still a *VDQS*, it produces a growing range of good light reds, rosés, and even whites, thanks to recent moves to outlaw duller grape varieties such as the Carignan and Ugni Blanc. The best villages (whose names are permitted to feature on labels) are St. Remèze and Orgnac.

Finally, Hermitage Vin de Paille is a glorious, ancient style that, like its counterpart in Alsace, has been revived by a number of top producers including Chave, Chapoutier, Grippat, and Guigal. The drying process, which allows the grapes to lose three-quarters of their water content, produces glorious sweet wines with extraordinary longevity.

DOMAINE DE LA CITADELLE
Here is the proof that the Côtes du Lubéron can make reds worthy of its recently won appellation *status.*

THE FOOD OF THE RHÔNE

Like the Loire valley, the Rhône valley is made up of several separate regions connected by one great river. Inevitably, there are huge differences between the cuisine of Lyon, in the heart of the country, and Châteauneuf-du-Pape, which is closer to the Mediterranean. But, like the red wines of the Rhône, the traditional dishes here share a single quality in their intense flavors.

IF YOU WERE TO ASK a number of French gourmets to name the city where they would most like to spend a few days, Lyon would no doubt be among the most popular choices. Situated right on the border between the Rhône and Burgundy regions, this has long been the home of numerous great restaurants as well as some of the finest charcuteries in France. Traditionally Lyonnaise, the spiced, dry, salami-style sausages *rosette* and *saucisson de Lyon* are now famous all over France and are made by *charcuteries* in other regions. Harder to find outside this city, however, is *saladier lyonnais*, once prepared with sheep's testicles, but now more commonly made with sheep's feet and chicken livers, and

ANDOUILLETTES À LA LYONNAISE
In this dish from Lyon, andouillettes, or tripe sausages, are stuffed with veal and served with fried onions.

ROSETTE DE LYON
Made of meat from leg of pork and served in chunky slices, rosette de Lyon is the most famous of Lyon sausages.

POULET À LA DEMI-DEUIL
To make this dish, also known as poularde à la lyonnaise, the chicken is poached in white chicken stock and stuffed with truffled forcemeat. Small pieces of truffle are also inserted under the skin and the dish is served with vegetables cooked in the chicken broth.

CLAFOUTIS
This cherry flan is made with locally-grown, dark cherries covered in a dough and laced with Kirsch, a cherry liqueur.

cervelas lyonnais, a brioche filled with boiled sausage mixed with pistachio nuts and truffles.

Throughout the northern part of the region, veal is cooked in white wine to make *blanquette de veau.* The main ingredient here, though, is the onion, which goes into *soupe à l'oignon* (onion soup) as well as *sauce soubise,* a simple onion sauce that can be used with sausages.

Pike fished from inland rivers is used as the basis of *quenelles de brochet,* sausages made with a fish mousse. At its best, with plenty of flavorsome fish and a sauce made with crayfish, this is a delicious appetizer.

Moving south, the focus of this region's food shifts toward Mediterranean flavors: of ratatouille and tapenade, of wild herbs, saffron, tomatoes, peppers, and olives. Whereas the northern part of the region cooks with butter, here olive oil is far more commonly used.

The river is also the source of eel, used to make the well-known *matelote,* a fish stew from Barthelasse island on the Rhône river near Avignon.

But the best fish come from the ocean. There is *rougets grillés aux feuilles de vigne,* red mullet cooked with grape leaves and fennel, and all kinds of fish soup, the most famous being *bouillabaisse* served with *rouille,* a mayonnaise made with oil, garlic, chillies, and stock. Just as interesting, though, is *bourride,* a fish stew that comes with *aïoli,* a mayonnaise made with egg yolks and garlic.

The Rhône valley isn't a haven for the sweet-toothed, but it is the place to find nougat as well as *bugnes lyonnaises* (lemon fritters) and a bread tart made with almonds and *kirsch.*

PEPPERS
Further south in the Rhône valley, the cuisine adopts a Mediterranean flavor and peppers, tomatoes, and olives are more commonly used.

REGIONAL CHEESES

When cheese lovers refer to the Rhône, they are usually thinking of the Rhône-Alpes to the east and northern part of the region, where a variety of, often quite pungent, cheeses are made. Among those associated with the region are the various Fourmes from Forez, the goat's milk Chevrotins, the Grataron d'Arèches from Savoie, and the rich, creamy, but relatively low-fat cow's milk Tommes, made in small farms in the Alps. These cheeses all go well with light Rhône reds and, more particularly, whites

FOURME D'AMBERT
Famous since the 17th century, the blue cheeses produced in the Forez region have an individual, mild character that sets them apart.

CHEVROTIN DES ARAVIS
Similar to the more famous Reblochon, this goat's milk cheese comes from Savoie, but is popular in the Rhône, where it goes well with white wine.

SOUTHWEST FRANCE

THIS REGION IS AN IDEAL HUNTING GROUND FOR

ANYONE WHO WANTS UNUSUAL FLAVORS AND

GOOD VALUE ALTERNATIVES TO BORDEAUX.

Southwest region

T HE SOUTHWEST IS AN area where frontiers have been drawn up with more regard for convenience than logic. There are several *appellations* here that grow the same grape varieties as are used in neighboring Bordeaux *(see pp.70–95)*, and which might, but for an accident of geography and history, be classified as part of that region. Bergerac *(see p.224)*, for example, was an important wine region long before the Médoc *(see p.81)* began to earn its reputation. Indeed, the second-class status of Bergerac today owes more to the efforts of Bordeaux merchants to discriminate against it than to the quality of its wines. Though never great, when made with care and skill the wines of Bergerac can compete easily with many pricier wines from Bordeaux. The same is true of wines from the sweet white *appellation* of Monbazillac *(see p.228)*, and of more expensive wines from *appellations* such as Saussignac and Pécharmant *(see p.229)*.

Even more interesting, to my mind, are a number of *appellations*, including Gaillac *(see p.226)*, Cahors *(see p.225)*, and Irouléguy *(see p229)*, that make their wines from local grape varieties such as the Tannat, the Fer, the Gros and Petit Manseng, and the Len de L'Elh, which are grown almost nowhere else in the world. These wines are often resolutely unfashionable, like hand-made pots in a

A TASTE OF THE PAST
Many vineyards in the Southwest region are small and family-owned, like this one run by the three Laplace brothers. Using the traditional Tannat grape, the brothers make rich red wines that are distinctive and attractively old-fashioned.

🔺 32,400 acres (13,000 ha): 220 million bottles.	▦ Ranging from the gravelly clay of Cahors to the sandy soils of the Côtes de Duras and Tursan.
🌡 Very varied in this large region, but the Atlantic Ocean to the west and the Mediterranean to the southeast give most of the area a maritime climate that keeps winters warm and summers cool.	🍇 Red: Cabernet Sauvignon, Merlot, Cabernet Franc, Fer, Tannat, Malbec, Gamay. White: Gros & Petit Manseng, Picpoul, Clairette, Ugni Blanc, Colombard, Sauvignon.

shop full of machine-made crowd pleasers. Although varied, the reds tend toward the rugged and tannic, made to accompany the hearty stews for which this region is known. The whites, at their best, have a fresh and gently tangy character all of their own. Perhaps inevitably, in recent years the so-called real world of international commerce and technical

NEW SHADES OF BLACK
The tough, tannic "black wine" from the Cahors vineyards may be a rarity these days, but there are delicious modern versions.

innovation have begun to make an impact on these wines. While Cahors, for example, has traditionally produced intense, inky dark wines, modern techniques are now being used here to make light and medium-bodied reds, too. So, until you pull the cork, there is often no way to know whether the contents of the bottle will be richly tannic and best drunk with a *cassoulet*, or light and fruity to go with a plate of cold meats. Throughout the Southwest region a new generation of wine makers has responded to the demands of the international marketplace by learning new ways to bring out the best qualities of their vineyards and local grape varieties, and to replace rusticity with refinement. It is no coincidence that, after centuries of disdain, the grandees of Bordeaux have recently begun to consider including both Bergerac and Monbazillac within their *appellation*.

SOUTHWEST FRANCE
Despite the high quality of its wines, this diverse region has historically been overshadowed by neighboring Bordeaux, where merchants often took steps to prevent rival wines from reaching overseas markets.

KEY

⬜ Bergerac	🟦 Irouléguy
🟦 Buzet	⬜ Jurançon
⬜ Cahors	🟦 Madiran (including Pacherenc du Vic-Bilh)
⬜ Côtes de Duras	🟦 Pécharmant
🟦 Côtes de St. Mont	— *Département* boundary
⬜ Côtes du Frontonnais	— Other AOC and VDQ areas (including Monbazillac, Marcillac, Montravel, Tursan)
⬜ Côtes du Marmandais	
🟦 Gaillac	

BERGERAC

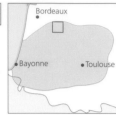

Bordeaux

Bayonne • Toulouse

THE WINES OF BERGERAC have for a long time been kept in the shadows, with Bordeaux (*see p.77*), across the Dordogne, taking the limelight. Vines have been cultivated in this picturesque region since Roman times, with exports of wine to England recorded as early as 1250. Today, Bergerac is the biggest *appellation* in the southwest and the wine produced here is often similar to Bordeaux.

In fact, Bergerac wines made from Bordeaux grape varieties (mainly Merlot and Sémillon) and grown on similar soil to that found in Bordeaux are so like the wines produced in the fringes of that region that in the late 1990s it was suggested that Bergerac might one day be accepted as a sub-region of Bordeaux. Another *appellation*, the Côtes de Bergerac, exists for red wines with a higher minimum alcohol content (11 rather than 10 percent).

BERGERAC
A magnet for thousands of fans of the play "Cyrano de Bergerac," Bergerac is a small, pleasant, country town that is only now beginning to gain a good reputation for its wines.

CHÂTEAU TOUR DES GENDRES
Good white Bergerac, like this, easily outclasses wines like Entre-Deux-Mers (see p.79) and basic, white Bordeaux.

❋ AC Bergerac, AC Côtes de Bergerac, AC Bergerac Sec.

🍇 Red: Merlot, Cabernet Sauvignon, Cabernet Franc.
White: Sauvignon Blanc, Sémillon, Muscadelle.

🍷 Medium-bodied reds. Dry or sweet whites. Dry rosés.

🏠 Ch Belingard, Court-les-Mûts, des Eyssards, de Gouyat, Grinou, Jaubertie, le Raz, Richard, Ch Tour des Gendres.

🍴 White: Grilled carp.

🗓 Red: 1996, 1995.

⏳ Red: 3–5 years. White: 1–3 years.

BUZET

Bordeaux

Bayonne • Toulouse

FORMERLY KNOWN AS THE Côtes de Buzet, the vineyards located between the towns of Agen and Marmande date back to Roman times. As with many *appellations* in this area, Buzet suffered when the importation of wine into Bordeaux (*see p.77*) was banned following the Hundred Years War. More recently, however, Buzet's wines were blended with the wines of Bordeaux, until *appellation* laws made this illegal. Today, Buzet's red wines are better than many of the more expensive Bordeaux reds that are sold as Haut-Médoc (*see p.83*) and St. Émilion (*see p.89*). Those of Châteaux de Gueyze, Baleste, du Frandat, and de la Tuque can all be recommended and are made by the *coopérative*, which ages its production in oak barrels and produces most of Buzet's wines. Sadly, its rosés and whites are less interesting.

BUZET VINEYARDS
Despite its lack of international prestige, Buzet benefits from vineyards that can, in good years, provide grapes that are as ripe as those found in most parts of Bordeaux.

LES VIGNERONS DE BUZET
Wines like this illustrate how efficient coopératives can compete on level terms with small estates and merchants.

❋ AC Buzet.

🍇 Red: Merlot, Cabernet Sauvignon, Cabernet Franc.

🍷 Bordeaux-like reds that often benefit from being aged in small oak barrels.

🏠 Ch Baleste, Ch du Frandat, Ch de Gueyze, Pierron,

Sauvagnères, les Vignerons de Buzet (whose wines are sold under the names of individual estates such as Ch du Bouchet and de la Tuque).

🍴 Lamb casserole with spring vegetables.

🗓 Red: 1998, 1996, 1995.

⏳ 4–8 years.

CAHORS

Bordeaux

Bayonne • • Toulouse

THE ONCE FAMOUS "BLACK WINE" of Cahors takes its name from the Malbec grape that, prior to phylloxera, produced dark, inky colored wines. Said to have been appreciated in London since the 13th century, the merchants of Bordeaux (see p.77) banned its sale in Britain after the Hundred Years War. In order to sell their wines, the producers developed their own market in Holland, where drinkers preferred these "black wines" to the paler varieties of Bordeaux. However, the use of the Tannat and Merlot grapes as blending partners and new wine making methods make today's Cahors a lot paler and more appealing to most wine drinkers. Fans of traditional Cahors should head for the limestone flats, while those seeking lighter, plummier reds will be more impressed with wines from the sand and gravel hillsides.

PONT VALENTRÉ
With its imposing towers, the fortified bridge over the river Lot illustrates the importance the town enjoyed in the Middle Ages, when it was the trading center for a wide variety of goods.

CLOS LA COUTALE
Although this Cahors is not "black," it does have some of the depth traditionally associated with this appellation.

✴	AC Cahors.	Coopérative, Gautoul, de Hauterivem, Haute-Serre, Lagrezette, Lamartine, Latuc, Paillas, Rochet-Lamothe, Clos Triguedina.
🍇	Red: Malbec, Tannat, Merlot.	
🍷	Dark, tannic, long-lived traditional reds. Supple, fruity, modern reds.	🍴 Bayonne ham.
🍴	Ch de Caix, La Caminade, Ch du Cèdre, Clos la Coutale, Clos de Gamot, Côtes d'Olt	🗓 1996, 1995, 1990, 1989.
		📅 5–15 years.

CÔTES DE DURAS

IF BORDEAUX (see p.77) ever wanted to expand the boundaries of its region, the wine makers could quite easily join up with the Côtes de Duras, whose slopes carved out by the river Dourdèze are actually an extension of the Entre-Deux-Mers (see p.79). Even the grape varieties used here are primarily the same as those used for Bordeaux. As for the quality of its wines, while there are no Côtes de Duras wines that provoke excitement, there are plenty of decently made reds and whites that are as good as, if not better, than similar Bordeaux wines.

MOULIN DES GROYES
A classic, dry white, this example of the Côtes de Duras could easily be sold as Bordeaux.

✴	AC Côtes de Duras.
🍇	Red: Cabernet Sauvignon, Cabernet Franc, Merlot. White: Sémillon, Sauvignon Blanc, Muscadelle.
🍷	Bordeaux-like reds. Dry or sweet whites.
🍴	Amlard, Moulin des Groyes.
🍴	Red: Lamb in brioche.
🗓	Red: 1998, 1996, 1995.
📅	Red: 2–5 years. White: 1–3 years.

CÔTES DU MARMANDAIS

SURROUNDED BY ENTRE-DEUX-MERS (see p.79), the Côtes de Duras, and Buzet (see p.224), this *appellation* for red, white, and rosé wines extends over both sides of the Garonne river. The Côtes du Marmandais' often rustic reds are prevented from being too Bordeaux-like (see p.77) by the stipulation that only 75 percent of its wines can be made from the three main Bordeaux grape varieties: Cabernet Franc, Merlot and Cabernet Sauvignon. The whites are mainly made from Sauvignon Blanc, mixed with Sémillon and Ugni Blanc.

CHÂTEAU DE BEAULIEU
The presence of local grape varieties gives the wines of the Côtes du Marmandais a somewhat "gamey" character.

✴	AC Côtes du Marmandais.
🍇	Red/ rosé: Cabernet Sauvignon, Cabernet Franc, Merlot, Abouriou, Fer. White: Sauvignon Blanc.
🍷	Light reds. Dry whites. Dry rosés.
🍴	Ch de Beaulieu, Cave de Beaupuy, de Cocumont.
🍴	Red: Game casserole.
🗓	1996, 1995.
📅	3–5 years.

GAILLAC

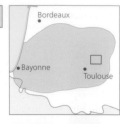

ONE OF THE MOST ANCIENT wine regions in France, Gaillac is enjoying a minor renaissance due to a growing interest in traditional grapes and styles. The Gamay, which used to produce Gaillac's feeble red wines, is on its way out and local varieties, like the Duras and the Fer, are being encouraged. In the making of white wines, the Mauzac, the Ondenc, and the Len de l'Elh are making a similar comeback. Luckily, the authorities have recognized that these grapes produce better wines if blended with more familiar varieties such as the Syrah and the Sauvignon Blanc. Gaillac produces a wide variety of wines, from light reds and pale rosés to appley, perfumed, dry, and honey-sweet whites. Gaillac's appley, sparkling wines are its most interesting product and are sold as Méthode Gaillaçoise and Méthode Gaillaçoise Doux.

PATTERN OF LIFE
The vineyards of Gaillac, some of which are among the oldest in France, are grown alongside a wide range of other crops.

DOMAINE DES PERCHES
This is a lovely, tangy example of new wave Gaillac made from the Sauvignon Blanc.

✴ AC Gaillac, AC Gaillac Doux, AC Gaillac Mousseux.	de Labarthe, Ch de Lastours, Mas d'Aurel, des Perches, Robert Plageoles, René Rieux, Clement Termes, des Terrisses, de Très-Cantours, de Vayssette.
⬡ Red: Duras, Gamay, Syrah, Cabernet Franc, Merlot. White: Mauzac, Sauvignon Blanc, Sémillon, Ondenc.	
	🍴 Veal brisket stuffed with Swiss chard.
⬛ Soft reds. Still and sparkling whites.	▥ Red: 1998, 1996, 1995.
⦀ De Bouscaillous, de Gineste,	⬗ Red: 3–5 years.

JURANÇON

GIVEN THE MODERN VIEWS against giving alcohol to children, there is something rather quaint about the legend that drops of Jurançon wine were placed on the lips of Henri IV at his baptism in 1553. Jurançon is one of France's oldest *appellations*, and its delicate white wines have always been fiercely protected. Situated on the foothills of the Pyrenees around the town of Pau, most of the area's vines are at an altitude of 980 ft (300 m) and are often trained on trellises to avoid frost damage. The local varieties Gros Manseng, Petit Manseng, and Courbu are grown, with the best dry and sweet wines sharing a tangy bouquet of pineapples and peaches, and a combination of richness and acidity that comes from the underrated Manseng grape. The *appellation* has good producers and its wines deserve to be better known.

VIEW FROM THE TOP
Some of Jurançon's best vines are grown on the very steep, hillside slopes of the appellation, while other crops are grown on the flatter land beneath.

DOMAINE CAUHAPÉ
This producer is well worth remembering for both its dry and sweet Jurançon wines.

✴ AC Jurançon, AC Jurançon Sec.	Bru-Baché, Cauhapé, Clos Guirouilh, Clos Lapeyre, Clos Uroulat, Cru Lamouroux.
⬡ White: Gros Manseng, Petit Manseng.	
⬛ Fresh, dry, and lusciously sweet whites.	🍴 *Roquefort* (cheese) and walnut tart.
	▥ 1998, 1997, 1996, 1995.
⦀ Bellegarde, Jean-Pierre Bousquet, Brana,	⬗ 3–6 years.

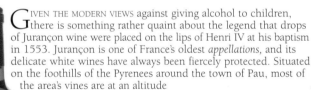

MADIRAN

Bordeaux
□
Bayonne • Toulouse

ONE OF THE ONLY *APPELLATIONS* to produce red wines made from the Tannat grape, this region has a distinctive, old-fashioned character. Dating back to Roman times, Madiran's wine-making heyday was in the Middle Ages, when its reds were relished by pilgrims en route to Santiago de Compostela. The vineyards of this *appellation* are on mainly clay and limestone soils, and the climate is tempered by the Atlantic to the west. The use of the Tannat and Fer varieties gives the wines of Madiran a rustic character that can take a long time to soften. Although the Tannat must now represent 40 percent of the blend, the Cabernet Franc and Cabernet Sauvignon are also used in order to soften the wines, providing them with a fruitiness they might not otherwise have shown in their youth.

CHÂTEAU BOUSCASSÉ
One of the best, most progressive producers in the area, Alain Brumont produces barrel matured Madiran at this château.

DOMAINE PICHARD
The toughness of the Tannat grape variety is beautifully balanced by the fruitiness and richness of this Madiran red wine.

✱ AC Madiran.	Ducourneau, Lanestousse, Lafitte-Teston, Lenclos, Montus, Moureou, de Peyros, Pichard, Cave de Plaimont.
🍇 Red: Tannat, Fer, Cabernet Sauvignon, Cabernet Franc.	
🍷 Full-bodied, traditional, tannic reds.	🍴 Roast pigeon in Armagnac and red wine.
🍽 Aydie, Barréjat, Berthoumieu, Bouscassé, Diana, la Chapelle, Crampilh.	▤ 1996, 1995.
	➤ 5–10 years.

MARCILLAC

Bordeaux
•
□
• Bayonne • Toulouse

THE SAVAGE AUVERGNE COUNTRYSIDE is one of the few places in which the Fer, or Mansois, grape is found. The Fer variety produces reds and rosés that tend to be fiercely tannic when young, becoming peppery and almost perfumed with age. Once there were thousands of acres of Fer vines in this *appellation* where, today, there are only a scant hundred left. If the authorities had not elevated Marcillac's status from *VDQS* to *appellation contrôlée* in 1990, the area's producers might even have given up wine making.

Recent regulations stipulate that the Fer must represent a minimum of 90 percent, with the Merlot, Cabernet Sauvignon, or Cabernet Franc making up the balance. The reds are now more approachable in their youth than in the past, but the rosés still tend to be fairly dull.

SUN-BAKED TERRACES
The vines of Marcillac are planted on steep slopes, where grapes ripen and develop thick skins that can give toughness to the the red and rosé wines.

DOMAINE DU CROS
Domaine du Cros' peppery, perfumed wines are some of the most characterful and reliable wines produced in Marcillac.

✱ AC Marcillac.	et Fils, Cave du Vallon-Valady.
🍇 Red/ rosé: Fer, Cabernet Sauvignon, Cabernet Franc, Merlot.	🍴 Chicken stuffed with eggs, ham, and chopped garlic and cooked with tomatoes and herbs.
🍷 Peppery, ideally aromatic, but often toughly tannic reds. Dry, full-bodied, peppery rosés.	▤ Red: 1998, 1996, 1995.
🍽 Du Cros, Lacombe Père	➤ Red: 3–5 years. Rosé; 1–3 years.

MONBAZILLAC

ONBAZILLAC, WHOSE VINEYARDS were originally planted on the hill of Mont Bazilhac 900 years ago, enjoyed its heyday in the 16th and 17th centuries, when its main customers were Dutch wine merchants. Later, following the impact of phylloxera, Monbazillac was relegated to the role of "poor man's Sauternes" (*see p.94*) and most of its wines were produced accordingly.

Generally, the grapes used to make excellent sweet wines are best picked by hand, but here the grapes were often machine-harvested. However, in 1993 the producers decided to pay more attention to the quality of Monbazillac wines and as a result machine-picking was outlawed. Today, emphasis is placed on harvesting genuinely nobly rotten grapes in successive pickings; the resulting wines should be deep golden in color, often with an orange tinge.

CHÂTEAU DE MONBAZILLAC
One of the most imposing châteaux in Monbazillac, this is also the source of some of the best, longest-lived wines produced in the appellation.

CHÂTEAU THEULET
The care taken in the vineyard and cellar of Château Theulet has resulted in oaky wines that are often better than Sauternes.

✳	AC Monbazillac.	
❀	White: Sémillon, Sauvignon Blanc, Muscadelle.	
🍷	Sweet, orange flavored, botrytized, dessert whites.	
🍴	Ch Belingard, la Borderie, la Brie, Fonmourges, Grand Marsalet, Lajonie, les Marnières, Ch de Monbazillac, de Pecoula, Septy, Theulet, Tirecul la Gravière, Treuil de Nailhac.	
🍽	Foie gras with Monbazillac jelly.	
▤	1997, 1996, 1995, 1990.	
⧖	5–15 years.	

MONTRAVEL

THIS SMALL REGION follows the river Dordogne westward from Ste. Foy-la-Grande to the border between the Gironde and the Dordogne *départements*. Boasting three separate *appellations* for its white wines, Montravel produces crisp wines made mainly from the Sémillon and Sauvignon grapes, while the Côtes de Montravel and Haut-Montravel cover the more traditional semi-sweet, medium-sweet, and late-harvest whites. Some of the best producers of white wine here also offer good examples of red Bergerac (*see p.224*).

CHÂTEAU PIQUE-SERRE
This white wine, with its dry, peachy flavor, is typical of Montravel.

✳	AC Montravel, AC Côtes de Montravel, AC Haut-Montravel.
❀	White: Sémillon.
🍷	Dry or sweet whites.
🍴	Ch du Bloy, Ch de Bondieu, Ch Pique-Serre, De la Roche-Marot, Viticulteurs de Port Ste. Foy.
🍽	Grilled trout.
▤	1998, 1997, 1996.
⧖	2–4 years.

PACHERENC DU VIC-BILH

ONE OF THE LITTLE-KNOWN GEMS of the French wine world, Pacherenc du Vic-Bilh has an unusual Gascon name and is produced from 247 acres (100 ha) of vines to the west of Auch and north of Pau. The dry, medium-sweet, and sweet whites are made from the local Ruffiac grape, the Petit Courbu, the Petit Manseng, and Gros Manseng, better known for their role in Jurançon (*see p.226*) and the Sémillon and Sauvignon. At their best, the wines of Pacherenc du Vic-Bilh have a fruity flavor, with the occasional touch of new oak.

PLAIMONT
An excellent, sweet, honeyed example of Pacherenc du Vic-Bilh from the Plaimont coopérative.

✳	AC Pacherenc du Vic-Bilh.
❀	White: Gros Manseng, Petit Manseng, Ruffiac, Petit Courbu.
🍷	Dry or sweet whites.
🍴	Ch Berthoumieu, du Boucassé, Brumont, Capmartin, des Crouseilles, Laffitte-Teston, Plaimont.
🍽	Grilled foie gras.
▤	1997, 1996, 1995.
⧖	5–10 years.

PÉCHARMANT

T HE RED WINES OF PÉCHARMANT, an *appellation* covering 445 (acres180 ha) to the east of the town of Bergerac, put many Bordeaux (*see p.77*) red wines to shame. The Cabernet Franc, Cabernet Sauvignon, and Merlot vineyards are located on the banks of the river Dordogne, where the soil's high iron content contributes to the rich structure, flavor, and longevity of the wines. A number of producers here are dedicated to making the most of the region's potential and its wines are ideal accompaniments to the traditional Perigord cuisine.

✴	AC Pécharmant.
❖	Red: Merlot, Cabernet Franc, Cabernet Sauvignon.
▦	Medium- to full-bodied reds.
▥	Ch de Biran, Champeral, des Costes, Grand Jaure, de Tiregand.
▐	Pigeon with turnips and morels.
▤	1996, 1995, 1990.
▨	5–8 years.

CHÂTEAU DE TIREGAND
Not only is this château a fine old building, it also produces subtle and supple wines.

TURSAN

M OST OF THE WINES MADE in this small *VDQS*, located to the west of Armagnac, are produced by the local *coopérative*. The often tough, berryish reds and fruity rosés are mainly made from the Tannat grape, but must contain at least 25 percent Cabernet Franc, Fer, or Cabernet Sauvignon. Tursan's traditionally dull whites, made from the Baroque grape, have recently been uplifted by the Michelin-starred chef Michel Guérard's Domaine de Bachen. His aromatic, barrel-matured wines benefit from the use of Sauvignon and Gros Manseng grapes.

✴	VDQS Tursan.
❖	Red: Tannat. White: Baroque.
▦	Tannic reds. Aromatic whites
▥	De Bachen, Cave de Tursan.
▐	White: Grilled shad or herring.
▤	Red: 1996, 1995.
▨	Red: 3–7 years. White: 1–4 years.

CAVE DE TURSAN
Tasty, robust reds like this are ideal when served with strongly flavored dishes.

OTHERS

A MONG THE OTHER WINES of the southwest are the interesting red wines of Irouléguy, richly spicy if tannic reds made from a blend of Tannat and Cabernet grapes. These are easy to spot on a wine merchant's shelf: they're the ones whose Basque names tend to include unexpected consonants such as the excellent Cuvée Bixintxo. Rosés here can be fair, but the whites are dull. The red wines of the Béarn *appellation*, made nearby from similar blends, are lighter and less interesting, though the whites and rosés can be aromatic when young. The Côtes du Frontonnais, whose wines can also be sold as Fronton or Villaudric depending on the village in which they were produced, are characterful country reds that owe their spicy, berryish flavors to the Negrette grape, which must make up at least 60 percent of the blend. As sweet wines develop a greater following, Saussignac and Rosette are worth watching. Saussignac is made from the Sémillon, Sauvignon Blanc, Muscadelle, and Chenin Blanc grapes and must have a minimum of 0.6 oz (18 g) of residual sugar per liter. At its best, this wine is full-bodied with a rich flavor. Rosette must contain between zero point three and two ounces (8–54 g) of residual sugar per liter and is softer than Saussignac. Produced close to Bergerac (*see p.224*), under whose name their reds are sold, these are good alternatives to Sauternes (*see p.94*).

Bordeaux

Côtes du Frontonnais

• Bayonne   □ • Toulouse

□ Irouléguy

IROULÉGUY
The picturesque countryside around Irouléguy is some of the moodiest and most beautiful in this part of southwestern France.

DOMAINE ETXEGARAYA
Berryish, red Irouléguy like this is delicious served with Basque dishes made with tomatoes and herbs.

VINS DE PAYS

FRANCE'S VINS DE PAYS, *OR COUNTRY WINES,*

ARE INCREASINGLY THE UNEXPECTED DRIVING

FORCE BEHIND THE FRENCH WINE INDUSTRY.

IN THE EARLY 1990s, a reliable way of
bringing a disdainful look to the face of a
Parisian wine snob would have been to
utter the three words "*vin de pays.*" California,
Australia, and South Africa were, he might
grudgingly have conceded, starting to make
palatable country wines, but in France, to
get something worthwhile, you had to
choose from the *appellations contrôlées.*

The *vins de pays*, he would argue, are
merely 141 handy designations created in
the 1970s for areas that had previously turned
out basic *vins de table.* This wine was either
sold by the liter in plastic or returnable glass
bottles, or poured directly into the European
wine lake. Admittedly, the *vins de pays* were
subject to legislation that dictated where
they could be made and which grapes could
be used, but the rules were far looser than
they were for *appellation* wines. *Vins de pays*
could be made by combining grapes that
were never blended elsewhere, and fruits
from vineyards hundreds of kilometers apart
were often blended in the larger regions.

In a sense, the snob's dismissal of the *vins
de pays* was, and still is, largely valid. While
there have been occasional exceptions to the
rule, such as the Vin de Pays de l'Hérault
made by Aimé Guibert at his Mas de Daumas
Gassac estate, most of the wines sold under
this designation are still basic fare, carelessly
produced by ill-equipped *coopératives* from

COTEAUX D'AIX-EN-PROVENCE
Most of the red vin de pays *produced in
the* département *of Bouches-du-Rhône comes
from the area of Coteaux d'Aix-en-Provence.*

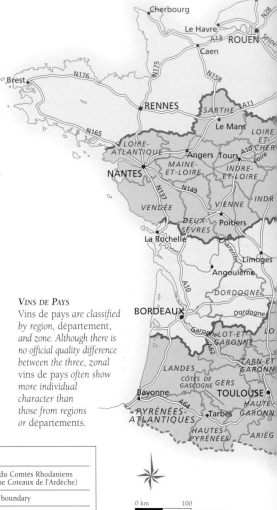

VINS DE PAYS
Vins de pays *are classified
by region,* département,
*and zone. Although there is
no official quality difference
between the three, zonal*
vins de pays *often show
more individual
character than
those from regions
or* départements.

KEY TO REGIONS

◻ Vin de Pays du Jardin de la France

◻ Vin de Pays du Comté Tolosan
(including the Côtes de Gascogne)

◻ Vin de Pays d'Oc (including Hérault)

◻ Vin de Pays du Comtés Rhodaniens
(including the Coteaux de l'Ardèche)

— *Département* boundary

— Regional boundary

0 km ___ 100

0 miles ___ 100

HÉRAULT
This vin de pays département produces more than 11 million cases of wine a year, with red accounting for more than 85 percent.

LILLE
Amiens
PARIS
Reims
Metz
MEUSE
STRASBOURG
NANCY
Orléans
LOIRET
Auxerre
YONNE
Mulhouse
CHER
Dijon
Bourges
NIÈVRE
Mâcon
Clermont-Ferrand
PUY-DE-DÔME
LYON
St-Étienne
GRENOBLE
Valence
ARDÈCHE
DRÔME
AVEYRON
GARD
Nîmes
ALPES-DE-HAUTE-PROVENCE
ALPES-MARITIMES
Montpellier
HÉRAULT
BOUCHES-DU-RHÔNE
VAR
NICE
MARSEILLE
AUDE
Perpignan
PYRÉNÉES-ORIENTALES

CORSICA
The island of Corsica is not a département but a vin de pays zone.

Calvi
Bastia
ÎLE-DE-BEAUTÉ
(CORSE)
Ajaccio
Bonifacio

badly tended grapes grown on poorly sited land. However, behind the scenes, this picture has begun to change.

Pioneers like Yves Grassa in Gascony and Robert Skalli have introduced New World wine-making methods and marketing techniques, and have begun to play the New World producers at their own game by producing smartly packaged, modern, fruity wines in France. Throughout the Vin de Pays d'Oc vineyards of Languedoc-Roussillon, dull Carignan and Grenache Blanc vines have been replaced by the Chardonnay, Sauvignon Blanc, Merlot, and Cabernet Sauvignon, all of whose names feature on *vin de pays* labels in the same way as they do on bottles from California and Australia. Another influence has been the arrival of outside investors and "flying wine makers" who, like vinous mercenaries, have been sent into French *coopératives* by British supermarkets to make the modern wine that their customers demand.

Vins de pays now represent over a quarter of all French wine and a growing proportion of France's vinous exports. There is still room for improvement, but the best examples not only easily outclass the least distinguished efforts from *appellation contrôlée* regions like Bordeaux and the Loire, they are also commanding higher prices for their quality.

HOW THE VINS DE PAYS WORK

Just as *appellation contrôlée* wines are placed in a quality pyramid that rises from basic regional wines to the fruits of the *grands* and *premiers crus*, the *vins de pays* have a pyramid of their own. At the base are the four regional designations, Vin de Pays du Jardin de la France, Vin de Pays du Comté Tolosan, Vin de Pays d'Oc (which includes Languedoc-Roussillon, parts of the southern Rhône and Provence), and Vin de Pays Comtés Rhodaniens.

Next come the 39 *vins de pays départements* that produce nearly half of all *vins de pays* and are, as their name suggests, named after the *départements* in which the wines are made – unless this already forms part of the name of an *appellation contrôlée*.

Finally, there are nearly 100 zonal *vins de pays*. Between a quarter and a third of the total, they are often smaller than many established *appellations*.

BOUCHES-DU-RHÔNE

THE *DÉPARTEMENT* of Bouches-du-Rhône stretches from the sharp peaks of the Alpilles to the flat marshlands of the Camargue, and from the city of Marseilles to the marooned port of Aigues-Mortes. Most Bouches-du-Rhône wines come from the Coteaux d'Aix en Provence area, with 80 percent of the wines being reds that are made from the Merlot, Carignan, Grenache, Syrah, Cinsault, and Cabernet Sauvignon grape varieties. Many Bouches-du-Rhône rosés are in fact better than a lot of Provençal rosé wines that are produced as *appellation contrôlée*.

✴	Bouches-du-Rhône.
▩	Red/ rosé: Carignan, Syrah, Grenache, Cinsault, Merlot, Cabernet Sauvignon. White: Clairette, Ugni Blanc
▨	Soft, fruity reds. Dry whites. Dry rosés.
▥	De Beaulieu, des Gavelles, Mas de Rey, de Trévallon.
▯	Lamb with garlic.
☰	Red: 1998, 1996, 1995.
▨	Red: 1–7 years.

DOMAINE DES GAVELLES This rich red wine definitely deserves better status than vin de pays.

COTEAUX DE L'ARDÈCHE

ALTHOUGH THIS AREA comes under the regional category of Comtés Rhodaniens, most wine makers here prefer to sell their wines as Coteaux de l'Ardèche. The Burgundy merchant Louis Latour's Grand Ardèche Chardonnay is made from grapes grown in the limestone soil here; and the Beaujolais merchant Georges Duboeuf, who has planted grapes in partnership with 120 grape growers and seven *coopératives*, helped put the area on the map. Only 10 percent of the wine is white and 10 percent rosé, but 30 percent of the wines are sold as pure varietals.

✴	Coteaux de l'Ardèche.
▩	Red/ rosé: Syrah, Grenache, Cinsault. White: Marsanne, Ugni Blanc, Roussanne, Viognier.
▨	Medium-bodied, often fragrant reds. Dry rosés.
▥	Ardèchois, la Clapouze, Combelonge , Louis Latour.
▯	Red: Pigeon with olives.
☰	White: 1998, 1997.
▨	1–5 years.

VIGNERONS ARDÈCHOIS Wine makers Ardèchois produce attractive, peppery, light red wines.

CÔTES DE GASCOGNE

UNTIL THE 1970S, this region produced little but Armagnac. Thanks to the efforts of the Domaine du Tariquet and the Plaimont *coopérative*, the Colombard and Ugni Blanc varieties are now used to make fruity, dry wines as an alternative to brandy. Modern methods of fermentation and the addition of the Sauvignon Blanc and Manseng to the blend have given the white wines a more lifted, aromatic quality. Unfortunately for the Côtes de Gascogne, however, wines from many warmer regions further south are giving them a lot of competition.

✴	Côtes de Gascogne.
▩	Red: Gamay, Cabernet Franc, Cabernet Sauvignon, Duras, Tannat. White: Colombard, Ugni Blanc, Chardonnay.
▨	Light- to medium-bodied reds. Crisp, dry whites.
▥	Grassa, Plaimont.
▯	White: Cheese tart.
☰	White: 1998, 1997.
▨	White: 1–3 years.

DOMAINES GRASSA This dynamic producer and the Plaimont coopérative have greatly improved the reputation of this region.

HÉRAULT

THE REPUTATION OF THIS huge *département* was given its biggest boost by the success of the Mas de Daumas Gassac estate to the north of Montpellier. Aimé Guibert, the man behind this estate, planted an eccentric mixture of vines on fine, volcanic soil that was deemed by the well-known Bordeaux geologist Professor Enjalbert to be capable of producing wines of *grand cru* standard. Plots of land like this are rare, but vine-growing and wine-making skills are improving, and many *vins de pays* are as good as *appellation* wines produced nearby.

✴	Hérault.
▩	Red: Carignan, Cinsault, Grenache, Syrah. White: Clairette, Ugni Blanc Macabéo, Grenache Blanc.
▨	Medium- to full-bodied reds. Dry whites. Dry rosés.
▥	De Bosc, Capion, Mas de Daumas Gassac.
▯	Red: Beef casserole.
☰	Red: 1998, 1996, 1995.
▨	Red: 3–10 years.

MAS DE DAUMAS GASSAC This eccentric blend is produced by one of the most famous estates in southern France.

ÎLE DE BEAUTÉ

THE GENEROUS WAY IN which *appellation contrôlée* designations have been allocated here leaves little room for wines to be labeled *vins de pays*. However, there are interesting experimental wines being produced here, including a number of promising early attempts with the Pinot Noir grape variety. Although the Pinot Noir has been used with some success, the designation encompasses an excess of local varieties as well as Italian ones, making it very hard to generalize about the overall quality of the Île de Beauté's reds, whites, and rosés.

		PRODUCTEURS RÉUNIS
❌	Île de Beauté.	*This attractive*
❀	Red/rosé: Nielluccio, Cabernet Sauvignon, Pinot Noir. White: Vermintino, Muscat.	*wine has the herby, Italian character of most Corsican red wines.*
🍷	Herby reds, Light, fruity whites. Herby rosés.	
🏾	Laroche, Producteurs Réunis, Sette Piana.	
🍴	Red: Mixed pork meats.	
⊟	Red: 1998, 1997, 1996.	
🥂	1–3 years.	

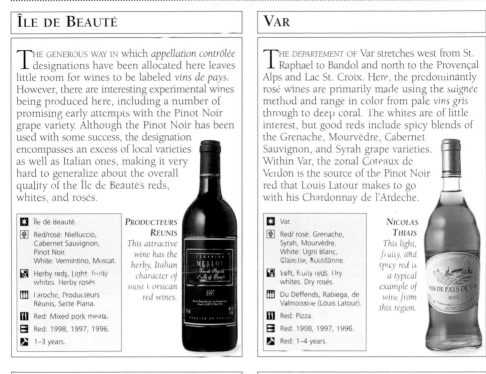

VAR

THE *DÉPARTEMENT* OF Var stretches west from St. Raphael to Bandol and north to the Provençal Alps and Lac St. Croix. Here, the predominantly rosé wines are primarily made using the *saignée* method and range in color from pale *vins gris* through to deep coral. The whites are of little interest, but good reds include spicy blends of the Grenache, Mourvèdre, Cabernet Sauvignon, and Syrah grape varieties. Within Var, the zonal Coteaux de Verdon is the source of the Pinot Noir red that Louis Latour makes to go with his Chardonnay de l'Ardèche.

		NICOLAS THIAIS
❌	Var.	*This light,*
❀	Red/ rosé: Grenache, Syrah, Mourvèdre. White: Ugni Blanc, Clairette, Roussanne.	*fruity, and spicy red is a typical example of wine from this region.*
🍷	Soft, fruity reds. Dry whites. Dry rosés.	
🏾	Du Deffends, Rabiega, de Valmoissine (Louis Latour).	
🍴	Red: Pizza.	
⊟	Red: 1998, 1997, 1996.	
🥂	Red: 1–4 years.	

VIN DE PAYS D'OC

THE HUGE REGION of Oc takes in the *départements* of Pyrénées Orientales, Aude, Hérault, and Gard and produces most of the best *vins de pays* in southern France. These *vins de pays* have done particularly well outside France, partly due to the easy recognition of the name and because of the quality and "international" style of the wines made by producers here: Skalli Fortant de France and Domaine Virginie; Australian companies such as BRL Hardy and Penfolds; and by "flying wine makers," who are employed by chains of British wine retailers.

		FORTANT DE FRANCE
❌	Vin de Pays d'Oc.	*This recently*
❀	Red: Merlot, Grenache, Syrah, Cabernet Sauvignon. White: Sauvignon Blanc, Chardonnay, Marsanne, Viognier.	*lauched, top red wine is made by one of the region's most ambitious producers.*
🍷	Medium- to full-bodied, fruity reds. Dry whites.	
🏾	De la Baume, Fortant.	
🍴	Red: Mixed pork meats.	
⊟	Red: 1998, 1996, 1995.	
🥂	Red: 1–6 years.	

OTHERS

COMPARED TO OC, the three other main *vin de pays* regions seem fairly insignificant. The designation of Jardin de la France, stretching from the mouth of the river Loire at Nantes to Auxerre, produces wines from 14 *départements*. Although it is best known for its dry white wines, most of its produce is in fact red. Comté Tolosan, which follows the rivers Garonne, Lot, and Tarn and takes in the Pyrenees and Auvergne, produces mainly red wines that are made from a wide range of varieties. Comtés Rhodaniens, which encompasses eight *départements*, stretches south from Mâcon to the Ardèche and east into the Alps; this name can only be given to wines that are already zonal *vins de pays*. Outside these three main regions lie the *départements* of Dordogne and Puy de Dôme and, between Champagne and Alsace, the *département* of Meuse.

CLOS DE CRAY
The Jardin de la France in the Loire valley can produce delicious Chardonnay like this.

GLOSSARY OF TECHNICAL TERMS

For a glossary of descriptive terms see pp.40–41.

Appellation Contrôlée/ Appellation d'Origine Contrôlée (see pp34–5)
Quality designation that guarantees origin, grape varieties, and production methods for what are, theoretically, the best of French wines.

Caves Coopératives
Vineyards and wineries owned jointly by a number of members are known as *caves coopératives*. More than half of all French vineyards are currently collectively owned, but numbers are slowly declining.

Climat
Specific vineyard site, defined by its climatological and geographical characteristics. The terms *climat* and *terroir* are interchangable.

Commune
French for village or parish.

Cru Classé
The best wines of the Médoc district of Bordeaux are split into five *crus*, from *premier cru classé* (best) to *cinquième cru classé*, with an additional sixth, *cru Bourgeois*.

Dégorgement (Disgorgement)
Following *remuage*, this is the final stage in the *méthode Champenoise* of sparkling wine production: the removal, by freezing, of yeast deposits.

Grand Cru
Literally "great growth," this classification is awarded to the finest vineyards and to the wines they produce. The term has different meanings in Bordeaux, Burgundy, Champagne, and Alsace.

Grand Vin
The best wine of an estate, as opposed to the "*second vin.*"

Méthode Champenoise
Method used to make all high-quality sparkling wines, involving, among other things, a second fermentation in the bottle.

Phylloxera
Yellow aphid that has periodically devastated French vines, killing them by feeding on their roots.

Premier Cru
Quality indicator, applied in Burgundy to wines classified just below *grand cru*, and used in various ways in Bordeaux and elsewhere.

Remuage (Riddling)
Part of the *méthode Champenoise*, *remuage* is the shaking process by which dead yeasts are moved to the neck of the bottle after the second fermentation.

Vin de Table (see pp.32–3)
Quality classification applied to the lowest level of French wines.

Vin de Pays (see pp.32–3)
One step above the **vin de table** quality classification, and one below **VDQS**, these are mostly simple country wines with a regional character.

Vin Délimité de Qualité Supérieur (VDQS) (see pp.32–3)
Quality classification for wines better than **vin de pays** but not as good as those of **appellation contrôlée** status.

SUPPLIERS

US

Acker, Merrall & Condit
160 West Seventy-Two,
New York City, NY 10023
Tel: 212 787 1700
Fax: 212 799 1984
Email: vinogod@aol.com

Anna's Cafe
5618 East Thomas Road,
Phoenix, AZ 85018
Tel: 480 945 4503
Fax: 480 423 5771

Beekman Liquor
500 Lexington Avenue,
New York City, NY 10017
Tel: 212 759 5857
Fax: 212 753 4534
Website:
www.beekmanliquors.com

Bel-Air Wine Merchant
10421 Santa Monica Boulevard
West,
Los Angeles, CA 90025
Tel: 310 474 9518
Fax: 310 475 2836
Email: sales@belair2020.com

Calvert Woodley
4339 Connecticut Avenue
Northeast,
Washington, DC 20008
Tel: 202 966 0445
Fax: 202 537 5086

Crossroads Wines
55 West Fourteenth Street,
New York, NY 10011
Tel: 212 924 3060
Fax: 212 633 2863

Dubis Discount Liquors
30 Chauncy Street,
Mansfield, MA 02048
Tel: 508 339 3454
Fax: 508 339 3941
Email: dubs@freshcatchinc.com
Website: www.freshcatchinc.com

Gabriel's Wine & Spirits
4445 Walzem Road,
San Antonio, TX 78218
Tel: 210 654 1123
Fax: 210 655 5763
Email: gabrielis@txdirect.net.

Kermit Lynch
Wine Merchant of Berkeley,
1605 San Pablo Avenue,
Berkeley, CA 94702
Tel: 510 524 1524
Fax: 510 528 7026
Email: klwmgb@aol.com

Mills Wine & Spirits Mart
87 Main Street,
Annapolis, MD 21401
Tel: 410 263 2888
Fax: 410 268 2616
Email: millswine@toad.net.
Website: www.millswine.com

PJ Liquor Warehouse
4898 Broadway,
New York City, NY 10034
Tel: 212 567 5500
Fax: 212 567 2743

Premier Cru
5890 Christie Avenue,
Emeryville, CA 94608
Tel: 510 655 6691
Fax: 510 547 5405
Website: www.premier-cru.com

**Rochambeau Wines
& Liquors**
389 Broadway,
Dobbs Ferry, NY 10522
Tel: 914 693 0034
Fax: 914 693 0039

Sherry-Lehmann Inc.
679 Madison Avenue,
New York City, NY 10021
Tel: 212 838 7500
Fax: 800 811 WINE

John Walker & Co.
175 Suiter Street,
San Francisco, CA 94104
Tel: 415 986 2707
Fax: 415 421 5820

**The Wine & Spirit
Company of Greenville**
4025 Kennett Pike,
Greenville, DE 19807

Tel: 302 658 5939
Fax: 302 658 0808
Email: wnsco@aol.com

CANADA

**British Columbia Liquor
Distribution Branch**
30200 East Broadway
Vancouver, VC V5 M1Z6
Tel: 604 252 3217
Fax: 604 252 3200

**Andrew Hilton Wine
Merchant**
212 3rd Avenue,
South Lethbridge,
Alberta, TIJ 0G9
Tel: 403 686 1980
Fax: 403 320 9157

**Liquor Control Board
of Ontario**
55 Lakeside Boulevard East,
Toronto,
Ontario M5E 1A4
Tel: 416 365 5900
Fax: 416 864 6864

GENERAL INDEX

Acknowledgments

Additional Photography
Max Alexander, Andy Crawford, Phillip Dowell, Neil Lukas, Ian O'Leary, Neil Mersh, Stephen Oliver, Guy Ryecart, Kim Sayer.

Picture Credits:
t: top, tl: top left, tlc: top left center, tc: top center, trc: top right center, tr: top right, cla: center left above, ca: center above, cra: center right above, cl: center left, c: center, cr: center right, clb: center left below, cb: center below, crb: center right below, bl: bottom left, b: bottom, bc: bottom center, bcl: bottom center left, br: bottom right, d: detail.

The Publisher would like to thank the following individuals, companies and picture libraries for permission to reproduce their photographs:

AKG, London: 11c, 61t/b, 202t; **Ancient Art & Architecture Collection**: 3c, 174b; **Anthony Blake Photo Library**: 45b; **Bridgeman Art Library**, London and New York: Archives Nationales, Paris 72t; Biblioteca de Catalunya, Barcelona 73t; British Library, London 13b; Buhrle Collection, Zurich 13t; Giraudon/Musée Conde, Chantilly 100t; Musée d'Orsay, Paris *Palais des Papes 1900* by Paul Signac © ADAGP, Paris and DACS, London 1999 203t; Musée National du Moyen Age et des Thermes de Cluny, Paris 10–11, 14b; Museo Archeologico Nazionale, Naples 14tl; Museo dell'Opera del Duomo, Florence 12t; Private Collection 72b, 57 (insert); Private Collection/Roger-Viollet, Paris 203b; Staatliches Museum, Schwerin 12b; Victoria & Albert Museum, London 60t; **Cephas Picture Library**: Nigel Blythe 174t; Mick Rock 155c, 175t/br, 130b, 161tr; StockFood 44bl; TOP/Christine Fleurent 44br; TOP/Pierre Hussenot 47, 141tr, 193c; TOP/Tripelon/Jarry 69tr; Wine Magazine 39t; **Jean Loup Charmet**: Musée Carnavalet 15t; **Robert Joseph**: 171br; E. T. Archive: Cathedral Treasury, Aachen 14tr; **Institut National des Appellations d'Origine (INAO)**: 34tl, 35bl/br; **Interior Archive**: Jonathan Pilkington 49t; **Pol Roger**: 145b; **Retrograph Archive**, London: Martin Breese 144t; **Scope**, Paris: Jean-Luc Barde 1, 2–3, 8, 18t/bl, 19cl, 23b, 24b, 25b, 26bl, 29cr, 30, 32, 35t, 39b, 45t, 50t, 51, 55b, 71, 80tl/bl, 83tr, 88b, 93cr/b, 95t/bl, 97tr, 99, 106t/bl, 107tl/tr/b, 109t/b, 110t/bl, 111br, 119br, 120t/bc, 121tr, 122tr, 123t, 124br, 126tr, 128br, 132br, 159tr, 162, 163, 165t/bl, 166tr/br, 167tr, 168tr/br, 169tr/br, 171tr, 219t, 222, 223, 224tr/br, 225tr, 226tr/br, 227tr/br, 228tr, 229br, 231; Philippe Beuzen/Îles Images 199tr/br; Philippe Blondel 20t, 172, 181br, 191bl/t, 199br; Charles Bowman 50b; Daniel Czap 42t; Jacques Guillard 4, 5br, 6tl, 16, 17tl/tr, 19tr/br, 20b, 21t, 22t/bl, 26t/br, 28t/b, 29tl, 38b, 46, 48t, 49b, 52t, 54t/b, 56 - 57, 58t, 60b, 62, 63t/c/b, 64br, 65tr/br, 66tr, 67tr/br, 86tl, 100b, 101b, 102cl/br, 103t/c, 104t, 105t/c/br, 108bl, 111t, 112bl, 113tr/c/b, 114br, 115t, 116br, 117tl, 118tr, 119tr, 122br, 125tl, 127t/bl, 128tr, 129t, 130tr/c, 131cl/bl, 132t, 133t, 134br, 136br, 137bl, 138bl, 139t/bl, 143t, 144b, 145t, 146b, 147t, 152bl/br/bl, 156, 157, 158t/bl, 160br, 161br, 173, 176, 177t, 178tr/br, 179tr, 180tr/br, 181tr, 182tr/br, 183t, 184cl, 185tr, 186t, 187bl, 188tr/br, 189t, 190bl, 194, 195, 196br, 201, 202b, 204t, 205, 206tr/b, 207t/bc, 208tr/br, 209tr, 210bl, 211t/b, 212t/bc, 213tr/br, 214t/bl, 215tr/br, 216tr/br, 217tr/br, 218tr/c/b, 219bl, 230; Michel Guillard 17b, 18br, 21bl, 22br, 23t, 24t, 25t, 27t, 29b, 36t, 38t, 43t, 48b, 52b, 64tr, 73b, 74t/b, 75, 76t/b, 77t/b, 79br, 82tl, 83br, 84tl, 85t/c/b, 87tl, 88tr, 89tl, 90t/bl, 91cr, 92t/cl, 93tr, 94t, 121br, 135tr, 177b, 189bl, 196tr, 204b; Frederic Hadengue 21cl; Noël Hautemanière 44t, 164tr, 170t; Francis Jalain 5tl, 27t, 126br; Sara Matthews 55t, 98; Michel Plassart 34b, 37t/ca/cb/b, 66br, 101t, 118br, 142, 183bl; Jean-Luc Sayegh 15b; **Clive Streeter**: 221c.

Cover: All special photography except **Cephas Picture Library**: Mick Rock front cover tcl, bc; **Martin Preston**: back flap t; **Scope**: Jean-Luc Barde back cover br; Jacques Guillard back cover tl; Michel Guillard front cover bl/br, front flap t.

THE WINE REGIONS OF FRANCE

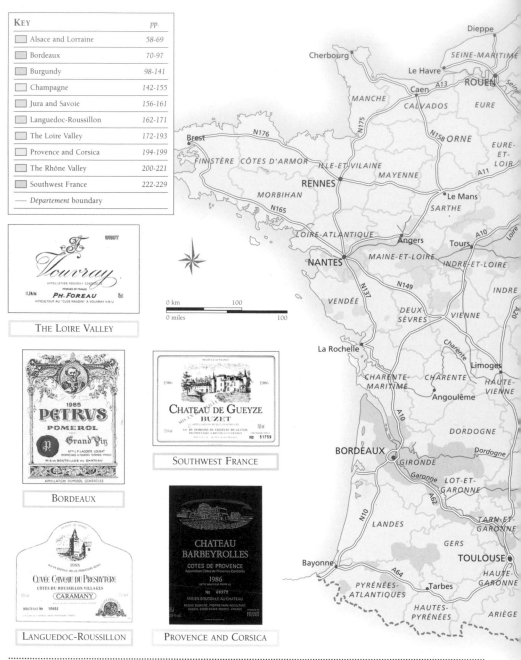

THE LOIRE VALLEY

BORDEAUX

SOUTHWEST FRANCE

LANGUEDOC-ROUSSILLON

PROVENCE AND CORSICA